THE MERTON ANNUAL

Studies in Culture, Spirituality, and Social Concerns

Volume 18	2005

Edited by

Victor A. Kramer

Book Reviews Coordinated by

David Belcastro

THE MERTON ANNUAL
Studies in Culture, Spirituality, and Social Concerns

THE MERTON ANNUAL publishes articles about Thomas Merton and about related matters of major concern to his life and work. Its purpose is to enhance Merton's reputation as a writer and monk, to continue to develop his message for our times, and to provide a regular outlet for substantial Merton-related scholarship. *THE MERTON ANNUAL* includes as regular features reviews, review-essays, a bibliographic survey, interviews, and first appearances of unpublished, or obscurely published Merton materials, photographs, and art. Essays about related literary and spiritual matters will also be considered. Manuscripts and books for review may be sent to the editor.

EDITOR

Victor A. Kramer
University Catholic Center for Emory
1753 North Decatur Road
Atlanta GA 30307
Email: victorak@bellsouth.net

PRODUCTION MANAGER

Glenn Crider
University Catholic Center for Emory
1753 North Decatur Road
Atlanta GA 30307
Email: wcrider@emory.edu

Grateful acknowledgement is expressed to The Merton Legacy Trust for permission to publish from the St. John's University manuscript version of "Three Poems" and to republish the articles "The Monk and Sacred Art" and "Art and Worship" originally appearing in Sponsa Regis. We also thank *The Banner*, St. John's University, for allowing revision of the articles by Hollas and Durken. The Merton Legacy Trust has also granted permission to use illustrations for both Sunderman's article and to include illustrations for the Lipsey collection of Merton-Reinhardt correspondence. The Estate of Ad Reinhardt has graciously given permission to publish Reinhardt's letters to Merton.

PUBLISHED BY:
Fons Vitae
49 Mockingbird Valley Drive
Louisville KY 40207
502.897.3641
Email: Fonsvitaeky@aol.com
http://www.fonsvitae.com

SPONSORED BY:
International Thomas Merton Society
Thomas Merton Center.
Bellarmine University
2001 Newburg Road
Louisville KY 40205
502.452.8187 or 8177
Email: merton@bellarmine.edu
http://www.merton.org/ITMS/

Also available through The Thomas Merton Foundation, 211 Payne Street, Louisville, KY, 40206; 502.899.1991; Email: info@mertonfoundation.org

Further details about membership and subscribing to *The Merton Seasonal* and *The Merton Annual* are available at http://www.merton.org/ITMS/membership.htm or by contacting the Thomas Merton Center at the above address.

For members of the International Thomas Merton Society, available for $15.00, plus shipping and handling. Individual copies are available through bookstores and direclty from the publisher for $19.95. *Copyright*: All rights reserved.

Cover artwork is a drawing by Thomas Merton. Used with permission of the Merton Legacy Trust and the Thomas Merton Center at Bellarmine University.

Library of Congress Control Number: 2005XXXXXX

ISBN 1-887752-854

The Merton Annual

Volume 18 2005

Victor A. Kramer
Introduction: Monastic Awareness, Liturgy and Art:
The Benedictine Tradition in Relation to Merton's
Growing Artistic Interests 7

Thomas Merton
"Three Prayers" Written for Frank Kacmarcik 11

Thomas Merton
Edited by Victor A. Kramer and Glenn Crider
"The Monk and Sacred Art" (1956) and
"Art and Worship" (1959) 15

Kevin Seasoltz
Frank Kacmarcik and the Cistercian Architectural Tradition 22

Charlotte Anne Zalot
A Merton Connection: Frank Kacmarcik, OblSB, Monk
and Artist (1940-2004) 33

Eric Hollas, Daniel Durken and Stefanie Weisgram
Three Comments about Benedictine Monastic
Community Reading:
I. "Food for Thought: Monastic Table Reading";
II. "A Record of Books Read"; and
III. "Table Reading in the Monastery Today" 59

Ernesto Cardenal
Transcribed and Edited by Dennis Beach with an Introduction
by Patrick Hart and Note by Corey Shouse
"Remarks Following a 2004 Poetry Reading" 65

Anthony Feuerstein
  A Discovery: Thomas Merton's Poetry as Art Song;
  Compositions by Bryan Beaumont Hays, OSB:
  A Bibliographical Note   73

Conducted and Edited by Victor A. Kramer and Glenn Crider
  "Unadorned Ideal": An Interview in Two Parts with
  Methodius Telnack, OCSO   77

Dewey Weiss Kramer
  Contemporary Architectural Witness to the Lived
  Cistercian Ideal: The Abbey Churches of Gethsemani
  and Conyers   96

Michael Griffith
  Thomas Merton on William Blake: "To Look Through
  Matter into Eternity"   109

Jeffrey A. Cooper
  Divining the Inscaped-Landscape: Hopkins, Merton
  and the Ascent to True Self   129

Malgorzata Poks
  Encounter in a Secret Country: Thomas Merton and
  Jorge Carrera Andrade   142

Marilyn Sunderman
  Jewels Upon His Forehead: Spiritual Vision in the Poetry
  and Photography of Thomas Merton   169

Ross Keating
  Wisdom, Sapiential Poetry, and Personalism: Exploring
  Some of Thomas Merton's Ideas for Values Education   189

Chris Orvin
  The Conflict Not Yet Fully Faced: Thomas Merton
  as Reader in His Journals   208

Paul M. Pearson
  A Monk with the Spiritual Equipment of an Artist:
  The Art of Thomas Merton   240

Roger Lipsey
Do I want a small painting? The Correspondence of
Thomas Merton and Ad Reinhardt: An Introduction
and Commentary   262

A Bibliographical Note and Index of Images
by Glenn Crider and Paul M. Pearson
Art in *The Merton Annual*, Volumes 1-5   315

Malgorzata Poks
Reading Merton from the (Polish) Margin:
2004 Bibliographic Review   320

REVIEWS

Victor A. Kramer
Szabo, Lynn (ed.) *In the Dark Before Dawn[;] New Selected*
Poems of Thomas Merton   349

Patrick F. O'Connell
Montaldo, Jonathan, *A Year with Thomas Merton:*
Daily Meditations from His Journals   352

Christine M. Bochen
Kownacki, Mary Lou, *Between Two Souls:*
Conversations with Ryokan   355

Joy A. Schroeder
Chittister, Joan, *Called to Question: A Spiritual Memoir*   360

Dana Greene
Kirvan, John, *Grace through Simplicity:*
The Practical Spirituality of Evelyn Underhill   362

Glenn Crider
Patterson, Richard B., *Writing Your Spiritual Autobiography*   363

Angus F. Stuart
Nouwen, Henri J.M., *Out of Solitude: Three Meditations on the Christian Life* and Ford, Michael, *Eternal Seasons: A Liturgical Journey with Henri J.M. Nouwen*   364

William H. Shannon
O'Malley, John W., *Four Cultures of the West*   367

Contributors   371

Index   377

Monastic Awareness, Liturgy and Art: The Benedictine Tradition in Relation to Merton's Growing Artistic Interests

Victor A. Kramer

I

The materials which make this volume of *The Merton Annual* have resulted from many different contemporary currents which reflect trends in liturgical design, monastic life and art, music and aesthetics in relation to Merton's own interests in monasticism, art, liturgical renewal and poetry. While this volume was not planned as a tribute to Merton as artist, the many pieces gathered here conjoin to reflect both his formation as artist and his monastic development which parallel movements within Catholic artistic circles during the years Merton lived the Cistercian life (1941-1968).

Merton's ideals and interests clearly parallel those of Frank Kacmarcik, and as we see in the two opening essays here which focus on Kacmarcik, these brother-artists shared much of the same urgency of aesthetic. The three poems written by Merton for Kacmarcik (revised later, as printed in *The Merton Annual*, Volume 2) are here reproduced as part of this volume as one of our "unpublished pieces" as first written at Kacmarcik's request. Both of these artists stand as towering representative figures who brought the best of Benedictine spirit to the modern world.

The confluence of Merton and the *Zeitgeist* during the movement of transition from the modern to post-modern age is refracted throughout these scholarly articles about art, poetry, reading, liturgical reform and music. Our two other Merton "obscurely published" articles, which have been relatively unknown, appeared first in Sponsa Regis. Both of these essays exemplify Thomas Merton's conviction that the monastic impulse should serve to improve the wider Church.

Much of the other material included in this volume provides illustration of how the Benedictine-Cistercian monastic impulse moves in a rhythm which remains in tune with its culture. The pieces which document accomplishments of Father Bryan Beaumont Hays and Ernesto Cardenal, both as artists clearly influenced by Thomas Merton, each indirectly illuminate aspects of Merton's fundamental love of simplicity and good art. And as we can see from the articles which examine monastic reading, by Eric Hollas and Stefanie Weisgram, any living monastery is constantly breathing in new ideas from the wider culture.

Adaptation is the key. It is this constant living exchange within the Benedictine-Cistercian ideal, and a love and concern for the culture in which we all live, that makes monasticism remain alive and vital. In the article by Ross Keating we see how the wisdom tradition remained alive for Merton.

When we examine the two pieces included here which are about the Monastery of the Holy Spirit in Georgia, by Methodius Telnack and Dewey W. Kramer, we see how the very ideas and ideals which stimulated Merton find new breath in a new setting. Father Methodius, as a near contemporary of Father Louis, has worked in the same traditions. His community's Conyers Church, which began as a definite copy of the Kentucky Gethsemani Church, evolved into a place quite appropriate just for Georgia and in part because of its simple glass and evocation of the past. As Jean Leclerq, OSB, once mentioned in conversation in 1975 "...a nineteenth century dream," but clearly a clean monastic building which echoes the earliest traditions of Cistercian art and which also draws seekers in steady numbers in the 21st century.

II

One thing then to be learned from the articles in our Volume 18 is that true Benedictine and Cistercian monasticism honors all things and adapts as needed. Art, Merton knew, sanctifies the ordinary. Thus, in the articles here which examine the continuing influence of William Blake and Gerard Manley Hopkins upon Merton, or the articles which trace parallels between his accomplishments and Andrade or Zen, we see always his love of the immediate. I think that important connection with the immediate is something Jonathan Montaldo has recognized well in his recent editing work of Merton for *Dialogues with Silence* which combine Merton's drawings with prayers. Montaldo combines selections of line drawings with prose and poetry which function as prayer. Most of the time what Montaldo does is to pull materials out of a hidden context so that the viewer or reader will be illuminated. What is significant is that these texts are often not formal prayers, and Merton, himself, kept doing this over and over in journal entries and poems.

Montaldo's *Dialogues with Silence* is both roughly thematic and somewhat chronological, although there is apparently little attempt to be systematic in terms of giving any overview of Merton's artistic accomplishment or prayerful vision. Nevertheless in the words and images, as selected, Montaldo approaches Merton with his own editorial eye and provides an emphasis which allows the reader to enter into a particular contemplative moment.

The drawings in *Dialogues* fall into several distinct groups: I) Portraits, or Impressions, of Saints or Holy Men; II) Monks, sometimes autobiographical; III) Women, often "portraits" of the Blessed Virgin Mary; IV) Crucifixions; V) Realistic sketches of places familiar to Merton; VI) Abstract flowers and other objects; VII) Calligraphies with some representation; VIII) Semi-representational calligraphies (such as the figure of the animals suggesting the ark); IX) Stark clean simple drawings—such as the Big Oval which Merton repeated many times and which we are honored to use on our cover for this year's volume. These nine groupings fall into three sets, roughly early figures which suggest holiness or asceticism; other realistic pictures of Christ and places Merton knew; and finally calligraphic representations. We move toward the more abstract, but also the more universal, and the immediate. So too in all good liturgy, in good poetry, in good music, in good connections of the monastic ideal with contemporary culture.

In the article by Pearson and commentary by Lipsey we see how Merton as artist was always somehow involved in the world he loved and was constantly seeking ways to make connections both by drawing and through sophisticated correspondence. The bibliographical note about Merton's art in Volumes 1-5 of *The Merton Annual* should serve to help future scholars to appreciate all the diverse pieces of Merton's work which often reflect his focus on the immediate.

I believe Merton's sure love of the particular is the whole reason for his journal project. What is rewarding and refreshing is to see reflected in much of the work in this volume of *The Merton Annual* is that so much of the Benedictine-Cistercian impulse toward successful activity never forgets the particular. Chris Orvin's reading of Merton's journals shows this. Still another recent editing job by Montaldo also deserves mention. Montaldo's idea of arranging his newly released *A Year with Thomas Merton: Daily Meditations from His Journals*, reviewed in this volume, is simple and tremendously effective because it uses particular seasonal materials. As a day book, as a record of Merton's seasonal moods, and as a challenge to all who need to get to the essence of being, this compilation provides guidelines. It does so by remaining grounded in Merton's words which honor the immediate. This is the essence of effective art.

III

The comments by Malgorzata Poks, within this year's bibliographic analysis, about Merton's "vision of the solitary who withdraws to the margin of society to become a diaphanous center of awareness" (p. 33) are also quite on target in terms of Merton's sustained perceptive insights as a religious writer. This insight stands also as a metaphor into art, liturgy and the wider world of responsibility which the successful Christian artist indirectly assumes must never be forgotten.

The new man, redeemed in Christ is both nowhere and everywhere. The artist on the margin must make the watcher, or reader, aware of this eternal gift. Merton's ability both to keep his focus on his own personal "journey" as a monastic yet also to keep his eyes open to the beauty of the world is reflected in many of the scholarly articles which make up this book. In the same way in the insightful book reviews, coordinated by David Belcastro, we see many more connections fruitfully examined.

Merton could always, it seems, keep his love of God in the forefront. Yet he knew as did Julian of Norwich, whom he considers in his journal entry for December 27th, 1961 that despite the distractions, even horrors of the contemporary moment, within a true school of charity, reinforced by attention to good monastic and aesthetic principles, all things can be brought with love to the Lord's service.

"Three Prayers"
Written For Frank Kacmarcik

Thomas Merton

Editorial Note: A revised version of these three poems was included in Volume two of *The Merton Annual* (pages 115-117) with the heading "Three Prayers on Sacred Art." The manuscript at The St. John's University Alcuin Library is entitled "THREE PRAYERS." Each poem is clearly a distinct unit. The poems are not separately headed with Roman Numerals as in the later version. These prayers were written for Frank Kacmarcik as artist and are, therefore, for the artist, not about sacred art.

THREE PRAYERS

First Prayer: <u>For Vocations in the Realm of Sacred Art</u>

Almighty God, Father of all light, Maker of the World
Who has made man in Your image, a seer and a maker,[1]
Look down into the abysmal darkness of our hearts
And see the unutterable destitution into which our spirit
     and our art have fallen, since we have grown blind to
     the splendor of Your truth.
O Lord, Who once heard the cry of Israel, Your son,
     enslaved in Egypt
Who delivered him, with great power,
And led him, with Your prophet Moses into the desert:
Send us now men of vision who will open our eyes
     once again
To see Your incorruptible light.
O Lord, Who showed to Moses on the flaming mountain
The plan of a perfect Tabernacle, in which a fitting worship
     could be offered to Your Majesty,
Send us chosen messengers and teachers,
Men of worship and men of art,

Who will restore with chaste and noble works
     the beauty of Your House!
May they teach us to see, with pure hearts,
The Splendor of Your Son, Jesus Christ,
And to express what we have seen in images
     worthy of so great a vision:
Through the same Jesus Christ, Your Son,
Your Logos, Your Art and Your Splendor
In Whom all things subsist
And through Whom, by the power of the Holy Spirit,
All are called to be united with You forever.[2]

Second Prayer: In Selecting an Artist for a Sacred Work

Lord, God, Father Almighty, Whose art and Whose wisdom
     delight at all times to play, before You, in the great
     mystery of the works[3] You have created:

Look down upon us and bless our ardent desire to create, in
     our turn, a sacred"world," a mystical Eden of spiritual
     symbol and form,
In which we may converse familiarly with You as
     Adam our Father once did in Paradise.
Send us, therefore, a wise maker of sacred buildings[4] to
     construct[5] a visible house for Your invisible glory.
Enlighten us, and let us choose the one who has received
     wisdom, from You, to do this work with all humility,
     and reverence, and perfection.
Teach us to choose him, not in the way the world chooses its
     servants,[6] not by his empty fame, not by the price of
     his service, not by his conformity to ephemeral
     fashions: but show us how to find, by the inspiration of
     Your Holy Spirit, the one whom that same Holy Spirit
     will guide and strengthen for his Task: for without
     Your Holy Spirit, Lord, no man can serve your
     worthily or make anything that will give you honor.
But with His guidance and inspiration, all
will be done in praise of your everlasting glory, through
Christ our Lord. Amen.

Third Prayer: <u>For the Artist[7] and for the Work in Progress</u>

Lord Jesus Christ, Who by Your Holy Passion and Death and
    by Your glorius Resurrection, restored the mined[8]
    world to its pristine perfection and ushered in a
    New Creation,
Be mindful, we beg You of your servant _____,[9] and
    stand by him in the work he has undertaken for Your
    Glory.
Strengthen his soul in his struggle to create a new and living
    form: Sustain him in his wrestling with the inertia of
    wood and stone, defend him against the lure of cow-
    ardly solutions, falsity, insincerity and
    servility to worldly standards.
Grant him patience, humility and understanding.
Endow his heart with incorruptible wisdom, his mind with
    subtlety and wisdom[10], his hands with dexterous skill.
May he be sanctified in his work, may his work itself be
    holy, and may it raise all our hearts to You in prayer:
Thus may we all, priests and people, artists and workers be
    united in one great act of praise and thanksgiving on
    the day when, by Your grace, we shall happily dedicate
    this[12] work in all its[13] splendor, to the glory of Your
    Heavenly Father. Amen.

Notes

1. This line is expanded in the revised version to "Who have given to Man the power to conceive sacred forms and to create/Works of art in Your honor,/"

2. "Amen." added in revised version.

3. "world" in revised version.

4. "ikons" substituted in revised version with "[or buildings]" following.

5. "adorn" substituted in revised version with "[construct]" following.

6. [:] added, not comma in revised version.

7. , (comma) added after "Artist" in revised version.

8. "mined" replaced with "ruined" in revised version.

9. "[Name], the architect [or sculptor, painter, etc.]" added in revised version.

10. "discipline" substituted for "wisdom" in revised version.
12. "new" added in revised version.
13. "sacred" added in revised version.

"The Monk and Sacred Art" (1956); and "Art and Worship" (1959)

Thomas Merton
Edited by Glenn Crider and Victor A. Kramer

Editorial Note: These articles first appeared in <u>Sponsa Regis</u> (Liturgical Press, Collegeville, MN). They have not been reprinted since their original appearance. The essays succinctly reflect the early convergence of Merton's ideas about art, monasticism, liturgy and worship.

The two articles are also especially appropriate for inclusion in this volume of *The Merton Annual* since we have the good fortune to include several other articles about Benedictine and Cistercian art, liturgy and life.

We are thankful to Sister Stefanie Weisgram, OSB, at The College of St. Benedict and of St. John's University, who suggested, in conversation, that the <u>Sponsa Regis</u> Merton contributions could be researched for their connections with Merton's artistic vision.

"The Monk and Sacred Art"
By Thomas Merton

IN THE TWELFTH CENTURY it was possible for St. Bernard to ask how much a monk could do without art, how much he could sacrifice it. That question is no longer as intelligent for us as it was for him. One cannot sacrifice what one does not possess. Before we can go to God "without art," we must learn to go to Him with it. That was something the men of the twelfth century acquired with the very air they breathed. Bernard of Clairvaux was raised in the country of Vezelay, Cluny, Paray-le-Monial, Tournus, Saulieu. The rich imagery of his prose is precisely the imagery of romanesque sculpture. He could afford to "renounce art," when his imagination, his character, his whole being were steeped through and through in the romanesque.

We, on the other hand, not so. Reared in a degenerate and tasteless eclecticism, passively carried this way and that by the winds of artistic doctrine, we need to hear a voice that will steady us in our confusion, enable us to recognize, in the art of the past and that of the present, what belongs to us and what is alien to us as Christians. And it is normal and right that this voice should come to us from the monasteries, from monks trained in the great tradition which is more than a culture—deep and pure religious cult.

Art and worship are inseparable in the Christian view of life, and where a true and healthy asceticism has stripped art of its non-essentials, the result has been a revival of art and worship. In either case, where art is rich, lavish, magnificent, or where it is severe, austere and strong, it needs to be *seen* before it can fulfill its function as an aid to worship.

Today we speak of the monk as a "contemplative"—a vague, abstract term which is not always free of pagan connotations. The Fathers said the same thing much more concretely by calling the monk a *prophet*. Both the prophet and the contemplative are men who see what others do not see. They see the inner meaning of things. They see God in the darkness of faith. Yet the difference between the word "contemplative" and the word "prophet" would seem to be this: that the contemplative sees essences, while the prophet sees persons and things. And the contemplative, while indeed capable of "sharing with others his contemplation", does not do so in the same way as the prophet, who sees the things of God and announces them as the instrument and the mouthpiece of God.

The monk, then, is a prophet who sees and speaks the things of God. He is a *videns*, a seer, whose very vocation is vigilance on the frontiers that divide the flesh and the spirit, so that he may "see" what things are coming over the horizon and "announce" to others what they are.

Christian art is prophetic in this sense, because it is spiritual, and mystical. It is part of the *conversatio* by which the Christian lives in heaven while still living on earth. It fully and uncompromisingly accepts the limitations of matter, but spiritualizes and elevates its material element, making all the creatures of God transparent symbols of God's great work in the world of men, symbols of the Mystery that reestablishes all things in Christ.

The difference between a Prophet like Isaias and the nameless prophet who carved the magnificent capitals of the "martyred Church," Saulieu, is that Isaias foresaw the Mystery of Christ as a future thing, the sculptor of Saulieu saw it as a present reality which was still, nevertheless, hidden by the veils of faith. Isaias said: "These are the things that will happen." The artists of the twelfth century said: "This is what is now happening, what is now being fulfilled in us." And the voices of the monastic "prophets" of our time join in the solemn chorus: "Yes, we too see that this is what is happening." But all together turn their eyes to the future, expecting the great consummation that is finally to come.

If the monk is a *seer*, it is also because he is a *maker*. Far from being an antiquarian, or an academician, the monastic "seer" studies not "rules" and "canons of beauty," but *how to make things*— how to form an earthenware vessel on the potter's wheel, how to carve a saint's image in applewood. In so doing he does not elevate himself into a kind of academic superego, dictating norms and imposing them upon the rest of the human race with severe sanctions ("you must believe this is beautiful, or you will pay the penalty of not being thought a man of culture"). He simply looks, and responds to what he sees. All his life is a looking, a making, a praising. It is in this way that he imitates God, by imitating the Son who is always busy doing what He sees the Father doing. The monk learns to see the things of God, and God's creation, by himself participating in God's creative work. This he does in his manual labor in the fields, in his artistic creative work in the studio, in his meditative reading of the Scriptures, in his guidance of other souls. In all these activities he is praising God the Creator, learning the greatness of God and the beauty of creation by making for himself and his brothers a whole new world of his own which mirrors the hidden purposes of the Almighty. The monk who has made something with his own hands and his own mind is entitled to speak, modestly, of the sacredness of a creation which God has made. He too has looked upon the world through the eyes of Him who made the world, and has seen that all things are "very good."

As a *seer* and a *maker* the monk is attuned to what is. He knows by instinct the difference between the solid and the artificial, the sincere and the false in art. He knows what is "right" and, therefore, also what is "sacred," because he himself is right. He has reestablished in himself by self-denial and prayer and love the rectitude with which man was made in God's image (*Deus fecit hominem rectum*). And from the depths of his own simplicity the monk can then praise God in Himself and in all His creatures. Filled with the life that God gives to His sons, the monk is attuned to sacredness wherever it is found, and it is found everywhere, because the imprint of God's creative hand is upon everything that is. Everything that is, is holy.[1]

But there is more. The monk sees also that all things have their special holiness in Christ. All things are good because they are blessed by the word of God and by prayer. The world is sanctified by the Mystical Body of the Risen Christ. The monk sees that all things are holy because he sees them only in Christ. "He is the image of the invisible God and the firstborn of every creature. In him were all things created, in heaven and on earth …[.] And he is before all, and by him all things consist" (Col. 1:15-17). Christ, the Logos, is the "art" of the Father, the Creator of the world. But in Him and by Him the fallen creation is redeemed, saved, sanctified, transfigured and offered once again to the Father. Sacred art is then a prophetic participation in the consciousness of the Mystery of Christ, which is the great work of the Father. This prophetic participation cannot be content merely to look: it must imitate, it must praise. That is why sacred art is inseparable from Liturgy, from adoration, from prayer. It enters into the great complex of means by which the Christian communes with God and with his fellow Christian. Sacred art is, therefore, another means of verifying our communion in Christ. As all true Christian art enters into the setting of the infinite act of worship which the Mystical Christ offers to God, all true art is Eucharistic. The *tympan* of Vezelay is a picture of what St. Thomas would call the *Res sacramenti* of the Eucharist, the final and perfect union of the faithful in the risen Christ.

The vocation of the monk is, therefore, in the highest sense prophetic. The message of the monk is the message of seers, *videntes*, who remind the sacred City of Jerusalem of her true identity as the Body of Christ. The monk is not merely trying to tell us about art, but about ourselves, not merely how to identify a work of art, but how to identify ourselves, how to find ourselves in Christ. This means finding ourselves in the art of the past, creating for ourselves our own art in the present, handing on to other generations the awareness of the Mystery which is coming closer and closer to its final manifestation. In a word, it is the message of Isaias: "Arise and be enlightened, O Jerusalem, for thy light is come and the glory of the Lord is risen upon thee" (Is. 60:1). All sacred art that is worthy of its name is but a faint reflection of the glory of Christ's transfiguration. No one who sees that light can help but say, "It is good for me to be here."

"Art and Worship"
By Thomas Merton

MAN THE IMAGE of God has a vocation not only to rule and exploit the world, but to transform it and to draw forth from it the hidden glory which has been placed in creation by its Creator. Hence man cannot be complete if he is only a scientist and a technician: he must also be an artist and a contemplative. Unless these elements in his life reach a proper balance, his society and culture will be out of harmony with the spiritual needs of his inner life. Hence art has a vitally important place to play not only in keeping man civilized but also in helping him to "save his soul," that is to say, to live as a Child of God who has knowledge, understanding and love of the things of his Father.

Unless man fulfills his vocation as artist, technology will tend to blind him to the things of God. By artistic and creative insight, man rises above the material elements and outer appearances of things and sees into their inner nature. By the disciplined exercise of his art he is enabled to draw forth the glory of God that is hidden in created beauty and make it manifest in the world.

The traditional definition of glory is *clara cognitio cum laude*—clear perception with praise. This definition contains what is most essential about the aesthetic experience—a combination of discovery with admiration. Art is not merely an interior appreciation of ideal beauty. It implies also a workman-like and disciplined use of tools and materials to produce a work of art which is a visible embodiment of the ideal form which the artist has seen in his contemplation of nature.

One of the marks of a secularized society is the stunting and degradation of art, both as contemplation and as discipline. This is inseparable from the decline of spirituality and prayer, but also results from the culture of our age which is top heavy with technology and fails to satisfy some of the deepest and most elementary needs of man's nature.

Our phenomenal advance in scientific investigation and technique has been accompanied by a kind of regression in spirit and also in instinct. We can find out all sorts of things about the most distant stars but we have lost the capacity to "see" a chrysanthemum in the garden or the beech trees on the hill side. The reality that is all around us has become alien and unreal to us, and while our senses are subjected to a constant bombardment of useless and obnoxious stimuli, we are out of contact with the very things that would keep us healthy and sane. Nothing is familiar any longer except what is alien to our true nature.

Twentieth century art is endowed with great vitality and immense aspirations for discovery, but it is flourishing in the darkness of the prison house. Why is this? Because in a technological society art loses its roots in spirituality and religion, and tries to take root in the dead world of subjective abstraction. Not that there is anything wrong with abstract art: it can be very much alive and have a great deal to say. But no art, whether abstract or not, can get anywhere if it does not exercise a transforming and spiritual action in the world of visible things, revealing in its midst the reflected glory of hidden and spiritual forms.

This is another way of saying that art cannot be content with simply copying the outward aspect of visible things. To copy nature is to falsify it. The artist is not simply reproducing the thing he paints, but creating something new, an *eikon*, an image which embodies the inner truth of things as they exist in the mystery of God. Such an *eikon* or image may be a very striking and suggestive representation of a scene or of a person—witness the intense spiritual clarity of Japanese painting. The "realism" of such a picture is nevertheless all the more real in proportion as it *suggests* rather than *copies* the object. What is real in such a case is not the picture but the experience of the one looking at it.

An *eikon* then, does not reproduce the reality of an object, but contains that reality, in a spiritual or "sacramental" form within itself, so as to communicate it wholly and directly to the spirit of the one who sees it. In this sense, the word *eikon* might be translated as "symbol," but not as a "symbol" that has to be figured out through ratiocination. It is a symbol which directly and intuitively communicates, by a sign, the reality of the thing symbolized. The realm of art is then the realm of intuition, and not of reasoning.

Modern art, flying further and further from the pedestrian logic of straight representation, has tried to live up to its vocation to grasp the inner spiritual reality of things. But in order to do this the artist must be a spiritual man. Now in some modern artists who have not painted "religious" subjects at all, there can be found a deep and original spiritual quality: for example in Cezanne's *eikons* of landscape, or in Paul Klee's mysterious cult-like symbols, or in the painstaking dreamlike evocations of the jungle by Le Douanier Rousseau.

In spite of this, modern art remains to a great extent frustrated in its search for valid symbols, because it is out of touch with God who gives meaning as well as existence to the world of images and to the world of things. As S. Boulgakov has said: "The inspiration of art attains its completeness of insight only when it is enlightened by religion; only in religion does art become truly symbolic; only in religion does it fully understand its symbolic nature as a witness of the invisible through the medium of the visible."

This statement would not be fully acceptable if it meant that art was only fully itself when associated with a religious *cult*. Art can have an essentially religious quality even when not having anything directly to do with worship. "Even when art is not strictly an art of the cult it remains religious as long as it is *true* art because it reveals beauty, that is the hand of God in the world.... It always retains a connection with the world of essential spiritual values, i.e., with religious values."

While all true art is spiritual in the above sense, sacred art does even more. It seeks not only the "inner meaning" of things, it seeks to represent in some way the reality of God Himself. Now the divine nature as such cannot be represented by any material form, but the Incarnate Word, Jesus Christ, is Himself an *eikon* or manifestation of the divinity. For Christ, the author of Hebrews says, is "the brightness of (God's) glory and the figure of His substance" (Hebrews 1:3).

Sacred art therefore seeks to represent the hidden things of God as they are manifested in those beings, Christ, His Blessed Mother and His saints, who are themselves *eikons* of God.

Notes

1. This echo of William Blake is fundamental to the aesthetic of Thomas Merton.

Frank Kacmarcik and the Cistercian Architectural Tradition

R. Kevin Seasoltz

A number of contemporary critics of the Vatican II reforms of the liturgy have accused the reformers of being unduly influenced by the tenets of the Enlightenment. Most of the fathers of the council and the members of the Consilium who were responsible for implementing the liturgical directives of the Constitution on the Sacred Liturgy would be surprised and probably chagrined by the accusation. Included here would be the names of Giacomo Cardinal Lercaro, Franz Cardinal König, Archbishop Denis Hurley, Pierre-Marie Gy, Pierre Jounel, Balthasar Fischer, Godfrey Diekmann, James Crichton, and Frederick McManus. These distinguished scholars were above all steeped in the history of the Church, especially the patristic period; they were not friends of philosophical modernity. Furthermore there has been the charge that architects and liturgical consultants responsible for the construction and reform of church buildings in the last forty years have simply opted for mathematical rationalism and dualism and have been basically anti-traditional.[1]

There is no doubt that after the council many contemporary church buildings were hastily renovated simply so that Mass could be celebrated facing the people, and that new churches have been built by incompetent architects who have had little sense of liturgical tradition and have responded poorly to liturgical briefs set out in official church documents. Those documents rightly emphasize the importance of the entire liturgical assembly as the primary celebrant of the liturgy and the consequent importance of the altar, baptistry, ambo, and presider's chair.

Frank Kacmarcik was certainly not influenced by either modern or post-modern philosophers nor by the spirit of the Enlightenment. He was influenced primarily by his early association with the Benedictine monastic tradition and formed by that tradition. In the 1940s he entered the Benedictine novitiate at Saint John's Abbey in Collegeville where he worked closely with Brother Clement Frishauf, OSB, an influential liturgical artist trained in the Beuronese school of religious art.[2] Brother Clement became a devoted mentor, inspiring Frank to see himself as a faithful disciple of this influential but humble liturgical artist. Other monks who contributed to his early spiritual formation were Fathers Gregory Roettger, OSB, and Paschal Botz, OSB.

Frank's early artistic style was both challenged and broadened after the Second World War by his experience at the Acadèmie de la Grand Chaumière and the Centre d'Art Sacré in Paris. During his teaching years at Saint John's University in the early nineteen-fifties and for many years thereafter he was profoundly affected by his friendship with Father Michael Marx, OSB, whose life and scholarship were deeply rooted both in biblical studies and in the early monastic tradition.[3] When Frank first met with potential clients who were interested in either renovating an existing church or building a new one, his primary concerns were ecclesiological. He inquired about and insisted that the community come to grips with very basic questions: Who have you been as a community? Who are you now? And who do you want to become? Especially when working with monastic communities, he was aware of the Benedictine tradition and the emphasis that the experience of God flourishes in a climate of hospitality in which people are present to one another as the body-persons they are, as members of the body of Christ, comfortable with one another, gathered together with each other, capable of seeing and hearing all that is enacted within the worshiping assembly. He insisted that an attractive beauty in all that is said and done, used or observed is the best way to facilitate the experience of God as mystery, for God is not only goodness and truth, God is also beauty. He asserted that it is above all God's Spirit in our hearts and communities that gives access to the otherness, the transcendence, and holiness of God.

Certainly the New Testament, which is normative for Christians in their evaluation of their life of faith, asserts the primacy of persons and communities over things. It is the paschal mystery of Jesus Christ celebrated by the Christian assembly that provides the foundational meaning for all places of worship. Their meaning is always derivative; apart from the centrality of the paschal mystery and the assembly which is the body of Christ, they easily degenerate into mere monuments, often very impressive monuments, but monuments none the less. The buildings themselves certainly have a symbolic meaning, but that meaning should be rooted in and reflective of the paschal mystery which is celebrated within the space. Over the centuries, the architectural forms of Christian churches and their artistic appointments have taken diverse shapes reflective of the structure of the liturgical rites and the theological underpinnings of such rites. However, the church buildings themselves and their appointments have also conditioned both positively and negatively the ways in which the liturgy has been celebrated and the theological understanding of the liturgy. Architectural and artistic styles have reflected both the phenomenon of inculturation and that of tradition. In fact architectural and artistic traditions are simply records of inculturation from the past; as such they provide us with a storehouse of models and resources for proper inculturation today.[4]

Among the most satisfying and successful projects both for Frank Kacmarcik and his clients were the renovation of the Cistercian church at New Melleray Abbey in Peosta, Iowa, and the construction of the new church for the Cistercian community at Mepkin Abbey in South Carolina. They reflect communities that struggled with their identity as Cistercian monks—who they had been in the past, who they were when they considered a building project, and who they hoped to become as a monastic community in the future. Certainly Cistercian monasteries in general made a strenuous effort to renew their lives as monks and nuns in the years immediately following the Second Vatican Council. In renewing and reforming both their liturgy and the spaces in which they worshiped, they carefully attended to the Cistercian architectural tradition.

Cistercian Architectural Tradition

In the middle ages, monastic complexes sometimes became so large that they tended to collapse under their own weight. That seems to be what happened at Cluny in the eleventh and early twelfth century. Consequently there were various monastic reform movements in the late eleventh and the twelfth centuries, chief among them being the Cistercians. The order, named after the first foundation at Citeaux in Burgundy, France, was founded by St. Robert of Molesmes (d. 1111), a former abbot of the Benedictine abbey at Molesmes. In 1098 he founded the monastery at Citeaux to institute a life of poverty, simplicity, and eremetical solitude under the Rule of Benedict. The order flourished, especially under the leadership of St. Bernard, who in 1113, with about thirty companions, applied for admission to Citeaux, became the founder and first abbot of Clairvaux, and died in 1153.[5]

The Cistercian order played an important role in the history of sacred architecture and art. Their buildings, especially the churches, were originally distinguished by their simplicity and absence of ornamentation. This style of architecture formed an integral part of Cistercian spirituality. The relationship between their spirituality and architecture was linked to the way in which they understood their relationship with God and consequently their relationship with the environment they created for themselves. They felt that the life of God was manifested in the material world. Their practice of *lectio divina* resulted in a careful pondering on their structures and their decoration. The mysterious quality of spaces that were open and closed, with clean lines and shadows and shafts of light, all invited the eye to behold the beauty of God, just as the play of sounds in their churches invited the ear to hear the word of God. They were convinced that the human mind and heart should be drawn beyond what it sees and hears. Hence they wanted space in their buildings for the eye to see in a way that inclined its vision to go beyond the sight and the ear to go beyond the word proclaimed. Their spirituality was one that emphasized the importance of place, light, and word, but they wanted all to sustain and foster the contemplative dimensions of their lives.[6]

The Cistercians wanted to be poor with Christ who was poor. As a result they sought to reject anything that might appear to be luxurious, whether in their worship, their clothing, or their food. In architecture, they rejected the construction of bell towers, and the appointment of their places with paintings and sculptures. These commitments were vigorously set out by St. Bernard in his famous *Apologia* addressed to his friend William, the Benedictine abbot of Saint-Thierry. He protested against the splendor of Cluniac churches and their grand size, as well as the decoration and ornamentation of the capitals in both the churches and cloisters. Bernard acknowledged that representations of biblical scenes could be instructive and could edify the faithful, but he wondered what use they could be for spiritual men vowed to a life of poverty.[7]

There is, however, really no such thing as an authentic original Cistercian architectural style. Just as the order evolved, so also the buildings were the result of complex cultural, organizational, and religious phenomena intermingling with and influencing one another. A great variety of building styles existed, reflecting the context in which they came into being. Furthermore, a description of a distinctive Cistercian architectural style is not to be found in the documents of the general chapters of the order. Although the order was in some sense quite centralized, a certain autonomy was always characteristic of each of the abbeys. St. Bernard has often been taken as speaking with the authority of the whole order; his prestige was great, but his views did not always reflect those of the other abbots. The general chapters sought to keep unity within the order, but unity was not the same as uniformity, since each monastery functioned within a complex web of ecclesiastical and secular politics.[8]

Drawing on the architecture itself, we can conclude that Cistercian art and architecture manifest many different forms of expression. Not surprising, the architectural style at the time of the great expansion of the order was romanesque on its way to becoming Gothic. Hence, this style was adapted by many of the early Cistercian buildings in Burgundy and their daughter houses, but the style of these buildings is not much different from other abbeys in Burgundy. As the order expanded, local styles often fused with the styles that prevailed in the mother abbeys. Furthermore, the development of technology made it possible for the monks to improve their architectural designs as time went on.

The key element lying behind the architectural choices made by abbots and their communities was the silence prescribed by the Rule of Benedict. Life in community was meant to provide a context in which the monks could develop a deep interior life of solitude. The environment in which the monks lived and worked was just as important an instrument for formation as were the books, sermons, and instructions in the community. Although silence is normally a description of an auditory condition, it relates also to the visual realm. There is regularly a near-absence of narrative and color in Cistercian buildings. The decor is achieved by using bands and moldings of various widths, thickness, profile, or material to emphasize the architectural lines. In the twelfth and thirteenth centuries, figurative sculpture was quite uncommon in Cistercian churches. It was the crucifix in the refectory that had the greatest impact on the monks and nuns. Their imaginations were nourished above all by the images to be found in scripture and other sources of sacred reading. Perhaps what distinguishes Cistercian buildings most of all is the presence of much light. Sunlight animates the buildings by day, outlining the nooks and crannies, highlighting all the architectural details. It is the silence of the abbeys that draws attention to the visual subtleties, for there are few distractions.

After a long period of more or less faithful building in the romanesque style, the Cistercians adopted the Gothic style and contributed to its expansion all over Europe. Ultimately they succumbed to the trends of their time and built enormous churches decorated with both sculpture and painting.

In addition to their important contribution to architecture, the Cistercians also produced distinguished illuminated manuscripts; the oldest coming from the scriptorium at Citeaux contained ornamented letters and illuminations of a high quality. But about 1150, under Bernard's influence, there was a decree of the order's general chapter, which ruled that only one color should be used for the initial letters of a text. As a result the copyists devoted their care to the quality of the parchment, the outline of the letters, and the arrangement of the text on the page. But soon the chapter's prohibition was forgotten and illuminations reappeared.[9]

Both the Cistercian communities at Peosta in Iowa and Moncks Corner in South Carolina sought to retrieve the best theological and spiritual themes in their tradition and to articulate them in their building projects. They did that with the full support and challenge offered by Frank Kacmarcik as their liturgical / architectural consultant. These monastic communities, following the Rule of Benedict and their Cistercian Constitutions, stand in the biblical tradition, but they have also sought to bring that tradition into dialogue with contemporary culture and technology. They have tried to be responsible for the environment, the place which is their gift, their promise, and their challenge.

Abbey of Our Lady of New Melleray, Peosta, Iowa

In 1973, the Cistercians at the Abbey of Our Lady of New Melleray near Dubuque, Iowa, voted to remodel the north wing of their monastery for the permanent location of their church.[10] The monastery was founded in 1849 by monks from Mount Melleray in Ireland. Following the Civil War, the community engaged a local architect, John Mullany, to design a complex of permanent buildings. Mullany had been associated for a time with Augustus Welby Pugin, the distinguished English architect and designer. Mullany's designs reflect Pugin's influence in his preference for pitched roofs and arched windows, and his use of asymmetry and vertical forms. By 1875 the north and east wings were occupied by the monks. Their church was temporarily located on the second floor of the east wing, until it was moved in the 1920s to the second floor of the north wing. Mullany's plans called for a permanent church to be constructed as the south building running parallel to the north wing; however, when construction was resumed on the south wing in the 1950s, the original plans for the church were set aside. When the monks turned their attention to a permanent church in the 1960s, it was suggested that the north wing be razed and a circular church built in its place, but those plans were not accepted by the community. By 1973 they decided instead to remodel the north wing to house a permanent church and hired Willoughby Marshall, Inc., to draw up the original architectural plans.

A second floor was removed from the north and old kitchen wings so as to allow the use of the full height of the north wing for the church and of the old kitchen wing for a chapter house. As a result, an open space of great simplicity was created. Under the direction of Frank Kacmarcik and Theodore Butler, a distinguished architect from Minneapolis, the project was carried through to completion. With the unnecessary partitions and ornamentation stripped away, a space of exceptional beauty emerged as a marvelous shelter capable of revealing God as mysteriously transcendent but also warmly immanent in wood and stone, and above all in the community of monks and their guests gathered for worship. The beams and purloins were sand-blasted so as to appear in natural finish. Douglas fir was used for decking in the roof which arches forty-nine feet above the red-gray tile used as paving throughout the project. The native honey-colored sandstone walls have been left bare; they are pierced by arched windows running along both sides of the building and filled with clear glass so that sunlight plays on the walls and furnishings, thus changing the mood of the church throughout the day. In a sense the space is grand, but it does not dwarf those who gather for worship; it rather generates an atmosphere that is unified, mysterious, and inspiring.

In order to offset the length of the church, the sanctuary at the east end and the guest area at the west end have been elevated somewhat, thus facilitating visibility and pulling the two ends of the building toward one another. As a monastic church the building is used primarily for the celebration of the liturgy of the hours seven times a day and also for the daily celebration of the Eucharist. The latter has rightly placed the strongest claims in determining the furnishings of the space, but through effective lighting the sanctuary area recedes in prominence during the liturgy of the hours. A gray-black opalescent granite altar centers the space in the sanctuary. On each side of the church is a single row of choir stalls; a tracker-action organ stands at the foot of the choir stalls on the right. Pews at the rear of the church rest on slightly raised tiers, accommodating about eighty guests. The community at the time of renovation insisted on a single wrought-iron grate separating the monks from the guests, which is problematic during the Eucharist, above all during the Communion rite.

Of special interest is the successful handling of the place for the reserved Eucharist. The monks wanted to emphasize the primacy of the eucharistic celebration, but they also wanted the reserved sacrament related to the larger eucharistic space. Hence the reserved sacrament stands in a large tabernacle house of red oak directly behind the presider's chair in the sanctuary. The edifice provides an effective backdrop for the sanctuary area and can accommodate several monks for eucharistic devotion and personal prayer. Apart from the processional cross, the only image in the church is an icon of Our Lady of Vladimir mounted on a wrought iron stand. This is in keeping with the Cistercian tradition which on the one hand has maintained a strong devotion to the Mother of God but on the other hand has been reserved in its attitude toward paintings and sculptures in monastic buildings. The overall effect of the renovation project is powerful; it has been and will continue to be formative of both the monastic community and their guests. It rightly received an honor award from the American Institute of Architects.

Mepkin Abbey Church, Moncks Corner, South Carolina

The new church and other monastic buildings at Mepkin Abbey in South Carolina are eminently successful from both architectural and liturgical points of view. In 1949 a group of Trappist monks came from the Abbey of Gethsemani in Kentucky to bring the monastic life to Mepkin. The property, a splendid old plantation, belonged to Henry and Clare Booth Luce, who donated it for the foundation of a new monastery. The monks built a provisional church in 1950 and worshiped there for about forty years. In 1989, before the arrival of hurricane Hugo, the community began discussions concerning a renovation of that temporary edifice. The arrival of the hurricane and the destruction it left in its path, however, delayed the project until 1991 when the community, now under the direction of a vibrant young abbot, Francis Kline, took up the process once again.

After interviews with several liturgical/architectural consultants, the community chose Frank Kacmarcik with Theodore Butler as architect. They discussed at length their identity as a community—how they worshiped together, how they prayed as individual monks, how they celebrated the liturgy with retreatants and guests, and how the Eucharist and the liturgy of the hours related to one another in their daily life. During their deliberations they found they were examining the whole of their monastic life: what it had been, how it was currently expressed, and what they hoped for in the future. It was clear that a monastic, theological and liturgical program was uppermost in their minds, rather than a particular style of building. It was also clear that the emerging floor plan of an entirely new church and the relationship of proposed spaces in the church were, in fact, expressing their identity as a Cistercian community and their vision for the future. The centrality of the altar to the entire space; the relation of the choir to the altar; the relation of the retreatants to the monastic community; the placement of casual visitors; the creation of a smaller, more intimate space for personal prayer and eucharistic devotion; the very location of the building itself in the monastic complex—all these factors they discovered spoke of a theology of Cistercian monastic life, their vision of church, and their faith in the risen Lord.

The new church provides both monks and guests with a wonderful experience of both God's transcendence and immanence in the community. One is aware of others, but not too aware. There is a profound sense of beauty in all that is there—in the altar, in the lighting, in the organ, in the wood-work, especially the ceiling, in the holy water font, and above all in the people. The church was dedicated in November, 1993. Since then an impressive bronze statue of Mary and the young Christ Child, designed by the Jewish sculptor, Alexander Tylovich, has been placed at the head of the choir, near the presider's chair. After winning, along with Theodore Butler, the 1995 American Institute of Architects award for religious architecture for the Mepkin church, Frank went on to guide the community through a large building program from 1997 to 2001. There is a new monastic wing for the elderly and infirm monks, a new refectory for the monks and their guests, and a spacious library and conference center.[11]

Frank Kacmarcik had an extraordinary influence on the positive development of American church architecture and art. He was involved in the design or renovation of over two hundred church buildings in this country. In the Cistercian tradition, his buildings reflect his conviction that the church is not primarily a monument but is rather a place for the celebration of the paschal mystery by the community of God's faithful people. He felt that sacred spaces should be characterized by a certain visual silence, that the space should communicate a discreet sense of absence without the assembly of God's people. He was one of the first to accentuate the importance of a gathering place so that the community might assemble in preparation for the liturgical celebrations. The furnishings, the vessels, the utensils that are used in worship should have a profundity, a *gravitas,* an inner content about them. He was committed to natural art, basic art, fully tactile art. His passion was for beauty, honesty, proportion and truth. His ministry with Cistercian communities confirmed him in that passion.

Notes

1. See Robert Barron, *Bridging the Great Divide: Musings of a Post-liberal, Post-Conservative Catholic,* A Sheed and Ward Book (Lanham, MD: Rowman & Littlefield Publishers, Inc., 2004), pp. 11-21, pp. 68-84.

2. See Desiderius Lenz, *The Aesthetic of Beuron and Other Writings* (London: Francis Boutle Publishers, 2002); *Sacred Art: Beuronese Art at Saint John's* (Collegeville: Saint John's, 1998).

3. See RKS, "Brother Frank Kacmarcik Obl.S.B. 1920-2004," *Worship,* 78 (May 2004), pp. 194-99.

4. Peter Jeffery, "A Chant Historian Reads *Liturgiam Authenticam* 3: Language and Culture," *Worship* 78 (May 2002), p. 236.

5. C. H. Lawrence, *Medieval Monasticism: Forms of Religious Life in Western Europe in the Middle Ages* (New York: Longman, 1984), pp. 146-52.

6. See Terryl N. Kinder, *Cistercian Europe: Architecture of Contempla- tion* (Grand Rapids: Eerdmans, 2002); idem, *Architecture of Silence: Cistercian Abbeys of France,* Photography by David Heald (New York: Harry N. Abrams, 2000); *Studies in Cistercian Art and Architecture,* ed. Meredith Parsons Lillich; 4 vols. (Kalamazoo, Michigan.: Cistercian Pub- lications, 1980, 1984, 1987, 1993); Anselme Dimier, *Stones Laid before the Lord: Architecture and Monastic Life: A History of Monastic Architecture,* trans. Gilchrist Lavigne (Kalamazoo, Mich.: Cistercian Publications, 1999).

7. *Cistercians and Cluniacs: St. Bernard's Apologia to Abbot William,* trans. Michael Casey (Kalamazoo, Mich.: Cistercian Publications, 1970); Conrad Rudolph, *The "Things of Greater Importance": Bernard of Clairvaux's Apol- ogy and the Medieval Attitude toward Art* (Philadelphia: University of Penn- sylvania Press, 1990), pp. 287-83.

8. Kinder, *Cistercian Europe,* pp. 374-88.

9. See Janet Backhouse, *The Illuminated Manuscript* (Oxford: Phaidon, 1997).

10. The history of the monastery and church is set out in a booklet: *An Historical Sketch of the Abbey Church* (Dubuque, Iowa: New Melleray Abbey, n.d.); the spirit of the community is described in another book- let: *New Melleray Abbey: Cistercians of the Strict Observance* (Dubuque, Iowa: New Melleray Abbey, n.d.). See also R. Kevin Seasoltz, "L'Abbaye Notre-Dame de New Melleray," *Art d'Église,* XLVII (Janvier-Février-M ars 1979): 1-7; idem, "From the Bauhaus to the House of God's People: Frank Kacmarcik's Contribution to Church Art and Architecture," *U.S. Catholic Historian,* 15 (Winter 1997), pp. 114-15.

11. See Seasoltz, "From the Bauhaus to the House of God's People," 120-21; "A Tribute to Frank Kacmarcik," *Chapter and Verse,* Newsletter from Mepkin Abbey (Fall 2004).

A Merton Connection: Frank Kacmarcik, OblSB, Monk and Artist (1920-2004)

Charlotte Anne Zalot

I. Biography and Background

On February 22, 2004, a man who was, like Thomas Merton, both a monk and an artist, died peacefully yet unexpectedly in his sleep. His name was Frank Kacmarcik, a claustral oblate of Saint John's Abbey in Collegeville, Minnesota. One might wonder why an article about him appears in *The Merton Annual*, yet it will not take long to see that, in fact, this interdisciplinary journal is the rightful kind of place for this analysis.

Brother Frank Kacmarcik, OblSB, artist-designer and consultant in the sacred arts (1920-2004), and Thomas Merton (1915-1968) were friends. Remnants of written correspondence trace this; passing mention of Kacmarcik in some Merton writings, and journal, supports this; prayers written by Merton for Kacmarcik evidence this; and a log of this author's personal conversations with Kacmarcik confirm this. While their interest in art might seem to be the foremost link in their association, the connective strands supporting and sustaining their relationship were many: rich yet simple, real yet fundamentally spiritual. Their journeys, although different in some ways were remarkably similar in others. They shared a profound sense of vocation; they respected and used their gifts so that God would be glorified; they were tireless in promoting what was right and good. Kacmarcik and Merton were artists, each in his own right. Kacmarcik and Merton were also theologians, each in his own right. Kacmarcik and Merton were monastics, each in his own right.

On March 15, 1920, Frank Kacmarcik, an ordinary man of extraordinary talents, was born to parents of Polish-Slovak descent who led a life given to hard work, family ideals and the pursuit of a God relationship through the practice of religion. Raised in this strongly devout Catholic family where regular church attendance and daily prayer were the norm, the initial molding of Kacmarcik's religious consciousness began at a young age. In time, as these seeds took root, this faith force grew to motivate and animate Kacmarcik in every aspect of his life. Faith sustained by religion and devotion not only shaped Kacmarcik's life but greatly strengthened his character and his person.

Art was instinctive and natural to Kacmarcik in much the same way that art was instinctive and natural to Merton. It was part of who he was. For as long as he was able to remember, Kacmarcik was drawing and designing. It was a talent that was intuitive and innate, a natural gift which Jacques Maritain, the French philosopher who influenced both Merton and Kacmarcik, described as being "indispensable" to the creation of genuine art.[1] However, Kacmarcik had no formal study in art until he won a scholarship to the Minneapolis College of Art and Design (MCAD), in 1938 (then the Minneapolis School of Art.) It was during this time that Kacmarcik became a trained artist. He used his travel time to and from the school on the street car, a daily total of four hours, to read and study art books that were available in the school library. This insatiable quest for art knowledge also put Kacmarcik in touch with a number of important figures, among them the artist Eric Gill (1882-1940), who figuratively became a friend to Kacmarcik during his college years.

Gill's art work and writings strongly influenced Kacmarcik in his art and in some of his attitudes. Gill was a man who embraced the truth in his life, religion and art. When he converted to Catholicism he said: "I would not have anyone think that I became a Catholic because I was convinced of the truth, though I was convinced of the truth. I became a Catholic because I fell in love with the truth, and love is an experience I saw. I heard. I felt. I tasted. I touched."[2] Gill had a love affair with truth that resulted in a commitment to truth in any and all circumstances. His passion for truth and honesty was strong. His words and his deeds, and most certainly his art work, reflected this reality. "Compromise with truth was impossible for Gill."[3] Consequently, Gill was known, not only for his inability to compromise at any cost but for his directness in expressing his feelings and opinions. The same may well be said of Kacmarcik and Merton, both of whom possessed a courage for the truth that was free in its expression, significant in its meaningfulness, and challenging in its provocation.

Kacmarcik was known for not mincing words. Through the years various people noted this, not least among them Kacmarcik himself. One of his most influential mentors, Michael Marx, OSB (1913-1996), explained it this way: "[Frank has] salty speech but I hope it has the salt of the Gospel. [He] does not spare the individual and that can be painful in the face of the reality of the truth."[4] In an article written a dozen years ago, Kacmarcik's friend, Abbot Patrick Regan, OSB, said: "Frank is quick to express his opinion, express it freely and accurately, but without always considering how the opinions are going to be received by other people."[5] While it is true that Kacmarcik's outspokenness more than likely built up a list of people who disliked him, it seems that the truth he spoke, always candidly and frankly, likewise earned him the respect of many. Kacmarcik's faithfulness to his talents and his mind to speak the truth, regardless of its impact, allowed it to be said that "Frank is one who would see his children whimper now and live forever rather than be satisfied in the moment."[6] With that greater good in mind, Frank did not think about himself and how he would be accepted or not accepted, liked or disliked. Surely this would have earned him the admiration of Merton who, in his view of the modern world, believed that "many [people] seemed to be losing any ability to distinguish the true: appreciation of truth was apparently being lost because of increasingly greedy, cruel, and lustful pressures common to a society which encourages [a person] to ignore the truth and to be primarily concerned with fitting in, or with his [or her] own satisfaction."[7]

Similarities between Kacmarcik and Gill do not end with the avid proclamation of truth at any cost. Gill is recognized as having used the gifts of mind and will that God had given him, not only to create things but to respond creatively to the direction his life took. In so doing he was able to complete what God had begun in him and to become a whole person.[8] The introduction to Gill's autobiography (Beatrice Warde) sums it up well:

> For Gill stands, to many of us, as the good man who knew what he was good for and knew for what he was good: the type of artist, craftsman and artisan—whether in sculpture, wood-engraving, carved lettering or controversial writing— who will stand fast though he attract passionate opponents and joyous adversaries with every provocative stroke of chisel or pen .... [9]

This could well be said of Kacmarcik and Merton. Both were attuned to God as the root of their talent and the One to whom all glory and credit should be given for their accomplishments. The evolution of their wholeness resulted from their complete and total response to the gifts of God that resided within their person and took shape through their work.

In addition to becoming acquainted with Gill's work during his college years, Kacmarcik also became fascinated with the liturgy and learned about Saint John's Monastery in Collegeville, Minnesota. This happened as a result of having come in contact with the periodical *Orate Fratres*, now known as *Worship*. Kacmarcik was profoundly affected by the information and knowledge that he learned through reading this scholarly magazine. It fed his hunger to know as much as he could about the liturgy and inspired his ideas for designing church buildings that would enable people to truly worship God in the fullest way possible. Furthermore, because of its origin as a publication of the monks in Collegeville, he learned of this community of Benedictines, a learning that changed his life forever.

While Kacmarcik was inhaling everything he possibly could from the art library at MCAD, he discovered that there were such persons as brother-artists. He was fascinated by the work at Maria Laach Abbey. This famous Benedictine Abbey in Germany was the nascent home of the liturgical movement and its beginnings. It was here that a great deal was done in liturgical studies, including liturgical art and architecture, and Kacmarcik found this most alluring. When he discovered Saint John's in Collegeville and came in contact with Brother Clement Frischauf, OSB, an influential liturgical artist trained at the Abbey of Beuron, a new hope took root within him. Not only did his desire to be a liturgical artist deepen; now the possibility of being an artist within the context of the vowed life became plausible. When asked whether this was his awakening to the possibility of a religious vocation, Kacmarcik replied: "No, this was not the beginning of the stirrings of a religious vocation. The stirrings had always been there. It wasn't until I realized that there were such things as brother-artists that it became clarified."[10]

II. Early Years and Basic Aesthetics

In 1941, the same year that Merton entered the Cistercian Abbey of Gethsemani in Kentucky, Kacmarcik entered the Benedictine Abbey of Saint John's in Minnesota. Although hopeful that he would be able to pursue his art, there was no guarantee of this.

Despite that, he entered the community anyway to pursue his heart's desire to seek God. It was a story similar to that of Merton, about whom it has been said that "as a monk Merton never desired to relinquish fully all hopes to be a successful writer; but it is significant that as a young monk he was willing to cease writing if that appeared to be God's will."[11] While Kacmarcik admitted that there were not many opportunities to develop his artistic talent and interest, he simultaneously acknowledged that he was provided with more opportunities than might have been considered typical in those days. As a result of that, Kacmarcik was able to make his artistic mark on Saint John's.

When it came time for his first profession of vows, however, the community vote did not go in his favor and Kacmarcik was asked to leave. His forthrightness and honest expression of truth had not served him well; it suggested that he would never be able to fit into community life. The consequences of Kacmarcik's manner of veracity caused a very painful period in his life. He believed strongly in his Benedictine vocation but it was not to be at that time. The Abbot told him to go out into the world to mature and get more experience. Kacmarcik, without losing his love for Saint John's or his longing to be a monk, moved on with his life. In hindsight, he acknowledged that what happened was providential. He came to understand that his novitiate sojourn provided an important time in his personal formation.

After leaving the monastery Kacmarcik was drafted into the army. Kacmarcik admitted that he was not in favor of the war. However, unlike Merton, Kacmarcik did not seek conscientious objector status. Based on just war principles it is known that Merton did apply for noncombatant conscientious objector status. He never knew whether this was granted because with his entrance into religious life this became a non-issue. On the other hand, Kacmarcik became an army sergeant. During World War II he was in noncombative duty and served first as a surgical technician and then as a chaplain's assistant. This was a fortuitous happening as it permitted Kacmarcik to travel throughout Europe. Far from bringing a halt to his education, the years Kacmarcik spent in the Army, from 1944 to 1947, were important ones in his personal growth and artistic development. After the war, he went back to MCAD for one more year before he returned to Europe to study in Paris from 1948 to1950. While in Europe Kacmarcik traveled extensively; he visited churches and monasteries, museums and monuments, all of which contributed to the critical maturing of his background in church art and architecture. It was a time in which Kacmarcik's creativity was nurtured and stimulated. As a result, he was eventually able to respond to the art needs of the Church in very significant ways.

When his European study neared its end Kacmarcik was invited back to Saint John's, where he became a teacher in the art department. Although Kacmarcik was glad to be back at Saint John's as a professor of art, teaching and promoting the importance of sacred art and the vocation of sacred artists, it was not always smooth sailing for him. His honesty and frankness continued to be an irritant. Un-Christian he was not; straightforward, without concession, he was. Oddly enough, it was while doing work close to his heart that he was once again asked to leave Saint John's.

During Kacmarcik's tenure at Saint John's University the Benedictine community undertook a building project for the construction of a new Abbey church. Kacmarcik was asked to be the Art Coordinator for this effort. However, as the endeavor evolved, the Abbot feared the monks would not accept the plans if Kacmarcik's name was associated with them. The memory of Kacmarcik as an unreservedly opinionated young monk, combined with the experience of Kacmarcik as an authoritatively outspoken young professor, constituted Kacmarcik as a risk. Hence, despite having proved himself a successful teacher of great merit, Kacmarcik again left Saint John's and embarked on a journey that would have far-reaching and long-lasting effects in the liturgical world of the Catholic Church. As an artist, typographer, collector and liturgical consultant, Kacmarcik made an indelible mark, one that exemplified his creativity.

In describing Kacmarcik as creative, the word is not used lightly. In a Merton essay entitled: "The Catholic and Creativity," Merton set out to develop a theology of creativity. Basically, what Merton came to understand was that there is no genuine creativity apart from God: "The dignity of [a person] is to stand before God on his [or her] own feet, alive, conscious, alert to the light that has been placed in him [or her], and perfectly obedient to that light."[12] Merton went on further to say that one's creative gifts should be used "for the good of others and for the glory of God instead of exploiting them to draw attention to [oneself]."[13] Undoubtedly, Kacmarcik was creative in this truest and finest sense of the word. As stated by Merton, creativity becomes possible insofar as one can forget one's limitations and selfhood and lose oneself in "abandonment to the immense creative power of a love too great to be seen or comprehended."[14] Kacmarcik was a liturgical artist and designer who did that very thing; he was able to give himself over to the gifts and talents and abilities that he knew and was fully convinced were God-given. At the same time, while using his artistic ability in service to the Church as artist-designer and consultant in the sacred arts, he had a keen sense of the importance of investing self without imposing self. Particularly in his work of designing liturgical space and furnishings, Kacmarcik was clear that an artist did not have absolute freedom to do whatever he or she wanted to do. Any art or design in service to the Church would seek to emphasize and clarify the action of the Church and its liturgy and not compete with it. According to Kacmarcik, the artistic design of the space and furnishings, as well as any art work in the space, should never dominate the action of the liturgy. In response to questions about this, Kacmarcik was quite clear that, while not imposing themselves, artists do have distinctive styles: "You can't avoid yourself. If you did, you would be nothing. Every person is given a personage and there is no reason why they should hide it. Of course, they have to govern it in the circumstances but they should be true to themselves."[15] Merton's thoughts on artistic freedom extend the discussion:

> True artistic freedom can never be a matter of sheer willfulness, or arbitrary posturing. It is the outcome of authentic possibilities, understood and accepted in their own terms, not the refusal of the concrete in favor of the purely "interior." In the last analysis, the only valid witness to the artist's creative freedom is his [or her] work itself. The artist builds his [or her] own freedom and forms his [or her] own artistic conscience, by the work of his [or her] hands.[16]

Being true to yourself without imposing yourself or giving in to "sheer willfulness" or "arbitrary posturing," and instead allowing the honesty of function and the confession of truth in art and design to be primary, is a challenge for the liturgical artist. It is a challenge Kacmarcik accepted and handled quite well. In large part this is due to his view of himself as a sacred artist. In the words of Daisetz Suzuki, a spokesman of Zen who was greatly admired by Merton and whose contacts with the West allowed him to explain his basic Zen idea of art in Christian terms: "The greatest productions of art, whether painting, music, sculpture or poetry, have invariably this quality—something approaching the work of God. The artist, at the moment when his creativeness is at its height, is transformed into an agent of the creator."[17] This is a concept that Kacmarcik also took seriously. He never credited his work to himself but to the gifts and special talents from God that enabled him to do what he did. It is probably the reason why he was the successful designer of the covers and interior layout for *Worship* from 1950 until his death, why he received numerous awards for his work in book design and graphic arts, why so many of the more than 200 churches in whose design he was involved were so successful and very often award-winning.

Kacmarcik had specific ideas about what it meant to be a sacred artist. He professed that a sacred artist is one who is "to serve as a spokes[person] and minister of the Christian mystery, to provide a prophetic and priestly mediation of God's truth to God's people."[18] As a sacred artist, Kacmarcik felt a large responsibility to put himself at the service of truth, of the mystery, so as to glorify God by the service he rendered to the Church through his work. For Kacmarcik, his service as an artist-designer and consultant in the sacred arts became his vocation. It was a way of serving God and God's people. It was a way of joining self and service. "True vocation begins in the self where we know we are here on earth to be the gifts God created"[19] and in so doing to use the gifts God gives in order to satisfy that purpose. While vocation is related to one's work it was clearly much more than that for Kacmarcik. Essentially, the biblical understanding of vocation is rooted in the belief that God is the fundamental source and initiator of vocation. God is the One who calls and therefore, a vocation is from God. Merton believed a vocation was a personal call. Kacmarcik, too, embraced this sense of vocation, one in which God initiated and he responded. "A vocation means that one lives in responsible obedience to God in the way that God has so destined" and to this end, although the actual work is not the vocation, "it is the significant opportunity for the person to give evidence of the calling given them."[20]

Those who discern a vocation sort through the movements of their heart and unfold the truth of who they most deeply are. It is discernment that reveals the best way to live in truth before God. When Kacmarcik looked deeply into himself and when, with typical Kacmarcik integrity, he defined his true self and his God-given gifts, he knew that to be a sacred artist was his calling in life. He said: "And since then, I have never had any question about my vocation in life. I have been spared that uncertainty and indecision . . . [T]he conviction that I was going to be some sort of church artist has remained with me."[21] Looking at this part of Kacmarcik's life and his dedication to it allows one to conclude that the energy of the religious vocation that was not meant to be his in the early 1940s fueled what he then considered to be his true vocation as artist-designer and consultant in the sacred arts. To amplify, I quote Parker Palmer, internationally renowned teacher, author and education activist: "We must take the no of the way that closes and find the guidance it has to offer—and take the yes of the way that opens and respond with the yes of our lives."[22] This is what Kacmarcik did. He responded with a full and resounding yes to the way that opened to him when he was first asked to leave Saint John's Abbey and then several years later, when he was likewise asked to leave Saint John's University.

III. Kindred Spirits in Relation to Vocation

Kacmarcik and Merton seemed to have been kindred spirits in their understanding of vocation. It has been written:

> Retrospectively, it is clear that Merton conceived of his vocation as fundamentally that of a writer—a monk striving to find God through language. . . . What the mature writer knows is that God chose to place him in a monastery, but since he was first a writer, and a monk second, God allowed him to work his way closer to the Divine through the writing.[23]

In Merton's own words: " . . . it is not possible to doubt that I am a writer, that I was born one and will most probably die as one . . . this seems to be my lot and my vocation. It is what God has given me in order that I might give it back to Him."[24] Similarly, Kacmarcik said: "I can't sing. I have no charm. I have no beauty. But I do have gifts in art. I cannot take pride in this. It is from God. It could be lost in a moment."[25] These statements are like a clear window into the souls and motivations of these two artists and monks. Both were committed to their God-given gifts and talents. Both took their gifts seriously and spent their lives stewarding them. There are not many people who have such confidence in their gifts and who are able to acknowledge them so truth-fully. However, when one has an accurate view of him- or herself this is humility at its best and the kind that brings with it the free-dom to respond to the gifts and talents that have been given so they do not become sterile or ineffective. For Kacmarcik, and like-wise for Merton, their vocation as sacred artist and writer respec-tively, was never a goal to be achieved. Rather, it was a calling to be received, responded to, and lived. It was a gift that became an obligation. It was a gift to be lived out in service. "True vocation joins self and service."[26] This is what Kacmarcik, and undoubt-edly Merton as well, did. Each of them joined who they were with service and as a result of that partnership were able to make re-markable contributions.

In 1947, the year that Merton professed his solemn vows, Kacmarcik became involved in his first church project. It was the year that *Mediator Dei* was promulgated by Pope Pius XII. This is the document believed to have given official endorsement to the American Liturgical Movement. From then until his death in 2004 Kacmarcik rendered considerable and distinguished additions to the artistic sphere of the liturgical movement, designing worship spaces that both anticipated and supported the liturgical renewal called for by Vatican II and the *Constitution on the Sacred Liturgy* (1963). It has been said that "it was not until Frank Kacmarcik came onto the scene . . . that modern church architecture took its rightful place within the liturgical movement, with the creation of high-quality, uniquely American structures for the gathering of the Mystical Body of Christ."[27] Like Merton, Kacmarcik was a prophet of sorts. While it is true that he did not necessarily dis-cover new things, Kacmarcik was able to make fresh designs from a deep understanding of tradition and thus create that which would be able to speak to people of the present age in a manner that was both timeless and enduring. Moreover, the prominence and effec-tiveness of Merton and Kacmarcik resulted from one of the essen-tial characteristics of a prophet: the courage to be critical. Both men were known for outspoken criticism in their respective fields. It cannot be denied that if one is truly to be a prophet, the ability to be penetratingly demanding is imperative. Critical confrontation, whether in written word or visual art, provided it is based on truth and rooted in love, can be a positive propheticism calling the Church and the people of God to be more. In this regard, Kacmarcik, along with Merton, excelled.

Kacmarcik's contributions to the development and design of liturgical space and furnishings in American Roman Catholic churches for more than fifty-five years are noteworthy. They are contributions that called the Church and the people of God to be more. A vision that grew from within enabled Kacmarcik to pioneer the role of liturgical consultant. By honoring his truest self and his authentic talents Kacmarcik was able to set the standards and identify an essential ministry in the Church. This ministry proved itself to be indispensable to the proper renovation and design of church buildings and furnishings for worship. Taking the responsibility seriously and using his talented response-ability Kacmarcik gave shape and form to a role in the Church that would more than likely not have been had otherwise. "Liturgical Consultant" is the title that Kacmarcik first coined in 1954 and subsequently sanctioned by his work. Although this ministry was accepted and valued by many, it was not given official recognition until 1978 when *Environment and Art in Catholic Worship* (EACW), guidelines for the building and renovation of liturgical space, was issued by the Bishops' Committee on the Liturgy of the United States Catholic Conference of Bishops. In this document the liturgical consultant is acknowledged for the first time as "an invaluable partner of the architect, for the purposes of the space can be imagined and the place creatively designed only by a competent designer who is nourished with the liturgy's tradition ..." (EACW, Article 48). Kacmarcik was indeed a competent designer but he viewed himself as more than a designer. As a liturgical consultant Kacmarcik considered himself a deacon and a visual theologian, roles that he took most seriously.

The word deacon is known to be derived from the Greek word *diakonos* meaning servant and helper. In the early centuries of the Church it referred to a specific office. The designated mission of the deacon was one of service to the people of God. While it is true that the role of deacon had its ups and downs, thus causing its importance to shift and decline throughout the centuries before being reinstated by Vatican II as a permanent ministry of service in the Catholic Church, its essence was always about service.[28] This is primarily why Kacmarcik described himself as a deacon. Although his ministry and service as a liturgical consultant was not an ordained one in the literal sense, for him it was holy and sacred, one conferred on him by the power of God. Kacmarcik believed strongly that a sacred artist is one who has a Christian vocation, a diaconal ministry as it were, just as surely as does a priest. His belief was rooted in an understanding of the common priesthood, the priesthood of all believers.

The Church teaches that Christ, high priest and mediator, has made the Church "a kingdom, priests for his God and Father" (Revelation 1: 6). The whole community of believers, by virtue of their baptism, is priestly. They exercise their priesthood through their vocation and participation in "Christ's mission as priest, prophet and king."[29] In the Dogmatic Constitution on the Church, *Lumen Gentium*, promulgated by Pope Paul VI in November of 1964, it is clear that the faithful share in the one priesthood of Christ. Articles 10-12 of Chapter II, "The People of God," are a well-defined description of the dignity of the people of God as they are called to be participants in the kingship, priesthood and prophetic office of Christ. The concept of the common priesthood is dealt with extensively and finds its basis in strong biblical foundations.[30]

The ministry of the people of God derives its nature from the ministry of Jesus Christ. All believers, by virtue of their baptism, are participants in the priestly ministry of Jesus Christ and are called to use their gifts in service to the Church. In quoting Martin Luther it can be further explained:

> Luther said, "All Christians are priests and all priests are Christians." Luther argued that the simple milkmaid or tailor with the Word of God in his or her hands was able to please God and minister the things of God as effectively as the priest, the prelate and the pope himself (*Babylonian Captivity of the Church* 2.284).[31]

This kind of explanation and understanding gave Kacmarcik the validity he felt was necessary to call himself a deacon of the visual arts:

> I have the role of deacon. It is not yet formalized but we already have the power. We are baptized into the common priesthood and into ministry. And I started that right off from the beginning. There has been no following consultant who quite operated the way I do. I always insisted that my service was a religious service.[32]
>
>   I function as a deacon. In the 1940s you knew that was officially an impossibility but when you already have the power you do not worry about such trivialities.[33]

It is conceivable that the nature of Kacmarcik's work also contributed to his view of it as a religious service, a ministry. Being involved in the design of liturgical space and furnishings meant that the fruit of his labors would impact the worship of the people of God. Likewise, it would influence the people's understanding of their participation in the mission of the Church to which they are called by virtue of their baptism. Kacmarcik's consciousness of the priesthood of the laity could not help but impact his church design. His understanding of the priesthood of believers not only shaped his role as a "deacon" of the arts but likewise shaped his design work as a liturgical consultant.

Although Kacmarcik never earned a degree in theology or formally studied theology, he still considered himself a theologian, specifically a visual theologian. According to the *Instruction on the Ecclesial Vocation of the Theologian*, issued in 1990 by the Congregation for the Doctrine of Faith, the role of the theologian is to seek the truth which is the living God, to respond dynamically and to communicate that truth.[34] If a theologian is one who seeks, responds to and communicates truth, then a theologian such as Kacmarcik, a sacred artist, would be one who accomplishes that through the visual arts. The artist, in the role of teacher of knowledge and truth, imparts a visual theology through the work of art and design.

Another interesting insight into the definition of a theologian is proposed by Jürgen Moltmann. His thesis is that every believer is a theologian: "Every Christian, man or woman, young or old, who believes and thinks at all about that belief is a theologian."[35] Moltmann recognizes that theology is about seeking understanding and theologians are those who teach that understanding. At the same time, it is his conviction that theology does not aim to know its object, God, in order to dominate God; rather:

> Theology belongs to the sphere of knowledge that sustains existence, [which] gives us courage to live and consolation in dying. It is the knowledge that lends us bearings, the knowledge we seek in order to perceive the path we are to take.[36]

While one might wonder what this has to do with the design of liturgical space, it can be clarified in the work of Kacmarcik who saw himself as a visual theologian who strove for the truth and who believed that the theology and truth communicated by the design of the space is indispensable for the Church and the educa-

Saint Francis of Assisi Processional Cross
Raleigh, North Carolina
1995

tion and spiritual growth of its community of worshiping faithful. Kacmarcik was a fervent believer that the liturgical environment has a purpose far greater than the designer behind it and is about much more than advanced technology and pure aesthetics. As leading Lutheran architect Edward Sovik has said, the design of liturgical space "is a means not simply of accomplishing technical intention, but of dealing with ideas, and at its most serious, with the disclosure of truth."[37] Although not specifically using the term "visual theology," Sovik is clear that architecture can, and must, reflect "commitment to truth and to the authentic" and as such, church architecture "ought to be absolutely forthright, entirely authentic" in its expression of the truth which it is about.[38]

As a liturgical consultant and as a visual theologian, by his design of liturgical space and furnishings Kacmarcik was a communicator. As an artist, and in the role of teacher of knowledge and truth, Kacmarcik imparted visual theology through his work. Visual theology, according to Frank Nieset, has three parts. Several years ago, Nieset spoke of visual theology in terms of the how, the what and the why. He specified that it is the artist's talent that enables the how of the expression; the sincerity in the spiritual life based on true knowledge of theology that brings about the what of the expression; and the courage of the artist to combine the how and the what for the education and enlightenment of others that defines the why of the expression.[39] In light of this explanation Kacmarcik stands as an example of one who was talented and sincerely spiritual; he was courageous in using those two traits to produce visual arts that were theologically sound. An example would be the Glorified Crucifix, a major theological symbol in Kacmarcik's work and one that appeared frequently throughout his career as an artist-designer and consultant in the sacred arts.

Kacmarcik had strong feelings about the crucifix that finds its place in a worship space. Early in his career he was encouraged by friend and mentor, Paschal Botz, OSB, to design a Glorified Crucifix. It was designed for homes, offices, classrooms and sick rooms but almost immediately became his inspiration for the crucifix to be used in a worship space as well. The Glorified Crucifix is a perfect specimen of visual theology. Botz taught Kacmarcik that a crucifix of this type would be a return to the glorified conception of the cross that had prevailed in the Church for many centuries, the concept of which prevails in the liturgy. It is a type of crucifix that preceded the sorrowful type. However, it does not deny Christ's sufferings and this is apparent in Kacmarcik's design. The corpus that graces the cross always shows the wounds of Christ while visualizing the living Christ "in the glorified state in which he now exists."[40] It does not deny the way of the cross for Christians but recalls that the full Christian mystery is suffering, death and resurrection. It serves as a strong reminder that the vision of the Glorified Christ is the power that transforms ordinary suffering into Christian suffering. A message of faith is conveyed as well as a challenge of hope. This is the visual theology that is manifested in the crucifixes Kacmarcik advocated for a worship space. Through the years many different designs revolving around the theological concept of the Glorified Christ on the cross were fashioned by Kacmarcik. The designs, while most pleasing, are, more importantly, theologically sound and in possession of context and truth. This was very important to Kacmarcik. The visual theology that the design communicated was the theology by which the worshiping assembly would be shaped. That the crucifix will allow an assembly of believers to imagine the entire paschal mystery is a conviction that Kacmarcik maintained throughout his entire career as a liturgical consultant. Informed by sound Catholic doctrine, created with intuitive artistic talent, and exhibitive of a reliable visual theology, the designs of Kacmarcik's Glorified Crucifix have endured through the years and continue to be viable. The integrity of their message and design is of a quality that is indeed timeless and a confidence that was both accurate and precise.

As a visual theologian Kacmarcik had a "homiletic," a message as it were, an instruction that he preached faithfully throughout his life. It was simple yet profound and it was his mantra as a liturgical consultant. Based on the famous words of Winston Churchill, "we shape our buildings, and afterwards, our buildings shape us," Kacmarcik consistently stated over and over again that "we are formed or deformed by the art and environment we experience around us."[41] Whether it was a workshop or a seminar, a symposium or an interview, a conference or a consultation, Kacmarcik always found a way to convey this message to any and all audiences.

It was Kacmarcik's opinion that the visual environment is not merely about aesthetics, and thus he was insistent that at all times people should be in touch with the realization that the environment, any environment, is very influential. Comprehension of this fact leads to an alertness and awareness that will unfold in critical discernment, judicious evaluation and a demand for quality in the renovation or design of liturgical space. Kacmarcik saw this as a huge challenge as a result of what he termed visual literacy.

Back in the 1960s Kacmarcik made the headlines when he said that 98% of the clergy were visually illiterate and a somewhat higher percentage of the hierarchy.[42] His audacity to say such a thing caused quite a furor. Although it meant losing a job or two his integrity and his certainty of accuracy in this regard prevented him from any retraction of the statement whatsoever. Several years later, while in a panel discussion about the need artists and clergy have for one another, Kacmarcik reiterated this same view and said quite strongly:

> Most clergymen are visually illiterate. If the church needed the artist in the past, it needs him [or her] more than ever today because we are living in the most visual age in history. Through visual environment, we form or deform people spiritually. Religious leaders should be concerned about the witnessing power of a visual setting.[43]

Liturgical space is a teacher and this is what Kacmarcik hoped to convey by his firm conviction that as teacher it has the potential to form or deform. In support of this position William Seth Adams makes an important statement:

> The setting, the environment in which the liturgy is celebrated is where the body of Christ is formed, edified, nourished. Liturgical spaces are profound teachers of the nature of the church and they are central to the process of formation. Thus, theological deliberation about liturgical space, about spatial expression, about "meaning," is fundamental to the making of Christians.[44]

Everything about liturgical space, everything that contributes to its arrangement and quality, has the ability to shape the faith community who gathers in it. Therefore, the space must possess an honesty that allows it to be faithful and true to its function, thus enabling it to form rather than deform the worshipers. This honesty must be one that evolves from truthfulness in design, in use of materials and in the actual building of the place. This is a concept that was roundly supported by Sovik:

Architecture is an expression and communicative medium, revealing and echoing the minds of its builders and forming or deforming those who subject themselves to its message. Therefore, a church will attempt in its configuration of space and substance to be a faithful and lucid evocation, a shelter which asserts in the language of architecture the self-understanding of the community and thus helps it to become what it is.[45]

Sovik strongly believes in the power of a church building to communicate and if it was to communicate well, then it must be true and honest in every respect. In his book, *Architecture for Worship*, he outlines some misconceptions about church architecture, all of which could lend to making a liturgical space more deformative than formative. It is his contention that good church architecture is about more than skillful solutions to technical problems, more than a pleasant appeal to the senses, more than a space that simply provides an exciting sensual experience, and more than a matter of self-expression.[46] True and lasting meaning must be suggested, inspiration as to the purpose of community must be imparted, and spiritual significance must be conveyed so that values not communicable by any other means can be expressed and embraced, taught and learned. It is only when guided by an understanding such as this that a liturgical space can indeed be formative as it should be.

This corresponds well to some of Merton's feelings about architecture. Merton was convinced that Cistercian architecture was beautiful primarily because it was right: "Our Fathers did not build according to canons of beauty, but according to notions of what was right for monks."[47] Merton suggested as well that what was "right" was also formative. In one of his journals he made a correlation between the architecture and the prayer of Cistercians saying that "Cistercian architecture explains many things about our rule and life. A church . . . is born of prayer and is a prayer. Its simplicity and its energy tell us what our prayer should be . . . ."[48] Consequently, in its effective telling the environment makes an impression and is thus able to be formative. The liturgical space influences and impacts the individual and the community and has the potential to shape and enable the community's prayer.

Another liturgical consultant, Robert Rambusch, a contemporary as well as a friend of Kacmarcik, also supported Kacmarcik's

idea about the ability of the liturgical environment to form or deform:

> The designs of church buildings will either encourage and en-
> hance participation or limit and frustrate it. Whatever is newly
> built has consequences; whatever is left unchanged has conse-
> quences. We are formed or deformed by our worship envi-
> ronment. If you are going to build a church you are going to
> create something that speaks. It will speak of values and mean-
> ings, it will go on speaking. If it speaks of wrong values it will
> go on destroying.[49]

Clearly, this insight gives credence to the power of a liturgical environment and the reality that the created and established space
will, by its very nature, continue to have an effect long after the
last stone is laid and the doors are opened. The articulation of
theology with stones and mortar makes of itself a lasting image
and one that is not easily reworded. Therefore, great care must be
taken to insure that the expressed theology is indeed one that is
true so as to be formative in the best possible sense. As Rambusch
further explains, "Church architecture is not only a reflection of
values, it is an imposition of values."[50] As such, those values must
be carefully thought out and planned for in design and representation. Kacmarcik had remarked on more than one occasion that
the Church structure forms the people's spirit. Therefore, liturgical design is not something that can be taken lightly or done
thoughtlessly. Much is at stake in the liturgical, theological and
spiritual formation that will result because of it.

Marchita Mauck, a teacher and author who also works as a
liturgical design consultant, expresses the importance of the environment being a vehicle of liturgical theology but also adds to the
concept:

> Building and renovating is about translating a liturgical theol-
> ogy . . . and beauty into three dimensions. It is about forming
> a holy people whose lives are transformed, motivated, formed
> and sustained by their experience in that place.[51]

While the space is indeed formative or deformative, what happens in the space is likewise formative and deformative. Her thesis is that buildings themselves don't do the forming or deforming; rather, the buildings can "invite experiences" that enable the
forming or deforming.[52] Her point is well made and is certainly

not at odds with Kacmarcik's "homiletic." Undoubtedly, this is the basis for a design solution with the potential to be formative: an understanding of how the building is to function, an understanding of what is to take place in the building. Building or renovating liturgical space is about much more than construction. At its very best it is about instruction, about a space that teaches and communicates, about a space that forms and transforms. While it is true that a liturgical space should delight the worshipers, it is equally true and doubly important that it direct the worshipers. It must be a space that leads them to an ever-growing and ever-deepening understanding of what it means to be the mystical body of Christ at work together in the celebration of God in worship.

Essentially, Kacmarcik had an intuitive sense of the ability of a liturgical space to be a teacher. As well-stated, again by Adams, "Liturgical spaces are powerful teachers. They teach the Church about the Church: about who we are, how we work, what we do, what is important to us, who is important to us; and they teach us about God."[53] In this respect, Kacmarcik's knowledge and understanding of the power of sacred art and architecture cannot be minimized. His commitment to authentic truth is foundational to the visual theology to which his designs and works give form, forms whose value could be easily acknowledged by an explanation given by Romano Guardini (1885-1968), one of the generators of the Liturgical Movement: "Authentic religious [sacred] art [and architecture] is essentially a way to God and vice versa."[54]

IV. Parallels in How Kacmarcik and Merton Function as Theologians

Kacmarcik functioned as a theologian in much the same way that Merton did. Insight into Merton as "theologian" is particularly apropos: "In a profound way, Merton is a 'theologian' in the oldest sense of the term—not as a professional thinker in the service of ideas and not as a person of systematic theological reflection, but as someone who knows how to speak of God authentically."[55] Like Merton, who knew how to speak of God authentically through his writings, Kacmarcik knew how to speak of God authentically as a deacon of the arts and a visual theologian. As a Visual Theologian, Kacmarcik's "homiletic" was his first and foremost impulse of design. Respecting and reverencing the power of a liturgical environment to be either formative or deformative is what enabled Kacmarcik's works to be both exceptional and distinguished. As such, they are sometimes acclaimed and other times roundly criticized, acknowledged though not always appreciated. Nevertheless, it was work that became noteworthy and important to the development of Roman Catholic liturgical space and furnishings both before and after Vatican II, making its mark over a period of more than fifty-five years and continuing to have impact to the present day.

As theologians, each in their own right, Merton and Kacmarcik not only spoke of God, they led others to God. Through their words and their works, their lives and their living, they guided and inspired, persuaded and convinced. Merton strongly adhered to the belief that authenticity made a good monk and a good theologian. The Truth upheld was to be genuine; the Truth served was to be undisguised. Throughout his career as a liturgical consultant Kacmarcik had been clear that sacred artists perform a spiritual service through their work and as a result, are to be considered spiritual directors of the visual form. By taking his role as theologian seriously, he became a master who performed his duties well. His work was a service and as servant, Kacmarcik served the Church and its tradition with sensitivity and excellence, creating images and spaces that had the power to speak with clarity and distinction. The value of any art work or design as regards liturgical space is the instruction and inspiration it provides. Kacmarcik understood this and had a clear perception of how the artist-designer and consultant in the sacred arts, the liturgical consultant, functioned as a visual theologian.

Merton knew Kacmarcik as a liturgical consultant and champion of the arts. He expressed that he was "glad Frank [Kacmarcik] is keeping his head above water and defending the cause of sacred art step by step."[56] To this end, Merton further supported him by responding to Kacmarcik's request in the 1950s for specific prayers related to his cause and composed three prayers: the first, "For Vocations in the Realm of Sacred Art;" the second, "In Selecting an Artist for a Sacred Work;' and the third, "For the Artist and for the Work in Progress." Kacmarcik used these prayers throughout his career, particularly the one for more vocations in Sacred Art, a vocation he believed in and lived, embraced and encouraged. At the same time, he never gave up his monastic heart and, as he was fond of saying, "after maturing and getting experience out in the world for forty-five years," he found his way back to the monastery. He was accepted as a claustral oblate and made his promises in 1988. For Kacmarcik, it was a homecoming for which he had longed and nothing gave him greater pleasure than to live the life of a monk, welcomed by his brother monks as a community member of Saint John's Abbey in Collegeville.

Kacmarcik and Merton were men committed to their faith, to their God-given gifts, to their monastic vocations. Robert Rambusch, good friend of Kacmarcik and admirer of Merton, recalled visiting Gethsemani with Kacmarcik around 1960. He said that Merton knew Kacmarcik's work and was appreciative of it. His observation of Kacmarcik and Merton interacting with one another clearly revealed Kacmarcik and Merton as two men who shared a love for art as well as a love for monasticism. Rambusch said, "They were real gangbusters; they were both exciting and successful and they shared vigor and zeal." Rambusch particularly appreciated the openness they exhibited and recounted Kacmarcik's extreme reaction to the room where they were received at the monastery. The reception room was, in Kacmarcik's opinion, a very sensual purple. When Merton arrived to greet them, Kacmarcik asked him whoever chose such a color, one that Kacmarcik declared made the room "look like a brothel." Merton heartily agreed while adding that it was "reminiscent of [his] pre-*Seven Storey Mountain* days!" Rambusch further recounted that Kacmarcik had a knack for enlivening conversations and remarked that "interesting people were interested in him and it was not surprising that he and Merton hit it off so well." Combine this with Merton's ability to unleash inquisitive minds and you find that any time shared by Merton and Kacmarcik was more than likely a real heyday for both of them.[57]

As artists and as monks Kacmarcik and Merton lived their lives powerfully motivated to glorify God in all things. By embracing their talents and using them in service to God and God's people, they were successful. The contributions they made to the Church and to the world were exceptional as a result of their entering deeply into their Christian vocation and as a result of their being faithful to their unique abilities. However, perhaps in the end, what was most important was the communion with God that their vocation as monk and artist provided them for it is without doubt that the "Divine Being pulsed through [their] talent"[58] and took flesh in exciting and innovative ways through their creative genius.

It is well known that Eric Gill said that the artist is not a special kind of person, but every person is a special kind of artist. This same idea was supported by Ananda Coomaraswamy (1877-1947), friend of Gill and admired by Merton. Merton took the concept a step further and suggested that it applied not only to artists but to Christians and proposed that "the creative Christian is not a special kind of Christian, but every Christian has his [or her] own creative work to do, his [or her] own part in the mystery of the 'new creation.'"[59] As such, Kacmarcik and Merton, good artists as well as good Christians, accepted the responsibility to participate in "the work of restoring all things in Christ" through their creative activities and, as a result, brought God to fuller revelation in the world. No doubt, from their home in eternity they both echo the words Merton wrote for Kacmarcik and together pray: "Send [them] now people of vision who will open [their] eyes once again to see your incorruptible light . . . teach [them] to see with pure hearts the splendor of your Son Jesus Christ and to express what they have seen in images [and words and actions] worthy of so great a vision: through the same Jesus Christ, your Son, your logos, your Art and your Splendor, in whom all things subsist and through whom, by the power of the Holy Spirit, all are called to be united with you forever. Amen."[60]

Notes

1. Jacques Maritain, *Art and Scholasticism,* trans. J. F. Scanlan (London: Sheed and Ward, 1930), p. 42.

2. Eric Gill, *Autobiography* (New York: The Devin-Adair Company, 1941), p. 247.

3. Graham Carey, "Eric Gill: 1882-1940," *Liturgical Arts* 9, no. 1 (1940): p. 25.

4. Henry Fehrenbacher, "Catching the Soul of Frank Kacmarcik," Unpublished manuscript (undated), Kacmarcik Archives, Saint John's University, Collegeville, MN.

5. Julie Inglebret, "Bound to Books," *St. Cloud Times,* 25 October 1992, p. 10.

6. Fehrenbacher.

7. Victor A. Kramer, *Thomas Merton: Monk and Artist,* Revised ed. (Kalamazoo: Cistercian Publications, 1984), p. 93.

8. Conrad Pepler, OP, "The Life and Teaching of Eric Gill," *The Catholic Art Quarterly* 11, no. 2 (1948): p. 88.

9. Gill, p. xii.

10. Frank Kacmarcik, Interview by author, Transcribed tape-recording, Saint John's Abbey, Collegeville, MN, 6 February 2003.

11. Kramer, *Thomas Merton: Monk and Artist*, Preface.

12. Louis Merton, O.C.S.O., William Davidson, M.D., and Brother Antoninus, O.P., "The Catholic and Creativity," *American Benedictine Review* (1960): p. 209. Reprinted as "Theology of Creativity" in Thomas Merton, *Literary Essays*, ed., Brother Patrick Hart (New York: New Directions, 1981) p. 367.

13. Merton, Davidson and Antoninus, *American Benedictine Review*, p. 209; (*Literary Essays*, p. 367).

14. Merton, Davidson and Antoninus, *American Benedictine Review*, p. 210; (*Literary Essays*, p. 368).

15. Frank Kacmarcik, Interview by author, Transcribed tape recording, Saint John's Abbey, Collegeville, MN, 28 February 2003.

16. Thomas Merton, "Answers on Art and Freedom," in *Raids on the Unspeakable* (New York: New Directions), p. 175.

17. Merton, "The Catholic and Creativity," p. 207; (*Literary Essays*, p. 364).

18. Frank Kacmarcik, "The Bible and Creative Imagination," *Liturgical Arts* 32, no. 2 (1964), p. 65

19. Frederick Buechner, *Wishful Thinking: A Seeker's ABC* (San Francisco: Harper and Row, Publishers, 1993), p. 119.

20. David J. Maitland, "Vocation," in *Handbook of Christian Theology*, ed. Marvin Halverson and Arthur A. Cohen (Cleveland: The World Publishing Company, 1958), pp. 320-321.

21. Frank Kacmarcik, "The Berakah Award for 1981," *Worship* 55, no. 4 (1981), p. 361.

22. Parker J. Palmer, *Let Your Life Speak* (San Francisco: Jossey-Bass, Inc., 2000), p. 55.

23. Kramer, *Thomas Merton: Monk and Artist*, Preface.

24. Thomas P. McDonnell, ed., *A Thomas Merton Reader*, Revised ed. (Garden City, NY: Double-Day Image, 1974), p. 17.

25. Frank Kacmarcik, *Talk Given to Catholic University Law School* (Washington, 1993), Videocassette.

26. Palmer, *Let Your Life Speak*, p. 16.

27. Keith Pecklers, *The Unread Vision, the Liturgical Movement in the United States: 1926-1955* (Collegeville: The Liturgical Press, 1998), p. 255.

28. James Monroe Barnett, *The Diaconate: A Full and Equal Order*, Revised ed. (Valley Forge: Trinity Press International, 1995), p. 16.

29. *Catechism of the Catholic Church, Libreria Editrice Vaticana* ed. (Liguori: Liguori Publications, 1994), p. 386.

30. Aloys Grillmeier, "Dogmatic Constitution of the Church, Commentary on Chapter II," in *Commentary on the Documents of Vatican II*, ed. Herbert Vorgrimler (New York: Herder and Herder, 1966), p. 156.

31. R. Paul Stevens, *The Other Six Days: Vocation, Work and Ministry in Biblical Perspective* (Grand Rapids: William B. Eerdmans Publishing Company, 1999), pp. 173-174.

32. Frank Kacmarcik, Interview by Author, Transcribed tape recording, Saint John's Abbey, Collegeville, MN, 8 February 2003.

33. Frank Kacmarcik, *Lecture on Architecture*, 28 February 1994, Audio-tape.

34. *Instruction on the Ecclesial Vocation of the Theologian*, (Congregation for the Doctrine of Faith, 24 May 1990, accessed 11 July 2003); available from /congregations/ cfaith /" www.vatican.va/. /congregations/ cfaith / documents/ re____con cfaith/doc_ 19900524_theologian-vocation_en.html.

35. Jürgen Moltmann, *What Is A Theologian* [Internet Article] (Princeton Theological Seminary, Princeton Lectures on Youth, Church and Culture, 1999, accessed 16 July 2003); available from http:// www.ptsem.edu/iym/research/ lectures.

36. Moltmann, *What Is A Theologian*, (accessed).

37. Edward Sovik, *Architecture for Worship* (Minneapolis: Augsburg Publishing House, 1973), p. 44.

38. Sovik, *Architecture for Worship*, p. 55.

39. Frank E. Nieset, "A New Order According to Michelangelo," *The Josephinum Review: A Catholic Bi-Weekly* 8, no. 15 (1954), p. 12.

40. Paschal Botz, OSB, *The Saint Paul Statuary Presents the Glorified Crucifix*, Advertisement Pamphlet, 1947, Saint Paul Statuary Company, St. Paul, MN.

41. Kacmarcik, "The Berakah Award for 1981," p. 363.

42. Dick Cunningham, "He Teaches Clergy Their Artistic ABCs," *Minneapolis Tribune* (1960s), p. 15.

43. "Panelists Say Artists, Clergy Need Each Other," *The Minneapolis Star*, 5 October 1974, 10A.

44. William Seth Adams, "Theology and Liturgical Space," *Liturgy* 6, no. 4 (1987), p. 29.

45. Edward Sovik, "*Esse Quam Videri*: Notes on the Building of Churches, 1969," Unpublished Manuscript, Kacmarcik Archives, Collegeville, MN.

46. Sovik, *Architecture for Worship*, pp. 44-50.

47. Quoted from "Notes on Sacred Art, " (p. 24) and found in Hongchang Yew, "Thomas Merton's Journey with Art: A Study of Thomas Merton's Spiritual Aesthetics" (Ph.D. Dissertation, Drew University, 1999), p. 159.

48. Thomas Merton, *Entering the Silence: Becoming a Monk and Writer*, ed. Jonathan Montaldo (New York: HarperSanFrancisco, 1996), p. 37.

49. Robert E. Rambusch, "What Mean These Stones? A Theology of Church Building," in *Jesus Christ Reforms His Church: Twenty Sixth North American Liturgical Week, 1965*, ed. The Liturgical Conference (Baltimore, Portland, Chicago: The Liturgical Conference, Washington, D.C., 1966), p. 122.

50. Rambusch, p. 122.

51. Marchita B. Mauck, *Places for Worship: A Guide to Building and Renovating* (Collegeville: The Liturgical Press, 1995), p. 7.

52. Mauck, *Places for Worship*, p. 9.

53. Adams, p. 33.

54. Romano Guardini, "Sacred Images and the Invisible God," *Cross Currents* (1957): p. 219.

55. Lawrence S. Cunningham, *Thomas Merton and the Monastic Vision* (Grand Rapids: William B. Eerdmans, 1999), p. 188.

56. Thomas Merton, *The School of Charity: Letters of Thomas Merton on Religious Renewal and Spiritual Direction*, ed. Brother Patrick Hart (New York: Farrar, Straus & Giroux, 1990), p. 128.

57. Robert Rambusch, Interview by author, Transcribed telephone conversation, 21 April 2005.

58. Francis Klein, O.C.S.O., "Frank Kacmarcik: A Mepkin Tribute," *Worship*, May 2004, p. 202.

59. Merton, "The Catholic and Creativity," p. 212; (*Literary Essays*, p. 370).

60. Adapted from Merton's prayer for Kacmarcik, "For Vocations in the Realm of Sacred Art."

Three Comments about Benedictine Monastic Community Reading

Eric Hollas, Daniel Durken, and Stefanie Weisgram

Editor's note: These three short articles hint at the rich variety of table reading which has been done regularly within Benedictine and Cistercian houses and are included with the hope that other related research might follow about monastic reading. Bibliographic note reprinted from *The Abbey Banner*, Spring, 2003, pp. 10-11.

I. "Food for Thought: Monastic Table Reading"

Benedictine life has never been entirely at home with modern mores. A glaring example is the case of meals. In the age of fast food, Benedict's regimen for the table includes carefully prepared dishes, monks who take turns serving the community, prayers to introduce and complete the dinner, and reading that should always accompany the meal. Benedict refused to reduce meals to mere caloric intake. Rather, they were a time for spiritual, intellectual and physical nourishment.

Always sparing when it came to instruction, Benedict neither specified the books to be read nor the purpose for reading. Thus Benedictines through the centuries have adapted table reading to suit their own purposes.

At Cluny, for example, the monks continued passages from Scripture that they had begun in choir. This allowed them to cover major sections of the Bible in short order. At Durham, the monastic archives indicate that the monks read heavily from the lives of local saints and regional histories. Still other monasteries had a steady diet of spiritual texts.

At Saint John's that tradition continues, and monks from ages past would recognize in the ritual of dinner in Collegeville a familiar pattern. Today's meal opens with a prayer, follows with a chapter read from the *Rule of Benedict*, continues with fifteen minutes of reading from a book selected by a specially appointed committee, and concludes with a prayer. Afterwards the monks are free to leave or to linger over coffee and conversation.

What do modern monks read? Many factors influence the selection of texts to be read. Seasons play a part, so during Lent the readings tend to be more spiritual in nature. Current events can influence the selection as well, but in general biography and history tend to be the areas from which most books in the refectory at Saint John's are drawn.

Eamon Duffy's recent book, *Saints & Sinners: A History of the Popes*, was well received at the monastic table. So too was Joseph Ellis' *Founding Brothers: The Revolutoinary Generation*, a book that detailed the lives of some of America's original political personalities.

David H. Donald's biography of Abraham Lincoln, simply entitled *Lincoln*, held monks' attention for many weeks, though its length came to weigh heavily. None of the monks approved of Lincoln's assassination, but it did bring both an end to his presidency and the book, as well as an audible sigh of relief.

Do the monks like everything that is read to them? Decidedly not! Within the past twenty or thirty years many books have not reached the finish line. Many years ago the biography of the Mayo brothers came to an abrupt end when the chapter on their pioneering surgical techniques proved too much for some sensitive stomachs. A history of Mexico likewise was moving along very nicely until the author began to provide overly graphic descriptions of Aztec human sacrifice. Still other books have remained unfinished because the subject matter turned out to be far more tedious than initially supposed.

Topic alone is not the sole factor affecting the reception of a book, a fact that Benedict recognized when he specified that not just anyone should take up the book and read. Some voices can make the blandest book seem wildly interesting, while others have prompted the abbot to reach for the bell to signal a premature end to a day's reading.

Further complications can arise when pictures and graphs pop up in the middle of a text, leaving the best of readers at loss for what to do. And in a phenomenon not unique to Saint John's, unfortunate mispronunciations have achieved legendary status in the folklore of most monasteries since the time of Benedict. One reader thought "mis*led*" was pronounced "*mize*led."

No one book has ever enjoyed universal acclaim in the monks' refectory at Saint John's, and perhaps that is as it should be. In an age when the various media and diverse academic pursuits vie for the attention of the individual monk, reading in refectory provides one of the few moments of shared intellectual experience in the monastery. Ironically, it is the book that animates conversation and even disagreement that goes the furthest in forging the bonds of community. (EH)

II. "A Record of Read Books"

An Abbey Archives' treasure is a small volume entitled "Record of Books Read in the Refectory." From 1939 to 1968 this journal contains the titles, authors, dates when a book or article was read and occasional concise evaluation. For example:

1941: *The Man Who Got Even with God*, M. Raymond, OCSO. Not quite finished. We had enough of it.

1950: *The Trapp Family Singers*, Maria Trapp. Seemed to be well liked.

1951: *Kon-Tiki*, Thor Heyerdahl. Most generally appreciated book read in years.

1952: *The Little World of Don Camillo*, Giovanni Guareschi. Treats a serious topic in a very humorous way. Enjoyed by all.

1953: *Sign of Jonas*, Thomas Merton. Reactions mixed but almost everyone agreed that it went on too long.

1957: *St. Benedict and His Monks*, Theodore Maynard. A thoroughly unhistorical, subjective meditation on our Holy Father Benedict, packed with unsupported generalizations and misconceptions.

1957: *The Nun's Story*, Kathryn Hulme. This book found everyone an interested listener and raised perhaps more discussion than any book read in the refectory. Liked very much by most and even those who disliked it agreed that it was very well written.

Books recently read:

Wounded Prophet: A Portrait of Henri J. M. Nouwen, Michael Ford
Benjamin Franklin, Edmund S. Morgan
The Question of God: C.S. Lewis and Sigmund Freud Debate God, Love, Sex, and the Meaning of Life, Dr. Armand M. Nicoli, Jr.
Faithful Dissenters: Stories of Men and Women Who Loved and Changed the Church, Robert McClory (DD)

III. "Table Reading In The Monastery Today"

In speaking with members of St. Benedict's Monastery regarding table reading, one thing immediately becomes clear. There is definitely a "before" and "now" for most members, especially those who came to the monastery before, during, or immediately after the Second Vatican Council. It also becomes clear that there are as many opinions regarding table reading as there are members, although the opinions tend to fall into two general categories.

Table reading in the past was at the noon meal and the evening meal with conversation allowed only on special feast days and sometimes only after a short reading. Readers were generally chosen with care—sisters who would prepare in advance by reading through the material and checking pronunciations when necessary to avoid either amusement or pain for the listeners. This was usually successful, although some readers were known for their occasional wry tone in editorial comment.

The material chosen for reading was usually different for noon than for dinner. The noon reading was more often a biography, a travel book, or a book deemed of both interest and educational merit. Two all-time favorites still remembered with pleasure are *The Lost World of the Kalahari* by Laurens Van der Post and *Kon-Tiki: Across the Pacific by Raft* by Thor Heyerdahl. *The Gentle House* by Anna Perrott Rose is also mentioned over and over by sisters whose faces light up in memory, as are *My Left Foot* by Christy Brown and *Karen* by Marie Killilea. In the areas of biography Ida Gorres' biography of St. Therese of Lisieux, *The Hidden Face*, was popular as was Russell Baker's *Growing Up*.

The reading during the evening meal was usually of a more reflective kind, but it always began with the saint of the day from *Butler's Lives of the Saints*. Because often there was more than one saint for each day, it seemed that some effort was made to read about more obscure saints. One sister remembers, as a novice, one Halloween night waiting on the novices' table and listening to the life of St. Quentin, a martyr in Gaul whose fingernails were torn out, his throat was cut, and his body was thrown into the river. The unfortunate sister's name was Quentin. She had not read *Butler's* before suggesting receiving that name when she entered the novitiate.

Generally, table reading in the past was enjoyed, especially the noon reading which was lighter and easier to become engaged with whether eating or waiting on table. But what many sisters found of special interest and looked forward to were the letters from our own sister missionaries in Taiwan, Japan, Puerto Rico, and the Bahama Islands. These sisters were all known by the older sisters and soon became known by the younger members through their letters to the community.

These letters were the writers' first hand accounts of living in another country and culture, and they were fascinating to many of the sisters. Even more, they gave the sisters at home a sense of being in on a particular mission endeavor—as in a real sense they were. Much later, when these missions became dependent priories, and still later when they became independent, the sisters at St. Benedict's could rejoice with the sisters in these countries while at the same time feeling both a sense of loss and disconnection and a sense of pride in the growth of these priories.

Table reading today is a different story. Because of the variety of ministries the sisters engage in today, for many sisters the evening meal is the only meal eaten with the community. For this reason many enjoy the opportunity for conversation at the meal. However, more importantly, many find table reading difficult simply because of distractions. In the past, with many members in the community, meals were served family style. With fewer members meals are served in a buffet style with sisters invited table by table to the serving tables. This means there is both more activity and more noise to distract from the reading. Still other members feel that their life is filled with words coming from all directions, so listening to table reading becomes arduous at the end of a long day, especially if the reading is more reflective.

In spite of all of the opinions, table reading has not disappeared entirely from St. Benedict's Monastery. Each month on the first Saturday the community observes a Day of Recollection. Usually this includes a conference from the prioress and a day of silence and reflection. Sisters are asked to keep this day as free as possible from work and distraction. Appropriate table reading is often chosen by the prioress on the general topic of the morning's conference. The reading is for approximately 15 to 20 minutes followed by silence for the rest of the meal.

During the days of community retreats the noon meal has table reading in support of the retreat theme or on monastic topics. Classical music is played during the evening meal. Because of the reflective nature of the retreats and the silence throughout the day, the reading is both expected and appreciated, especially by sisters who live away from the monastery who have no opportunity for table reading.

Table reading during Lent has gone through several evolutions. At one point the evening meal had table reading daily. Tuesday night, however, is community night with the sisters eating with their living groups, some of them not in the common dining room, so the continuity of the reading was lost for some sisters. Because of this, table reading often became more stressful than fruitful, so the reading was changed to Monday, Wednesday, and Friday. Eventually Friday was dropped. Lenten reading is usually a book that has a theme of interest to the sisters and one that can be missed at times while still benefiting from the reading.

One particularly successful book was Daniel Homan and Lonni Collins Pratt's *Radical Hospitality: Benedict's Way of Love*. Table readers report that when the reading is especially interesting to individual sisters, as this one was, they often ask to see the book and then borrow it from the library for private reading. Sisters who are hard of hearing sometimes ask to use the book for a short time to see what they missed!

During the Triduum the table reading is from current periodicals like America, U.S. Catholic, and St. Anthony Messenger. The articles are chosen to enrich the sisters' participation and appreciation of the Triduum services. Again, the general atmosphere of silence and reflection helps in both the experience and in the appreciation of the reading.

Table reading at St. Benedict's is always open to change and to comment. What the sisters have learned is that the way it was done at one time is not necessarily how it will be done today or tomorrow. What they do prefer is something that is lighter and easier to follow through the distractions of the dining room rather than something that is heavily reflective or theoretical. (SW)

"Remarks Following a 2004 Poetry Reading"

Ernesto Cardenal

Transcribed and Edited by Dennis Beach with
an Introduction by Patrick Hart and a Note by Corey Shouse.

In April 2004, the Nicaraguan priest and poet Ernesto Cardenal gave a public poetry reading at Saint John's University in Collegeville, Minnesota. Home to Saint John's Abbey—and down the road from its sister campus, the College of Saint Benedict and the monastic community of women there—this Benedictine setting provided a unique occasion for reflection on the perhaps mystical union of religion, poetry and politics in Ernesto Cardenal's life and work. What follows is a brief introduction to Ernesto Cardenal, the person and former Trappist novice at Gethsemani Abbey in Kentucky, by Brother Patrick Hart. Then follows an overview of the themes of Cardenal's poem *Cosmic Canticle*, and, finally, the transcript of the Question and Answer session that followed the poetry reading.

Ernesto Cardenal was born in Granada, Nicaragua, in 1925, and was educated at the University of Mexico and Columbia University in New York. He is considered one of the significant poets of Latin America, along with fellow Nicaraguans Rubén Darío, José Coronel Urtecho, and Pablo Antonio Cuadra. Cardenal was involved in the political resistance movement under the dictatorship of the elder Somoza and this experience is reflected in his *Epigrams*, as well as a long political poem, *O Hora O*, both written before he entered Gethsemani. He also had a ceramic exhibition at the Pan American Union in Washington shortly before entering the novitiate at Gethsemani in 1957.

As a novice, Don Ernesto received the name Frater Lawrence, and was in daily contact with Father Louis as the Novice Master. He continued modeling in clay, as well as writing some poetic sketches which were later developed into poems and published in a volume under the title *Gethsemani, KY* (Mexico City, 1960). Thomas Merton translated some of these poems into English and published them in *Emblems of a Season of Fury* (New York, 1963). Merton

65

and Cardenal became good friends as a result of this experience, as their voluminous correspondence testifies.

Poor health and a nearly tone-deaf ear brought Frater Lawrence the advice that he leave Trappist life at the end of his two-year novitiate, but he continued his priestly studies and was eventually ordained. He established a lay monastic community on the inland archipelago of Solentiname in Nicaragua, a community which was later bombed by the Somoza regime. He joined the Sandinista revolutionary movement, and when it took over the government in 1979, Cardenal became Minister of Culture, while his Jesuit brother Fernando Cardenal became Minister of Education. Under church pressure, both resigned from politics, but continued their ministry as priests in Nicaragua. In his "retirement," Ernesto Cardenal also served as director of the Casa de los Tres Mundos, a cultural centre in Granada, Nicaragua. (PH)

* * * * *

In the poetry reading at Saint John's University, Cardenal read sections of *Cosmic Canticle* (1989), an expansive five hundred page free verse poem that explores the nature of the universe through the language of metaphysics, astronomy, spirituality and evolutionary science. As the poet José Coronel Utrecho has said of Cardenal's masterpiece, "more than an explanation, *Cosmic Canticle* is a representation of the universe itself, a poetic rendition of an astronaut's photos." Revealing Cardenal's lifelong fascination with the ideas of thinkers such as Charles Darwin, Sir Fred Hoyle and Thomas Merton, *Cosmic Canticle* embraces the discoveries and contradictions of our age, weaving these into hope-filled verse that searches for the divine amid the material, ethical and intellectual conditions and limitations of human existence. As in all of Cardenal's poetry, *Cosmic Canticle* is also deeply marked by the political, historical and spiritual context of his life as a priest, activist and revolutionary. Reminiscent of the popular poetry workshops Cardenal directed during his work as the Sandinista Minister of Culture, *Cosmic Canticle* evokes the hardships and dreams of contemporary Nicaragua through colloquial Nicaraguan speech, testimonial accounts of the Somoza dictatorship and reflections on the poet's work in the Christian base community of Solentiname. It also denounces the legacy of the Spanish Conquest and the abuses of American imperialism through poignant and often humorous examinations of Nicaraguan history, pop culture, U.S. foreign policy, the Contra War, and world media. Most impressively, in *Cosmic Canticle* Cardenal distills a seemingly endless number of source materials, insights and inspirations into an authentic poetic language that rings with a conversational tone, verbal elegance and sense of humanity reminiscent of Walt Whitman's *Leaves of Grass*. Fusing faith, science, poetics and politics with urgency and grace, Cardenal's *Cosmic Canticle* has earned him distinction as one of Latin America's most significant revolutionary voices and greatest poets. (CS)

* * * * *

Transcript of the Question and Answer Session for the Poetry Reading of Ernesto Cardenal at Saint John's University, Collegeville, Minnesota, April 14, 2004.

Q: Good Evening, Sir. I would like to ask a question about another poem I have read, the *Cantares Mexicanos*. Could you talk to us a little about ancient ideas and how they blend with modern ideas?

EC: I would like to ask if you believe that it could be of interest here that I speak about a poem that I didn't read, that perhaps others don't know. It's a question that I ask.... Perhaps they will not understand what I say because the others don't know the poem?

    However, I can tell you one thing. I learned from a North American poet, Ezra Pound to put the ancient together with the new or to make the old new. And this poem of which she speaks is a poem from old Mexico, from the Aztecs, from the poet Netzahualcoyótl and I took his texts and remade them, updating them in a way, as if they were truly from our time. The new and the old, the modern and the historical, and what I'm telling you is that my teacher in this was Ezra Pound, who did this often. And he, too, had other teachers.

Q: What does the religion that you embraced represent to you?

EC: I did not embrace religion; I embraced God. God showed himself to me as love in beauty. I fell in love with the beauty of God, who is the author of all beauty. Of your beauty, and that of everyone here present, men and women, and that of all the universe: the author of the beauty of the whole world. God revealed himself to me as beauty, and I fell in love. And so I entered a very strict religious order, the Trappist Order, which stems from the Order of Saint Benedict, to which this monastery belongs. Thus I could say that I embraced mysticism rather than religion.

Q: What do you think will happen to you when you die?

EC: Union with God.

Q: With God?

EC: And with the whole universe, which is God's body. I imagine that God is like the soul of the universe and that the universe is his body. Perhaps this is not very exact, very logical, but that is how I imagine it. And therefore I would be transformed into the universe and the body of God.

Q: How could you explain the religion of revolutionary Christianity?

EC: There should be no need to explain it because Christ came to bring a revolution, to say that another world is possible. This is what he said when speaking of the kingdom of heaven or of the kingdom of God: a world different than that which we have is possible. A world of justice and equality, without rich and poor, without exploiters and the exploited. And this message is one that we ought to continue to announce on the earth. When he spoke in his time of the heavenly kingdom, that was like now talking about revolution. And for this reason he died, for this they killed him.

Q: How does this conception differ from other conceptions of the Christian religion?

EC: There is no other Christianity than the one I'm talking about.

Q: Saint Benedict said that he could see the universe in the rays of the sun. Is there anywhere you have seen the universe in some moment of your life?

EC: I have not had this mystic experience. Some have had it, and among them, Saint Benedict. There is present here a Benedictine father, right? You're not? But isn't there a Benedictine here?

[Monk in the audience]:   Yes, I am a Benedictine, but I haven't had mystical experiences either!

EC: Yes, but you do know the anecdote, the one that tells how Saint Benedict saw the whole universe in a single ray of light? Other mystics have had the same experience. It seems that it is a well-testified phenomenon, but only for those few who are mystics.

Q: Don Ernesto, you speak of how the driving force of the universe is love, but other poets claim it to be war. For example, the ancient Greek poet or philosopher Heraclitus said that everything comes from war: "Strife begets all." How can two people, two poets, view the same universe and one say that its engine is love and another say that it is war? At root are these the same thing?

EC: I will say that this must have been a metaphor, speaking of love and calling it "war." I don't think there is a single poet that defends war. Bush defends it, but he's not a poet.

Q: Don Ernesto, you speak much about the sciences and evolution. In your view, are there contradictions between science and faith?

EC: For me there is no contradiction at all. For me science and faith complement one another. True, there are many scientists who do not have faith, but there are some that do. But today the majority do not believe them to be in conflict, but to be two different things. Still, for me they can also be complementary. The fact that the universe was born in the big bang, from a great explosion, and that everything else developed by evolution since that time, for me this is a revelation of the grandeur of God. God is the author of the big bang and of evolution and of everything else that exists on this planet and of everything that would be found on many other inhabited planets in the heavens. I very much enjoy reading books that recount scientific discoveries and these also fill me with love for God. And they also inspire me to write poetry, such as this that I read to you.

Q: When you read the passage about the individual, I thought of Rubén Darío and the poem *"Lo Fatal."* What is your relationship to Darío and his poetry?

EC: Rubén Darío, the subject of the question, is the great national poet of Nicaragua, and he has a very large following there. But he has not influenced me in my poetry. The influence I had was from the poetic literature of the United States.

Q: Who? Which people?

EC: Ezra Pound, T.S. Eliot as well, Marianne Moore and Robert Frost, Robinson Jeffers, William Carlos Williams, Allan

Ginsberg, and many more: Walt Whitman, also Carl Sandburg, the great poet of Chicago.

Q: Thank you very much.

Q: In Nicaragua, you worked with the Sandinista government, which fought to lift up and to give power to the people. You talked about how you used your poetry to empower the people in Nicaragua, with the elements of mysticism and humor. How did you use poetry to empower the people in Nicaragua?

EC: My role was to be the Minister of Culture, and this meant to be the minister of poetry, of theater, of painting, of dance. Also folklore, libraries, publications and handicrafts. Poetry was very important in this ministry. At that time I created something there that exists in the universities here in the United States—poetry workshops. But here they are in the universities and the universities are not for everyone, for they are expensive. At that time we created there poetry workshops to help the whole populace, for the poor barrios, for the indigenous communities, for those of the countryside and workers and laborers and for everyone in the country. And we also had a publication for them of poetry from all over the world. There was much poetry from the United Status, of those poets I just enumerated. Also poetry from ancient Greece and Rome, translated into English by some of these same poets, also Americans. And poetry as well from ancient China and Japan, and from many parts of the world, from Latin America and Europe. A British periodical, *The Tablet*, said that it was impressive that the workers and *campesinos* were reading that kind of poetry. And impressive as well that we taught them rules for writing poetry taken from a poet who was so difficult, even in English, as was Ezra Pound.

Q: Now that the Sandinista revolution is over, how is it? Do you feel defeat on behalf of the Sandinista revolution, that the revolution has been defeated?

EC: Insofar as we—all of us who participated in the revolution— were part of it, then, yes, we are defeated. Not that it is a personal defeat for me, but for all, and, I believe, for people from other countries such as right here as well. In the same way as I feel that God was also defeated in those elections. And it's not the first time that God was defeated in an election. In the Bible we find God being defeated in an election, in the Book of Samuel. God recounts how the people of Israel had voted against him when Yahweh was the King of Israel and Israel wanted to have another king and elected Saul. Samuel did not want them to elect a king, because God was King of Israel, and so God says to him, "It is not you that they have defeated, but me." I believe that every time a people makes a bad election, then they are also defeating God.

Moderator: One more question.

Q: How do you see the relationship between poetry and politics? I ask especially because you mentioned Ezra Pound a couple of times. And his politics, of course, are very far to the right. So how do you see the relationship between them?

EC: What's important for me is the poetry, not the political ideas. Even when speaking about a poet, for me what is important is his poetry and not his ideology. I am not interested in Ezra Pound for the ideology he had, which was a defense of fascism, or of Mussolini rather than fascism itself, for it was the person of Mussolini that he defended and not the fascist party. Rather, it is his poetry that interests me. As far as his political ideas go, he was simply wrong. It was pure error. He believed that Mussolini was a great person, or that he could be such, to the point that he wrote a little pamphlet called *Jefferson and/or Mussolini*, comparing the two of them.

A Discovery:
Thomas Merton's Poetry As Art Song;
Compositions by Bryan Beaumont Hays, OSB:
A Bibliographical Note

Anthony Feuerstein

Bryan Beaumont Hays, OSB, is an accomplished composer whose music has been created largely within the context of his monastic vocation at St. John's Abbey in Collegeville, Minnesota. Among the numerous compositions which he has completed are many works which utilize Thomas Merton's poems.

Fr. Bryan Beaumont Hays was born in 1920. Before he entered St. John's Monastery in Minnesota, he pursued an active career in music. Father Hays was born on a farm near Clarksville, Tennessee. His Southern roots remain strong even after 48 years as a monk in St. John's Abbey in Collegeville, Minnesota.

After serving in the Pacific during World War II, he returned to school and obtained a Master's Degree in music composition in the late 40s at the Chicago Music College (now the Music Department of Roosevelt College in Chicago). Hays won the Gershwin Memorial Award for a short orchestral composition, *Pastorale and Allegro* in 1949. This piece was performed at Carnegie Hall during the annual Gershwin Memorial Concert. He was awarded a summer scholarship to Tanglewood where he was a student of Aaron Copeland in 1950. That fall two of his compositions were performed at a concert of contemporary music at McMillan Hall, Columbia University in New York City.

In 1951, Hays received the first of two Guggenheim Fellowships in Music Composition and spent two years in Italy composing and listening to opera. In 1957 he entered St. John's Abbey, a Benedictine monastery in Collegeville, Minnesota where he has served as a teacher of French and English. He has composed five operas, numerous art songs, choral music and music for chamber ensembles.

In 1995, some of his choral and organ music was performed at St. Mark's Cathedral in Minneapolis. Hays continues to compose for available local performers. The selections presented on a recent CD represent only a small portion of the vast collection of beautiful songs Bryan Beaumont Hays has composed for voice, piano and a variety of instruments.

He commented when this recording was released:

> I am a frustrated opera composer in as much as I have not had my operas performed. But perhaps this has been a blessing. Maturing musically late in life, I realize now that I am a lyric poet. I generally prefer short poems that make their point quickly.
>
> Although I occasionally write instrumental pieces, my true love is for the art song.
>
> To me there is nothing so lovely and expressive as the human voice. I shall devote the rest of my creative life to this vocal genre. I am the poet of the short line, not the long. Not for me is the spinning of endless melody. As my device, I adopt the lines of Alfred de Musset: "Mon verre n'est pas grand,/ mais je bois de mon verre." (My glass is not a big one, but I drink from it.)

Hays's musical accomplishments are well represented on the CD released in 2000, entitled <u>Uncommon Daisies</u>. These songs reflect the range of his work only to a limited degree. Frequently, his songs are written in the tradition of the Nineteenth Century Art Song. This recording includes twenty-three pieces arranged in five categories. These are: 1) Six English Epitaphs; 2) Six Autumn Songs; 3) Five Spring Songs of Francis Ledwidge; 4) Nine Songs to Poems of Isaac Rosenberg; and 5) Two Trios. The recording, copyright 2000, is available from Granite City Records.

Hays's voluminous work also includes considerable Choral Music (A Cappella or with instruments); duets and trios (for women's voices and one duet for bass-baritone and soprano); instrumental music, operas and oratorios as well as considerable more songs for solo voice than those written "to poems by Thomas Merton." His work is ambitious and artful. He has written a full opera for Flannery O'Conner's "Parker's Back," and when asked once if he was disappointed about it not ever being produced, commented: "Oh, it would take a very good company ...."

Hays's interest in Thomas Merton's writing has been substantial. He has composed for at least 43 of Merton's poems. These compositions are arranged in 7 sets, grouped loosely according to

Merton's thematic interests. Hays's songs arranged for poems by Thomas Merton are designed within the following groupings:

Songs to Poems by Thomas Merton

7 sets, voice and piano. (These are listed chronologically.)

Songs to Poems by Thomas Merton, Set. No. 1

for baritone and piano.
1. Love Winter When the Plant Says Nothing
2. For my Brother: Reported Missing in Action, 1943
3. Song for Nobody
4. A Messenger from the Horizon

Orchestra version exists.

Songs to Poems by Thomas Merton, Set No. 2

for low voice.
1. The Messenger
2. Saint Jason
3. Song for Our Lady of Cobre
4. The Flight into Egypt
5. The Winter's Night
6. Evening
7. Carol
8. The Man in the Wind

Orchestral version exists.

Songs to Poems by Thomas Merton, Set No. 3

for soprano and piano.
1. The Greek Women
2. Calypso's Island
3. Ariadne
4. Ariadne of the Labyrinth

Orchestral version exists.

Songs to Poems by Thomas Merton, Set No. 4

for high voice and piano

1. The Candlemass Procession
2. The Heavenly City
3. St. Paul
4. Trappists, Working
5. Poem
6. Dirge for a Town in France

Orchestral version exists.

Songs to Poems by Thomas Merton, Set No. 5

for high voice and piano
1. St. Agnes: A Responsory
2. Crusoe
3. Advent
4. When in the Soul of the Serene Disciple ...
5. April
6. O Sweet, Irrational Worship
7. Song from Crossportion's Pastoral

Orchestral version exists.

Songs to Poems by Thomas Merton, Set No. 6

for Baritone or mezzo-soprano and piano.
1. Night-Flowering Cactus
2. Landscape
3. What to Think When it Rains Blood
4. Song: In the Shows of the Round Ox
5. An Elegy for Five Old Ladies
6. Spring Storm

Orchestral version exists.

Songs to Poems by Thomas Merton, Set No. 7

for high baritone or mezzo-soprano
1. Lent in a Year of War
2. In Memory of the Spanish Poet-Frederico Garcia Lorca
3. The Captives—A Psalm
4. Aubade-Harlem
5. In the Rain and the Son

6. The Guns of Fort Knox
7. Elegy for the Monastery Barn
8. The Moslem's Angel of Death

Orchestral version exists.

Seven Sets of Songs to Poems of Thomas Merton

Complete set scored for full orchestra.

Hays's work is published. The Merton Poem Cycles are available through KSM Publishing Co., P.O. Box 3819, Dallas, Texas, 75208. The poems of Set No. 1 (for low voice and piano) include "Love Winter When the Plant Says Nothing," a composition of 6 pages.

This introductory note will alert future Merton scholars and musicians to the existence of Bryan Hays's sophisticated use of Merton's poetry as the foundation for so many compositions. Some of these works have been performed at St. John's University and Abbey, Collegeville.

This body of work would clearly afford an excellent opportunity for a knowledgeable Merton scholar. It draws largely on the more lyrical Merton. Study of Hays's compositions would clearly afford an opportunity for drawing specific connections with contemporary music. Such study might add to performances at future Merton-related gatherings.

"Unadorned Ideal": An Interview in Two Parts with Methodius Telnack

Conducted and Edited with Notes
by Victor A. Kramer and Glenn Crider

I

The first segment of this interview was conducted as part of "The History of The Abbey of Our Lady of The Holy Spirit" (1984) by Victor A. Kramer. It is excerpted here to emphasize aspects of the continuing Cistercian aesthetic tradition. The second segment was conducted in 2005 by Glenn Crider.

As director of the Stained Glass Shop at the Conyers, Georgia Monastery, Father Methodius has supervised the design and construction of scores of stained glass projects throughout the Southeast during the past four decades. He has also been active as a musical composer. His vocation, as a Cistercian who was a contemporary of Thomas Merton, clearly reflects many of the Cistercian ideals which Merton articulated during a period of great monastic change and adaptability. As artists, both are intensely aware of the important influence of art upon the formation of community.

(1984 Interview) Conducted by Victor A. Kramer

Kramer: Would you care to say something about when you first came to this monastery and the nature of the monastery at that time?

Telnack: I entered in 1949, I came down on an Easter retreat from Catholic University. I didn't really intend to join a monastery at that time. I was studying architecture and had been two years in the Marine Corps. I was in my first year of architecture when I came here on a retreat, and I liked what I saw.

Later that year one of the first things I saw when I returned to Georgia ... and I had gotten into Atlanta to get on a bus, was that there were seats in the back of the bus, so I went to the back to sit down. There were empty seats all through the bus as the bus went from one town to another all the way from Atlanta. The seats filled up but there were still seats in the front of the bus. There was a black lady standing right next to us, although there were plenty of seats up in the front of the bus. And I thought it was funny that she didn't sit down. Finally she said, "Would you please move up to the front of the bus; these seats are our seats." And that kind of shook me. So, something about the racial conditions in the South is also what influenced my entering here.

Kramer: When did you actually enter here? Did you enter the same year?

Telnack: Yes. My first visit was in April and then I came back in June after school was out and I entered in August. It was on my June visit that I got on that bus and had the experience with the blacks. I was very much aware of black and white race relations. And so that was a very strong motivation for my entering this particular monastery, although I was never attracted to any other monastery.

Subsequently I found out that the Cistercian vocation is a "vocation to the place"…says Saint Stephen Harding, the second Abbot of Citeaux. That is very much my own orientation. I would not want to be a monk any place else.

Kramer: So you feel that is very crucial, the vow of stability.

Telnack: For me that is essential. Everyone is different. There is room for everybody. And also we as a community are involved with people.

Kramer: In 1949 there were already a large number of men here. I think the monastery was not at a high point in members just yet, but there were a lot of people.

Telnack: Yes, at least 67 people. And I worked with the monks …on the second visit. The first visit was during Holy Week, so it was mostly just attendance at Mass and choir services, and I thought that was pretty wonderful, although I had been familiar with the Liturgy at the cathedral in Baltimore and such things in other churches. But when I came the second time, I worked with the novices, and then Dom Robert [McGann] himself. When you saw him, you admired and liked him.

Kramer: So he was the Abbot at that time. Who was the Novice Master?

Telnack: Father Joseph, who was then called Father Mary. I did not meet him until I actually entered. I may have talked to him on the second visit, but I do not think I did. I'm not sure.

I don't remember him until after I entered. And he wanted to have me enter the monastery on the feast of the Assumption. I think at that time they had some sort of rule that you had to arrive the day before, which I did. I arrived on the 14th. But he had to expedite my getting in on the 15th as he knew of my desire. Very nice, though.

Kramer: Were you then immediately involved in construction work?

Telnack: Well, they had not started at that time. It was when they had run out of money. They had just put an addition on to the old building, actually two additions—the infirmary wing was built, and the novitiate wing, just before I came, that same year in 1949, I believe. So the work on this building had stopped because they ran out of money, and Dom James had been sent off to Gethsemani and had cut off the funds. There was considerable hostility toward Dom James at the time as I can remember, because he just cut off the funds saying we could not expect Gethsemani to continue the financing. But Dom Robert took over in 1949. He was elected Abbot, and it was really a blessing. I guess it was January, 1949. So he was the new Abbot here when I came, and his intention was to continue building, but we did not get enough money to start until 1952. I am not sure of the dates though.

Kramer: So for roughly two or three years, you were not involved in any kind of building?

Telnack: Correct. And as work we had common work a couple of times a week at least, but for the most part, the novices had the garden; we had somebody in charge. I think it was Brother Dominic when I first came in, who was Brother Thomas. I think he was already professed, and he was in charge of the garden and I used to help him, or we cut wood because we had a wood-burning boiler, and that was also in common. So we worked a lot together, which was fun, but it was not particularly fulfilling. I do not know how monastic it was, but at that time, it was part of the ideals. It was very romantic. We would walk out in single file with our hoods up and our shovels over our shoulders, like the seven dwarves or something. It really was very romantic. In fact, the whole time was kind of a romantic period.

Kramer: Well, then along about 1952 or 1953, plans were started up again, in terms of actually building the Church?

Telnack: The big thing was the selection of an architect, which Dom Robert did pretty much by himself on the advice of, I understand, Father Joseph Smith, who is buried in the cemetery. Father Smith recommended Mr. Logan as the best gothic architect in the South. There was not much good gothic architecture, but he had done the building at Agnes Scott and a few Presbyterian churches. Logan and Williams, I think was the name of the architecture firm, but we never did see much of Mr. Williams. And Logan was an old man at the time, too. So, he sent out some drawings. They could have been begun either by Dom Robert, himself, or by the council. I never thought to ask. In those days, no one really questioned the Abbot's decision on anything. So, he sent out a drawing which in general we were pretty favorable to because he decided on a concrete rather than brick structure.

We had initially started in brick and we had to tear it down, a whole story of brick over in the infirmary wing that was up to the first floor. We tore that all down, and blasted up the foundation and changed it and then started the concrete. We were very pleased with that. We were not pleased particularly with Logan's approach to the monastery, because he wanted to build a pretty box. Father Bob and I (Father Bob is a graduate architect. He even actually taught for a while.) both felt architecture should start from the inside out and that we should care what particular use the building would be put to, and then build around that. Whereas Logan's idea was to build a pretty box and leave us, the committee, to put rooms inside the box, which was really inside-out-architecture. Plus, there were a lot of fancy things that he was doing which we did not find appropriate.

Kramer: What do you mean by fancy?

Telnack: Well, a lot of decoration on the building. If you look at the buildings at Agnes Scott, or the Presbyterian Church on North Decatur Road, you'll get the idea. Of course, it was not exactly like those. Well, this was the plan until Mr. Logan got sick. The rest of the building was pretty much complete. One thing should be mentioned which I would like to see it in any kind of archival collection of remembrances. I think it was when Father Cyprian was Prior, and he was on the building committee. Dom Robert and Mr. Logan were talking about a groined vault in the cloister, which means plaster and lath, and none of us wanted that. It was a matter of just maintenance for one thing. You just cannot keep something like up, and we were thinking in terms of centuries. So, there had to be a key support put into the wall on the refectory side of the cloister. I may be wrong, but I think Father Cyprian and I were aware of the fact that the key should be put in, but it was not put in because of someone's oversight. The key was not put in and we just let it go, and so the construction went on for several months. Then Dom Robert went to General Chapter, and while he was there, it was discovered that this key had not been placed in the poured concrete.

Father Cyprian called up long distance to Rome, which at that time was not such a common thing to do, and Dom Robert got the telephone call. He asked, "How much does this cost?" And Cyprian explained to him that the key was not put in where it should be, and there was not enough height in the cloister ceiling to put a plastered vault. We would just have to put in a more simple ceiling with arches. And all Dom Robert could think of was the cost of that phone call, I guess, because he said, "Oh, Lord, do whatever you think is right," and hung up. So we were happy because we were then able to just put the concrete as it exists, first with the plaster ceiling with the arches and, now, with monolithic concrete. It should last for centuries. That was kind of the first coup, a triumphant coup. Then when it came to the Church building, we were 22 feet 4 inches up when Mr. Logan had a stroke. We could not very well change the structure of the Church by that time.

We had worked on other schemes for the Church, other design schemes, but Dom Robert was not inclined to go along with Father Bob or me; he wanted to go along with Mr. Logan. But it got to 22 feet 4 inches. Dom Robert then became worried that the Church was too high. He saw the scaffolding and he said, "My, it's dangerous to work up that high." Father Cyprian said, "Yeah, that's less than a third of the height [of Mr. Logan's plans]." Dom Robert said, "Oh, that's too high." So we cut it down.

Then they gave that job to me. So, I was able to take 10 feet out of the clerestory and then change a lot of details, the window details. For example, in the nave of the Church I simplified the windows. I redesigned them without a jam so that you could see the actual structure—a fortified arch that goes over the windows which is a big, thick concrete arch. And I thought that should not be lost and disguised with window jams so that you could see through the transparent glass. You can see that 4 foot thick arch. It is a dramatic church. And then the rear wall had to be changed. Originally that wall was round, the way Gethsemani was years ago. But we changed that early on, but then the actual design of the wall had to be changed.

Kramer: The rear wall had to be changed?

Telnack: That was originally a round apse which was then changed to be squared off, and simplified a great deal.

Kramer: And then did you have to change the roof also in terms of the way the arches come up?

Telnack: The angle of it may have been changed some. We did not change the structure because the arches were pretty much Logan's details. He worked that out, and I liked it. But there was talk at one time, of course, also in building a plaster vault within the Church, but that was rejected by the committee and Logan agreed with that. But the facade of the Church, when we took the 10 feet off, had to be changed dramatically. (By the way, I have in the glass shop a lot of architectural drawings that I did. You can see them there.)

As a matter of fact, I did several alternative facades. Dom Robert went up to New York; he had some contact up there with an architect. I do not know who it was—somebody he had confidence in. And the architect up there actually took the simplest drawing I did, which would have changed the roof line considerably, flattened the roof considerably. But for, I think, structural reasons, the work we had already done on the facade, there were certain things we could not do as we had originally drawn it up. So we had to change that, with the result that the gable in the front, the facade, comes up way over the roof on the west end. So, it was really a false gable, but that was about the only thing we could do and maintain the whole design through the building.

Kramer: So that it looks finished. Yes.

Telnack: Yes, there are problems with the work that had already been done. The front of the Church appears to be a little heavy; it had to be tapered off some way. We needed a certain amount of height to do it gracefully. That is why the Church looks that high.

Kramer: I think it looks quite good.

Telnack: I am happy with it, but I think if we were able to start just a few feet sooner, down lower, we could have....

Kramer: I was going to say something about the windows. The general shape of the windows would also have to have been changed in height. And in terms of the actual glass, that would come later in terms of the design.

Telnack: Yes, but I think I was thinking of the glass. In fact, I know I was thinking of the glass already.

Kramer: You were aware these windows would have to accommodate glass? And the windows in the front and the rear, you also had to be thinking in terms of what kinds of windows would go in there?

Telnack: That is right. And we knew we did not want a window, for example, on the east side that would be a big glare. So that window was put up high, so that we did not have the sunlight in our eyes. I already knew what I wanted for stained glass even though I did not have the project as my responsibility. They would have to be planned ahead. It was just a matter of really not even a year, I suppose, the time lag between those details and getting the stained glass into them.

Kramer: What year would that have been?

Telnack: It was 1955 because we did not start the stained glass until ... we had our birthday on April 10th in 1957. The reason I use that date is because we went on a trip to the Blenko Glass Company in West Virginia, where we got all our glass.

Kramer: That is the name of the company, Blenko? Is that a family name?

Telnack: It is a family name. It is a British family that came over three generations ago. The son, who was an old man at that time in 1957, was the founder. Bill Blenko was his name. He was very helpful and encouraged us. We tried to get all the information about stained glass which we could, and we got a lot of encouragement. We wrote the stained glass association, who were very helpful, very nice. As a matter of fact, Muriel Willett (who is the wife of Henry Lee Willett who died last year: Muriel died some ten years ago) was the secretary, or something, for the association, and she wrote us and was just as nice and helpful as she could be.

Also, she sent us a book called *Stained Glass For Amateurs* by Ruth Case Almy. I was kind of insulted. I thought, now we're not really amateurs. We have got a real project underway here, and I did not really look at the book for maybe six months or so. And then, just one day I picked the book up and looked at and read it. It was absolutely fascinating. It is a wonderful book on stained glass, and I was really mortified. In fact, I had not appreciated it. So I wrote to Mrs. Willett and I also wrote to Mrs. Almey, telling her that I really thought the book was wonderful and I appreciated it. Her theory of stained glass was really good.

Kramer: Did any of these people come here?

Telnack: Not at that time. Mrs. Almey came five or six years later. I think it was in the 1960s, 1964 when she finally came with her husband. He was a Presbyterian minister, retired, and they were taking a trip around the country to see all their friends. So they stopped off here and spent a couple of days and parked there in the parking lot in an Airstream trailer. We had a very nice visit with both of them. I suspect they are dead now because they were old.

Kramer: In terms, then, of your making decisions about getting into the stained glass business, did you then go visit these people in West Virginia, or how did you ...?

Telnack: Not to get "into the stained glass business." Let's see, how did it work? It was obvious we had to get some stained glass for the church. The Abbot General came, Dom Gabriel Sortais, and saw the plans. He said, well you have to have some stained glass in this latitude. Pretty far south. We are the same latitude as the Sahara Desert and also Nineveh, and so he said that the Cistercian proscription against stained glass does not apply because that was done through northern climates, France, for example. I think Paris is like Nova Scotia, in latitude. So we were pretty far south. So we wanted the go ahead with the recommendation from the Abbot General and Dom Robert wanted it. So we decided something had to be done. But the problem was a matter of man-power, that we had a very small, limited number of people to put into stained glass work.

Dom Robert told us to do the Chapter Room first, and he said, "If I like that, then you can go on with the rest of the building." He kept out of the Chapter Room all the time we were working on it ... did not bother us. And after a year (he gave us a year to do it) well, specifically, it took us about a year to get that done. When he saw it, he said, "I like it and you can go on with the rest of the building."

We started the project, and then there was a young novice who may have been professed by that time, named David Richards. He had been an art student at Chouinard, an art school in Los Angeles, and he started the project with me. Then soon after that, there was a Father Anselm Atkins, who had a lot of artistic ability. He was actually going through a nervous crisis and people were looking for something for him to do to get him interested, and I kind of liked him, and thought I could work with him as a person, and got him into stained glass. So we did it. The Chapter Room designs were complete.

Atkins did some sketches for that, some very simple geometric designs. I did the same thing then as I do now. I try to let anybody who has worked in the glass shop be creative and express, get to use their artistic talent. I try to utilize their artistic talent as best I can. But with the glass in the buildings, since I did have a lot to do with the architecture of the building, I had pretty much in my mind what I thought it should be and what I wanted for the Chapter Room and the Sacristy, since both of those, the windows of the Sacristy and the windows of the Chapter Room are the same side, both on the cloister and on the outside and they had to reflect the same on the outside. So we used just a simple geometric design. I did not know too much about stained glass colors.

So we went up to West Virginia. Father Joachim drove us in those days. None of us had licenses except for a few who were drivers in the community, and Father Joachim, I think was Prior at that time. So he took David Richards and me up to the stained glass company in 1957. And while we were there, Mr. Blenko and Bill took a liking to us and saw the project we had. They realized it was a big project and suggested we talk with his designer named Wayne Husted, and that was the beginning of a friendship that has lasted all these years. Bill and his wife Jeanne and I are still good friends. And Wayne and his wife Betty, who is also a designer and David and I just had sort of a brainstorming session, and we showed them what we wanted to do, and they made some suggestions about the colors and gave some very interesting insights about stained glass. He was the first one to point out to me that the colors of glass situate themselves in space, so that blue is at infinity and the other colors progress forward.

Working with stained glass is actually a three dimensional art, which was my dimension anyway, because as an architect I was working in three dimensions. Then he also pointed out the work of Robert Sowers who was very popular about that time. He did the stained glass for the American Airlines terminal at Kennedy Airport. Sowers was using deep, dark colors with a lot of light colors, so there was a lot of contrast in his windows and it was very obvious he was working with depth. So we experimented then with the Chapter Room. We got into a very deep blue and a darker green with a very light blue, and then red and also yellow colors come forward. The point Wayne made was that this is what happens automatically and you have to organize your colors for a pleasing effect, and it is a matter of organizing in three dimensions.

So with the Chapter Room, we got the stained glass started and then did the Sacristy. The Sacristy colors are not all that bad, except that the yellow was very heavy. We went up to the glass works and picked out our colors for the Chapter Room when the three of us were actually up there. Father Joachim did not have anything to do with it—just David and me. But when it came to the Sacristy, I thought, we'll just order from the samples we had here. Well, the yellow we ordered was a very bright yellow. When it came in the box, it was the same number but just various parts of the sheet. The part they had cut the sample from was maybe a thin part of the sheet, so that the yellow came out very heavy; and actually the color that looks purple in there, we thought was green. On the order, I ordered so much of this particular number in green that actually looks purple next to the yellow. And if I had gone up there to the glass shop and had seen the full sheets we would have understood what to work with. This was just sight unseen. But we put it together because I realized they were not really too bad, and it was kind of interesting, that yellow-violet, which are complimentary colors. But I'm still not as pleased. I think those colors would have been better if we had not had that accident. So, that was an indication that when we did the church, we would have to make sure what the colors looked like in the full sheets.

Kramer: Well, then how did you come to the decision that the church colors would be the colors that you have?

Telnack: That was done at the same time. It was Wayne, I think, because Bob Rambush did the design for the eastern Salve window. That was a bit of, I guess, politics. I had to make a decision there. I would have loved to design something for the Community, but Anselm had kind of a reputation of being the "designer" which he really was not.

Kramer: Anselm Atkins would have been a fairly young man.

Telnack: He is five years younger than I. He is just 50 this year and I am 55, and he would have been not that young because he had a college degree, so he would have been 24, I guess. How long ago was that? ... 20 years, 30 years?

Kramer: Roughly middle 50's. So he would have been in his middle 20's.

Telnack: Yes. I would say about that. As you get older, that seems young, but to a person who is 25 years old .... So, anyway, I thought it would be a bad idea. I knew what he would do with the design because I had seen his designs. He did the two windows in the back of the Church, Saint Bernard and Saint Stephen Harding, which some people like very much. I like them for what they are, but they are a little comical and there is a little cynicism involved. As a matter of fact, recently Anselm Atkins was asking me if I wanted to change the face of Saint Bernard. I said, no, leave it like it is. And I think he would have got the same thing in the Salve window which I would not have been happy with. And then I did not want to put myself up to do it. I thought, if they do not like me, or they get mad at me, when that window is lit up at Compline, when we sing the "Salve Regina" and they light that window, it could ruin their prayer life. So it seemed advisable, the most political thing to do, to get someone from outside the community and Bob Rambush was our architectural consultant. He was the son of the establishment of Rambush Church Decorating. They are an old company. As a matter of fact, just about this time the liturgical revival started up, and they started to call it "surgical art," not "liturgical," but "surgical" because all the Churches were tearing out all the old art and redoing their churches and making them more simple. This company was really involved in that. Bob was a very talented artist, very talented stained glass artist. He did the lady chapel at the Baltimore Cathedral which is a very fine stained glass installation. Anyway he did this design. He gave us just a sketch, and I selected the glass colors.

But the trapezoidal figures in the back of that window sort of determined our plans. Because if we were going to use that for our most prominent window in the Church, then it would have to influence the rest of the stained glass. So this was decided then in that first trip up to Blenko when David and I talked with Wayne and Betty. It was decided at that point then to use the trapezoidal shape for the clerestory windows and to use a softer shape down below. There again, Anselm had done some curvy shapes which suggested what is there right now. What he had done with the colors would not have been good stained glass.

II

Father Methodius's work as stained glass artist and as musician reflects his grounding in the ideals of the Benedictine-Cistercian life. His friendship with Thomas Merton has, as we can see in the 2005 interview, fed into his community work as well as helped develop and articulate Father Methodius's identity as a Cistercian artist. This interview further reveals a particular Cistercian aesthetic present in both his glass work and music. Key to this aesthetic is the analysis of Beauty as a reality of God's ephemeral yet tangible presence. Drawing on early monastic wisdom, Father Methodius shows how Beauty reveals itself through simplicity and unfolds in multidimensional ways so that one's experience of God remains dynamic and evolutionary.

(2005 Interview) Conducted by Glenn Crider

Crider: What can you say about your continuing glass design and production work in particular as it relates to the Cistercian ideal?

Telnack: Well, Saint Bernard himself, even though he had been accused of being the first Puritan because of the simplicity of the Cistercian churches built during his time, made a disclaimer about simplicity and how it did not apply to parish churches or cathedral churches. He recognized that there are different needs for different churches—different needs for the liturgy, the worship, and the people. Since I have been doing most of my work outside the monastery for parishes, I have not used any particular Cistercian ideals except—and this is true for St. Bernard as well—an analysis of beauty. He recognized Beauty as a transcendental quality of God: Truth, Goodness, Being.

Beauty which St. Thomas later developed as an entity of God. Saint Thomas says that we approach God more as a passion than as an activity. God draws us by beauty, for example. We're drawn by beauty. And St. Bernard says that the pursuit of beauty is the pursuit of God. And with all the necessary ramifications and qualifications and cautions, ontologically speaking, truth is beauty and goodness. Those are transcendental qualities. So what I can say is that the Cistercian ideal of the pursuit of truth is seen in simplicity.

Clearly, I think that sense of clarity in Cistercian architecture, a single-minded and unadorned ideal, is what I have used throughout all the work I have done. But I do not know if all my work is necessarily Cistercian, that what I create is necessarily Cistercian. I hope it is beautiful though. And if it is beautiful then it is in accord with the principles of Saint Bernard.

He was an artist in literature. He quotes the Fathers—he says that they may read poetry more beautifully than he can write it. They can say it more beautifully, and that beauty is persuasive. When the Word is expressed beautifully, it is more effective. And so that is one art form—poetry—a particular use of words. When I make stained glass, I am not in a verbal mode. To show beauty I pick a combination of colors and beautiful lines.

Crider: If you were preparing glass for a Cistercian monastery versus a parish church, what immediate differences and similarities become apparent?

Telnack: I think it would be a mistake to think that we have to repeat the designs of the original Cistercian churches. Why do that?

Crider: Yes.

Telnack: They were great works of art—what we have left. They were called "Cistercian Glass." They were not allowed to use colors. That was proscribed by St. Bernard. It should not be tinted or colored. But that did not keep the artist down. Consider the size of glass that they had to use; they did not have very big sheets of glass like we have now. They had very small pieces of glass to work with. And when they put them together, they put them together in very intricate geometric, or sometimes floral, type designs. It was really complex. The design of those windows was not simple. Yet it contributed to the Cistercian style of simplicity because of the color of light coming through the glass. The glass itself was a grayish green. They called "grisaille." The typical Cisterican glass was intricately put together. It proves that you just cannot keep the artist down. They will find a beautiful way to do it.

With our own church, we had not thought of stained glass initially. Part of the Church was already roofed when the Abbot General came through in 1952. And it must have been the hottest June in history, I think. The Abbot had just come from Africa. He came from Africa to Georgia and said he had never felt such heat until he arrived here. He walked through the Church as it was under construction and look around and said, "You're going to have to put colored glass in here to cut down the intense sunlight." So it was really the Abbot's mandate that got us thinking about stained glass. I had done a lot of the architecture by that time. The architect had a nervous breakdown so I had to take over.

Simplicity was in my mind. And in the spirit of simplicity, rather than having a painting or a statue, we decided to put a stained glass window of the Virgin Mary in the Church. But it was not designed by me. It was designed by our liturgical consultant, Bob Rambush. I, of course, built it, enlarged it, colored it and painted it. But the initial design was his.

Crider: What year did that take place?

Telnack: It must have been around 1957. The stained glass was not installed or hung in the Church until 1959. It took that long because we had so much work to do including getting materials and so forth. But the rest of the windows—we were not on a tight schedule but we had to get the building enclosed before winter—were done on a sort of a mass production scale. The design could not have been any more simple because they were just straight lines. I figured out a design scheme which was just a—it is kind of difficult to explain. There are two colors: pink and blue, of various shades. And the shades go from light to dark. So you have a counterpoint of pink and blue and light and dark. There were actually twenty-three colors in each window. And I figured out how many pieces of each color we put in each window.

So we cut that glass out and put it on an easel. I had at that time a mathematician living with us, a young scientist, who was working at Cape Canaveral. We built two big easels out of chicken wire, and I said take these trapezoidal pieces of glass and put the same amount of colors in each window, but put them in differently. We would put one up and critique it, and put another up and critique it, and so on. We used this method as a critique, or as a way to see what looked best. So we would examine each window and ask if it should be darker here, or lighter there. Should this section have more blue? Should this piece go somewhere else?

So now when you look around the Church, there is one window that is almost like a checkerboard. It is light-dark-light-dark-light-dark-light-dark. It does not show up in the photograph, but there in the Church you can see it. It is very regular. But all the other windows are a commentary and a departure from that regularity. And the goodness of that is that there is an emotional element to each of those windows. Because when you see how the designs are distributed— again, it is difficult to describe, but it is an emotional thing. It is not rational. It affects your emotions when you look at the window. And they are always fresh because they are so simple.

We decided to put curves in the lower windows. It is just a simple art. And we did the same thing. We would put them up on an easel. As a matter of fact, we have Br. Louis here who lost one of his legs. He was actually born deaf but eventually he got hearing aids and was able to hear. He was an Italian boy from a poor family from, I guess, New York or New Jersey. Anyway, he did the windows on the south side of the Church. The windows on the north side were done by Father Andrew who was a professor of philosophy and theology for us. But he had no particular artistic background at all.

There is a logic in it, but it is not the kind of thing you can reason to. It is something felt. And I think it is completely within the Cistercian spirit because, I mean, how simple could you get? So, even though we used colored glass which is not traditionally Cistercian, I think the designs proclaim Cistercian simplicity.

I have not done that any place else because these were particular designs for this Church. Although I know that the chapel at the airport has the same sort of trapezoids that we have here. (I think it was done by Anselm after he left the monastery.)

Crider: How might your work here within the monastery compare to your work outside the monastery?

Telnack: Every job that I have done outside the monastery has been along with a particular community—either the pastor, architect, or the building committee. I like working with the architect because he can sell the idea to the church better than I can myself. And with my particular background, I speak the same language as the architect. I think the best work I have done has been along with an architect.

Crider: You had mentioned that stained glass evokes a feeling or an emotion. I assume you see your work more as a way to predispose others to contemplation. Is that true?

Telnack: Yes. It does the same thing as a text, a scriptural text. It is not the words, it is what is behind the words. It is not the picture. And I have been kind of against pictures because we are so sated with pictures through the media. It is not the picture that is communicated. What is communicated is that somehow through the beauty something spiritual is communicated. At least, that is the area that I hope I have been working in. The windows are alive in that respect.

Crider: Do you think this possible spiritual or contemplative connection is the motivation behind people wanting stained glass in churches in the first place?

Telnack: I do not know the exact cause and effect, but whatever is the cause, many feel that their church is not complete until it has stained glass. Just the words "stained glass" has a kind of magical connotation. Now there are many churches who want clear glass, and I think that is wonderful. If they want stained glass, I would be glad to do it. But as it is, the plain, white glass is pretty wonderful. You do not necessarily need the colored glass.

Every church does not necessarily need stained glass but it adds another dimension, another possibility of communicating contemplation. It can become another element in disposing people to a contemplative mood. Of course, that is another thing seen in Saint Bernard. The materials themselves are beautiful. But when the artist uses the materials wisely, Saint Bernard says that wise use is according to the "Truth," it adds another dimension to that experience of beauty, which is ultimately an experience of God.

Crider: Two contributors to the projected *Merton Annual*, Kevin Seasoltz and Charlotte Zalot, are writing articles about Frank Kacmarcik as a contemplative artist and visual theologian. What can you say about your connection to, or awareness of, Kacmarcik and his work?

Telnack: Well, Kacmarcik knew Merton, or Merton knew Kacmarcik. They had at least some correspondence and once Kacmarcik consulted at Gethsemani. I do not think that Father Louis was all that drawn to Kacmarcik. Father Louis also knew Bob Rambush who was our liturgical consultant.

Father Louis referred to Rambush as a "gentleman" but did not use that same term with Kacmarcik! I met Frank at Mepkin. That was the last time I saw him. Our meeting was cordial but I cannot say that we were friends because we had not had the opportunity of meeting until then. Of course, I was familiar with his work. I think there are couple of things to say about Mepkin. I do not think it is built well which may have to do with the resources they had. It is already showing signs of age. The stucco is discolored. Of course, with the climate, you might expect that. But it is impressive in its simple lines and that reflects Cistercian simplicity. I appreciate that. Do you know Richard Meyer who did the High Museum?

Crider: I am somewhat aware of him.

Telnack: I recently discovered a church Richard Meyer designed for the diocese of Rome which is in the suburbs. It is called the "Jubilee Church" and was designed in honor of Pope John Paul's twenty-fifth anniversary of ordination. It is a very contemporary building, much nicer than the High Museum. But the Church has no stained glass yet it is quite beautiful, very peaceful and, I think, contemplative.

Crider: With Kacmarcik, do you notice any differences in his work as a Benedictine versus a Cistercian?

Telnack: It just occurred to me that there is sometimes a sense of grandeur with his work. Even with Mepkin which is not a big church, there is a sense of grandeur which is not common to Cistercian tradition. Cistercian Churches can be huge but they do not say "grandeur." I had not thought of this before, but there is that different sense of spirit between the two. I had not identified that before, but when you think of the Benedictine churches like St. John's in Collegeville, you see the grandeur. I am not sure how much Kacmarcik had to do with St. John's. Marcel Breuer was the architect. I think Kacmarcik did some of the altars and perhaps crucifixes around the building which were very simple. Those were his designs. We actually have one of his designs here in our scriptorium.

Crider: Would you like to comment on your relationship with Thomas Merton as it might relate to this theme of Cistercian art and contemplation?

Telnack: I met Father Louis in 1957 which is when I started the stained glass work. As a matter of fact, I was at Gethsemani for eight weeks for a music class conducted by a French Benedictine named Ludo Berone who was a master of the interpretation of Gregorian chant. While I was there—of course Father Louis was well known by then—one of the first things I did when I saw the Abbot, Dom James Fox, was ask him to meet Father Louis. He said he would arrange it before I left. So I was there for several weeks and preparing to leave. And my ordination was coming up in a couple of weeks. Then I reminded Father James that I wanted to meet Father Louis. He said sure.

At that time, Father Louis was the Novice Master so I met him in his office in the novitiate which was piled with manuscripts and books. He was very cordial and very friendly. We had a nice, long talk. But I did not think much of it except that I really liked him.

A couple of months later, I had a chance to go back because of some glass work. It was probably around August of 1957. And I got to meet with him again. After that, I was able to visit at least once a year, and sometimes several times per year for quite some time. By that time he had moved into the hermitage, so I met him there often and we had some really nice talks. I am sure anyone who had contact with him would tell you the same thing—that he was their friend. He had that personality and was so easy to talk to. He was my friend.

Interesting enough, while I was there I met his confessor. He had a German name. I think he was John of the Cross. In any case, over the years I was able to see Merton. I was Cantor here at the time. And I had the idea of singing the Chant with English words. The Episcopalians had been doing it for years since they had adopted the Anglican translations which were very beautiful. So I talked to Father Louis about this idea, about singing the Chant in English. He said this would be an opportunity to do something different and original. So his suggestion was my impetus to make that transition, and not adapt the Gregorian melodies.

I did the whole Sunday schedule of Mass in English with my own melodies. Well, there were three or four hymns I adapted, but the rest was original. I incorporated a melodic line as opposed to the usual Gregorian lines which had a lot of notes going up and down. This was to give a simple yet strong melody, and be easy to sing.

Crider: Is your music used here still?

Telnack: Yes, it is used for Sunday Masses but we combine Mass with Lauds, so the Graduals and communion verses are not sung. So it is truncated. Two of the important pieces of Mass are not sung anymore. Unless we have a Mass at a later hour which we did at Easter and Christmas, then we sing the longer versions. It is interesting though because the choir itself knows the melodies better than the cantors. The cantors try too hard. You just have to attend to the melody.

Crider: Perhaps a concluding note on your glass work would be helpful. Do any of your jobs really stand out to you?

Telnack: I did some windows for Atlanta University, for their Lyke Catholic Center. There is clear glass only. The designs are sandblasted and glue chipped. We did forty windows. There is no stained glass at all. I think that is one of the most beautiful works I have done. It also depends on the circumstance, the Church and the architecture itself. If I see a church that is really well done with no colored glass, I really appreciate that.

Contemporary Architectural Witness to the Lived Cistercian Ideal: The Abbey Churches of Gethsemani and Conyers

Dewey Weiss Kramer

Introduction

Two mid-twentieth century churches stand as proof of the vitality of the Cistercian ideal being lived today: the church of the Abbey of Our Lady of Gethsemani, renovated in the mid-1900's, and that of the Abbey of Our Lady of the Holy Spirit near Conyers, Georgia, the first daughter house of Gethsemani, constructed between 1954 and 1960. While the two projects proceeded nearly simultaneously and there was clearly extensive and regular contact between founding and daughter houses, the two communities worked rather independently on their churches. However, although the resulting sacred spaces differed from each other, both turned out to be profound expressions of the Cistercian charism. Both churches are strikingly contemporary, yet both echo the twelfth and thirteenth centuries as well. Neither a staid nor merely academic influence, the Cistercian medieval heritage as it was re-examined and rediscovered during the twentieth century constitutes a development in the Order's self-identity. Through its focus on the architecture of two Cistercian communities and the changes made in it, this paper shows the increasing significance of the original Cistercian ideals as a workable basis for monastic life in the contemporary world. The "medieval" element exists in lively interaction with the modern, so much so, that as will be seen in the example of the glass work at Conyers, the life of the mid-twentieth Cistercians spontaneously produced an artistic expression which combined the spirit and goals of both the founding and the current era.[1]

Cistercian Spirituality

The Cistercian order was a reform movement which reacted particularly against the wealthy and comfortable Cluniac Benedictinism of the late eleventh century. Citeaux's founders were

determined to restore and to live St. Benedict's *Rule* in its original
and pure form. To do so, they created a spiritual and physical
environment conducive to their goals, ramifications of which profoundly affected the spirituality, the architecture, and the art of
Europe for at least two centuries.

Cistercian spirituality was centered in the reality of divine love,
a love that could and would lead the monk to his ultimate aim of
the union of the soul with God. Contemplative prayer was the
monk's main task, and his physical environment, especially the
monastery church, should further this task. It should be a workshop where meditation could proceed unhampered. The key to
such an environment was simplicity. St. Bernard's famous attack
on the Cluniac style and his refusal to have it part of the Cistercian
environment, rather than being a puritanical aversion to the aesthetic realm, affirmed his aesthetic sense and his recognition of
the power of art to affect persons.[2] Imagery was necessary for common folk, but it was both unnecessary and counterproductive for
monastic spirituality. In the monastery, the threshold of the spiritual vision, he found all images wanting. Thus the architecture
was to be clean, stripped of unnecessary distractions, including
figurative stained glass. Instead, the carefully proportioned spaces
were decorated with simple, meaningful forms which stressed the
orderliness of transcendental truths, and produced an atmosphere
of calmness. One of the main functions of Cistercian art and architecture seems to have been to discourage emotional, irrational
reactions, and to encourage a sense of composure, necessary pre-
disposition to contemplative prayer.[3]

From its earliest appearance in the Egyptian deserts of the third
century, monasticism had recognized the necessity of creating an
environment to further the life. By choosing deliberately a form
of life apart, monks were free of the constraints of society to some
extent and thus were able consciously to form their surroundings.
This aspect of the conscious creation of one's environment in order to further a particular life style and thus to attain an ideal mode
of existence, makes the monk the precursor of modern urban plan-
ners. Throughout history, no other group of people has exercised
to such an extent as monastics rational choice in the creation of
their environment, realizing—perhaps not always consciously—
that the environment one creates and shapes around oneself also
shapes and forms one in return. And of all monastic orders, probably no group was more successful than the Cistercians in this
regard.

This aspect of the conscious choice of life-style and environment is germane to an examination of the Gethsemane and Conyers abbey churches.

The Nineteenth Century Monastic Revival

The Cistercian order underwent various declines and reforms after its thirteenth century florescence. The best known of the reforms was that initiated in the late seventeenth century by Armand de Rancé at the abbey of La Trappe in France. De Rancé's concept of the Order's charism was that of penance, reparation, austerity, suffering, not the emphasis of the twelfth century founders. Yet he and those who followed his reform down into the nineteenth century believed they were returning to the original spirit, and they saw themselves as an island of medieval life and spirit within the modern world, an interpretation cultivated especially in the nineteenth century monastic revival and which continued well into the twentieth century, perhaps even up to the Second Vatican Council. The rigid adherence to the external trappings of the middle ages, anachronistic as they appear today, was really another manifestation of that basic need for the nurturing environment. And the conscious choice of the externals of a past style reinforced the conscious choice to persevere in that life which they believed had produced such externals and which they were convinced was still valid.

Perhaps the whole nineteenth century Romantic Movement was a necessary step in rediscovering the medieval contribution to the modern era, after this contribution had been denigrated by the renaissance with its emphasis on classical antiquity and by the enlightenment with its dream of infinite perfectibility and a secular paradise. For the restored monastic orders of the nineteenth century, aspects of medieval style and thought, even in their misinterpretations, helped raise in monastics the awareness both of their otherness and of the value of the monastic heritage as vital part of the continuum of European history. Thus the nineteenth (and twentieth) century monastics constituted in their very selves a bridge between history and modernity.

The Gethsemani Church

The Gethsemani pioneers came to the Bardstown area of Kentucky in 1848, a colony of monks from a France threatened by revolution and by virtue of its militant secularism inimical to their life. Kentucky was the end of a long arduous journey into the wilderness. Yet harsh geographically as it was, it was an area of Catholic settlement, including several religious communities, from one of which they purchased their land.

They built their monastery during the Civil War years, thick brick walls, hand-hewn timber roof supports, a church largely rectangular, based on the ground plan of the thirteenth century Abbey of Melleray in France. But within that rectangular brick and wood space they also constructed the interior shell of a neo-gothic building out of laths and plaster. Later on, neo-gothic windows were also introduced into the large rectangular window areas of the original building. They also constructed an imposing steeple above it all, visible for miles around.

Now this building was an admirable reflection of the community's life style, a witness to and support of their ideals. First, it looked like what the nineteenth century thought Catholic churches had "always" looked like. Thus it was a statement that this community stood in the continuity of unchanging (as they then thought) centuries. Second, the church would have been awesome to the inhabitants of the rural Kentucky environment. So it helped to impart to those who worshipped in it a sense of the mystery of their life. Its otherness was a forceful statement of the otherness of their existence in the United States of "manifest destiny" and expansionism. Further, since most of the founders—as well as subsequent arrivals during the next decades when native U.S. vocations were scarce—came from Alsace, it transmitted a sense both of home and of their essential unity with the mystical body. Third, the fact that this church in its neo-gothicized form differed from the other buildings of the monastery built among the Kentucky knolls emphasized the spiritual orientation of their life. Though the specifically "Trappist" interpretation of Cistercian spirituality over-stressed penance, the purpose of each man's being there was still spiritual. And the awesome church served well as sign thereof. It also served as sign of the type of prayer stressed. The original Cistercian balance of contemplative / private prayer with communal prayer of the Divine Office had shifted toward reliance on the latter. The *Opus Dei* had also gradually taken on extraneous details, not unlike those plaster excrescences of the neo-gothic shell. Finally, the complexity and ornateness of the church also reflected that awareness of the need for and the validity of beauty which has always characterized all forms of cenobitical monasticism. And amid tremendous changes in American life, this church remained essentially unchanged for almost one hundred years.

The Monastery of Our Lady of the Holy Spirit in Conyers

A century after its own founding, Gethsemani established its first daughter-house in rural Georgia. Several aspects of the Conyers foundation fit the Cistercian tradition very precisely. For example, Cistercian monasteries historically had followed the same ground plan while allowing for adaptation to the specific geography, and had established links to the surrounding countryside. The Conyers foundation was planned to reproduce the Gethsemani plan exactly. And the subsequent sixty years have shown that the Community has been most receptive to its surroundings.[4]

Holy Spirit's founding abbot, Frederic Dunne, had clear notions of what he wanted done there, and these were essentially those of nineteenth century Gethsemani. But Abbot Frederic, for all his conservatism, was also the abbot who admitted to his monks at Gethsemani that after him the Trappist life was bound to change. And in Georgia it began to change. Some of the changes were common to the order as whole, in part as response to Vatican II, and these paralleled those at Gethsemani. Others were the result of the Georgia environment and the need to be **not** Gethsemani. In keeping with this paper's thesis, these changes gained visible expression in a building—this one now of poured concrete and modern stained glass. The physical plan of the monastery evolved in interaction with the development of the monastic community and its evolving sense of identity.[5]

The Conyers pioneers started with almost no physical facilities. An existent barn was converted into a tiny monastery, with dormitory, scriptorium, chapel. And the life was led in the traditional manner. But the lack of a large physical plant as at Gethsemani, the rigorous labor required in building, the radical change in geographical locale, all this produced a sense of a new beginning and furthered a closer sense of community. Inevitably, the regimen deviated from the strict **ordo** of the mother house. As the community developed on its own, it came to value its difference, so that eventually recourse to "That's the way it's done at Gethsemani" would prove counter-productive in getting something approved. This community was also more dependent on the non-monastic populace than was Gethsemani, and the openness that came with such necessity was very early recognized as a positive aspect of the monastery's mission, serving the diocesan priests for retreats and counsel, then gradually all religious faiths. Holy Spirit's means of livelihood—bread, plants, glass, etc. spread its presence into the area. The final form of the monastery as a whole even reflects this mission, for Conyers has the largest guest house in the Order. The present guest house had started out as a novitiate. The change in plans resulted in part from the decline in the great post-war influx of novices. But an equally important consideration was the increased need for hospitality, acceptance and affirmation of a mission thrust on the Community from their unique situation.

The Abbey Church at Conyers

The abbey church planned by Dom Frederic for the new community was to be a copy of Gethsemani's, same floor plan, also of brick. But at first the war effort precluded construction of "nonessential" buildings. Then brick was unavailable. Then funds were unavailable. And when some years later construction on a church was again feasible, the Conyers community would make its own plans. A copy of Gethsemani was no longer the plan. However, the plan adopted in the early 1950's was still in the traditional mold. An Atlanta architect famous for tudor gothic churches was retained, and the plan proposed was to have a grandiose statement of Catholicism in rural Georgia, not unlike Gethsemani's statement for rural Kentucky a century earlier.

Radical modifications developed during the building process, modifications which reflected the character of **this** particular community of monks. Concerned that the architect did not know their life (which the designer of the later Gethsemani renovation **did**), the community worked to affect changes that would reflect their life style. They managed to avoid the intricate gothic detail-work of the blueprints by recourse to the fact that such intricate work required trained artisans, not available from within the monastery. More importantly, of course, the resultant clean lines **did** express the Cistercian ideal as the architect's vision could not have. The enormous height could be shown to be too dangerous for the monks to cope with. But the ostentation which would have been part of such impressiveness would have misrepresented the religious witness being lived by this community, "the poor men of Citeaux."

Modifications were further determined by the make-up of the growing community. Conyers had among its members gifted men who had studied art history, architecture and sculpture. Thus the final product was truly the result of the **community's** work and was an expression of its values.

Gethsemani

While Conyers was expressing its developing identity in the poured concrete and stained glass of its twentieth century, yet quintessential Cistercian church, Gethsemani was going through a similar process of discovering the best way to express its evolving identity. Dom Frederic's prediction of changes to come after his time (He died in 1948.) came true. The great influx of vocations after World War II had brought new views into the monastery. James Fox's abbacy, 1948–1968, encouraged new emphases and approaches, so that when Vatican II (1965–68) called on all religious orders to reexamine their life, purpose, style, and original charism, these monks had already begun that process. A thorough-going renovation of monastery buildings and church, necessitated by their one hundred years of constant use, would provide that community a challenge to self-exploration and self-expression similar to that faced by their Georgia daughter house.

The work of general renovation undertaken in the early sixties and carried out over several years gave them a chance to express a different spirit that was already in evidence. In their planning they consciously aimed at changes which would reflect their life as well as be suitable for the functions they needed.[6] For example, a crucial question centered on the extent to which guests might participate in the liturgy. The question was finally decided in terms of the local tradition and the past attitude of aloofness toward the guests: separation was maintained, and thus the guests' gallery was kept apart from the monks' church. Not a "modern" or popular decision, the decision was nonetheless an honest expression of identity of **this** particular community and accordingly took visible form in the arrangement of the church. In comparison, the Conyers guest area was less distinct and more accessible to the main church, in keeping with that community's mission.

The overall impression of the renovated Gethsemani church is one of simplicity and strength. The steeple is gone. Twelfth century Cistercian statutes had proscribed steeples along with stained glass, elaborate decoration, etc., and this twentieth compliance with the statutes has resulted in greater integrity for the building. Natural materials are in evidence—the plain brick is painted white, the choir stalls in light oak are hung scapular-fashion over concrete slabs. The overhead supporting beams have been exposed, recalling thereby the monastic ties to nature. Further, the act of uncovering these beams hewn from Kentucky timber by the Gethsemani founders emphasizes the community's ties to their founders, their Kentucky home, and as well to those first Cistercian fathers of the forests of twelfth century Citeaux. Such a detail manifests Gethsemani's participation in Cistercian tradition, U.S. life, its geographical environment, and ultimately in the mystical body of Christ. As mentioned above, the abbey church was originally constructed according to the floor plan of the French Abbey of Melleray. In its renovated form the church's affinity to the Cistercian structures of Citeaux's founding generations is unmistakable.

In the several decades following the completion of both church projects, however, both monastic communities have grown increasingly aware of their call to witness beyond cloister walls and this stance finds expression in the churches as well. Gethsemani today seems far more welcoming than just after the renovation. Guests are encouraged to come into the sanctuary on Sundays. Similarly, at Conyers aspects of the church have been modified to open it up. Extra altars and the high abbatial choir stall have been removed and guests are invited to stand with the monks at all Offices and during Mass.

The Stained Glass

The treatment of the windows in both Conyers and Gethsemani is an intriguing instance of how the monastic life manifests itself visually. The similarity of both abbey churches' windows to Cistercian glass of the thirteenth century would seem to offer artistic proof that the Cistercian monastic life being led in contemporary America has definitely recovered the essence of the Order's founding generations.

Possibly as early as 1134 and certainly by 1151 there were statutes proscribing the use of stained glass in Cistercian churches. In place of the figural, colored windows of the then current gothic era, the White Monks developed Cistercian *grisaille*, clear or white or grey-tinted glass with strictly geometric or stylized floral designs.[7] The prohibition was not primarily an economy measure, to insure poverty, as once was thought. Rather, it tied in with the attempt to create a physical environment in accord with, and capable of furthering, the Order's spiritual goal—contemplation. Instead of distracting the mind with images (as Bernard observed the romanesque grotesques tend to do, for instance), the Cistercian imageless patterns would free the mind from obstacles to contemplation. Today one might say that the *grisaille* windows function somewhat as *mandalas*.[8]

Gethsemani

The original Gethsemani windows were full of colorful figures, nineteenth century interpretations of fourteenth to sixteenth century European stained glass. No doubt awe-inspiring, they inspired devotion, perhaps, but not apophatic prayer. The contemplative ideal which had required and called forth the early Cistercian *grisaille* had been replaced by the **Trappist** commitment to a life of utmost penance, reparation, and suffering, "the hardest life in the Catholic Church."[9]

The return to the sources responsible for the form the renovation took at Gethsemani demanded new treatment of the windows. As noted above in regard to the decision to maintain space between guests and the monastic community, retention of stained glass was deemed essential.[10] In keeping with a return to the unadorned raw materials of the church edifice and the resultant affirmation of the community's natural environment, and with the Cistercian commitment to simplicity, the restored church now has windows composed of large geometric abstract designs in earth tones.

Conyers

The Conyers community inherited no glass, of course. As in the case of the church itself, the community was able to find its own way. Also as in the case of the church architecture, the monks were thrown on their own resources—financially, artistically, and spiritually—so that the resultant glass program clearly reflected the community's life.[11]

The financial situation required that if there was to be stained glass, the monks would have to make it themselves. One of their number learned the craft and taught the technique to his fellow monks. A basic plan was developed which was simple enough for non-artists to produce, so that several members of the community could become involved. Each window had a set number of pieces of each color, but the specific arrangement of the pieces was decided by the individual monk responsible for it, working a few hours a day over a period of weeks. In this way individual personalities found expression within a communal effort. And each window **does** have its own character, a fact that becomes ever clearer the more one gazes on them. Due to this mode of construction, the windows shared in the unique Conyers experience of community, for the character of this monastic family is due in great part to the experience of building the whole complex from scratch with their own labor.

The visible results of the glass project suggest this monastery's grounding in the wider complex of Cistercian life through the centuries. For although the design of the windows appears to the casual visitor as "modern," and no doubt does reflect the taste of the nineteen-fifties, the affinity to the thirteenth century Cistercian *grisaille* windows is striking. The reliance here on geometric patterns, on a tightly restricted number of patterns repeated again and again throughout the church, produces the same effect as that intended by the *grisaille*—the windows are non-distracting, they calm, they predispose to contemplation.

Blues predominate in the nave, recalling the European cathedrals of the high middle ages and thus Conyers' participation in the continuity of the faith. The sanctuary, by contrast, is flooded with golden light due to the use there of exclusively white and yellow glass, albeit again with the same forms. The contrast focuses attention on the Real Presence in the Eucharist and on the celebration of the Mass as the central act of worship.

The Lady Window

The windows manifest the charism of the monastic community in yet another way. The dominant motif of the clearstory windows is a trapezoidal figure repeated over and over again in various shades of blue and rose. The source of this motif is found in the Lady Window above the main altar, a work executed for the community by an outside artist. This window, an icon of Our Lady of the Holy Spirit, can therefore be seen as the artistic generator (or generatrix, to speak in theological terms) of the major stained glass program of the church. Further, the color scheme of the whole church relates to this window-icon as well. As the worshiper's eyes are drawn toward it, so too do the colors in the church progress toward it. Starting in the back, the eastern rose window shares its luminosity with its gems of red, the blues in the nave reflect it, the high narrow windows of the transepts join their reds and yellows to it, and the yellows and oranges are then added in full array in the sanctuary.

Such repetition of basic, simple motifs stands firmly in the Cistercian artistic tradition. In this case, though, artistic practice proclaims a spiritual truth, namely the central role of the Mother of God in Cistercian spirituality. Just as the Lady Window motif expands throughout the whole building, so too does the spiritual reality imaged there of the Mother of God, the Contemplator *par excellence*, permeate the life being lived in the community.

Since Cistercian art is subtractive, i.e., less is preferred, what elements remain should serve significant aesthetic and iconographic purposes. The window of itself could proclaim the centrality of the Virgin, constituting as it does the sole figurative art in the church, aside from the crucifix. But through its interaction with the windows, a physical relationship—which comes to light gradually through hours of meditation in their presence—makes the spiritual reality the more tangible.

Mary and Citeaux

The centrality of Mary receives artistic expression also in the renovated church at Gethsemani where, again, the sole figural artistic piece beside the crucifix is an icon of the Virgin and Child. Why is it that both the Gethsemani and the Conyers communities chose iconic representations of Mary?

Several reasons suggest themselves. First, iconic art has been rediscovered in the modern era. Collectors pay high prices for originals. Reproductions are popular, both in secular and religious art stores. Modern artists feel drawn to the style, perhaps because the icon's externally simple two-dimensionality is capable simultaneously of revealing many more dimensions. In any case, the style is part of the artistic milieu of the men whose lives find expression in these two churches.

Second, and more important, the icon represents a kind of religious art which corresponds well to Cistercian spirituality with its search for the direct experience of God. As art, the icon is neither primarily decorative nor didactic, but is rather a window into the world of the sacred. Just as Jesus Christ in the flesh imaged God in eternity, so the icon as "matter" permits a glimpse into the timeless world of religious mystery. One stands before the icon and speaks through its image to the reality behind it. Cistercian life has recovered its contemplative dimension, and the icon is essentially contemplative art.

Finally, the icon is affirmation of the rich heritage of eastern spirituality. It is the glory of Christian Orthodoxy, and so these images represent artistically the return of these Cistercian communities to the very origins of monasticism, to the wisdom of the desert fathers. Beyond this Christian context, the icon recalls the profound contemplative life of the Hindu and Buddhist traditions which have enriched both Christian and non-Christian spirituality mid-twentieth century American and continue to do so today.

How foreign such images would have seemed to the nineteenth century Gethsemani monk worshipping in his neo-gothic abbey church. To his twenty-first century counterpart, that image witnesses to the reality of a way of life that was valid in the fourth century, in the twelfth, and remains valid today. As such, it supports him in his commitment to a life-style which in a time of hecticity and materialism still focuses on "God alone."

Conclusion

The striking aesthetic simplicity which resonates from both these abbey churches calls forth in both visitor and worshipper an awareness of the presence of God. The visitor has probably consciously sought out a "Catholic" church, even more consciously, perhaps, a "monastic" church. And yet both these labels lose their significance once the person is immersed in this Presence. Such was the intent of the earliest Cistercian reformers, to help seekers **experience** God profoundly. This ideal continues to enliven the Cistercians of the twenty-first century.

Notes

1. This paper originated in work involved with the Oral Histories of Thomas Merton and Holy Spirit (Conyers, GA) conducted in the early 1980's (both published, 1985). The information led to my historical guide to the Conyers' monastery, *Open to the Spirit* (Conyers: Holy Spirit Monastery, 1st ed. 1986, 2nd ed. 1996).

2. Bernard, in his *Apologia to William of St. Thierry* in Bernard of Clairvaux, *Treatises I*, Cistercian Fathers Series Vol. I (1970), pp. 3-69.

3. See Emero Stiegman, "Saint Bernard: The Aesthetics of Authenticity," in *Studies in Cistercian Art and Architecture*, Vol. 2, ed. M.P. Lillich (Cistercian Studies Series: No. 65, Kalamazoo: Cistercian Publications, 1984), pp. 1-13.

4. This information on the early development of Holy Spirit Monastery is based on interviews conducted and recorded in the published Conyers *Oral History.*

5. The two-part interview of Father Methodius included in this volume of *The Merton Annual* constitutes a valuable complement to this paper, both as background and expansion of aesthetic and communal points being made.

6. Articles by some of those involved in Gethsemani's renovation project are collected in the August 1968 issue of *Liturgical Arts* (Vol. 36, August 1968, No. 4) the journal published by The Liturgical Arts Society: pieces by the architect, William Schickel; monks Thomas Merton and Matthew Kelty; designer Martin T. Gilligan are included.

7. There is copious scholarship on Cistercian *grisaille.* Foremost scholars include Meridith Lillich, editor of *Cistercian Art and Architecture*, Vol. 65, cited above. A helpful guide with illustrations is that by Helen Jackson Zakin, *French Cistercian Grisaille Glass* (New York: Garland, 1979).

8. The *mandala*, an arrangement of patterns, pictures, circles, squares, or rectangles representing the cosmos or wholeness has been central to Hindu and Buddhist practice for millenia. In the early twentieth century C. J. Jung recognized the healing potential of the mandala as well as its religious universality (present in early and medieval Christianity, both East and West, in native American religion, etc.). Since the mid-twentieth century the mandala as a valid means of approach to the Divine has become well established. For more information see: Giuseppe Tucci, *The Theory and Practice of the Mandala* (Mineola, NY: Dover, 1969); Judith Cornell, *Mandala: Luminous Symbols for Healing* (Wheaton, IL: Quest, 1994); C.G. Jung, *Man and His Symbols* (Garden City, NY: Doubleday, 1964) and C.G. Jung, *Mandala Symbolism* (Princeton: Princeton, 1973).

9. Fr. Francis X. Kavanagh interview in Conyers *Oral History*, p. 201–202.

10. An interesting parallel can be seen between the renovation of the church of the Gethsemani community and that of the neighboring Sisters of Loretto. When the sisters replaced their traditional stained glass windows, they opted for large wood framed ones of clear glass, symbols of their renewed openness to the world beyond the monastery. The monks chose to reaffirm their Cistercian heritage of a life lived "far apart from the haunts of men," thus commissioned windows which offer no views of the outside. The patterns and color scheme do, however, evoke the world of nature. This stance has been considerably modified during the recent decade.

11. See the Abbot General's recommendation that the church have colored glass in Methodius Telnack's interview, p. 84.

Thomas Merton on William Blake: "To look through matter into eternity"

[A Paper Developed from a Presentation at the Eighth Conference of the International Thomas Merton Society, University of British Columbia, Vancouver, Canada. June 4-8, 2003.]

Background

The literature on William Blake's impact on Thomas Merton is now extensive. At the 1998 Oakham Conference of the Thomas Merton Society of Great Britain, Sonia Petisco presented a paper "Recovering our Innocence: the Influence of William Blake on the Poetry of Thomas Merton."[1]   Later in the same year Michael Higgins published his book-length exploration of the shaping influences on Merton's radical spirituality: *Heretic Blood: The Spiritual Geography of Thomas Merton*.[2] In that work Higgins proposed that

> The... key to [Merton's] spiritual geography... is William Blake... the arch-rebel, provoking the establishment of his day and defying all convention with his madly experimental art and poetry.[3]

Higgins qualifies: "Artistically, spiritually, and intellectually, Merton laboured to achieve for his own time something of that visionary imagination of Blake."[4] This is an important scholarly insight. More recently, in 2001, Ross Labrie published his rather more measured study *Thomas Merton and the Inclusive Imagination*, which explores the links between Merton's spirituality and creativity and skillfully locates this centrally in what Merton learned from Blake. Labrie writes:

> As with Blake, for Merton, the font of the imagination, seen as a means of attaining a direct, ontological insight into being, awakened the mind at certain times to what, although frequently overlooked, was always and everywhere present.[5]

In support of these important claims I point out that in *New Seeds of Contemplation* Merton links poetry, music and art with the contemplative experience[6] and passionately expresses his belief that spiritual liberation can only be found through an acknowledgement of Blake's impulse of inclusiveness which, in its challenge to sanctimonious moralism, led to Blake's repeated declaration: "Everything that Lives is Holy":

> Let the Priests of the Raven of dawn, no longer in deadly black, with hoarse note curse the sons of joy. Nor his accepted brethren whom, tyrant, he calls free; lay the bound or build the roof. Nor pale religious letchery call that virginity, that wishes but acts not! For every thing that lives is Holy.

This is from Blake's "Song of Liberty" at the end of *The Marriage of Heaven and Hell.* Blake repeated this line in *Vision of the Daughters of Albion* and in *America a Prophecy.*[7] Merton, in his chapter "Everything That Is, Is Holy" in *New Seeds* translates this challenge to Catholic exclusiveness into the following exclamation:

> The only true joy on earth is to escape from the prison of our own false self, and enter by love into union with the Life Who dwells and sings within the essence of every creature and in the core of our own souls. In His love we possess all things and enjoy fruition of them, finding Him in them all. And thus as we go about the world, everything we meet and everything we see and hear and touch, far from defiling, purifies us and plants in us something more of contemplation and of heaven.[8]

There have also been numerous incidental references to Blake's impact on Merton's life and work prior to these recent sustained explorations. I am referring in particular to Monica Furlong's 1980 biography in which she places Blake at the center of Merton's spiritual development. About Merton's formative period she writes: "In a world of falsity and dangerous ambiguity, Blake seemed a trustworthy guide, prophet, and guru."[9] And she quotes Merton's own words:

> I have to acknowledge my own debt to him, and the truth which may appear curious to some, although it is really not so: that through Blake I would one day come, in a round-about way, to the only true Church, and to the One Living God, through His Son, Jesus Christ.[10]

So this essay, while not ground-breaking, attempts to bring together some of the key insights of all this good work. The essay also tries to present it from the context of someone working in Australia with a special interest focused on William Blake's impact on contemporary spirituality and the arts.

Blake's Presence in Merton's Life and Thought

My own chief interest is the way Blake's presence in Merton's life— both at the beginning and at the end— helps to throw into relief some of the most interesting tensions in Merton's spiritual and creative practice. These tensions are arguably the source of his true distinctiveness as poet and contemplative and are possibly the source of his liberating impact on his many audiences; these tensions lie behind the intensity of his commitment in every area of his life and they also lie behind the persistence of his revolt against solidifying structures: poetic, spiritual and personal.

Blake, I believe, was spiritually and artistically a profound influence on Merton's inner life and on the way that life ultimately found its deepest expression through the relationship between contemplative and creative practice. Briefly let me explain how I see the shape of this complex influence.

To begin with there is the paradoxical fact—we have heard Merton tell us—that Blake (iconoclast and hater of the established church) was the stimulus for his conversion to Catholicism; but it was not merely conversion to this faith, rather it was his taking on one of the most rigorous forms of this faith as a member of the Cistercian Order of the Strict Observance. Popularly known as Trappists, this Order sought to recover the strict asceticism and life of poverty expressed in the life and writings of St Bernard.[11] Against this background it seems initially paradoxical that Merton championed the author of "The Garden of Love" one of the great critics of the clerical garb and all it stood for:

> I went to the Garden of Love,
> And saw what I never had seen:
> A Chapel was built in the midst,
> Where I used to play on the green.

> And the gates of this Chapel were shut,
> And Thou shalt not. writ over the door;
> So I turn'd to the Garden of Love,
> That so many sweet flowers bore.

And I saw it was filled with graves,
And tomb-stones where flowers should be:
And Priests in black gowns, were walking their rounds,
And binding with briars, my joys & desires.[12]

Indeed rather than any kind of recoil, Merton's 1939 Master's thesis demonstrated a passionate interest into Blake as a poet and mystic expressing Thomistic and Maritainian insights into the nature of reality. As well as this, Blake served as a catalyst for Merton's own radicalism in artistic and spiritual matters. In the M.A. thesis, Merton drew on the aesthetics of Coomaraswamy, of Hinduism and of Neo-Platonism to indicate the ways in which Blake's thinking, artistically, religiously was a shaking of the foundations. Here is the conclusion of Chapter 1 of the thesis, where he quotes directly from Coomaraswamy; this clearly foreshadows Merton's own later search for "unitive," interfaith connections:

...because Blake is closer to Medieval Christians than to his own contemporaries, he is also closer to the religious thinkers of the East. Coomaraswamy says:

There was a time when Europe and Asia could and did actually understand each other very well. Asia has remained herself, but subsequent to the extroversion of the European consciousness and its preoccupation with surfaces it has become more and more difficult for European minds to think in terms of unity.[13]

Merton was here attuned to an insight that would radicalize Christian thinking in decades to come. In 1993 Karen Armstrong in her chapter "The God of the Mystics" in *A History of God* summarizes what she sees as the recent shift that has led to a trenchant critique of a Christianity that does not listen to its mystics:

Christianity made a human person the centre of the religious life in a way that was unique in the history of religion... Yet a personal God can become a grave liability. He can be a mere idol carved in our own image, a projection of our limited needs, fears and desires. We can assume that he loves what we love and hates what we hate, endorsing our prejudices instead of compelling us to transcend them... Since the West has never been very enthusiastic about mysticism, even during its heyday in other parts of the world, there is little understanding of the intelligence and discipline that is essential to this type of spirituality... Yet there are signs that the tide may be turning. Since the 1960's Western people have been discovering the benefits of certain types of Yoga and religions such as Buddhism, which have the advantage of being uncontaminated by an inadequate theism...[14]

Already in 1939, Merton was recognizing these limitations too and discovering, in the work of his hero William Blake, new sources for challenging "the extroversion of the European consciousness."

Merton's interest in William Blake did not stop with his 1939 thesis. In the year of his death, 1968, he published an essay "Blake and the New Theology." This was a review of Thomas Alteizer's book *The Radical Vision of William Blake.*[15] Merton strongly resists Alteizer's extreme appropriation of Blake into the "Death of God" movement and yet goes on to sing the author's praise for presenting a Blake who

...saw official Christendom as a *narrowing* of vision, a foreclosure of experience and of future expansion, a locking up of and securing of the doors of perception. He substituted for it a Christianity of openness, of total vision... not seeking to establish order in life by shutting off a little corner of chaos and subjecting it to laws and to police....[16]

From this perspective, Blake remained for Merton a potent source of the spiritual openness that he would develop in his last years, helping to express in practice and deepen the implications of the decree *Nostra Aetate*, which emerged out of Vatican Two in 1965:

The Church therefore has this exhortation for her sons: prudently and lovingly, through dialogue and collaboration with the followers of other religions, and in witness of Christian faith and life, acknowledge, preserve, and promote the spiritual and moral goods found among these men, as well as the values in their society and cultures (NA 2).

In *Mystics and Zen Masters* (1967) Merton would argue that without an acknowledgement of the "the spiritual heritage of the East" the West was hastening "the tragedy that threatens man and his civilizations."[17]

Merton's assimilation, at the core of his spiritual and creative life, of Blake's mystical poetry and painting, sheds further light on the sources of ambivalence in Merton towards his own creativity. As is well known, Merton determined to give up poetry on entering the monastery—partly as a result of his conservative critique of what he saw as his reckless bohemian youth—but later in life he came to accept his poetry as central to his spiritual practice. His essay "Poetry and Contemplation: A Reappraisal" (1958) is a key document for illustrating this progression in his thinking. Here in the *Author's Note* he writes:

> ...*the implied conflict between "contemplation" as rest and poetic creation as activity is even more misleading. It is all wrong to imagine that in order to "contemplate" divine things, or what you will, it is necessary to abstain from every kind of action and enter into a kind of spiritual stillness where one waits for "something to happen"*.... *Contemplation is not to be thought of as a separate department of life, cut off from all man's other interests and superseding them. It is the very fullness of a fully integrated life. It is the crown of life and of all life's activities.*[18]

Blake's Impact on Merton's Art

The comments on the nature of Blake's creativity in the M.A. thesis, also give insight into the nature of Merton's poetic practice and into the complexity of his relationship to this practice. At one point in this thesis, commenting on Blake's seeming lack of interest in the finished product, Merton writes mysteriously: "The created work is not art, it is the result of art."[19] What he means in the context is that art, poetry—their external forms—are the agents or tools for something higher; in and for themselves they are not so important. So Merton from this ground could be comfortable with a number of aspects of his own artistic practice.

Like Blake, he could often be less concerned with the finished product than some formalist artists. The essence was *in here*, not *out there* on the page; this will become evident in the discussions of particular poems later in this essay. Like Blake, Merton could also, paradoxically, be an artist *without* being an artist. There are those memorable last words of Blake recorded by the woman who heard him singing some of his songs on his deathbed and to whom he said: "they are not mine, not mine." So the insight that Merton had into Blake in 1939 would in fact develop and provide the ground for his mature assessment of the nature and purpose of his own creative output. There is a memorable journal entry in

1966 in which Merton explores the narrow line between that which is not art and that which is art. Indeed here "not art," mysteriously becomes the ground of that which is the basis of all art:

> I can't honestly say I know anything except that it is late, that I can't sleep, that there are fireflies all over the place, and that there is not the remotest possibility of making any poetic statement on this. You don't write poems about nothing.
>
> And yet somehow this nothing seems to be *everything*. I look at the south sky, and for some ungodly reason, for which there is no reason, everything is complete. I think of going back to bed in peace without knowing why, a peace that cannot be justified by anything, by any reason, any proof, any argument, any supposition. There are no suppositions left. Only fireflies.[20]

For the purpose of grounding some of these ideas in the texture of Merton's poetry, I would at this point like to return to the subtitle of this study "To look through matter into eternity" which is Merton's phrase for describing Blake's mode of seeing; "eternity" is also one of the most repeated words in Blake's Complete Works.[21] The phrase pinpoints the way Blake helped to evoke in Merton a creativity that looked to the transcendent and that could fly in the face of the canons of constructed, earthbound art. It also focuses attention on an outlook that would ultimately resolve Merton's conflicts between the poet and the contemplative and between the competing religious impulses in his life. While the phrase occurs in an early work, it is my contention that it is seminal in the effect it had on the rest of Merton's life.

This study will conclude with an exposition of how Merton illuminates this phrase and the bearing it has on two poems.

For Merton, as for that other great Catholic poet a century before him, Gerard Manley Hopkins (on whom Merton wanted to write a doctoral dissertation), poetic creativity would, from some points of view, seem at odds with the life of pure contemplation. Merton certainly experienced this tension and it took him a lifetime to come to a place where he could honour the experience of poetic creation as a vital tool in contemplative practice. To quote again from his 1958 essay "Poetry and Contemplation: A Reappraisal," Merton affirmed *"true contemplation is inseparable from life and from the dynamism of life—which includes work, creation, production, fruitfulness, and above all love."*[22] But in the early forties, in the early days of his monastic life, as Michael Higgins records "Merton was determined... to abandon poetry"[23] ... and may well have, had it not been for the work—behind the scenes—of Robert Lax and Mark Van Doren who helped to have his first poems published in 1944.[24]

With the hindsight of Merton's later development it is however possible to see that the groundwork for this understanding of the true relationship between creativity and the spiritual life was already being firmly laid in the 1939 M.A. essay on Blake. For Blake, while he was regarded with suspicion and contempt by the orthodox communities of his day, was profoundly committed to his experience of the spiritualising power of the imagination, both in its direct links to Jesus and in its liberating social power.

For Merton, as for Blake, the imagination was not something that distracted the mind with images of the natural world, taking it away from the heart of contemplation. This was the complaint of Hopkins's superior who felt that nature was a distraction and therefore suggested that Hopkins burn all his poems. Rather, imagination was a profoundly transformative agent. This is how Merton describes Blake's relationship to nature at the conclusion of his M.A. thesis:

> One of the most important ideas in Blake is that nature, simply as the eye sees it, is utterly unimportant to art.... [Blake] found it literally impossible to draw directly from nature. We have seen what confusion and despair he fell into when he tried to do so. Yet once nature had been assimilated and transformed by his imagination, it blazed before him in a vision fired with the glory of God. Nature, for Wordsworth, was God's greatest and most important creation, and so he, too, saw God in nature. But for Blake, nature is only the hem of God's garment.[25]

My contention is, that this passage give an important insight into how Merton ultimately was able to reconcile what he experienced in his life as a destructive tension between creativity and contemplation. This passage also helps to give some explanation of the Blakean texture of Merton's verse which like Blake is often less concerned with perfection of form and verisimilitude, and more concerned with spontaneity and symbolic resonances.

The Poetry: "Elegy for the Monastery Barn" and "Evening"

A poem such as "Elegy for the Monastery Barn," for example, literally and metaphorically transfigures an event in nature into "a vision fired with the glory of God." Its tone is casual, almost conversational, yet filled with a profound symbolism. With his wry humor Merton begins by personifying the burning barn as a woman stricken with vanity:

> As though an aged person were to wear
> Too gay a dress
> And walk about the neighbourhood
> Announcing the hour of her death…
> For: "Look!" she calls to the country,
> "Look how fast I dress myself in fire!"[26]   (lines 1–4, 9–10)

Soon the image shifts to a sense of nostalgia, past and present, at the meaning the barn has provided for all who knew her, the monks who laboured there during the summer & generations of cattle:

> She, in whose airless heart
> We burst our veins to fill her full of hay…
>
> Look! They have all come back to speak their summary:
> Fifty invisible cattle, the past years
> Assume their solemn places one by one.
> This is the little minute of their destiny.
> Here is their meaning found. Here is their end. (lines 15–16,
>   28–32)

But the imagery of the flames rising from the barn here serves Merton's purpose to reach into the deeper significance of this event, a potent reminder of the awesome and terrifying sacramental dimension of creation:

> Sweet Christ, how terribly her beauty burns us now! (line 19)

> Laved in the flame as in a Sacrament
> The brilliant walls are holy
> In their first-last hour of joy.

> Fly from within the barn! Fly from the silence
> Of this creature sanctified by fire!
> Let no man stay inside to look upon the Lord! (lines 33–38)

This terrifying "creature sanctified by fire!" echoes that mixture of awe and dread that accompanies Blake's reaction to the "fearful symmetry" of his Tyger:

> In what distant deeps or skies
> Burnt the fire of thine eyes?
> On what wings dare he aspire?
> What the hand dare seize the fire?

And the transfiguration of the wooden barn into something "brilliant," "holy" and sacramental echoes the poem "That Nature is a Heraclitean Fire." Here Merton's other poetic mentor, Hopkins, also dramatizes the cleansing and sacramental power of conflagration, particularly the power to change the most ordinary "matchwood" into "diamond":

> In a flash, at a trumpet crash,
> I am all at once what Christ is, | since he was what I am, and
> This Jack, joke, poor potsherd, | patch, matchwood, immor-
> tal diamond,
>   Is immortal diamond.[27]

About Merton's "Elegy for the Monastery Barn" Ross Labrie has written:

> .. the poem was not just an exercise in imaginative creation but also a technique by which the mind could be brought to apprehend different levels of reality at once, not unlike Blake's fourfold vision.[28]

While I agree with Labrie here with the purpose and outcome, I would question the word "technique." To me it seems more of an occasion of grace, of openness, which Merton allowed his pen to transcribe in response to this momentous event. Already in the 1939 essay Merton gave several telling examples of how he understands this mode of opening to different levels of reality to be operating in Blake's work; it is a mode that Merton links with that of the Christian mystic Meister Eckhart and with that of the Orient.

Merton writes:

> ... a special kind of artistic vision is necessary: vision to which the eye itself, by itself, is unimportant...

The man of imagination, the artist, because of the "virtue" of his art, sees more than his eyes present to him. He does not rely like Urizen entirely on the evidence of his senses, accepting nothing else at all. Urizen is always blind and in chains, and is trying continually to impose that blindness on the whole world. Los and Enitharmon on the other hand. [Merton here quotes from Blake's Prophetic poem the *Four Zoas*]:

... walk'd forth on the dewy earth
Contracting and expanding their all flexible senses
At will to murmur in the flowers small as the honey bee
At will to stretch across the heavens and step from star to
star (*Four Zoas*, Night the Second, p 34).[29]

Merton comments: "By virtue of artistic vision, they enjoy nature *sub specie aeternitatis* and not merely as it is in itself." He then quotes from these quintessentially Blakean lines from "Auguries of Innocence" which express Blake's experience of what theologians might call "the incognito of revelation":

To see a world in a grain of sand
And a heaven in a wild flower
Hold infinity in the palm of your hand
And eternity in an hour

Merton concludes this section of his essay by arguing that while Blake clearly loves nature, he is far from being a naturalist who might "love nature for its own sake."[30]

Merton's insight into Blake here and his celebration of Blake's freedom from the constraints of reason and materialism centres on the idea of *claritas* arising from his study of Plotinus, Aquinas, Coomaraswamy and Maritain, all of whom he refers to in the 1939 essay.[31] Merton writes: "Now this beauty is not perceived by the intellect alone... the brightness of *claritas* is the *splendor formae*; the glory of form shining through matter."[32]

A key word for Merton in this context is "virtue" ("the artist, because of the 'virtue' of his art, sees more than his eyes present to him").[33] Merton defines this term in great depth, drawing on all the thinkers just mentioned. In essence "virtue" is a quality of seeing, a quality related to the terms "intelligibility" and "*claritas.*" From Aquinas in particular, Merton draws the idea that material nature is not intelligible. Intelligibility is something that is imposed by the creative imagination. Here Blake and Aquinas intertwine in Merton's thinking. Merton writes:

> ...it is the forms poetry imposes upon matter that help to give it significance and keep us from falling into despair, because we would otherwise see nothing but chaos around us. [34]

This is a key statement for understanding why, despite all the contrary counsels, Merton was ultimately so reluctant to give up the work imposed by his creative imagination. Here is the seed for his own later affirmation of the inseparability of creativity and contemplative practice that I quoted at the start of this paper. For Merton the act of writing poetry was again and again an occasion of grace, a unique vehicle for opening his sensibilities to the extraordinary dimension of mundane reality.

There is a beautiful short poem that quietly celebrates precisely this dimension. The poem "Evening"[35] has the contemplative quality of some of Merton's personal journals.[36] In this poem he is attuned to the pregnant silence of the evening, when he hears the sounds of approaching children and enters imaginatively into their fantastical conversation: "They say the sky is made of glass,/ They say the smiling moon's a bride." As he does so, the children's voices merge with their surroundings and blossom-laden apple trees are transfigured into communion dresses. The poem ends with the sound of a "wakeful bird" set like a diamond against a panorama of fading night sky and wind in the poplar tree. It is a wonderful, understated epiphany, in which bird song is heard as a celebration of a moment of grace and in which bird song, implicitly, also becomes the poet's quietly resonating poem:

> Now, in the middle of the limpid evening,
> The moon speaks clearly to the hill.
> The wheatfields make their simple music,
> Praise the quiet sky.
>
> And down the road, the way the stars come home,
> The cries of children
> Play on the empty air, a mile or more,
> And fall on our deserted hearing,
> Clear as water.
>
> They say the sky is made of glass,
> They say the smiling moon's a bride.

They say they love the orchards and apple trees,
The trees, their innocent sisters, dressed in blossoms,
Still wearing, in the blurring dusk,
White dresses from that morning's first communion.

And where blue heaven's fading fire last shines
They name the new come planets
With words that flower
On little voices, light as stems of lilies.

And where blue heaven's fading fire last shines,
Reflected in the poplar's ripple,
One little, wakeful bird
Sings like a shower.

The Poetry: Merton's "Grace's House" and Francis Webb's "Five Days Old."

A poem that helps to draw together many of the ideas developed in this essay is "Grace's House," which as Ross Labrie notes, was written in response to a child's drawing.[37] The last few stanzas reveal Merton's extraordinary appreciation of the mundane, his opening to the mysterious luminous life contained in the drawing. Whether the child's name was actually Grace or not is in some ways irrelevant; this is an experience of the transfiguring power of Grace, while the last line is simultaneously an acknowledgement of how fleeting, even inaccessible is the path to this condition—especially for the adult immersed in the world of experience.[38]

O paradise, O child's world!
Where all the grass lives
And all the animals are aware!
The huge sun, bigger than the house
Stands and streams with life in the east
While in the west a thunder cloud
Moves away forever.
No blade of grass is not blessed
On this archetypal, cosmic hill,
This womb of mysteries.

I must not omit to mention a rabbit
And two birds, bathing in the stream
Which is no road, because
Alas, there is no road to Grace's house!

With a wonderful sense of paradox and the symbolic power in words, Merton transfigures the sense of distance or remoteness of Grace's world from ours (the fact that there is "no road" to this house) into the source of life, the stream harbouring these icons of spring—the rabbit and the two birds.

Merton has taken this child's drawing and poetically made its inner meaning "intelligible," made it glow with significance.

I think it is especially important in the light of what I said earlier, that he here chooses for his subject a child's primitive drawing for the locus of this quiet revelation. I understand the significance of this by comparison with two lines from a poem by our own Australian Francis Webb, Merton's contemporary, who in celebrating the awesome wonder of a five-day old child, represents the incognito of revelation in the lines:

> To blown straw was given
> All the fullness of heaven.

Just as Webb's "blown straw" is a wonderful metonymy for Christ in the manger, so the casual drawing of a child becomes a radiating source of "Grace," beckoning the jaded adult with wonder and gratuitous joy.

Here are a few more lines from Francis Webb's poem "Five Days Old"; they seem pertinent to an understanding of the inner meaning of Merton's "Grace's House":

> The tiny not the immense,
> Will teach our groping eyes…
> So cloud-voice in war and trouble
> Is at last Christ in the stable.
>
> Now wonderingly engrossed
> In your fearless delicacies,
> I am launched upon sacred seas,
>
> Humbly and utterly lost
>
> In the mystery of creation,
> Bells, bells of ocean.[39]

It may be valuable to know that while Merton was beginning his Trappist training, Francis Webb was training to be a Lancaster Bomber air-gunner here in Vancouver.

It is with reference to Merton's poem "Grace's House" that the other key term *"claritas"*—from Merton's Blake essay—comes into focus.[40] This term, like "intelligibility" is, for Merton connected with "Virtue" and is defined by Maritain, drawing on Aquinas and Plotinus, as "the glory of form shining through matter," indeed it is that which produces "intelligibility," revealing the essence of things, evoking God's Glory, enabling the mystical vision of heaven in a wild flower or the world in a grain of sand... or maybe even the Grace in the child's "huge sun."

For Merton, as for Blake "intelligibility," *"claritas,"* "virtue," were especially aspects of the vision of innocence of childhood; but they were also something that the poet, by virtue of his creative openness, could keep in touch with. Merton here, again using a Thomistic reference point, describes virtue, as it inheres in the artist, as "a quality which *perfects* the soul, and enables it to strive towards its ends with a stronger and purer life..."[41]

Lying behind both these ideas is Blake's profound belief in art and poetry as agents in the reconstitution, the awakening of the soul from its sleep of selfhood. In the text surrounding his engraving *The Laocoön*, which was his testament to the nature and function of art, Blake mysteriously wrote:

> Adam is only The Natural Man & not the Soul or Imagination
> The Eternal Body of Man is The IMAGINATION
>   God himself
> That is JESUS we are his Members
>   The Divine Body
> It manifests itself in his Works of Art (In Eternity All is Vision)

The most dramatic allusion to the state of sleep from which Art can have the power to arouse us is heard in the opening chapter of Blake's *Jerusalem*. In this poem Blake affirms his role as a poet whose primary function is to awaken us to our true nature, one that is open to others, informed by humility and not cramped by Selfhood. By virtue of these qualities it is also, by extension a gateway "into Eternity." The passage, which in its entirety, is beyond all theologizing, underscores the deepest motivations for Merton's phrase "to look through matter into eternity" which I took as the subtitle for this paper:

Awake! Awake O sleepers of the land of shadows, wake! expand!
Trembling I sit day and night… I rest not from my great task!
To open the Eternal Worlds, to open **the immortal Eyes**
Of Man inwards into the Worlds of Thought, into Eternity
Ever expanding in the Bosom of God, the Human Imagination.
O Saviour pour upon me thy Spirit of meekness & love!
Annihilate the Selfhood in me: be thou all my life![42]

Notes

1. *Thomas Merton: Poet, Monk, Prophet*, eds., P. Pearson, D.Sullivan and I.Thomson (Abergavenny: Three Peaks Press, 1998), pp. 109-118.

2. Michael Higgins, *Heretic Blood: The Spiritual Geography of Thomas Merton* (Toronto: Stoddart, 1998).

3. Higgins, p. 3.

4. Higgins, p. 3.

5. Ross Labrie, *Thomas Merton and the Inclusive Imagination* (Columbia: University of Missouri Press, 2001) p. 129.

6. Thomas Merton, *New Seeds of Contemplation* (New York: New Directions, 1961) p. 2.

7. *The Complete Poetry and Prose of William Blake*, ed. David V. Erdman (New York: Anchor Books, 1988) 45. See also Blake's *Vision of the Daughters of Albion*, ibid. p. 51 and *America*, ibid. p. 54.

8. Thomas Merton, *New Seeds of Contemplation*, p. 25.

9. Monica Furlong, *Merton: A Biography* (San Francisco: Harper and Row, 1980) p. 49.

10. Furlong, p. 49: quoted from Thomas Merton, *The Seven Storey Mountain* (New York: Harcourt, Brace and Company, 1948) p. 88.

11. Basil M. Pennington, Towards Discerning the Spirit and Aims of the Founders of the Order of Cîteaux in *The Cistercian Spirit: A Symposium in Memory of Thomas Merton* (ed. M. Basil Pennington, CS3, 1970) pp. 1-16; reprinted in Pennington, *The Last of the Fathers: The Cistercian Fathers of the Twelfth Century* (Still River MA; St. Bede's, 1983) pp. 3-14.

12. *The Complete Poetry and Prose of William Blake*, ed. David V. Erdman, p. 26.

13. "Nature and Art in William Blake" *The Literary Essays of Thomas Merton*, ed. Patrick Hart (New York: New Directions, 1985) pp. 422-423. The passage quoted from A.K. Coomaraswamy is from *Transformation of Nature in Art* (Cambridge, Massachusetts: Harvard University Press, 1934) p. 3.

14. Karen Armstrong, *A History of God* (Mandarin: London, 1994) pp. 242-245.

15. Thomas J.J. Altizer, *The New Apocalypse: The Radical Vision of William Blake* (Michigan: The Michigan State University Press, 1967).

16. *Literary Essays of Thomas Merton*, p. 6.

17. Thomas Merton, *Mystics and Zen Masters* (New York: Farrar, Straus and Giroux, 1967) p. 46.

18. *Literary* Essays, p. 339.

19. "Nature and Art in William Blake" *The Literary Essays of Thomas Merton*, ed., Patrick Hart (New York: New Directions, 1985) p. 434.

20. Thomas Merton, *Learning to Love: Exploring Solitude and Freedom*, ed., Christine M. Bochen (San Francisco: HarperSanFrancisco, 1997) p. 316.

21. This can be demonstrated by a search for "Eternity" in the *Digital Text Blake Project* at http://virtual.park.uga.edu/wblake/home1.html.

22. "Poetry and Contemplation: A Reappraisal" *Literary Essays of Thomas Merton*, p. 339.

23. Higgins, p. 34.

24. "... through the combined efforts of Lax and Van Doren [Merton] succeeded... in having his *Thirty Poems* published by New Directions in 1944, an achievement in which he took great, if slightly guilty, pleasure" (Higgins, p. 34).

25. "Nature and Art in William Blake" *Literary Essays*, p. 451.

26. Thomas Merton, *The Collected Poems of Thomas Merton* (New York: New Directions, 1977) p. 288.

27. *The Collected Poems of Gerard Manley Hopkins*, ed. W.H. Gardner (Oxford: OUP, 1970) p. 106.

28. Labrie, p. 155.

29. "Nature and Art in William Blake" *Literary Essays*, pp. 435, 436. Blake's terminology may need some explanation. Urizen is the domineering and limiting God of Reason of this world; Los, his antithesis, is poetry and the creative imagination: an aspect of the human psyche often buried; Enitharmon is spiritual beauty and Los's inspiration.

30. "Nature and Art in William Blake," *Literary* Essays, p. 436.

31. "Nature and Art in William Blake," *Literary Essays*, pp. 441-446.

32. "Nature and Art in William Blake," *Literary Essays*, p. 443.

33. "Nature and Art in William Blake," *Literary Essays*, p. 436.

34. "Nature and Art in William Blake," *Literary Essays*, p. 429.

35. First published in Thomas Merton, *A Man in the Divided Sea* (New York: New Directions, 1946). Republished in *A Thomas Merton Reader, Revised Edition*, ed. Thomas P. McDonnell (New York: Image Books, 1974) pp. 331-332.

36. See for example the following: "In the silence of the afternoon all is present and all is inscrutable in one central tonic note to which every other sound ascends or descends, to which every other meaning aspires in order to find its true fulfilment. To ask when the note will sound is to lose the afternoon: it has already sounded, and all things now hum with the resonance of its sounding", *The Intimate Merton: His Life from His Journals*, eds. Patrick Hart and Jonathan Montaldo (New York: HarperCollins, 1999) p. 248.

37. *The Collected Poems of Thomas Merton*, pp. 330-331.

38. See Merton's letter to Fulbert Sisson, *Road To Joy: The Letters of Thomas Merton to New and Old Friends* (Harvest Books, 1993).

39. *Cap and Bells, The Poetry of Francis Webb*, eds. Michael Griffith and James McGlade (Sydney: HarperCollins, 1991) p. 156.

40. "Nature and Art in William Blake," *Literary Essays*, p 444.

41. "Nature and Art in William Blake," *Literary Essays*, p 432.

42. *Complete Poetry & Prose of William Blake*, pp. 146-147.

Divining the Inscaped-Landscape: Hopkins, Merton and the Ascent to True Self

Jeffrey A. Cooper

Gerard Manley Hopkins was infused into the spiritual bones of Thomas Merton. From the moment when a young Merton declared that his reading was becoming "more Catholic" and the first books he took up were Hopkins' poetry, notebooks, and a borrowed "life of Hopkins,"[1] through his life-long love affair with nature and his keen awareness of how its inscaped landscapes shaped his spiritual landscape,[2] to every time, like a kingfisher, he caught fire, drew flame, and flung out the truth of his name,[3] the Hopkinsian spirit was an on-going force awakening him to his deepest Self. And because Merton was such a prolific writer we can easily find the enduring proof of this influence through the wealth of his written words. Merton literally wrote out the process by which his deepest identity, his interior, sacred landscape, was discovered via the relationship to the many exterior landscapes through which he walked. These exterior formations formed the interior man and became fertile ground for a true grounding in his own being, in *human* being, and in the Ground of All Being. So whether it was Dante's *Divine* Mountain by which he scaled his life, or Mt. Kanchenjunga, which haunted him near his death, influenced by Hopkins, Merton engaged the spiritual ascent through the alienated self to the True Self, exploring his messy but marvelous existence as both divinely human and humanly divine.

It is this ascent through vast and varied landscapes, without and within, and how these encounters between landscapes sparked recognition of the Divine Presence, that is not only the product of Merton's writing but the very fire that led him to put words to the page. So it is in his writing, especially within his May 1968 journal, *Woods, Shore, Desert*, that we can trace a path of spiritual growth that could be adequately described in the classic terms of Purgative, Illuminative, and Unitive, but even more richly described through the terminology of Hopkins' own poetic process of Inscape, Instress, and Selving. This poetic process, tied to these more classical terms, provides a "spiritual hiker's guide" to finding the way home, to the True Self, along the path moving from familiar to unfamiliar, from known to unknown while it also highlights the profound influence the Jesuit poet had on the Cistercian monk. The landscaped journeys of faith always move us out of an all too well-known country, the movement of Illuminative-Inscape, via a different country, a land called Purgative-Instress, to the unknown country of Unitive-Selving. The final movement is discovery of place as ultimately no place at all.

Merton came to know this landscape and, in a way uniquely his own, wrote about it all the way from *The Seven Storey Mountain* to *The Other Side of the Mountain*—a journey from a well-know life story, told, to the completely untellable, unknown and unseen, other side of the mountain. And Hopkins, who tread the path before him and along-side him, was always a beckoning spirit calling Merton to become in God's eye what in God's eye he was through seeing "Christ playing in ten thousand places." It was then in the recovery of these places as "no places" where Merton learned, and still teaches us today, "how to selve, to go ourselves, and our [truest] selves speak and spell."[4]

Hopkins' profound influence on Merton can be found most readily in *The Seven Storey Mountain*. It is in this autobiography, published in 1948, that Merton characterizes his conversion to Catholicism as a conversation between himself and the long-dead poet as he writes:

> I took up the book about Gerard Manley Hopkins. The chapter told of Hopkins at Balliol, at Oxford. He was thinking of becoming a Catholic. He was writing letters to Cardinal Newman (not yet a cardinal) about becoming a Catholic.
>
> All of a sudden, something began to stir within me, something began to push me, to prompt me. It was a movement that spoke like a voice.
>
> "What are you waiting for?" it said. "Why are you sitting here? Why do you still hesitate? You know what you ought to do? Why don't you do it?"...
>
> Hopkins was writing to Newman, at Birmingham, about his indecision.
>
> "What are you waiting for?" said the voice within me again. "Why are you sitting there? It is useless to hesitate any longer. Why don't you get up and go?" ...
>
> Hopkins had written to Newman, and Newman had replied to him, telling him to come and see him at Birmingham.

Suddenly, I could bear it no longer. I put down the book, and got into my raincoat, and started down the stairs. ...And then everything inside me began to sing–to sing with peace, to sing with strength and to sing with conviction.[5]

Time, and much more writing, would prove that Merton never changed this decidedly Hopkinsian tune. What started as a shared experience of faith conversion, across the years, over the boundary of life and death, developed into a shared vision of the natural world which was pivotal for the spiritual maturation of both men. It was a shared vision that allowed their spiritual landscapes to be awakened by the sacred landscapes that surrounded them. This is a spiritual vision best described as a poetic process, which Hopkins developed from experience and Merton lived.

Hopkins' unique terminology of Inscape, Instress, and Selving, like Purgation, Illumination, and Union, are almost interchangeable sets of concepts for describing the same dynamic process. The first two classical terms interpenetrate to the point that it becomes difficult to tell whether the fire of purgation is the illumination or is the moment of illumination which sets the fires of purgation alight? The same could be said of the relationship between the poetic terms Inscape and Instress. Hopkins highlights their interpenetrating relationship when he writes in his 1881 Notebook:

[The] energy of being by which all things are upheld [is] the natural instress which defines an inscape and keeps it in being–it is also the sensation of inscape–a quasi-mystical illumination, a sudden perception of the deeper pattern, order and unity which gives meaning to external forms.[6]

The Inscape itself is defined by the poet when he writes: "All things therefore are charged with love, are charged with God and if we know how to touch them, they give off sparks and take fire, yield drops and flow, ring and tell of him."[7]

It is this "touching," this illuminative Instress that reveals Inscape in landscapes "charged with love, charged with God," that then set off sparks which grow to a purgative fire. Instress, then, is the act of touching Inscape and illuminating it as it also maintains intensity. The moment of touching Inscape can be likened to a flash fire that casts a sudden and brilliant light on the relationship between the divine alive in nature and the divine alive in human nature. Instress is then the energy that both maintains and reveals the Inscape. It is the energy that illuminates the relationship between internal and external landscapes as it sets the purgative fire that unites them. This then leads to the Unitive stage which resonates with Hopkins' term Selving, which he simply defined as the act by which "the essential self is displayed."[8]

Merton himself gave voice to this dynamic process and the union which results, while reflecting on nature in *New Seeds of Contemplation*. In the chapter entitled, "Things in Their Identity," he comments that for animals, "Their inscape is their sanctity. It is the imprint of [God's] wisdom and of [God's] reality in them."[9] And he fleshes this out further in one of his journal entries written on Holy Saturday, April 5, 1958, just after a wren had landed on his shoulder:

> I want not only to observe but to *know* living things, and this implies a dimension of primordial familiarity which is simple and primitive and religious and poor.
> This is the reality I need, the vestige of God in His creatures.
> And the Light of God in my own soul.[10]

It is this relationship between the "vestige of God" in nature and "the Light of God" in the soul of the attentive viewer that sets off the spark of a true knowing that catches fire and burns. Purgative-Instress ignites and maintains the Illuminated-Inscape preparing the ground for the deeper union of Selving.

This then is the journey on which Merton, guided by Hopkins, embarked. And the trail map of his written words can lead spiritual seekers today along that same path through Illuminated-Inscapes, by Purgative-Instress to the Unitive-Selving and toward the recognition of True Self, which is also union with God. This is the spiritual ascent that leads to the "other side of the mountain." And since, in the spiritual topography of Thomas Merton, the mountain seems to be central, it will more than serve for a guiding image through this exploration of his own sacred landscapes.

In the *Woods, Shore, Desert* journal, Merton relates his reactions to a book given him entitled, *Mount Analogue* by René Daumal.[11] And in a wonderfully telling passage that he quotes from this text, he succinctly captures the heart of the journey described in the book, as well as, the heart of his own spiritual journey. While marveling at the canyons of New Mexico, Merton writes:

> From *Mount Analogue*: "How it is proved that a hirtherto unknown continent really existed with mountains much higher

than the Himalayas... how it happened that no one detected it before... how we reached it, what creatures we met there–how another expedition pursuing quite different goals barely missed destruction."[12]

And he follows this with a brief commentary:

The curvature of space around Mount Analogue makes it possible for people to live as though Mount Analogue did not exist. Hence, everyone comes from an unknown country and almost everyone from a too well known country.[13]

Often the curvature of the landscapes of our lives can lead us to live as if the spiritual mountain we ascend does not exist. It is often the too well-known country, the landscape of illusion, that we mistake for our deepest reality. But the spiritual quest always moves us from the too well-known country to the unknown country. And such a journey is sparked by attentiveness to the inscaped-landscapes of our lives. It is this attentiveness to the different countries we encounter, which awakens us to entire continents that we never knew existed even though our feet have always stood firmly upon them. Merton especially witnessed to this life of the examined-ascent, when he left the too well-known country of Kentucky and headed west.

It is on the first leg of his western journey, in the opening pages of *Woods, Shore, Desert*, that Merton, flying high above the vast landscape, catches fire somewhat like a kingfisher, and sets the tone for the spiritual awakening ahead, as he writes:

Snow-covered mountains. Thirty-nine thousand feet over Idaho. Frozen lakes. Not a house, not a road. Gulfs. No announcement. Hidden again. We are all secrets. But now, where there are suggested gaps, one can divine rocks and snow. "Be a mountain diviner!" Whorled dark profile of a river in snow. A cliff in the fog. And now a dark road straight through a long fresh snow field. Snaggy reaches of snow pattern. Claws of mountain and valley. Light shadow or breaking cloud on snow. Swing and reach of long, gaunt, black, white forks. The new consciousness. Reading the calligraphy of snow and rock from the air. A sign of snow on a mountainside as if my own ancestors were hailing me. We bump. We burst into secrets.[14]

Here we are given an ecstatic sounding poetic description of the landscape Merton encounters from the airplane window. He sees the play of rock and snow, white and black, shadow and light, darkness and illumination—all obvious opposites being held in tension, pushing toward some resolution. Merton immediately seems to draw flame as he touches the inscaped Idaho topography and divines a landscape charged with love, charged with God.

As is usually the case, such a spiritual journey begins with an absence of clear direction, until "no way" gives way to "a dark road straight through a long fresh snow field." It is the dark path of faith that is at one and the same time the blinding light of God. The spiritual air begins to thin with the recognition of secrets, things hidden, a call from within, contradictions held in tension, something familiar amid an unfamiliar landscape, "as if my own ancestors were hailing me." Then occurs the inevitable bump and the burst into illumination and the revelation of the ever deeper secrets of self in God.

W.H. Gardner, in describing Hopkins' poetic process, offers an apt explanation for the experience of Merton, that resulted in such a poetic outburst at "thirty-nine thousand feet over Idaho," when he writes: "poetic creation occurred when the poet's own nature (his own inscape) had been instressed by some complementary inscape discovered in external nature. ...all the world is full of inscape and chance left free to act falls into an order as well as a purpose."[15]

The inscaped-landscape, when attended to, provokes the illumination of Self-secrets, moves one out of a false light to the darkness that is God's light, from absence of direction to the revelation of a straight, dark, road cast upon a bright field. And like this dark road, the spiritual ascent begins to become visible, opening a way to union through the tensions of the seemingly impossible contradictions within and around us.

Merton's own inscape, then, is instressed by the complementary inscaped-landscape he sees and a secret is revealed as the inscape is "left free to act." And as "dragonflies draw flame / As tumbled over rim in roundy wells / Stones ring; like each tucked string tells, each / Hung bell's/Bow swung finds tongue to fling out broad its / Name..."[16] the vastly varied landscapes, the jumble of dark and light without become a metaphor to a revealed state within. The Illuminated-Inscape is triggered by, as it also triggers, the on-going Purgative-Instress.

Perhaps a helpful guide to understanding this more purgative leg of the ascent is one that Merton himself turned to during his western journey. It is a Hindu text entitled *Astavakra Gita*. The connections he makes, via this text, open the door for the reader into the deeper, interior process underway in the writer. Merton quotes the "Gita," which says: "When the mind is stirred and perceives things before it as objects of thought, it will find in itself something lacking."[17] Any illumination of secrets, on the spiritual quest, leads to a revelation of an ever deeper sense of lack, of internal alienation. We often discover our inner divisiveness, contradictions, dichotomies and utter lack, in the face of landscapes which mirror back to us our own poverty. Just as the landscape revealed high over Idaho touched Merton's own inscape, so too does another landscape awaken him to his own deeper poverty. Again in-flight, now with the Redwoods of California coming into view, Merton writes: "you can see where the hillsides have been slashed into, ravaged, sacked, stripped, eroded with no hope of re-growth of these marvelous trees."[18]

With this touching of the inscape the instressed illuminative spark feeds the purgative fires whose light and heat can be excruciating and Merton voices this as well. The "ravaged, sacked, stripped, eroded" landscape seems to reveal to him his own poverty and homelessness. He allows the instressed-inscape the freedom to act on him and by it he catches a glimpse of a personal reality which is universally true for all humankind: "I am the utter poverty of God. I am His emptiness, littleness, nothingness, lostness. When this is understood, my life in His freedom, the self-emptying of God in me is the fullness of grace."[19]

In this context then Merton again quotes the "Gita" which says: "The wise man [knows] the truth of the self."[20] And he also includes here the *Bhagavad-Gita*, in which it is written: "He [God] knows me, knows what in truth I am and who I am. Then having known me in truth, He enters into me."[21] This seems to hearken back to Merton's desire to "not only to observe but to *know* living things, [which] implies a dimension of primordial familiarity which is simple and primitive and religious and poor."[22] This represents knowledge achieved by first being known by the God who enters in and reveals the utter poverty at the heart of the human being. To enter this frightening and unfamiliar landscape is to know the truth of Self and no longer solely to observe life but to become Life itself. This is the place along the spiritual climb where the familiar becomes radically unfamiliar—what you thought you found becomes lost as the self-emptying of God within transforms into the fullness of grace. If the spiritual trekker can withstand the utter terror that this revelation incites, then he or she discovers home in homelessness and is freed from the too well-known country that fails to satisfy. The climbers awaken to find their feet firmly planted on "a hitherto unknown continent" that has always existed with "mountains higher than the Himalayas." As Merton himself would write later in the same journal: "The country which is nowhere is the real home."[23]

So the revelation of utter poverty is also the revelation of unutterable riches. Merton's Purgative-Instressed moment of truth is the realization of how our emptiness partakes in the self-emptying of God, in Christ, which then opens in us the space for the fullness of grace: God's promised union in the midst of impoverished human contradiction. Once the inscaped-landscape is left free to act of its own upon us, and we stand fast and endure the burning and illuminating fire of instress, we come to know the truth of Self as God enters in. Or, maybe better said, God's already existent presence within us is more fully actualized at the deepest center of our being.

This actualization of God's presence in us, this entering of God within us, is what I term here, Unitive-Selving. Hopkins himself captures this moment in the poem "As kingfishers catch fire" when he writes: "Each mortal thing does one thing and the same / Deals out that being indoors each one dwells / Selves–goes itself; myself it speaks and spells..."[24] Again for Merton the physical landscape of his travels in the Western U. S. provides a powerful and provocative manifestation of this divine union come to light. After his return to Gethsemani, Merton received the photos he took of his trip, and in a brilliant moment of revelation, he makes a profound connection between the exterior landscapes captured in a photo and his own interior human geography as he writes:

> John Griffin sent one of my pictures of Needle Rock, which he developed and enlarged. I also have the contact. The Afga film brought out the great *Yang-Yin* of sea rock mist, diffused light and half hidden mountain–an interior landscape, yet there. In other words, what is written within me is there, "Thou art that."[25]

Now we come full circle from those first impressions of the play of dark and light, snow and rock, absence and presence, poverty and riches, through the great "*Yang-Yin* of sea rock mist, diffused light and half-hidden mountain," all drawn into a unity revealing the consummation of humanity with divinity. After reading the "calligraphy of snow and rock" Merton comes into his own as a "mountain diviner," and amid *The Seven Storey Mountain*, Mount Analogue, and Mt. Kanchenjunga, he comes around to the other side of the mountain, the "half-hidden mountain" as his truest Self rises like a secret out of the clouds and is revealed: "Thou art that." Merton initially intuited how that Idaho mountain, viewed from the air, seemed to recognize him although his "own ancestors were hailing me." And now in this "half-hidden mountain" the secret is fully revealed as the hidden mountain within is made known.

Toward the end of *Woods, Shore, Desert*, Merton expresses what this climb through Purgative-Instress, Illuminated-Inscapes and Unitive-Selving has meant for him as he realizes:

> But I do have a past to break with, an accumulation of inertia, waste, wrong, foolishness, rot, junk, and a great need of clarification of mindfulness, or rather of no mind–a return to genuine practice, right effort, need to push on to the great doubt. Need for the Spirit. Hang on to the clear light![26]

As with any advance made along the spiritual ascent, the seeker realizes ever more deeply the on-going transformation to which he or she must surrender. Merton makes clear in this passage that the on-going transformation now takes place in a different light and one must continue the journey hanging on to this "clear light." I think we can get a richer sense of what Merton is expressing here by attending to this light.

In the 1982 edition of this journal, there is an especially intriguing and informative footnote concerning "the clear light" that Merton had found and so desired to hang on to. It is a quotation from Mircea Eliade who wrote:

> Death is a process of cosmic reabsorption, not in the sense that the flesh returns to the earth, but in the sense that the cosmic elements progressively dissolve into one another... When the process of cosmic reabsorption is complete, the dying man perceives a light like that of the Moon, then like that of the Sun, then sinks deep into the darkness. He is suddenly awakened by a dazzling light: this is his meeting with his real Self, which, according to the doctrine of all India, is at the same time the ultimate reality, Being.[27]

When anyone begins the spiritual ascent in earnest there is one piece of advice which needs to be followed and that is to "hang on to the clear light." This does not mean clinging to illuminations we might receive but instead allowing the light to move from moonlight to sunlight unto no light, purgation leading to death, with a trust that resurrects one into the dazzling light. It is this final light that is "the meeting with [our] real self" which is at the same time our meeting with Ultimate Reality. As Merton himself would put it:

> The secret of my identity is hidden in the love and mercy of God. But whatever is in God is really identical with Him, for His infinite simplicity admits no division and no distinction. Therefore I cannot hope to find myself anywhere except in Him.
>
> Ultimately the only way that I can be myself is to become identified with Him in Whom is hidden the reason and fulfillment of my existence.[28]

Merton demonstrates for us how this "secret" is revealed through attention to the relationship between our own particular inscape and the inscaped-landscapes of our world. Such a relationship, if left free to act, can then instress us into an ever deepening meeting with our True Self which is also the meeting with the Divine.

Both Gerard Manley Hopkins and Thomas Merton knew that this "dazzling light" of Selving was not the revelation of an outer glitter alone but that of an inaccessible inner glow. Merton himself once expressed intrigue about a Sufi notion he read about in the writings of Louis Massignon, "le point vierge" which is "the center of our nothingness where, in apparent despair, one meets God–and is found completely in His mercy."[29] He then goes on to write further on this same point stating:

> Again, that expression, *le point vierge*…. At the center of our being is a point of nothingness which is untouched by sin and by illusion, a point of pure truth, a point or spark which belongs entirely to God, which is never at our disposal, from which God disposes of our lives, which is inaccessible to the fantasies of our own mind or the brutalities of our own will. This little point of nothingness and of absolute poverty is the pure glory of God is us. It is so to speak His name written in us, as our poverty, as our indigence, as our dependence, as our sonship. It is like a pure diamond, blazing with the invisible light of heaven. It is in everybody, and if we could see it we

would see these billions of points of light coming together in the face and blaze of a sun that would make all the darkness and cruelty of life vanish completely.... I have no program for this seeing. It is only given. But the gate of heaven is every-where.[30]

All human beings are inscaped by God, "his name is written in us" as pure diamond, just as Merton found written in himself an interior reality instressed by an exterior landscape that gave way to the light expressed in "Thou art that." To suffer, as it were, the instresses of life is to be led up the spiritual ascent to that nothing-ness which first appears as utter loss, "our poverty, our indigence," and then reveals itself as "the face and blaze of a sun" that is the fullness of God's grace.

When any diviner of the spiritual mountain encounters their own absolute poverty it is a glimpse of this point of nothingness that is also the "pure glory of God." Merton knew that journey and he touched that point, as did Gerard Manley Hopkins who expressed it in the poem, "That Nature is a Heraclitean Fire and of the Comfort of the Resurrection":

> Flesh fade, and mortal trash
> Fall to the residuary worm; world's wildfire, leave but ash;
> In a flash, at a trumpet clash,
> I am all at once what Christ is, since he was what I am,
> And this Jack, joke, poor potsherd, patch matchwood,
> immortal diamond
> Is immortal diamond.[31]

The journey form "mortal trash" to "immortal diamond" is the heart of the climb up the spiritual mountain. It is an ascent al-ready begun simply by the desire of the spiritual seeker for True Self and Divine Union. And, in conclusion, it is important to re-member Thomas Merton's own words, that no matter how far we advance on this journey, "the climb has only begun."[32]

Appendix

> As kingfishers catch fire, dragonflies draw flame;
> As tumbled over rim in roundy wells
> Stones ring; like each tucked string tells, each hung bell's
> Bow swung finds tongue to fling out broad its name;

Each mortal thing does one thing and the same:
Deals out that being indoors each one dwells;
Selves– goes itself; *myself* it speaks and spells,
Crying *What I do is me: for that I came.*

I say more: the just man justices;
Keeps grace: that keeps all his goings graces;

Acts in God's eye what in God's eye he is–

Christ– for Christ plays in ten thousand places,
Lovely in limbs, and lovely in eyes not his
To the Father through the features of men's faces.

–Gerard Manley Hopkins

Notes

1. Thomas Merton, *The Seven Storey Mountain* (New York: Harcourt Brace & Company, 1948), pp. 211, 215.

2. Thomas Merton, *New Seeds of Contemplation* (New York: New Directions Publishing, 1962), p. 30. In the chapter titled "Things in Their Identity," Merton employs Hopkins' term "inscape" while describing how the things of nature share in the Divine identity.

3. W.H. Gardner (ed.), *Gerard Manley Hopkins: Poems and Prose* (New York: Penguin Books, 1953), p. 51. See end of this article for the complete text of the sonnet, "As kingfishers catch fire."

4. *Gerard Manley Hopkins: Poems and Prose*, p. 51.

5. Merton, *Seven Storey Mountain*, p. 215-216.

6. Gardner, *Gerard Manley Hopkins: Poems and Prose*, p. xxi.

7. Richard Ellman and Robert O'Clair (eds.), *The Norton Anthology of Modern Poetry* (New York: W. W. Norton & Company, Inc., 1973), p.68.

8. Ellman and O'Clair, *The Norton Anthology of Modern Poetry*, p. 68.

9. Merton, *New Seeds of Contemplation*, p. 30.

10. Thomas Merton, *A Search for Solitude* (Journals 3; ed. Lawrence S. Cunningham; San Francisco: Harper San Francisco, 1995), p. 190.

11. René Daumal, *Mount Analogue* (San Francisco: City Light Books, 1968).

12. Thomas Merton, *The Other Side of the Mountain*, ed., Patrick Hart (Journals 7; New York: HarperCollins Publishers, 1996), p. 107.

13. Merton, *The Other Side of the Mountain*, p. 107.

14. Merton, *The Other Side of the Mountain*, p. 94.

15. Gardner, *Gerard Manley Hopkins: Poems and Prose*, p. xxiv.

16. Gardner, *Gerard Manley Hopkins: Poems and Prose*, p. 51.

17. Merton, *The Other Side of the Mountain*, p. 104.

18. Merton, *The Other Side of the Mountain*, p. 96.

19. Merton, *The Other Side of the Mountain*, p. 102.

20. Merton, *The Other Side of the Mountain*, p. 91.

21. Merton, *The Other Side of the Mountain*, p. 103.

22. Merton, *A Search for Solitude*, p. 190.

23. Merton, *The Other Side of the Mountain*, p. 110.

24. Gardner, *Gerard Manley Hopkins: Poems and Prose*, p. 51.

25. Merton, *The Other Side of the Mountain*, p. 110.

26. Merton, *The Other Side of the Mountain*, p. 113.

27. Thomas Merton, *Woods, Shore, Desert: A Notebook 1968*, ed., Joel Wieshaus (Santa Fe: Museum of New Mexico Press, 1982), p. 58; from Mircea Eliade, "Light and the Bardo," *The Two and The One* (New York: Harper and Row, 1965), pp. 37-38.

28. Merton, *New Seeds of Contemplation*, pp. 35-36.

29. Thomas Merton, *Conjectures of a Guilty Bystander* (Garden City, NY: Doubleday Publishers, 1966), p. 136.

30. Merton, *Conjectures of a Guilty Bystander*, p. 142.

31. Gardner, *Gerard Manley Hopkins: Poems and Prose*, p. 66.

32. Merton, *The Other Side of the Mountain*, p. 107.

Encounter in a Secret Country:
Thomas Merton and Jorge Carrera Andrade

Malgorzata Poks

The purpose of my essay is to explore a kind of resonance between Thomas Merton's and Jorge Carrera Andrade's poetic visions. Since the bulk of my analysis is going to be based on Merton's English renditions of the Ecuadorian's poetry, I wish to start with a brief comment on Merton as a translator. It seems that the success of the monk's translating efforts lies in the fact that he did not merely read literature, but *meditated* on it until the deep truths contained in it became part of him, *connatural* with him—a term Merton the follower of Jacques Maritain applied to the experience of knowledge by identification, in art as much as in religion. Referring to the traditional definition of meditation as *inquisitio veritatis*, or the search for truth, Merton would repeatedly stress that it is not solely the function of intelligence, since meditation originates in love and leads to an affective identification with and a unitive knowing of ultimate reality. Contemplative meditation differs from its philosophical variety in engaging the whole person and all the faculties, speculative as well as affective. In *Spiritual Direction and Meditation* (1960) Merton specifies that meditation is a personal and intimate form of prayer, and as such it should integrate the mystery of one's own life with the mysteries of the Christian faith. In other words, in meditation we should try to see our life in the light of God's providential will for us and for humanity.[1] Merton's plea for spiritual realism in meditation makes it not only salutary but downright mandatory to see the mystery of Christ's Passion and Resurrection, which forms the very core of Christianity, reenacted in the sufferings and trials of individual human beings and whole communities. It is a contemplative's duty to confront the human condition in its entirety, even in its political actualization, for only a grasp of the inner sense of events and political pressures can provide a key to the liberation of the human being made in the image of God.[2]

Merton firmly believed that the contemplative experience should lead to dialogue and that the fruits of contemplation are to be shared. His meditations on the literary works of others, there-fore, resulted in the subsequent publication of numerous essays and highly praised translations, which, while remaining faithful to the original, reflect Merton's own lived and authentic experi-ence as much as they do that of the authors. Merton's working definition of translation as "a new creation emerging from com-munion in the same silence"[3] enables us to approach his English renditions of poetry in general, and of Carrera Andrade in par-ticular, as endowed with a life of their own, thanks to the translator's success in capturing what he calls a poem's "nativity or *natura*."[4] It bears stressing that, according to this definition, a translation, no matter how faithful to the original, will always be "a new creation" in so far as the translator, a unique individual with a unique perspective, first has to enter into another person's experience so deeply as to make it his own ("connatural" with him), and then, reemerging from this "communion in silence," has to transliterate this experience in his own idiom. Far from detract-ing from faithfulness to the original poem, the newness Merton speaks of is a necessary condition if a translation is to be alive.[5]

While a significant number of Merton's translations were first included in his 1963 volume of poetry *Emblems of a Season in Fury*, the posthumously published *Collected Poems of Thomas Merton* (1977) contains all his translating efforts, and these range over an impressive spectrum of languages and cultures: from the Latin and Greek of the Church Fathers (St. Ambrose, Paulus Diaconicus, Sedulius, Clement of Alexandria),[6] through the Chinese of Chuang Tzu and Meng Tzu and the Persian of the anonymous poem "Tomb Cover of Imam Riza,"[7] to the contemporary French poetry of René Char and Raïssa Maritain. The core of the section, however, con-sists of translations from the Spanish and Portuguese of the works of such poets as the Spaniards Rafael Alberti and Miguel Hernandez; the Nicaraguans Ernesto Cardenal, Pablo Antonio Cuadra and Alfonso Cortés; the Ecuadorian Jorge Carrera Andrade; the Chilean antipoet Nicanor Parra; the Peru-born cosmopolitan avant-gardist César Vallejo; Fernando Pessoa, once hailed as a Portuguese Whitman; and the Brazilian modernist Carlos Drummond de Andrade. However impressive the entire list of contents, that Merton gives a privileged place to the Ibero-Ameri-can continent in the arena of contemporary poetry is indisputable, especially in view of the fact that the list is incomplete, as Merton's premature death put an end to his larger-scale project of prepar-ing a personal Latin American anthology.[8]

The leading Cuban novelist Alejo Carpentier once defined Ibero America as the least Cartesian continent imaginable,[9] a view evidently shared by Thomas Merton, who praised the poets of the Southern continent for their natural openness to sapiential awareness. In contrast to a vast majority of their North American counterparts, they seemed "to be alive, to have something honest to say, to be sincerely concerned with life and with humanity."[10] In a letter to a literary scholar, the Gethsemani poet claimed: "There is some genuine hope left in them, or when they are bitter the bitterness has a maturity and content which make it respectable, and in any case I tend to share it in some ways."[11] To what extent he shared it becomes evident when we scrutinize the translations Merton originally included in *Emblems*, as if suggesting, by juxtaposing them with his own poetry, that his voice and the voices of the poets from the Southern continent echo one another; that they are participants in a conversation carried over ages and across distances in a kind of ceaseless musical harmony. Merton once said that "heart speaks to heart in the language of music" and "true friendship is a kind of singsong."[12] *Emblems of a Season of Fury*, consisting of original and translated poetry, gives the impression of having been intended by Merton as witness to such a heartfelt resonance between his entire being and "the entire being of the other," as he puts it in *Conjectures of a Guilty Bystander* (1966). "Resonances," his baffling 1963 volume seems to be saying: "here is a good choir."[13] And indeed, the parallelism between Merton's and the translated poets' themes and concerns, at the deepest heart of which is the spiritual destiny of man,[14] is exceptional. So, too, is the convergence of their poetic means and techniques. Thomas Merton's poetic idiom, which he characterized as "much more that of Latin America than that of the United States,"[15] was an asset in transcending the limitations of the Western mindset, dominated by discursive logic and Cartesian dualism, towards a reconciliation with another, though equally "American," order of perception: the Pilgrim Fathers' descriptions of the New World were as full of magical reality as Columbus's letters to the Catholic Monarchs.

A navigation of the country where the heart of Latin America was to speak directly to Merton's heart, and speak in the same key, might just as well start with the analysis of Merton's renditions of Carrera Andrade's poems in the hope that they will yield a rough map of this promised land of the poets, which, like in a

Zen koan, is everywhere and nowhere because it is within ourselves. It is in this nowhere land that the authorship of poetry seems
to lose importance; poetry is self-less and universal again, an asset
belonging to everyone and no one, as it used to be in premodern
times. Here poets once more become who they have always been:
listeners for harmonies hovering eternally in the air, their chan-
nels and transcribers.

Jorge Carrera Andrade (1902-1978) was born in Quito, the capital of Ecuador. He worked as a journalist at the age of fifteen, and
published the first book of poems at twenty-three. Then, in 1928,
he left his native country to study and travel in Europe. Throughout his life he was to shuttle between Europe, Asia, and the Americas in his capacity of diplomat and poet. The traveler's experience
of solitude and rootlessness helped him, paradoxically, to achieve
the planetary and cosmic awareness of communion with all being, as suggested by the title of his 1963 book of verse, *Hombre
planetario*. His books of poetry came out in such diverse latitudes
as, for example, Barcelona (*Boletines de mar y tierra*, 1930), Madrid
(*El tiempo manual*, 1935), Paris (*Biografía para uso de los pájaros*, 1937),
and Tokyo (*País secreto*, 1940). The titles of his later works sum up
the poet's growing concern with indigenous peoples (*Crónica de
las indias*, 1966) and the deepening consciousness of his own exile
(*El libro del destierro*, 1970). Carrera Andrade first came to the United
States in 1940 as Ecuadorian Consul General in San Francisco.
While serving his country on the political front, he disseminated
knowledge about the culture and literature of the entire Southern
continent through poetry, essays, and extensive correspondence.
In 1943 the Chicago *Poetry* magazine published his informative
article "The New American and His Point of View toward Poetry."
Three years later Macmillan brought out his *Secret Country*. In Muna
Lee's translation, it became the Ecuadorian's first major book in
English. Various other translations started to appear in anthologies, books, and magazines. In a recently published essay, Steven
Ford Brown finds most of them faulty or unaccomplished, with
one exception, however. He praises Thomas Merton for having
"managed to capture the flavor and delicacy of Carrera Andrade's
poems in a small collection of translations he included in *Emblems
of a Season of Fury* (1963)."[16]

Carrera Andrade's tourist and diplomatic experience in Europe, Asia, and the Americas left the Ecuadorian poet skeptical
about politics and the existent power structures. At the end of the

day he confessed his desire to embark "for the secret country, the country that is everywhere, the country that has no map because it is within ourselves."[17] In his inner journey there is something characteristic of the monastic spirituality of exile that Merton was to expound later in his writings on Albert Camus,[18] something that sets the pattern for Merton's other "monks" (in the sense of prophetic witnesses to truth and critics of existing power structures): they all have to travel light, in darkness and solitude, along a risky road often on the brink of infinite despair, with the determination to bring back to the world in crisis the seeds of hope out of which to grow "fruits able to calm the resentments and the rage of man." This was how Merton understood the role and responsibility of the poet, an understanding articulated in his "Message" for a congress of Latin American poetry, this "spontaneous explosion of hopes" and "a venture in prophetic poverty."[19]

Thomas Merton began to discover the poetry of Jorge Carrera Andrade in the late nineteen-fifties. Having obtained his address from the sculptor Jaime Andrade, he initiated correspondence with the "charming"[20] Ecuadorian poet. The admiration turned out to be mutual, and Andrade would soon call Merton "the world's conscience" and a "master of poets."[21]

Jorge Carrera Andrade inspired Merton with the idea of the secret country, even though, without knowing it, the author of *Emblems* had always been its citizen. For the Gethsemani monk this figurative place where "I have met Carrera Andrade, and [where] we have become good friends"[22] appeared to be, quite naturally, a distillation of all that was best about Ecuador—that "humble and delightful country."[23] Merton exalted Ecuador for being peripheral to the concerns of the industrialized world, and consequently unspoiled by aggressive greed and the will to power, and he saw the genius of this Central American republic fully incarnated in the poetry of Carrera Andrade. Little wonder that the author of *Hagia Sophia* would draw these irresistible comparisons:

The voice of Ecuador (which sings in his verse) is a soft, humble voice: a voice, oppressed but without rancor, without unhappiness, like the voice of a child who does not get much to eat but lives in the sun. Ecuador is a hungry wise child, an ancient child, like the child in the Biblical proverbs who was always playing before the face of the Creator. An eternal child, a secret Christ, who knows how to smile at the folly of the great and to have no hope in any of the strong countries in the world.[24]

In 1961 Merton translated six of the Ecuadorian's poems for *Directions 17*. While only five of them appeared in *Emblems*, all six can be found in *The Collected Poems of Thomas Merton* (1977). It is this posthumous volume of verse that I will use as the basis of my analysis.[25] The translated pieces present diverse facets of Carrera Andrade's poetry, but all of them—from the worshipful "A Man from Ecuador Beneath the Eiffel Tower" and "Cocoa Tree," through the messianic "Notes of a Parachute Jumper," the humorous "Radicals," and the metaphysical "The Mirror's Mission," to the light-hearted conceit of "The Weathercock on the Cathedral of Quito"— testify to the "humanity, tenderness, and wit in the sense of *esprit*"[26] that Merton discovered in their author.

The first poem, "A Man from Ecuador beneath the Eiffel Tower," alludes to Carrera Andrade's experience of homelessness and travel. Since he was robbed in Panama and penniless upon his arrival in Europe, the only burden he carried was "his light burden of poetry and of Indian blood," as Merton puts it.[27] With this imponderable, even if at times burdensome, load the Latin American traveler stood before the technological wonder of the world, the Eiffel Tower, which seemed to sum up to him the daring spirit of the industrial age. Overwhelmed by its size and its new aesthetics, the man from Ecuador bursts into a spontaneous song of praise:

> You turn into a plant on the coasts of time
> With your goblet of round sky,
> Your opening for the tunnels of traffic.
> You are the biggest ceiba tree on earth. [28]

At once humbled and exultant, the poem's speaker tames the Tower's strangeness by describing it in terms of the only reality he knows—that of his Latin American homeland. The familiar irrupts in the strange when the proud steel construction is exulted as "the biggest ceiba tree on earth" or seen stretching its neck like "a llama of Peru" (8). By domesticating the unfamiliar, this perception technique allows the expatriate to shake off the sense of alienation and feel at home in the harsh European reality. It also bears witness to the poet's childlike innocence and his capacity for wonder. In this sense Carrera Andrade is a truer devotee of the much celebrated American religion of wonder than many of his North American counterparts. Born and bred in a culture where every aspect of daily life was permeated by the marvelous, where

magic and reality blended seamlessly into a paradigmatic epistemology of the mestizo world "to convey a mode of existence that
is real enough, but strange to the rest of the world,"[29] he effort-
lessly picks up analogies between the seemingly incongruous, giving the tradition of the conceit a new lease of life. "A Man from
Ecuador" is a prime example of the poet's metaphoricity.[30] Rather
than describing, Carrera Andrade would frequently call an image
into existence by referring to other, mediating images, with which
the original would merge in interactive tension to yield a renewed
vision of reality. In the poem in question the result is, firstly, the
instantaneous annulment of distance between Latin America and
Europe. Secondly, the vegetative, animal, and technological realms
imperceptibly fuse into an organic view of reality, while the Eiffel
Tower, acquiring the status of the *axis mundi*, stands as a visible
symbol of the eternal marriage of heaven and earth.

The metaphor of the ceiba tree hints at the transcendental significance inscribed into the proud wrought-iron construction. The
massive tropical tree, with its buttress-like ridges along the trunk,
suggests associations with church architecture. A cathedral of the
natural world, popularly referred to as God tree, it overlaps with
the man-made "plant on the coasts of time" (1), vesting it with the
same character of religious awe. But the Eiffel Tower is a temple of
the new industrial age and of its optimistic spirit. As an "iron to
brand the flock of clouds" (23), it anticipates man's imminent
mastery over the world of nature, even as it continues its mediating function: the "first letter of a cosmic alphabet" (19), it spells
"an adventure above time" (13), its mast "pointing in the direction of heaven" (20). In the middle of the highly civilized world
stands the unrecognizable tree of life, its identity half-intuited only
by the pure of heart.

In the poem's catalogue of images and descriptive terms, many
are suggestive of the Tower's regal character. "Robed in folds of
winds" (9), with "a comb of constellations in your hair" (10), the
cosmic queen's towering presence commands the unruly elements,
confronting single-handedly "the circus of horizons" (12). Though
the poem seems to converge with futurist concerns, its
eschatological overtones, vesting the "sentinel of the industrial age"
(24) with implicit characteristics of the messianic monarch, suggest another, more theological reading. It is possible to see the com-
manding Eiffel Tower in terms of a global suzerain, a feminine-
gendered cosmic Atlas,[31] who rules over the world without sub-

duing it; who protects, sustains hope, reawakens people to the sense of their transcendent destiny. The poem's persona feels overpowered and humbled but not threatened; confident and hopeful rather than scared—an attitude contrasting sharply with that exhibited in the presence of a usurper-dictator who rules by terror. Like the messianic king of the Bible, Carrera Andrade's metaphorical queen performs the function of welcoming strangers, uniting what has been divided, and proclaiming the advent of a new era, not unlike that of the eschatological Kingdom.

Far from being an apotheosis of the merely human power as an end in itself, the poem concentrates on the beauty of the impressive human achievement as expressive of the most beautiful of all human dreams—the dream of unity and peaceful coexistence. The builders of the Babel Tower also wanted to unite heaven and earth, and provoked a disastrous catastrophe instead, as Merton illustrated in his 1957 morality play "The Tower of Babel." Yet, the hubris of haughty pride is totally absent from Carrera Andrade's poem, which depicts a truly worshipful humility of the speaker overwhelmed by the new aesthetic of the man-made cosmic tree in which he senses an authentic presence of the transcendent. The closing lines, "The tides of heaven / Silently undermine your pillar" (25-26), do not leave any doubt that the object of the poet's adoration is definitely not the *gloria huius mundi*.

While the poem resonates profoundly with Merton's eschatological and epistemological concerns, it is doubtful whether Merton would ever have eulogized a technological construction, no matter how pioneering or transcendental in character, as he was particularly alert to the reverse side of so-called progress. Technology in its growing autonomy from humans was to be feared rather than revered. Carrera Andrade's "Cocoa Tree," on the other hand, would have fallen neatly into the Merton canon. Visualized as "archangel tutor of the green parrot" (2)[32] or genuflecting worshipper ecstatically tuned in to the hum of bees, the virgin tree, sharing in virgin nature's transparency for the divine, is a privileged *locus theologicus* ("On your knees, hands joined,/ Hearing the hum of secret hives of bees / You let your happiness grow" [8-10]).

Combining the simplicity and innocence of a child with the wisdom of a sage, Carrera Andrade's cocoa tree is the jungle's happy and wise feminine child. In its "fragrant lessons" (7) dictated "with a heavenly vocation" (6) and transcribed by the Latin

American poet, Merton's sensitive ear could not fail to hear the voice of Hagia Sophia—once celebrated by the monk from Kentucky in terms of "life as thanksgiving, life as praise, life as festival, life as glory."[33] Protective and maternal, hailed by Carrera Andrade as "cool doctrine in a tropic land" (3) and a benevolent silencer of distracting noises, the cocoa tree simply "lets" its happiness grow (10), and this consent is all that is needed to bring happiness to fruition. Like a woman, it receives and gives its consent to the "life as thanksgiving, life as praise, life as festival, life as glory" that is already present in the depth of its very being; this humble *fiat* actualizing the original consent given to life by virgin nature.

A wise teacher of a merciful doctrine, a natural born poet and philosopher "rich in almond-shaped thoughts" (11), the cocoa tree is perceived as writing

> . . . upon the pages of the air,
> The virgin jungle's novel
> Even to the sweet smell of grandmother's cups
> In dining rooms, with silent doors,
> Where the wall clock drips
> Like a half-orange.

Addressees of the "fragrant lessons" are reached across the natural and cultural divide, in the jungle as well as in the safety of established city life. Much as the human and the vegetal imperceptibly blend in the description of the cocoa tree, the natural and the cultural interpenetrate to uncover a net of interdependencies, a hidden wholeness that normally remains unseen. Glimpsed only by a few, it is the same "mysterious Unity and Integrity" that Merton calls the "Mother of all."[34]

Carrera Andrade belongs to the few twentieth-century poets who remained responsive to spiritual values hidden in the landscape. Unlike Thomas Merton, he was not a "professional," cloistered contemplative, yet his poems demonstrate an awareness of natural symbolism that leads to the attainment of a new level of being and a transfigurative reading of reality. It was poets like him Merton had in mind when writing in "Poetry and Contemplation: A Reappraisal" (1958) that in the midst of ordinary life they find a new and transcendent meaning, and by this meaning they transfigure the whole of life.[35] Theirs is a true eschatology, defined by Merton as "the vision of a totally new and final reality, a cosmic reversal that brings ultimate meaning and salvation to the fallen world."[36] In Carrera Andrade's poetic universe vital symbols still abound and cosmic symbolism has not been "submerged under a tidal wave of trademarks, political party buttons, advertisements and propaganda slogans," which Merton once deplored as symptomatic of "an age of mass psychosis."[37] On account of the likes of Carrera Andrade, the world does not have to end in self-destruction yet. Merton once celebrated this innocence of vision in the following words: "O twenty poets, O ten poets, O five poets . . . the idol refuses to shine in us."[38]

In his essay on the Ecuadorian poet, Merton writes that during World War II Carrera Andrade "was silent, except for the quiet irony of his parachute jumper."[39] Silence seemed to be the only legitimate response to the barrage of words without content used on both sides of the conflict to legitimize death. When he finally spoke, he spoke of hope. His verse "Notes of a Parachute Jumper" depicts a paratrooper descending from heaven like a Messiah. In his "heavenly travel" (4), he traverses fantastic landscapes, vast and empty, save for "two birds and the wind" (1), occasionally dotted by flowers of condensed vapor and "rolled-up maps" of clouds (2).[40] The cloud-maps no doubt help him select the best way from among all "the roads of light and rain" (12) at his disposal, while the friendly steam-flowers, opening "to seek" him (3), neutralize the Messenger's fall. Before the expectant Earth can receive him into her "wet furrows" (14), like a caring mother would, the "friendly shrub" (13) further cushions the fall. Safe is the landing, warm is the welcome, all nature cooperates to shelter and protect the traveler from harm and from detection,

> For I come out of heaven
> As in prophecies and hymns,
> Messenger from on high with my uniform of leaves.

The "uniform of leaves" dissociates the wearer from any abstract nationalistic cause. Instead, it identifies him as a soldier of the earth who wears *its* colors and fights *its* cause—which is the cause of life—against the enemy death.[41] The son of Mother Earth, he returns home to liberate her from evil as ancient prophets have foretold. Inscribed within this mythic-eschatological framework, the jumper would almost from the start dissolve into the archetypal figure of the Messiah, the Prince of Peace, were it not for a few disquieting details. First of all, the title is the only place in the entire poem that identifies the speaker as a parachute jumper; what follows is his monologue—his "notes"—and *self*-identification, which might as well be self-projection into the messianic framework, inspired by the exhilaration of "falling from the sky" and the unearthly beauty of the airscapes. The poem's double perspective constantly causes the existential and the eschatological dimensions to overlap. Consequently, when the Messenger proclaims his arrival with "my supply of deaths and lives" (8), the attentive Merton reader might feel uneasy. As we cannot completely put out of our minds the reality of World War II, which is the poem's frame of reference, whose claim do we hear: the self-proclaimed or the anointed Messenger's? Who has he been sent by: a secular or a Higher Power? And how does he actually feel about his mission: is he enjoying his power over life and death or does it weigh on him like a burden? Only the latter response would make the Messenger credible.

Merton himself had long been struggling with the same contorted problem, the problem of "mission," which touches the very core of all human history, whether in its religious or secular dimension. His most profound poetic meditation on this theme (prior to *Emblems of a Season of Fury*, at any rate) is probably "Elias— Variations on a Theme." Forced to rethink his life and his mission, Elias, the great Old Testament prophet, discovers with shame that while prophesying God's vengeance on the unrepentant he was communicating his own power and innocence rather than God's concern for the chosen people. The moment his *own* message turns out to be *no* message, the difference between the prophet and those to whom he is sent becomes obliterated, as does the demarcation line between holiness and sinfulness. The stigmatized city with its misery and divisiveness is finally recognized as his "own city" and Elias is ready to accept his membership in fallen humanity. The newly-acquired awareness of solidarity with others and complicity in wrongdoing ("I would be lost together with others," confesses Elias[42]) heightens the sense of responsibility attendant on his mission. The test of a mission's authenticity, Merton suggests, is the Messenger's readiness to serve rather than be served, and his capacity for affective identification even with the enemy. Has this criterion been met by Carrera Andrade's character?

The poem is literally flooded with the lucid joy of the Messenger's coming. The speaker's openness to the world's visual beauty and his perceptual innocence, his compassionate concern for the suffering and his sincere desire to bring down the sky, momentarily dispel the readers' doubts. No trace of pride is detectable in him; in its place there is an unpretentious Franciscan lucidity. It is worth noticing that only a childlike, fresh, and innocent eye could have so de-familiarized and beautified the prosaic sight (at the height of the war frenzy) of the descending parachute. Now "swimming on air" (26) like a jellyfish, now drifting down like an umbel, it becomes a celestial umbrella protectively stretched over the earth, and a pledge of the traveler's heavenly mission. Images that fuse and metaphorical shortcuts are Carrera Andrade's signature.

Having happily descended on the continent troubled by atrocities, the speaker brings a potent message of hope, primarily to the destitute and the needy:

> Here I am, farmers of Europe.
> I come in the name of bread, of the mothers of the world,
> In the name of all that is white and bare,
> The heron, the lily, the lamb, the snow.

Earlier in the poem the jumper appealed to earth for help ("Earth, tell your wet furrows to receive me. / Tell that fallen tree to teach me / Color of a motionless form" [14-15]). He was the vulnerable one, the success of his mission dependant on her favorable response. The "motionless form" and the image of the Messenger buried like a seed in the wet soil hint at the necessity of patience for the success of his mission, a virtue he had yet to be instructed in by Mother nature. For him, covering the distance between heaven and earth, with the calculated risk of landing, was not unlike crossing the line separating life and death. On the other side of the "fall," however, is resurrection, and now, after what resembles the patient germination of a seed buried in the earth's furrows, roles can be reversed and the speaker can come out into the open to accomplish his mission of help-bringer sent to people impoverished by war, but continuing to care and "farm" the ravaged continent.

From "farmers of Europe" (stanza five) to "farmers of the world" (stanza seven), the span of the speaker's mission becomes all-embracing, his Messianic status confirmed by the Paschal imagery. Like Christ, he has been sent; like Christ, he comes *in the name* of the innocent and the pure who have been crucified by evil, and in the name of their grief-stricken mothers; he comes in the name of countless unknown martyrs of "historical necessity" whose clothes have been bleached[43] in blood ("the heron, the lily, the lamb, the snow"), and in the name of the desperately poor who do not have anything, and so all can only be given to them. In the optics of the competitive world, these are all people of no account and, therefore, the chosen of the Bible (the *anawim*). Depending heavily on others for their very survival, they alone have enough humility to be open to unexpected gifts; they know for certain that they are not solipsistic, self-enclosed universes. The Messenger comes *in the name* of bread, but he also *is* bread. By virtue of his compassionate identification with all the members of Christ's tortured body he does become Christ, the Lamb of God, the Living Bread. "Descending like daylight" (9), the Messenger comes to put an end to the long night of evil, to announce the dawn of a new, innocent world. "Farmers of the world, I have brought down the sky" (25), he proclaims. In actual fact, the mission has *already* been accomplished. Has anyone noticed it? Has anyone believed it?

The "quiet irony" of the poem is that the event is destined to pass largely unnoticed. The only addressees of the good news are farmers. Translating this into the language of the Bible, they are the humble of the Gospel, descendants of the shepherds and the country folk to whom the First Coming was proclaimed. The industrial society, as Merton would tirelessly point out, believes in war, not peace, and seeks to impose on others the utopias of its own making, mistaking its "final solutions" for the eschatological Kingdom-to-Come. What these people no longer believe in, they are least likely to see when it unexpectedly appears before their eyes. All the engineers of doom and worshippers of power deafened by explosions of their own making have no ear attuned to the gentler tones of the good tidings. If they watch the sky at all, it is through a telescope, or, in time of war, to scour it for portents of death. Farmers, on the other hand, are compulsive sky-watchers; from sky-scapes, from the shape of clouds, they read their fortune. Tracing the "roads of light and rain" (12), they read their own "deaths and lives" (8) in the estimated harvest. It is from the sky, then, that comes the great joy addressed to them. The very appellation, "farmers," additionally alludes to the deepest identity of man as revealed in the Book of Genesis: the moment the world-garden was entrusted to the stewardship of man, he became responsible for cultivating or "farming" it.[44] However, not all remained faithful to this hidden identity. The *Parousia* will inevitably reveal how well—or how badly—people have cultivated the garden of the world. Hence, having come "via the roads of light and rain," the Messenger brings "hidden lightnings," "a store of deaths, / But I also bring another year's harvests" (27-28). Death and life are two aspects of one reality, one depending on the other (*"but* I *also* bring"), complementing it, finally merging with it into a higher unity. As every farmer knows, perfectly sunny weather can be a curse if it is not interspersed with spells of rain and storm. This is the wisdom of the seed, which, received into the soil's "wet furrows" (14), by dying brings forth more abundant life. Yet, what life can abound on the debris of history? What crop can be harvested?

> I bring the quiet crop empty of soldiers,
> The window lighted again, driving out night.
> Routed forever. I am
> The new angel of our time.

Harvest is an explicitly apocalyptic image. It symbolizes the ripeness of time, the end of history. In "Notes of a Parachute Jumper" the consummation of history is announced by an angel-messenger, but, having traded wings for a parachute, he is even visually quite unlike his biblical counterparts. The new, uniform-clad angel speaks the language of his time and is firmly rooted in twentieth-century reality. His arrival is a hidden, almost marginal event, unaccompanied by any special signs. Or, to be more precise, the signs appear only to those who can still *see*, whose eyes are still open to natural symbolism, this preamble of supernatural faith. These signs are so "ordinary" and humble that people no longer heed them, expecting something more spectacular and violent as an announcement of the Messianic Kingdom. The aesthetic of escalation and noise has deafened the industrial society to the eloquence of the most elementary, most lucid symbols. Yet, through the quiet simplicity of his coming, the Messenger seems to be saying that there will not be another apocalypse. It is the present historical moment that contains the eschatological secret, the ripe crop of time. Interestingly enough, in the updated biblical parable of the wheat,[45] the subversive element in the harvested crop is not weeds but soldiers. This is another reminder that the eschatological Kingdom is to be the reverse of man-made utopias, in which peace is imposed and maintained by a well-trained army or militia.

Merton was deeply convinced that the tactic of war for the sake of (future) peace is self-defeating; that it only succeeds in feeding collective paranoia. After all, Hiroshima and Auschwitz were brain-children of the same mistaken retribution logic pushed to its limits, the same abstract categorizing ("we" versus "them") which reduces the unique, absolutely unrepeatable human person in his concrete existential situation to a one-dimensional label ("the enemy") and makes his or her liquidation a patriotic duty. In *New Seeds of Contemplation* (1961) Merton puts the following words into God's mouth: "I wish to make it impossible for anyone to be my enemy. Therefore I identify myself with my enemy's own secret self."[46] In the sixties the Merton credo is: solidarity with the world in crisis, divinization of the cosmos, transfiguration of *all* existential reality. The only war to end all wars is the war against illusion and the deceptions of facile propaganda that make us exiles from the truth and from ourselves, lost in the darkness of pseudo-knowledge, willfulness, and half-truths. Only if the house of our being can light up again will night be "routed forever" (31).

"Descending like daylight" (9) on the night-bound earth, the Messenger proclaims the dawn of a new world. His ontological status at this point is that of the light of the world coming to dispel the existential darkness forever. The Son of Man of the Hebrew prophets merges in the next image with the archetypal mythic hero, son of earth and sky, as an embodiment of the paradoxical conjunction of opposites, an integration of two realms of being divorced by the Fall:

Citizen of air and clouds,
I yet have earthly blood
Which knows the way and enters every house,
The road that flows beneath cars,

The waters that pretend to be the same
And that passed by before
The earth of animals, of plants, with tears,
Whither I go to light the day with my hands.

Having brought down the sky, the Messenger has, in consequence of his "fall" into the world, lifted up the fallen world back to heaven and restored to creation its original state of innocence, the second "fall" undoing the effects of the first. In the context of the poem's consistent Christological references, the metaphor of descent presupposes a complementary movement of ascent, which, although not explicitly there, is nonetheless implied in the suggested union of heaven and earth. In this symmetrical movement of the world's fall and assumption, the latter would cancel out the former. In consequence, time itself would be cancelled, and history would come round to the "final beginning" of eschatology. Consistent with the logic of the new beginning is the requirement that the new creation be innocent of the law (which resulted from the knowledge of good and evil); it is, therefore, necessary that the ethical order be supplanted by *ordo caritatis:* where mercy fulfills the whole law, the speaker's "earthly blood" can truly "enter every house." Now that *every* house of being has been marked by the lamb's blood, there are no more "enemies" to be destroyed and all God's creation can be spared from retribution.

This joint Carrera Andrade-Merton poetic meditation reaffirms the value of universal hope for the world: the "inconsistent" logic of mercy breaks through the "consistency" of justice, much like in the mystical vision of the fourteenth-century English recluse, Lady Julian of Norwich, who was a major influence on the Trappist contemplative poet's thought in the nineteen-sixties.

Impersonating the genius of his "humble and delightful" country,[47] Carrera Andrade could not have reacted to the abyss of history otherwise than as an involved, compassionate, observer and an attentive listener who, over "the harsh chorus of the prisoners in despair . . . has listened, silently, to other voices and other harmonies."[48] These other voices, other harmonies transcribed by him, e. g., in "Notes of a Parachute Jumper," made Merton wonder: "Can prophecy be so humble, so unassuming? Can the voice of a new world be so quiet? Is this the voice of the gray-green Andes, of the long-hidden America, of the dim and cool twilight of the Sierra dawn out of which peace, perhaps, will one day be born?"[49]

If "Notes" is central to Merton's private canon of the Ecuadorian poet's verse, another poem, "The Mirror's Mission," coincides with his own passionate defense of the metaphysics of presence and constitutes an interesting gloss on his poetic interest in reflected images of spiritual reality, often expressed by the motif of the self as a window—of differing stages of ontological purity (e.g., "The Blessed Virgin Mary Compared to a Window"). Endlessly projecting his image onto innumerable pages of journals—and struggling to break free from self-reflexivity and self-projections— the Gethsemani poet tirelessly explored possible ways of seeing, including non-seeing, in an effort to (re)educate his eyes. A sharp, penetrating glance of a bard, reaching to the depths of reality, is a prerequisite for prescribing corrective lenses for others.

"The Mirror's Mission" has an attractively regular pattern based on repetition and parallelism—the verbal analogue of the mirror's reflective power, of its "mission" to remember. The two opening lines introduced by the temporal conjunction "when" dramatize the advent of night:

> When all things forget color and shape,
> When walls, pressed by night, fold in
> And all else yields, or kneels, or blurs,
> You, O lucid presence, you alone stand![50]

First, darkness blurs the sharp outlines of reality, until finally all that is disappears in a seizure of universal amnesia, as if blotted out of existence. "All things forget color and shape," but, objectively, the color, the shape remain what they have always been, only the eye can no longer see them. Thus, absence would emerge as purely subjective, a matter of inadequate perception, of wrong epistemology, and, most importantly, of the loss of collective memory. Compressed to just one line is a penetrating diagnosis of the world's existential night. When—and the poet does not use the conditional "if," for he has no doubt that the metaphorical night falls as infallibly as the literal one—so when it comes, all seems to be lost. Blind, dissolving in the uniform nothingness, doubting its very existence, the besieged world experiences mounting panic; everything collapses, even the solid, mineral walls "fold in." Resistance is broken, the fortress of the self taken, its inhabitant enslaved, despairing, depicted in a supplicant position (kneeling). And since we have already ventured on the existential ground, hope and despair are naturally key concepts in the existential analysis. Despair can be defined, according to Gabriel Marcel, as an active denial of being, a form of spiritual suicide. The French philosopher clarifies the point, saying: "The soul which despairs shuts itself up against the central and mysterious assurance in which we believe we have found the principle of all positivity."[51] Void appears where fullness used to be, a void (non-being) that would engulf everything if it were not for the mirror and its "mission" of witnessing to what *is*, albeit at times what it witnesses to is invisible. "You, lucid presence," marvels Carrera Andrade, "you alone stand!" In obvious contrast to all else that "yields," the mirror has withstood the siege of the absurd, and now, by a symmetrical but inverted process, it makes "the shadows yield" to its "bright will." The mirror restores the rule of reality by recognizing absence for what it is: a substanceless shadow, a ghost of reality that ensnares us in a web of illusions to which we ourselves give substance by our consent. The "lucid presence"—lucid in its double meaning: firstly, bright, therefore opposing darkness; secondly, unambiguous, clear to the understanding, hence dispelling doubts and confusion—remains faithful to memorized images. It recollects them and by doing so, re-collects reality dispersed by night. When dark hours come, this "transparent witness" (11) will "recite" its "lesson learned by heart," the "lesson of light" (12).

The principle of symmetrical reflection would require that the third and final stanza be a creative echo of the first. Not surprisingly, the final stanza does develop the metaphor of shadow reality in order to give it its full-blown gothic twist:

Each chair opens out, waits in the night
To seat some unreal guest before a dish of shadows.

One is instantaneously reminded of that Emily Dickinson classic, "One need not be a Chamber—to be Haunted," or Edgar Allan Poe's disturbing projections of the same mental "Corridors—surpassing / Material Place."[52] The unnamed fear, the threat, the atmosphere of almost sinister anticipation culminate in a reversed image of the eschatological feast: the ghosts and dishes of shadows are markers of absence, substitutes for the promised revelation of the fullness of Presence. A "transparent witness" is desperately needed to break the fatal spell of unreality before we succumb to it for good. "You alone" (11), repeats the speaker addressing the mirror. Incidentally, the mirror's "lesson of light" is not unlike the "fragrant lessons" of the cocoa tree; both oppose the new code of consciousness that has proclaimed the death of God and reduced the human person to God's shadow, a self-enclosed object among other objects.

It is interesting to note how much the poem, in its metaphorical symbolism and even its linguistic suggestiveness, converges with Gabriel Marcel's metaphysics. For the author of "Outline of an Essay on the Position of the Ontological Mystery and the Concrete Approaches to It," the essential metaphysical step consists in what closely resembles Carrera Andrade's poetic reflection on (mirror) reflection. Marcel's "reflection squared" aims at a recovery of our unconscious intuition of the mystery of being through the mediation of "the modes of experience in which its image is reflected, and which it lights up by being thus reflected in them." It is recollection, continues the philosopher, "the most revealing ontological index we possess," in which this intuition can be recovered.[53]

The mirror cannot deny the image it reflects. Its essence is faithfulness. Lacking the power of denial, it is immune to betrayal and despair. Gabriel Marcel asserts that the concrete approaches to the ontological mystery should be sought in the *elucidation* of such data—spiritual by nature—as *fidelity*, hope, and love. Assuming with the French existentialist that the essence of the world, when viewed merely as a problem to be solved, is betrayal, and that man is forever implicated in the struggle against denial and introversion, it is easier to understand the urgency of the "mirror's mission." As a "lucid presence" it e-lucid-ates, that is, makes the truth perceivable, by virtue of its *fidelity*, understood as "the recognition . . . of an ontological permanency; a permanency which endures and by reference to which we endure."[54] Since permanency, presence, and being are synonymous terms, the mirror emerges as a model embodiment of Marcel's idea of a creative witness who "asserts himself in so far as he asserts Being and opens himself to it."[55] Additionally, Carrera Andrade's appellation "transparent witness" brings associations with the classic theological concept of creation as a window. When the window is transparent, when its surface is clean, it does not attract attention to itself and is capable of giving an undisturbed image of Reality. The transparent window of the self, the self that has been made in the image—not as a shadow—of God, remains thus *faithful* to the Exemplar.

The middle stanza of the poem, however, is the true pivot on which the whole turns. It is an affirmation of positivity amidst shadows and negativity, and the fullest demonstration of the mirror's mission. In its entirety it reads as follows:

You make the shadows yield to your bright will.
Your mineral silence glows in the dark.
Sweet messages to other objects
Fly out of you (your sudden pigeons).

The second line contains two crucial words: "silence" and "glows." Thomas Merton, a Trappist monk under the vow of silence, devoted innumerable pages to the exploration of silence as the principle of distinguishing between the real and the illusory. The mirror's "mineral silence" seems to echo the silence of the stone, which was the instructor in wisdom and patience of the Elias of Merton's poem. It was in silence that prophets and messengers encountered Reality (I Am Who I Am) and were entrusted with their mission. Additionally, the "mineral silence" of Carrera Andrade's mirror is far from mineral coldness. It is modified by the verb "to glow," which brings associations with warmth and kindness, a certain coziness and safety. A glow is dimmed light and (creative) witness to an infinitely greater Light, which would be blinding were it not clouded over; to a burning and consuming Fire, which can only be known in "the cloud of unknowing." The humble glow of the "transparent witness" is another veil of "the Blinding One," who in Merton's *Hagia Sophia* "speaks to us gently in ten thousand things, in which His light is one fullness and one Wisdom. Thus He shines not on them but from within them."[56] No wonder that the mirror's glowing mineral silence dispels the fiction of solipsism, and messages, like pigeon-grams, "fly out" of it to reach the other in a confirmation of a metaphysic of "we are."[57]

Carrera Andrade's "Radicals," on the other hand, is a lightweight, humorous poem, although with a serious twist, and a display of wit and fine irony. Though the title signals a rather serious, politically engaged theme, the verse flippantly develops the analogy between two unexpected allies in political extremism: "comrade locust" (1) and the poet[58] At first the ground of likeness may be far from obvious, yet the easily recognizable sound made by a swarm of locusts is as subversive to "the dictator: Man" (4) as the most politically committed poetry. "Comrade" insect, just like a compassionate poet sensitive to the needs and oppression of the common people, sings an uneasy song, "with a splinter in his throat" (2). Possessing nothing but the light burden of his troubled poetry ("Locust goes no place, singing his song"[6]), the little musical pest of the natural world is a radical poet's alter ego. From the commonsensical point of view, both "radicals" are marginal to the preoccupations of the world, whose order and structures they reject; the songs of both are equally "useless" to the profit-oriented society, and equally threatening to (dictator) man's will to power. All in all, the locust emerges as a somewhat unorthodox *monachos* and an embodiment of the Camusian Rebel:

Worker locust, you are right
To undermine the state
With your sagacious song.
We have one same song to sing,
Comrade! We are the world's
Extreme left wing.

Like "Radicals," also the baroque conceit of Carrera Andrade's
"The Weathercock on the Cathedral of Quito" lends itself to a surprising interpretation, an ironical—without ever losing its "glowing" warmth—comment, this time on life in the monastic enclosure. The tin cock perched on top of the cathedral spends his solitary life, a life of penitence and vigilance, on the world's frontier,
like a true monk. But upon seeing Anna del Campo, a local beauty,
"the cathedral ascetic" (22) turns into a blighted "tin Don Juan"
(14), sentenced to keeping his burning passion to himself,
unconsumed, even undeclared.[59] "The cock would like to crow"
(13), but "stuck on his belfry" (15) he is under the double vows of
silence and stability of place. "Paralyzed / In a desert of roofs"
(20-21), the hermit weathercock feels constricted by the rules he is
bound to obey—which are not unlike the Rule of St. Benedict,
whose rigorous interpretation would at times apparently immo-
bilize the spiritual growth of Merton and his fellow contemplatives.
"The burning bird flashes" (18) desperate messages of passion to
the vain girl, who remains quite ignorant of his existence. Finally
flashing "sun signals / To his friend, the lightning rod" (26-27)—a
stratagem resembling the Trappist practice of using sign language
to circumvent the rule of silence—he wishes at least to find a con-
fidant to share his secret with and, hopefully, an accomplice in
passing the message on. Anna del Campo has caused a grave vo-
cational crisis in the weathercock's life. A temptation appeared to
abandon the post between heaven and earth, a temptation that in
one form or another all prophets and prophetic witnesses to another reality have to experience as a test of faith. But the ascetic
seems decided to sate his long, self-imposed thirst, to trade his
noble mission for ordinary human happiness, and to turn into a
comfy husband living in easy circumstances at the side of a beautiful wife:

Anna, take me to the door
Of your house of flowers
Where bliss never ends.

Give me your cool dew
For my throat of sand.
Give me your lily field!

These temptations would soon be well known to the poem's translator in his struggle to disengage himself from his relationship with
the student nurse known as M.

The last two poems introduce a welcome break in the heavy
poetic diet, a humorous touch, which in itself is a subversive ges-
ture and an important contribution to solving a serious metaphysical problem facing the Western world. As has already been pointed
out earlier the mid-twentieth century discourse was characterized
by an almost dogmatic lack of a sense of humor, and this was to
Merton a telltale sign of the erosion of traditional values, the triumph of naturalistic reductionism, and the loss of the human
measure. One Merton poem from *Emblems of a Season of Fury* directly addresses this issue. "Elegy for James Thurber" is, in fact, a
double elegy, mourning simultaneously humor and spirituality—
those last bulwarks against doctrinaire matter-of-factness. With
the death of the celebrated humorist, an epoch has ended. "Humor is now totally abolished," mourns the Trappist poet, "The great
dogs of nineteen sixty-one / Are nothing to laugh at."[60] Having
reached its high point, human madness was absolutely beyond
parody or ridicule; from then on it could only be "solemnized."
Not surprisingly, contrary to this depressing pronouncement,
Merton continued to critique the world's madness through the
subversive use of humor in his poetry and prose, remaining faithful to the declaration he made in *Conjectures of a Guilty Bystander*
(1966): "I will keep laughing until they close my mouth with fall-
out."[61]

In the course of this analysis, two key terms have been found to
determine the landscape of the secret country inhabited by Carrera
Andrade and Merton alike: lucidity and humor. Reading the
Merton of the sixties one cannot fail to notice how often these two
terms (or such synonyms of lucidity as innocence and purity) appear in his critical essays and how regularly these concepts are
applied in his poetic practice. Naturally, the enthusiasm he feels
for poets of Ibero-America has much to do with what Albert Camus
called "'lucidity' in the presence of the 'denseness and strangeness' of the world."[62] Such lucidity, which combines perceptual
purity and transparency of style, clarifies man's awareness of his

true condition and, in doing so, enables him to transcend, in the affirmation of love and solidarity, the anguish that man experiences in consequence of his encounter with reality. In his brief sketches introducing Latin American poets to the North American reader, Merton cannot help but celebrate the Ibero-Americans' innocence and lucidity. He praises Carrera Andrade's innocent eye, which endows the Ecuadorian's verses with a vision of the underlying "is-ness" of daily reality in an analogue of the early Franciscan vision of God who simply "is." He appreciates the "lucidity" of Ernesto Cardenal's early poetry as encouraging "a profound renewal and change of perspective in which 'the world' is . . . seen in a clearer and less delusive light."[63] As for Ruben Darío, Merton hails his "limpid" "Sonnets to Cervantes" as harbingers of "the less rhetorical tastes of the later generation,"[64] of poetics that would see being in the concrete again and serve lucid consciousness to protect man rather than destroy him.

By that time, "Franciscan" for Merton had become a code name, synonymous with lucid consciousness, affirmation of all life in the concrete, unpretentious simplicity, poverty, and, in effect, revolt against the absurd. The idea of the early Franciscan as a paradigm of the Rebel—"poverty-loving, therefore liberated"[65]—was suggested to Merton by Camus. The French existentialist writer had an intuition that innocence, defined as the ability to live "without appeal" to systematic explanations, would be the end of the absurd. If this is so, there is another choice beyond the religious resignation of the yogi and the active revolutionary commitment of the commissar: *tertium datur*, and this third option is the "vocation to revolt."[66] What the author of *The Stranger* wrote in his *Notebooks 1942-1951* might have been written by Merton himself:

> The end of the absurd, rebellious etc. movement, the end of the contemporary world consequently, is compassion in the original sense: in other words ultimately love and poetry. But that calls for an innocence I no longer have. All I can do is recognize the way leading to it and be receptive to the time of the innocents.[67]

What else are Merton's translating efforts if not examples of such open-minded receptivity to the time of the innocents. Wherever he discovered innocence, he would want to make it known to the whole absurdity-infested Western world and, by the same token, annul the West's fatalistic legacy of violence. Compassionate love was to herald the end of history and the advent of, however hidden, eschatological fulfillment.

Notes

1. Thomas Merton, *Spiritual Direction and Meditation* (Collegeville: Liturgical Press, 1986), p. 88.

2. Merton, *Spiritual Direction*, p. 89.

3. Merton, letter to Esther de Cáceres, 9 Jan. 1965, *The Courage for Truth: Letters to Writers* (ed. Christine Bochen; New York: Farrar, Strauss & Gireaux, 1993), p. 166.

4. Merton, letter to Ernesto Cardenal, 11 Mar. 1961, *Courage for Truth*, p. 123.

5. While in his translations Merton happens to depart from the letter of the original poem, he manages to preserve its spirit. The task of comparing the Spanish versions with their English renditions, however, would require a separate study. I decided to abandon this, no doubt, intriguing task to a more specialized research, rather than attempting two ambitious topics simultaneously and not succeeding in either.

6. Merton's translations from Herakleitos ("The Legacy of Herakleitos") have been included in the "Uncollected Poems" section of *The Collected Poems of Thomas Merton* (New York: New Directions, 1977).

7. As Merton did not know Chinese or Persian, he relied on philological translations and the help of John Wu, a friend and Oriental scholar.

8. See Merton, letter to Clayton Eshleman, June 1963, *Courage for Truth*, p. 255.

9. Roman Samsel, *Bunt i gwalt* [Rebellion and Violence] (Warszawa: Czytelnik, 1978), p. 37.

10. Merton, letter to Stefan Baciu, 21 May 1965, *Courage for Truth*, p. 241.

11. Merton, *Courage for Truth*, p. 241.

12. Merton, *Conjectures*, p. 188.

13. Merton, *Conjectures*, p. 188.

14. I am retaining the existentialist terminology used by Merton. In order to avoid ambiguities, I wish to clarify that the word "man" will often be used here as an inclusive and gender-neutral term.

15. Merton, *Courage for Truth*, p. 241.

16. Steven Ford Brown, "http://jacketmagazine.com/andrade-intro-brown.html" "Jorge Carrera Andrade in America," *Jacket 12* (July 2000), online, *Jacket Magazine*, Internet, 26 Jan. 2003.

17. Qtd. in Merton, "Jorge Carrera Andrade," *Literary Essays*, p. 319.

18. Merton, "The Plague of Albert Camus: A Commentary and Introduction," *Literary Essays*, p. 206.

19. Merton, "Message to Poets," *Literary Essays*, pp. 371-74.

20. Thomas Merton, *Search For Solitude: Pursuing the Monk's True Life* (ed. Lawrence S. Cunningham, journals, vol. 3, 1952-60; San Francisco: Harper, 1997), p. 357.

21. Merton received two autographed books from Carrera Andrade: *El fabuloso reino de Quito*, inscribed: "Para Thomas Merton, uno de los más altos representativos de la consciencia del mundo, con mi admiración y en amistad" [For Thomas Merton, an outstanding representative of the world's conscience, with admiration and friendship] and *Retrato cultural del Ecuador*, inscribed: "A Thomas Merton, maestro de poetas. Homenaje de admiración y amistad" [To Thomas Merton, master of poets. A homage of admiration and friendship]. Archives of the Thomas Merton Center, Bellarmine University, Louisville, Ky.

22. Thomas Merton, "Jorge Carrera Andrade," *The Literary Essays of Thomas Merton* (New York: New Directions, 1985), p. 319.

23. Merton, "Jorge Carrera Andrade," *Literary Essays*, p. 318.

24. Merton, "Jorge Carrera Andrade," *Literary Essays*, p. 318.

25. For the most part, I will also follow *The Collected Poems* arrangement of Carrera Andrade's verse, which is alphabetical. Originally, in *Emblems of the Season of Fury*, Merton's renditions appeared in the following order: "Cocoa Tree," "The Weathercock on the Cathedral at Quito," "A Man from Ecuador beneath the Eiffel Tower," "The Mirror's Mission," "Notes on a Parachute Jumper." "Radicals" was omitted from the 1963 book of verse.

26. Merton, "Jorge Carrera Andrade," *Literary Essays*, p. 318.

27. Merton, "Jorge Carrera Andrade," *Literary Essays*, p. 319.

28. All quotations from Jorge Carrera Andrade's poem "A Man from Ecuador beneath the Eiffel Tower" come from Merton, *Collected Poems*, pp. 841–42. Parenthetical references in the text will indicate line numbers for the quotations.

29. Arturo Uslar Pietri, "The World Discovers Latin America," *Américas* (Nov.-Dec. 1985): 47.

30. See H.R. Hays, "Jorge Carrera Andrade: Magician of Metaphors." In his 1970 Vassar lecture "The Decade of My Poetry," Carrera Andrade explained: "In my poetry the image consists in putting two realities face to face through a system of analogies. It is different from surrealist metaphor . . . My metaphor rejects all excessive remoteness from reality and takes pleasure in bringing things and men closer in an effort to achieve universal coherence and harmony" (tr. Steven Ford Brown, *Jacket 12* (July 2000), online, *Jacket Magazine*, Internet, 26 Jan. 2003).

31. The benign Titan sustaining the world was the subject of two poems written by Merton: "Atlas and the Fatman" and "Martin's Predicament or Atlas Watches Every Evening" (Merton, *Collected Poems*, pp. 679–91 and 728–36, respectively).

32. All quotations from Jorge Carrera Andrade's poem "Cocoa Tree" come from Merton, *Collected Poems*, p. 842.

33. Merton, *Collected Poems*, pp. 368-69.

34. Merton, "Hagia Sophia," *Collected Poems*, p. 363.

35. Thomas Merton, *A Thomas Merton Reader*, ed. T. P. McDonnell (New York: Doubleday, 1989), p. 402. Rpt. in Merton, *Literary Essays*, pp. 338–54.

36. Merton, "Blake and the New Theology," *Literary Essays*, p. 10.

37. Merton, "Poetry, Symbolism and Typology," *Literary Essays*, p. 333.

38. Merton, "Prólogo," *Collected Poems*, p. 744.

39. Merton, *Literary Essays*, p. 320.

40. All quotations from Jorge Carrera Andrade's poem "Notes of a Parachute Jumper" come from Merton, *Collected Poems*, pp. 843-44.

41. What is meant here is existential, rather than physical, death. The nationalistic war rhetoric always divides people into two hostile camps and consequently reduces "the enemy" to abstraction in order to justify their extermination and to legitimize contempt for "the other."

42. Merton, *Collected Poems*, p. 244.

43. See St. John's Apocalypse 7:12.

44. Gen. 2:15.

45. Matt. 13: 24–30.

46. *Thomas Merton Reader*, p. 502.

47. Merton, "Jorge Carrera Andrade," *Literary Essays*, p. 318.

48. Merton, "Jorge Carrera Andrade," *Literary Essays*, p. 320.

49. Merton, "Jorge Carrera Andrade," *Literary Essays*, p. 320.

50. All quotations from Jorge Carrera Andrade's poem "The Mirror's Mission" come from Merton, *Collected Poems*, p. 845.

51. Gabriel Marcel, "Outline of an Essay on the Position of the Ontological Mystery and the Concrete Approaches to It," *Reality, Man, Existence: Essential Works of Existentialism* (ed. H. J. Blackham; New York: Bantam, 1965), p. 168.

52. Emily Dickinson, *The Complete Poems*, ed. Thomas H. Johnson (Boston: Faber, 1975), p. 333.

53. Marcel, "Outline of an Essay," p. 167.

54. Marcel, "Outline of an Essay," p. 168.

55. Marcel, "Outline of an Essay," p. 169.

56. Merton, *Collected Poems*, pp. 366-367.

57. See Merton's "Seven Essays on Camus," *Literary Essays*, pp. 181-301.

58. All quotations from Jorge Carrera Andrade's poem "Radicals" come from Merton, *Collected Poems*, pp. 844-45.

59. All quotations from Jorge Carrera Andrade's poem "The Weathercock on the Cathedral of Quito" come from Merton, *Collected Poems*, pp. 845-46.

60. Merton, *Collected Poems*, p. 316.

61. Thomas Merton, *Conjectures of a Guilty Bystander* (New York: Image, 1968), p. 75.

62. Merton, "Three Saviors in Camus: Lucidity and the Absurd," *Literary Essays*, p. 275.

63. Merton, "Ernesto Cardenal, "*Literary Essays*, pp. 324-25.

64. Merton, "Ruben Darío" *Literary Essays*, p. 305.

65. Merton, "Terror and the Absurd," *Literary Essays*, p. 241.

66. Merton, "Terror and the Absurd," *Literary Essays*, p. 245.

67. Qtd. in Merton, "The Plague of Camus," *Literary Essays*, p. 199.

Jewels Upon His Forehead:
Spiritual Vision in the Poetry and Photography
of Thomas Merton

Marilyn Sunderman

Thomas Merton expressed his spiritual vision in a variety of ways. This study views the poetry and photography of Merton as artistic jewels, precious gems, which serve as mediums Merton employed to render his spiritual vision emerging from his numerous experiences. The essay examines spiritual insights embedded in the following topics in Merton's poetic corpus: Zen, nature, city-emptiness, and incarnation. It then explores Merton's spiritual vision through the lens of his photography and, within that context, depicts Ansel Adams and Thomas Merton as Zen-type photographers. In essence, this investigation seeks to shed light on Merton's in-depth encounters with God by means of his poetry and photography.

Central to Merton's spiritual vision is his belief that to find one's true self a person must become self-forgetting and, thus, aware that he or she *is* only in God. Merton asserts that in the ground of one's being, a person is one with God, others, and all of reality. In essence, for Merton, being authentically human entails waking up, that is, developing a growing awareness of the truth of one's *isness*.

Another fundamental aspect of Merton's spiritual vision is the tenet that all of creation in some way reflects God's beauty. Regarding this, Merton asserts: "One of the most important ... elements in the beginning of the interior life is the ability ... to see the value and the beauty in ordinary things, to come alive to the splendor that is all around us in the creatures of God."[1] This belief correlates with the Zen insight that the sacred is experienced in and through everyday reality.

In Merton's spirituality, Jesus Christ is the person who simultaneously reveals the nature of God and humanity. For Merton, the Incarnation represents the self-emptying of God in God's becoming human. Since Jesus embodies God's fullness in emptiness, those who desire to follow Him must enter unreservedly into

167

the process of self-emptying in order to become wholly "in Christ." Taking oneness in Christ seriously, Merton declares: "If we believe in the Incarnation of the Son of God, there should be no one on earth in whom we are not prepared to see, in mystery, the presence of Christ."[2]

Merton's Artistic Vision

Merton inherited his interest in art from his parents, Owen and Ruth, who were both artists. For Merton, art is a window into the mystery of God. True art enables a person to come "alive to the tremendous mystery of being, in which ... all living ... things come forth from the depths of God and return again to Him."[3] God, the Mystery behind the reality that art seeks to penetrate,[4] communicates in and through art.

According to Merton, the artist is a dervish who dances in the water of life.[5] Merton asserts that "[T]oday the artist has, whether he likes it or not, inherited the combined functions of hermit, pilgrim, prophet, priest, shaman, sorcerer, soothsayer, alchemist and bonze."[6] The artist, whose role is multifaceted, perceives the inner meaning and integral nature of life.

Poetry as an Expression of Merton's Artistic Vision

As a graduate student at Columbia University, Merton wrote poetry. Mark Van Doren, one of Merton's professors at the university, described him as a "poet of promise." Referring to his own poetic process, Merton observes: "The dawn is breaking outside the cold windows... whole blocks of imagery seem to crystallize out as it were naturally in the silence and the peace, and the lines almost write themselves."[7] Additionally, reflecting on writing poetry during 1940-41 when he was an English instructor at St. Bonaventure University, Merton notes that "as the months went on, I began to drink poems out of these hills."[8]

William Blake's poetry also played an important role in the development of Merton's poetic vision. During the early years of Merton's life, his father Owen introduced his son to Blake's poetry by reading 'Songs of Innocence' to him. Later, while studying at Oakham, Merton poured over Blake's poems and, at Columbia University, chose to write his master's thesis on them. In this thesis, Merton concurs with Blake that experiences of nature reveal something of the transcendent.

Early in his monastic life, Merton struggled with how the poet and contemplative could peacefully co-exist within his own person. Eventually, Merton resolved this conflict by viewing poetry as an "act of pursuing a listening silence."[9] According to him, poetic expressions emerge from one's awareness of and attentiveness to the sacred encountered in solitude.

Some of Merton's early poetry expresses a flight from a world mentality that was the consequence of his embracing a dualistic theology that separated the sacred and the profane. In contrast, in Merton's later poetry, the world became the very ground of the experience of the sacred. During 1965-66, Merton lectured on the poetry of Blake, Hopkins, and Rilke to the novices at the Abbey of Gethsemani. Merton believed that the study of such poetry provided a way for his students to enter into communion with God by experiencing creation's hidden wholeness.[10]

For Merton, poetry and theology are essentially related. Both plumb the fundamental questions of life in search of Truth. Both are attuned to God and God's activity in the world. Concerning this nexus, Merton asserts: "You cannot have a decent poem that is not in some way close to theology."[11] Merton maintains that, "To the Christian poet, the whole world and all the incidents of life tend to be sacraments - signs of God, signs of His love working in the world."[12]

Zen Insights/ Christian Insights

Zen, a way of living and being fully awake, cuts across all religious denominations. Zen involves awe at the sacredness of being. It entails entering into a process of self-emptying in order to experience the reality of fullness being emptiness and vice versa. Zen teaches that to be nothing is to be everything. To do nothing is the highest activity.

Zen enlightenment refers to the transformation of human consciousness wherein one becomes aware that she or he is united with all that exists and learns to cherish each created thing. From a Christian perspective, Merton expanded this Zen insight to include a person's awakening to the realization that the beauty of created reality reflects God's unfathomable beauty. For Merton, Christian spiritual growth, rooted in Zen insights, involves learning to live life fully awake. Those awake or enlightened are emptied of self, since they have disappeared into God who is Love.

In Merton's life, a heightened sense of such Zen/Christian enlightenment occurred when he visited the statues of the Buddhas in Polonnaruwa. Merton reflected:

> Looking at these figures I was suddenly, almost forcibly, jerked clean out of the habitual, half-tied vision of things, and an inner clearness, clarity as if exploding from the rocks themselves, became evident and obvious.... All problems are resolved and everything is clear.... [E]verything is emptiness and everything is compassion.[13]

In Merton's poetic writings, there are many examples of Zen/Christian insights. What follows is a representative sampling. In his poem, 'All the Way Down', Merton writes: "I went down/Into the cavern/All the way down/To the bottom of the sea. / I went down lower/Than Jonas and the whale. /No one ever got so far down/ As me. /I went down lower/Than any diamond mine/Deeper than the lowest hole/In Kimberly/All the way down."[14] Here, the "diamond mine" is an image of the human journey inward that leads to the discovery of the jewel of one's true identity.   Diamonds symbolize the treasure of self-knowledge available to those who engage in the Zen process of self-emptying and go 'All the way down' to the lowest level of the psyche.[15]

In 'Early Blizzard' the poem's speaker ploughs the snow drifts and is "knee deep in silence/Where the storm smokes and stings..."[16] Finally, the speaker admonishes self to "Sink in the hidden wood/And let the weather/Be what it is."[17] Here is a fine example of the Zen principle of acceptance of the *isness* of reality.

In various sections of his lengthy prose poem, 'Cables to the Ace', Merton offers further Zen reflections. In Cable 37, he writes: "The perfect act is empty.... [S]top seeking. Let it all happen. Let it come and go. What? Everything, i.e., nothing."[18] Cable 38 states: "The way that is most yours is no way."[19] In Cable 58, Merton argues that

> For each of us there is a point of nowhereness in the middle of movement, a point of nothingness in the midst of being the incomparable point, not to be discovered by insight. If you seek it, you do not find it. If you stop seeking, it is there. But you must not turn to it. Once you become aware of yourself as a seeker, you are lost. But if you are content to be lost you will be found without knowing it, precisely because you are lost, for you are, at last, nowhere.[20]

In Cable 84, Merton describes the essence of "Gelassenheit," which means to let go in order to enter into the fullness of emptiness.

> Gelassenheit. Desert and Void. The uncreated is waste and emptiness to the creature. Not even sand. Not even stone. Not even darkness and night.... But the uncreated is not something. Waste.   Emptiness. Total poverty of the Creator; yet from this poverty springs everything. The waste is inexhaustible. Infinite zero. Everything comes from this desert Nothing.[21]

By piling cable upon cable in 'Cables to the Ace,' Merton conveys the Zen insight that no way is the way, i.e., that one must enter the void in order to experience everything in nothingness. One needs to stop seeking so that being lost, being nowhere, one can be found and be everywhere. Infinite zero is, in Merton's understanding, paradoxically everything!

In his poem, 'Elias—Variations on a Theme', Merton writes: "Listen, Elias, /... Listen to the woods, / Listen to the ground. / ... O listen, Elias/ ... Where passes One/ Who bends no blade, no fern. / Listen to His word. / 'Where the fields end, thou shalt be My friend. / Where the bird is gone/ Thou shalt be My son.'"[22] This poem develops the Zen/Christian insight that the human inward journey is one of waiting and listening for God in order to find one's true center in God. At the end of the poem, Elias, depicted as a "wild bird", is free because he has awakened to the fact that God, who is his friend, is in the center where the fields end, i.e., in the Void.

Merton's 'Grace's House' is a poem about the intersection of the sacred and the profane in the house that symbolizes Grace's center. One cannot find a map to Grace's house because the way to it, which is the inner journey to the true self, is unique to each person.

Merton's poem 'In Silence' includes: "Be still/ Listen to the stones of the wall/ Be silent, they try/ To speak your /Name. / Listen/ To the living walls. /Who are you? / Who/Are you? Whose /Silence are you?"[23] "Be still" is an imperative once again to enter into the timeless void wherein one discovers who one really is. By disappearing into the silence of God, one becomes one's truest self.

'Love Winter When the Plant Says Nothing' is a poem Merton wrote about the dark night of the soul. Hidden in the snow and barrenness, the Plant in this poem is the human soul that waits in creative darkness to experience the fullness of spiritual union with God. Merton's poem 'Night-Flowering Cactus' repeats the theme of 'Love Winter When the Plant Says Nothing'. Instead of a plant, there is a cactus that blooms in the dark of night. The blooming cactus, like the Plant that says nothing, symbolizes the experience of mystical union with God in the Void. In Zen/Christian terms, both poems convey the essence of transformed consciousness: utter awake-ness in God.

In 'Song: If You Seek' Merton depicts Solitude as a teacher who leads one into emptiness wherein one "disappears into Love in order to 'be Love.'"[24] In this poem, Solitude, the speaker and director of the soul, declares: "I go before you into emptiness, / I am... / The forerunner of the Word of God. ... / Follow my ways.../To golden haired suns, /Logos and music.../For I, Solitude, am thine own self; / I, Nothingness, am thy All. / I, Silence, am thy Amen!"[25]

'Song for Nobody' is one of Merton's most concise, meaning-packed poems:

A yellow flower/ (Light and spirit)/ Sings by itself/For nobody. /A golden spirit/ (Light and emptiness)/Sings without a word/By itself./ Let no one touch this gentle sun/In whose dark eyes/Someone is awake./ No light, no gold, no name, no color/ And no thought; /O, wide awake!/A golden heaven/ Sings by itself/A song to nobody.[26]

The "wide-awake" flower in this poem is self-accepting. It is content to simply be what it is. The flower, which has its existence in God, symbolizes the person who has shed ego-attachment in Zen/Christian self-emptiness and, thus, is able to enter into the fullness of God.

Nature

Thomas Merton, a lover of nature, soaked into his soul the beauty of God's creation. As an instructor at St. Bonaventure University in Olean, New York, he took long walks during which he gazed contemplatively at surrounding snow-covered hills.[27] During Holy Week in April, 1941, as a guest at the Abbey of Gethsemani in Kentucky, Merton journaled:

Tulips in the front garden have already opened their chalices too wide and have gone blowsy. The bees were at work, one in each flower cup, although it is still only April. Apple trees are in blossom, and every day more and more buds come out on the branches of the tall trees of the avenue before the gatehouse.[28]

These words indicate how attuned Merton was to the details of nature in his surroundings.

Later, as a monk at Gethsemani, Merton mused:

But my chief joy is to escape to the attic of the garden house and the little broken window that looks out over the valley. There in the silence I love the green grass. The tortured gestures of the apple trees have become part of my prayer. I look at the shining water under the willows and listen to the sweet songs of all the living things that are in our woods and fields. So much do I love this solitude that when I walk out along the road to the old barns that stand alone, far from the new buildings, delight begins to overpower me from head to foot and peace smiles even in the marrow of my bones.[29]

This passage from *The Sign of Jonas* indicates Merton's realization of the utmost importance of silence and solitude for the contemplative consideration of nature's beauty.

In another entry from this journal, Merton writes: "[T]he whole world is charged with the glory of God and I find fire and music in the earth under my feet."[30] Thus, for Merton, nature explodes with the revelation that God is encounterable in all of reality for those who have eyes to see and ears to hear!

In *Conjectures of a Guilty Bystander,* Merton contemplates the glory of the sunrise as "an event that calls forth solemn music in the very depths of man's nature, as if one's whole being had to attune itself to the cosmos and praise God for the new day, praise Him in the name of all the creatures that ever were or ever will be."[31] This reflection highlights Merton's attentiveness to the ingenuity of God who wakes up the world each day with the glory of the sunrise.

Viewing Merton as a nature mystic, Brother Patrick Hart writes: "He loved the woods and all of nature. He saw it as a sacrament of God's presence and was concerned about preserving it not only for our generation but for the generations to come."[32] Brother Patrick's comments point to the fact that eco-theological concerns are intrinsic to Merton's nature mysticism. Regarding this, Merton asserted: "[W]e Americans ought to love our land, our forests, our plains and we ought to do everything we can to preserve it in its richness and beauty, by respect for our natural resources, for water, for land, for wild life."[33]

In poetry, Merton expressed the role nature played in his spiritual vision. What follows is a brief treatment of several of Merton's nature poems. In 'Trappists Working', Merton writes: "Now all our saws sing holy sonnets in the world of timber/Where oaks go off like guns, and fall like cataracts, / Pouring their roar into the wood's green well."[34]   In this poem, the monks' physical labor that unites them with nature leads them to God. Merton continues: "Walk to us, Jesus, through the walls of trees./And find us still adorers in these airy churches,/Singing our other Office with our saws and axes./Still teach Your children in the busy forest,/ And let some little sunlight reach us, in our mental shades, and leafy studies."[35] For Merton, monks who draw close to nature by means of forestry work worship God, since closeness to nature is closeness to God.

In 'Stranger', Merton asserts: "When no one listens/To the quiet trees/When no one notices/the sun in the pool/When no one feels /The first drop of rain/Or sees the last star…/One bird sits still/ Watching the world of God:/One turning leaf,/Two falling blossoms,/Ten circles upon the pond."[36] Here, Merton stresses that whether or not anyone observes nature, it glorifies God by simply being what it is.

City-Emptiness

For Merton, city-emptiness imagery represents technological society that can make humankind more and more a "robot of its will."[37] The following description from Merton's writings depicts the technologically dependent city in a sterile and anti-spiritual way:

> One must move through noise, stink and general anger, through blocks of dilapidation, in order to get somewhere where anger and bewilderment are concentrated in a neon lit air- conditioned enclave, glittering with products, humming with piped in music and reeking of the nondescript, sterile…smell of the technologically functioning world.[38]

In his poem 'Dirge for the City of Miami,' Merton laments the materialism, selfishness and greed associated with life in such an urban environment. According to Merton, such city experience can deaden people's spirits and sensibilities. To remedy this situation, Merton proposes the development of an urban renaissance of Christian humanism.

'In the Ruins of New York,' a section of Merton's longer poem, 'Figures for an Apocalypse', he describes New York as a city "that dressed herself in paper money. / She lived four hundred years/ With nickels running in her veins."[39] In this poem, out of the eventual ruins of this city, Merton describes nature as rising up to create a spiritual renaissance:

> Tomorrow and the day after/ Grasses and flowers will grow/
> Upon the bosom of Manhattan…/There shall be dove's nests
> And hives of bees/In the cliffs of the ancient apartments. /
> And birds shall sing in the sunny hawthorns/
> Where was once Park Ave. / And where Grand Central was,
> shall be a little hill/ Clustered with sweet, dark pine. /
> Will there be some farmer, think you, Clearing a place in the
> woods, /
> Planting an acre of bannering corn/ On the heights above
> Harlem forest?[40]

Merton paints a picture of a renewed New York City wherein humans experience peace and harmony in an Eden-like way.

Merton's 'Aubade - Harlem' describes some of Harlem's poor persons "trapped in desperation and abandoned by the more affluent, but perhaps equally hopeless, residents of their city."[41] Anguish, sorrow, and woe characterize life in Harlem where "Daylight has driven iron spikes/ Into the flesh of Jesus' hands and feet: Four flowers of blood have nailed Him to the walls…"[42] In a dehumanized Harlem, Christ is once again crucified.

Merton's 'Aubade - The City' describes urban life as alienation from meaningful human existence.[43] Inside buildings, people isolated from the natural world are spiritually numb, restless, and discontent. They opt for the death of disconnection from God, others, nature, and themselves.

City imagery is also found in Merton's 'The Tower of Babel,' a prose-poem morality play. In this work, erecting the tower represents humankind's efforts to build a city of ambition. The tower symbolizes human pride and worship of technology. In the last section of this poem, Merton outlines his vision of building another kind of city, God's city, the city of love, which he contends is the true human vocation.

> Not the wisdom of men shall build this city, nor their machines, not their power. But the great city shall be built without hands, without labor, without money, and without plans. It will be a perfect city, built on eternal foundations and it shall stand forever because it is built by the thought and the silence and the wisdom and the power of God.[44]

In *The Geography of Lograire*, Merton employs city-emptiness imagery to depict the tyranny of Westerners' superimposition of their culture on the Mayan, Eskimo, Melanesian, and Native American peoples of the world. In the Cargo cults utilized in this poem, non-Westerners seek material goods not simply because they need them but because they have internalized the belief that such objects "will establish them as equal to the white man and give them an identity as respectable as his."[45] In the following poignant way in *The Geography of Lograire*, Merton describes the sterility of the city type commodity culture he believes the Western world has substituted for religious faith: "Please send tees, shutter, flaxens, needles, tocsins, suds, pumps, raglans, botanicals, turquoise acetate, tire valves, champagne crepe pantshifts. ... Send. Send. Send.... Send us all the whiskey."[46] In other words, seek to accumulate more and more possessions, regardless of need. That is the name of the Western game!

In essence, Merton's *The Geography of Lograire* communicates the profound moral truth that "in the process of defeating primitive peoples, toppling their gods and destroying their cultures,"[47] Westerners have lost their own belief in God, exhausted their culture, and defeated themselves. Instead of choosing to collaborate in constructing the city of God, they have opted to re-build the Tower of Babel.

Incarnation

As already mentioned in this essay, for Merton the Incarnation is the self-emptying of God. God became human so that, in and through the life, death, and resurrection of Jesus Christ, human beings could become one in Christ. A number of Merton's poems treat the enfleshment of the eternal Logos.

In 'The Annunciation', Merton's speaker reflects: "Deeper than any nerve/ He enters flesh and bone/ Planting His truth, He puts our substance on. / Air, earth and rain/ Rework the frame that fire has ruined. / What was dead is waiting for His Flame. / Sparks of His Spirit spend their seeds, and hide/ To grow like irises, born before summertime."[48] In the power of the Holy Spirit, the Incarnated Logos sets the world afire with love.

In 'The Quickening of St. John the Baptist,' the Virgin Mary, who has consented to God's desire to incarnate Godself in her flesh through the power of the Spirit, visits her cousin Elizabeth to share this news. In the following way, Merton addresses the yet unborn John in Elizabeth's womb: "Sing in your cell, small anchorite! / ...What secret syllable/ Woke your young faith to the mad truth/ That an unborn baby could be washed in the Spirit of God? /Oh burning joy!"[49] Truth finds a home in John who will announce, in future days, the arrival of the Messiah, the long awaited One, the incarnated Logos who is Truth: Jesus of Nazareth.

In 'Carol', Merton heralds the birth of Jesus with these words: "God's glory, now, is kindled gentler than low candlelight/ Under the rafters of a barn: / Eternal Peace is sleeping in the hay, / And Wisdom's born in secret in a straw-roofed stable."[50] The self-emptying Logos makes entry into the world in a lowly stable. In 'A Christmas Card', Merton describes the visitation of shepherds to the stable: "And one by one the shepherds, with their snowy feet, / Stamp and shake out their hats upon the stable dirt, / And one by one kneel down to look upon their Life."[51] Jesus, the incarnated One who is Life, reveals the nature of God whose triune life is abundant love.

Merton's prose poem 'Hagia Sophia' sheds still further light on Jesus as self-emptying Love. In this poem, the Virgin Mary "shows forth in her life all that is hidden in Sophia"[52] by crowning the incarnated One, "not with what is glorious, but with what is greater than glory; the one thing greater than glory is weakness, nothingness, poverty."[53] The following final lines of 'Hagia Sophia' poignantly portray the kenotic nature of the incarnation:

> A vagrant, a destitute wanderer with dusty feet, finds his way down a new road. A homeless God, lost in the night, without papers, without identification, without even a number, a frail expendable exile lies down in desolation under the sweet stars of the world and entrusts Himself to sleep.[54]

Here, Jesus' humble birth manifests His true identity as self-emptying Divinity.

Merton's Photography

Photography, like poetry, is a medium Merton often employed to render his spiritual vision. During the final years of Merton's life, it was John Howard Griffin who introduced his friend to the art of photography. Under Griffin's guidance, Merton honed his photographic skills.

Griffin reflected that Merton possessed a passion for photography and that this "passion was simply for another means for expressing his vision; the challenge to capture on film something of the solitude and silence and essence that preoccupied him."[55] During one of his visits with Griffin, Merton handled his friend's Alpa camera "as though it were a precious jewel."[56] When Griffin asked Merton if he would like to use the Alpa, Merton responded affirmatively. Griffin noted: "It was like placing a concert grand piano at the disposal of a gifted musician who had never played on anything but an upright."[57]

From 1964-68, Merton engaged in creative photography. During these years, he practiced the Zen principle of celebrating the world as it is by contemplating it through his camera lens. Merton's photos depict the spiritual core of whatever he filmed. In each photo, Merton captures a moment, as it will never be experienced again. Merton's photos represent his embrace of the immediate, of the here and now of the everyday world of the concrete. Merton's photos bespeak the truth that reality glorifies God by simply being what it is.

The range of what caught Merton's attention included the "movement of wheat in the wind, the textures of snow, paint-spattered cans, stones, crocuses blossoming through the weeds or... the woods in all their hours, from the first fog of morning through the noon-day stillness to evening quiet."[58]

Merton photographed with a "sense of childlike wonderment,"[59] wherein he sought to capture visually the sacredness of objects such as wooden stools, baskets, rocks, roots, chairs, rivers, oceans, statues of Buddhas and human faces and figures. Most of all, Merton desired to make manifest the inner essence of whatever he photographed. He wanted his photos to be self-revelatory, i.e., to express their object's hidden wholeness.

Merton's photographs testify to his keen observance of nature and his communion with reality beyond words and concepts. His photos are characteristically simple. In them, he juxtaposes opposites such as dark and light and black and white. This enables viewers to experience the meaning of fullness in emptiness and emptiness in fullness.

Figure 1 [60]

In order to enter more deeply into the spiritual vision evident in Merton's photography, let us now examine, in some detail, a sampling of them. In Figure 1, Merton draws the viewer into the solitude and silence of this space. One's eyes linger as one gazes at the natural beauty of a thicket of dark trees in vertical position in the background set against the lightness of the sky shining through the trees and a sea of winter snow in the middle and foreground of the photo. The focal point is a tree branch that stretches across the entire height, length, and width of the photo. Small leafy objects that appear on various parts of the branch serve as a poignant reminder that, though the branch seems dead, life past and present made it what it is and the future pulses in it.

Figure 2

Merton's Figure 2 captures beauty in the twisted, complex pattern of the branches on the left juxtaposed to the rounded, cascading leaves on the right. A play of light and shadow on both the branches and the leaves accentuates the darkness of the background in the photo. In this figure, life and death coincide; they exist harmoniously. Thus, this photo invites the viewer to reflect upon the paschal mystery at work in the world.

Figure 3

Figure 3 is Merton's photo of four water lilies in full, radiant bloom amidst a sea of leaves. Light almost translucent shines on the flowers. A single flower found in the lower left serves to balance the trinity of flowers in the center of the photo. Light and shadow appear in the flowers, whose multiple petals stand upright, as if at attention. The leaves are a kind of abstract configuration of grays and black that contrasts dramatically with the sheer whiteness of the flowers that signals a resurrection motif: the ever-abiding promise of new life. Furthermore, as the Zen principle indicates and Merton affirms, these flowers and their leaves are simply being what they are - beautiful examples of God's abundant creation.

Figure 4

Merton's figure 4 focuses on the concentric circles of a woven, wooden basket. There is real wholeness found in the circularity of this basket, whose cross beams are like spokes in a wheel. The viewer of this photo is drawn inward to its center. From there, the eyes of the beholder move outward to experience circle upon circle upon circle that gives the impression of infinity. Thus, the circularity of this woven basket serves as a reminder of God's being without beginning or end.

Figure 5

In Figure 5, Merton depicts the embrace of two light, leafless trees by the branches and trunk of a single darker tree. The lighter trees sport a somewhat smooth bark, whereas a scale like bark covers the darker tree. Accentuating the stability of seemingly barren trees, this photo points to nature's stark beauty. The focal point of this photo is the two lighter trees with shadows and light dancing across their lower trunks. In this skeletal fall/winter scene, the trees point heavenward as darkness and light stand together. This seems to be a clarion call to the viewer to embrace both the light and dark dimensions of his or her life. The photo reminds one of Jesus' command to allow wheat and weeds to grow up together. Weeds and wheat symbolize the sin/grace, dark/light dialectic at work in individuals' lives. In the final analysis, the wheat of life will be harvested and the weeds will cease to exist.

Figure 6

Merton's Figure 6 highlights the pristine beauty of a smiling, little girl with dark, bushy hair who is bundled up in clothing of simple folds. In her fully exposed, small left hand, the girl holds onto a circular object, while her almost completely covered right hand touches the edge of a sheet of metal, which she uses to balance herself in order to move forward. The vitality and softness of the girl contrast sharply with the inert, hard corrugated sheet metal and cracked concrete in the photo. The simple lines of the dark sheet metal stand out against the lightness of the concrete. To the right of the girl is a simple bowl (half-seen) that casts a large shadow on the concrete. Behind the girls stands an adult dressed in dark clothing. This person, whose face is invisible in the photo, seems to be watching over the movements of the girl. The adult figure and the little girl might be compared to God and each child of God. God, the giver and guardian of life, delights in the innocence and inquisitiveness of each little one.

Figure 7

Figure 7, a photo that Merton took in Polonnaruwa, highlights the serenity of the great silence of the Buddha. In the foreground of the photo is the massive, smooth line stone carving of the Buddha in a reclining position. The Buddha's head rests on stone. His left arm is positioned parallel to the length of his body. The ringlets of the Buddha's hair are a sea of small curls. His nose is slender and his eyes are closed. The Buddha's being exudes enlightenment and unending peace. The viewer of this photo has a sense of being in the eternal now.

Merton and Adams: Zen-type Photographers

Ansel Adams is considered one of the most admired American photographers of the twentieth century. He was a genius with the camera. His career as a photographer lasted seventy years during which time he produced more than 40,000 negatives, 10,000 fine prints, and 500 international exhibitions.

In 1980, at the ceremony during which President Carter presented the Presidential Medal of Freedom to Adams, the President declared:

> At one with the American landscape, and renowned for the patient skill and timeless beauty of his work, photographer Ansel Adams has been visionary in his efforts to preserve his country's wild and scenic areas, both on film and on earth. Drawn to the beauty of nature's monuments, he is regarded by environmentalists as a monument himself, and by photographers as a national institution. It is through his foresight and fortitude that so much of America has been saved for future Americans.[61]

Ansel Adams was basically a self-taught photographer. This was also the case with Merton, although (as previously noted) Merton's friend, John H. Griffin, oriented him to the basics of photography. Though Adams and Merton took some color photographs, both men also specialized in black and white photography.

During his lifetime, Adams published many books featuring his photography. Additionally, some of his writings deal with the Zone System[62] that he developed to enhance the craft of photography. Publications treating Merton's photography appeared only after his death. At the School of Fine Arts in San Francisco, Adams established the first academic department for the teaching of photography. He also became a lecturer in creative photography.

Merton never lectured on photography yet he and Adams can be characterized as Zen-type photographers. Both men were awake to the Zen insight that there is a spiritual core in all that exists. For both Adams and Merton, photography served as a vehicle for expressing the thoughts and emotions of the human soul. Regarding this, Adams wrote: "A great photograph is one that fully expresses what one feels in the deepest sense, about what is being photographed."[63] Merton and Adams agreed on the necessity of silence and solitude for the appreciation of the sacred *vis a vis* the medium of photography.

Unlike Merton, Adams had an opportunity to photograph a wide range of the American landscape, including vistas in the states of California, Alaska, Arizona, New Mexico, Tennessee, Maine, Utah, Colorado, Wyoming, Montana and Washington. After photographing in the American Sierra High Country, Adams reflected:

I saw more clearly than I have ever seen before or since the minute detail of the grasses, the clusters of sand shifting in the wind, the small flotsam of the forest, the motion of the high clouds streaming above the peaks. There are no words to convey the moods of these moments.[64]

Mountains, valleys and streams were fountains of life for Adams who had a keen sense of the redemptive beauty of the wilderness. Regarding his many American wilderness pilgrimages, Ansel wrote: "Sometimes I think I do get to places just when God's ready to have somebody click the shutter."[65] National parks and monuments and Native American people and lands interested Adams. He photographed Navajos as figures who belonged, in the most profound way, to the landscape.[66]

Adams' photographs include clusters of tall aspens, cascades of water in Yosemite Valley, rounded mountains in the Smokies, desert sands and brush, saguaro cactus, sprawling oak trees, rocks and limpets, hot springs in Yellowstone National Park, grounded icebergs in Alaska, wood grains, a moonrise in New Mexico, a Mormon temple, and cypress in the fog.

Unlike Adams, Merton did not often travel far to engage in his creative photography, though in his final year of life he journeyed to New Mexico, California, Alaska, and the Far East and, in these places, photographed mountains, the ocean, Native Americans, and Buddha statues. Like Adams, Merton had a great love of barns, trees, roots and rocks. Each one of these geniuses with the camera captured the beauty of these created objects in exquisite photographs marked by masterful attention to detail.

Photographing nature led both Merton and Adams to God. Merton wrote: "But the great, gashed, half-naked mountain is another of God's saints. There is no other like it. It is alone in its character; nothing in the world ever did or ever will imitate God in quite the same way. And that is its sanctity."[67] Merton reiterated this message about the sacredness of nature when he penned the following thoughts from his hermitage:

Up here in the woods is seen the New Testament.... The wind comes through the trees and you breathe it. ... One might say I had decided to marry the silence of the forest.... It is necessary for me to see the first point of light which begins to be dawn. It is necessary to be present alone at the resurrection of day, in the black silence when the sun appears.[68]

Echoing Merton's euphoria with nature, Ansel Adams captured his experience of the Grand Canyon in America's Southwest in the following way: "It is all very beautiful and magical here - a quality which cannot be described. You have to live it and breathe it, let the sun bake it into you."[69]

In essence, Merton and Adams are Zen-type photographers whose black and white images provide a visual feast reflective of these artists' awake-ness to reality.   On film, both men caught some of their moments of spiritual enlightenment. For these kindred spirits, photography served as a medium to communicate to others the grandeur of the jewel that is creation.

Photography provided a way for both Thomas Merton and Ansel Adams to search for and find the "hidden wholeness" of reality that testifies to the One who is the Sacred: God.   Perhaps Alfred Stieglitz's comment about Adams sums some of this up best: "But it's good for me to know that there is Ansel Adams loose somewhere in this world of ours...."[70] The same can be said of Merton. How wonderful it is that both men sojourned this earth for some of their years with a camera in their creative hands.

Conclusion

This study has explored various facets of Thomas Merton's spiritual vision through reflections on some of his poetry, his photography in general, and a few of his photos in particular. It has demonstrated that, for Merton, each of these mediums served as a vehicle for and expression of his quest for God. Thomas Merton, the poet and Zen-type photographer, has gifted the human community with the jewels of his poems and black and white photographs.

Notes

1. Thomas Merton, 'Art and Spirituality', in Thomas P. McDonnell (ed.), *A Thomas Merton Reader* (New York: Double Day Image Books, 1996), pp. 386-415 (386).

2. Thomas Merton, *New Seeds of Contemplation* (New York: New Directions, 1972), p. 269.

3. Thomas Merton, 'Reality, Art, Prayer,' *The Commonweal* LXI. 25(March 25, 1955), pp. 658-59.

4. See Thomas Merton, 'Notes on Sacred and Profane Art', *Jubilee* 4. 7(November 1956), pp. 25-32 (25).

5. See Thomas Merton, 'Message to Poets', in *Raids on the Unspeakable* (New York: New Directions, 1966), p. 161.

6. Thomas Merton, 'Answers on Art and Freedom', in *Raids on the Unspeakable*, p. 173.

7. Thomas Merton, *The Seven Storey Mountain* (New York: Harcourt, Brace and Co., 1948), pp. 389-90.

8. Merton, *The Seven Storey Mountain*, p. 304.

9. Lynn Szabo, 'The Sound of Sheer Silence: A Study in the Poetics of Thomas Merton', *The Merton Annual* 13(2000), pp. 208-22 (210).

10. See Gloria K. Lewis, 'Thomas Merton: Strategies of a Master Teacher of Poetry', *The Merton Seasonal* 22.3(Autumn 1977), pp. 17-20 (17).

11. Thomas Merton, Tape #54:6, 'Analysis of a Poem', 12.5.64, at the Thomas Merton Center, Bellarmine University, Louisville, Ky.

12. Thomas Merton, 'Poetry and Contemplation: A Reappraisal', *The Commonweal* LXIX.4 (October 24, 1958), pp. 87-92 (89).

13. Thomas Merton, *The Asian Journal of Thomas Merton* (eds. Naomi Burton, Patrick Hart, and James Laughlin; New York: New Directions, 1974), pp. 233-34.

14. Thomas Merton, *The Collected Poems of Thomas Merton* (New York: New Directions, 1977), p. 669.

15. See Robert Waldron, 'Merton Bells: A Clarion Call to Wholeness', *The Merton Seasonal* 18.1(Winter, 1993), pp. 25-28 (26).

16. Merton, *Collected Poems*, p. 651.

17. Merton, *Collected Poems*, p. 651.

18. Merton, *Collected Poems*, p. 421.

19. Merton, *Collected Poems*, p. 421.

20. Merton, *Collected Poems*, p. 452.

21. Merton, *Collected Poems*, p. 452.

22. Merton, *Collected Poems*, p. 240.

23. Merton, *Collected Poems*, p. 280.

24. Thomas Merton, *Love and Living* (eds. Naomi B. Stone and Patrick Hart; New York: Harcourt and Brace and Co, 1985), p. 20.

25. Merton, *Collected Poems*, pp. 340-41.

26. Merton, *Collected Poems*, pp. 337-38.

27. Ross Labrie, *The Art of Thomas Merton* (Fort Worth, TX: Texas Christian University Press, 1979), p. 47.

28. Thomas Merton, *The Secular Journal of Thomas Merton* (New York: Farrar, Straus and Cudahy, 1959), pp. 167-68.

29. Thomas Merton, *The Sign of Jonas* (New York: New Directions, 1986), p. 215.

30. Merton, *The Sign of Jonas*, p. 216.

31. Thomas Merton, *Conjectures of a Guilty Bystander* (New York: Doubleday, 1989), p. 280.

32. Patrick Hart, *Thomas Merton: First and Last Memories* (Bardstown, Ky.: Necessity, 1986), unpaged.

33. Thomas Merton, *The Road to Joy: The Letters of Thomas Merton to New and Old Friends* (ed. Robert E. Daggy; San Diego: Harcourt Brace Jovanovich, 1993), p. 330.

34. Merton, *Collected Poems*, p. 96.

35. Merton, *Collected Poems*, p. 96.

36. Merton, *Collected Poems*, pp. 289-90.

37. Therese Lentfoehr, 'Social Concern in the Poetry of Thomas Merton', in Gerald S. Twomey (ed.), *Thomas Merton: Prophet in the Belly of a Paradox* (New York: Paulist Press, 1978), pp. 111-37 (114).

38. Merton, *Conjectures of a Guilty Bystander*, p. 257.

39. Merton, *Collected Poems*, p. 144.

40. Merton, *Collected Poems*, pp. 144-45.

41. Patrick F. O'Connell, 'Thomas Merton's Wake-Up Calls: Aubades and Monastic Dawn Poems from A *Man in the Divided Sea*', *The Merton Annual* 12 (1999), pp. 129-63 (131).

42. Merton, *Collected Poems*, p. 82.

43. O'Connell, 'Thomas Merton's Wake-Up Calls', p. 131.

44. Footnote 45 in Therese Lentfoehr, *Words and Silence: the Poetry of Thomas Merton* (New York: New Directions, 1979) p. 96.

45. Thomas Merton, 'Arts and Letters', *Sewanee Review* 81(1973), p. 164.

46. Thomas Merton, *The Geography of Lograire* (New York: New Directions, 1969), pp. 50-51.

47. Merton, 'Arts and Letters', p. 164.

48. Merton, *Collected Poems*, p. 284.

49. Merton, *Collected Poems*, p. 200.

50. Merton, *Collected Poems*, p. 89.

51. Merton, *Collected Poems*, p. 185.

52. Merton, *Collected Poems*, p. 369.

53. Merton, *Collected Poems*, p. 370.

54. Merton, *Collected Poems*, p. 371.

55. John Howard Griffin, 'Les grandes amities', *Continuum* 7(Summer 1969), pp. 286-94 (291).

56. Griffin, 'Les grandes amities', p. 291.

57. Griffin, 'Les grandes amities', p. 291.

58. Thomas Merton and John Howard Griffin, *A Hidden Wholeness: The Visual World of Thomas Merton* (Dunwoody, Ga.: Norman S. Berg Publisher, 1977), p. 49.

59. Deba Patnaik, *Geography of Holiness: The Photography of Thomas Merton* (New York: Pilgrim Press, 1980), p. ix.

60. The photos in this essay are used with the permission of the Merton Legacy Trust. The Thomas Merton Center (Bellarmine University, Louisville, Ky.) catalogue numbers of these photos are as follows:

Figure 1: Photo 1171; Figure 2: Photo 56; Figure 3: Photo 0147; Figure 4: Photo 1227; Figure 5: Photo 0106; Figure 6: Photo 1007; Figure 7: Photo 1123.

61. Quoted in Basil Cannon, *Ansel Adams* (New York: Gramercy Books, 1999), pp. 54-55.

62. This system divides the range of light into eleven different zones from total black to pure white, which a photographer can utilize to determine and create different tones in a final print.

63. Ansel Adams, *Ansel Adam's Guide: Basic Techniques of Photography* (ed. John P. Schaefer; Boston: Little, Brown and Co., 1992), p. 3.

64. Quoted in Robert Turnage, 'Ansel Adams: The Role of the Artist in the Environmental Movement', *The Living Wilderness*, 43.148(March 1980), pp. 4-31 (5).

65. Quoted in Erich Peter Nash (ed.), *Ansel Adams: The Spirit in Wild Places* (New York: Todtri Book Publishers, 1995), p. 13.

66. Nash, *Ansel Adams: The Spirit in Wild Places*, p. 35.

67. Thomas Merton, *Seeds of Contemplation* (New York: New Directions, 1949), pp. 25-26.

68. Thomas Merton, 'Day of a Stranger', *The Hudson Review* 20.2 (Summer 1967), pp. 211-18 (214-16).

69. Ansel Adams, 'Letter to Alfred Stieglitz, Ghost Ranch, Aliquiu, New Mexico, Sept. 21, 1937', in Andrea S. Stillman (ed.), *Ansel Adams: The Grand Canyon and the Southwest* (Boston, Ma.: Little Brown and Co., 2000), p. 107.

70. Quoted in Nash, *Ansel Adams: The Spirit in Wild Places*, p. 670.

Wisdom, Sapiential Poetry, and Personalism: Exploring Some of Thomas Merton's Ideas for Values Education

Ross Keating

An understandable reaction to post-modern eclecticism by some traditional institutions and leaders is for them to strongly assert their particular set of values in an over-arching claim above the myriad of other conflicting perspectives. But instead of gaining expected attention, each of their voices becomes just one more vying for a greater "market share" in the growing uncertainty amongst people of what is true, what is the meaning of life (including self-identity), and how best to live. Unintentionally, or perhaps otherwise, these institutions and leaders join the ranks of those global marketing companies who are attempting to sell a lifestyle of meaning and purpose associated with their product. However, meaning and purpose are not values that can be bought. What today's market sells is brand mystique, in the hope of fostering a client's identity through association with a branded product and thus gaining long-term client allegiance. What this article suggests is that teachers should avoid promotional-type "marketing" strategies in the teaching of traditional values but rather attempt to awaken students to a presence of wisdom that is to be found within life and living. The essay will explore this idea in the light of Thomas Merton's ideas on wisdom, sapiential poetry and personalism.

According to Neil Postman, education should provide an alternative view to that which dominates society, so as to provide students with a more balanced outlook on life. This corrective role, Postman argues, needs to be built into a school's curriculum. In the late sixties and early seventies, he saw this role as a subversive one, and argued that students should be allowed to question authority and to approach learning as an act of self-guided exploration. Ten years later, in response to what he saw as largely a commercial, mass-media-driven society he promoted the idea of teaching as a conserving activity, and promoted the skills of critical analysis so that students could be made aware of manipulative self-interests acting within society.

In his latest book in this progression, *The End of Education* (1995), his most radical, he continues his appraisal of education in a society that he feels has lost its identity and sense of moral direction. This time he makes the point that schools should not attempt to serve the public but rather "create" a public; and that teachers need to make this their foremost responsibility. Postman's own solution for this present predicament is for teachers to start with a vision—a vision of their students entering public life "imbued with confidence, a sense of purpose, [and] a respect for learning, and tolerance." And for this vision to become reality, he argues, two things are necessary: "the existence of shared narratives and the capacity of such narratives to provide an inspired reason for schooling."[1] In his elaboration of this position he places an emphasis on the word "inspired." In his view, schools now need common "gods" more than common goals. Postman then goes on to suggest five such "gods" or overarching narratives that could possibly serve as sources of enduring inspiration for students.

All the narratives have a common underlying theme, which is the idea of unity within diversity. His first narrative is that without sacrificing one's cultural, national or religious identity a person "can be enlarged by adopting the role of Earth's caretaker."[2] This development of an environmental consciousness is something young people and schools have generally embraced. Second is the narrative that says the existential human condition in one of unknowing and in Postman's words "Therein lies the possibility of our redemption: Knowing that we do not know and cannot know the whole truth, we may move towards it inch by inch by discarding what we know to be false."[3] This creates an educational agenda that celebrates mistakes in learning not as failings but as points of clarification and opportunities towards better understanding. Under this narrative, Postman gives a more humble definition of science as "a method for correcting our mistakes" and not, as popularly imagined, "a source of ultimate truth."[4]

Thirdly, there is the narrative that encourages dialogue, debate, and experimentation and stands against hardened dogmatism. In Postman's view, "All points [of view] are admissible. The only thing we have to fear is that someone will insist on putting in an exclamation point [after their point of view] when we are not yet finished [our discussions]."[5] Fourthly, there is the narrative that says diversity is something to be celebrated as a source of vitality and creativity rather than suppressed in the interests of a contrived notion of shared "cultural literacy." In explaining this case, Postman points out "whenever a language or art form becomes fixed in time and impermeable, drawing only on its own resource, it is punished by entropy. Whenever difference is allowed, the result is growth and strength."[6] Lastly, there is the narrative of the power of language, about which Postman makes the comment, "There is, to be sure, a world of 'not-words'. But, unlike all the other creatures on the planet, we have access to it only through the world of words."[7]

Although much can be found within Thomas Merton's writings that directly addresses all of Postman's proposals, it is the last dimension of the power of language, and specifically poetic language, that I now wish to explore in the light of some of Thomas Merton's ideas. Merton has been described as a "spiritual master," a title he would have felt uncomfortable with, preferring himself to be known in later life simply as a writer.[8] His extensive writings reflect a person who had a profound understanding of the dignity of the human person: a poet, a seer, a questioner, a social critic, a humorist, and one who had the ability to reach into and express with clarity what lies at the heart of Eastern spiritualities and Western theology.

Knowledge, the Way of Knowing, and the Knower

In any learning situation, three dimensions are always present: knowledge, the way of knowing, and the knower. Various approaches to learning put a different emphasis and value on each of these dimensions. The most dominating epistemological framework of the twentieth century and still today is science, whose methodology has been adopted by modern philosophy, the social sciences, and significant areas of educational research. In this approach emphasis and value is placed on objective, quantifiable knowledge and a single way of knowing: essentially the inductive method. In this approach the subjectivity of the knower has no value except in recording results, and even this may be seen as introducing a distorting factor to the validity of empirical evidence. The dominance of scientific epistemology has led to what has been called the "religious-fication" of science,[9] while others have warned of its dangers, that it "edits out spiritual truths in the way X-ray films omit the beauty of faces."[10]

Recently, however, the actual categorization of scientific knowledge as a legitimate form of "knowledge" has come under question by contemporary theorists such as the social constructionist Kenneth Gergen, who writes that

> There is little reason to believe that we literally experience or "see the world" through a system of categories . . . However, we gain substantially if we consider the world-structuring process as linguistic rather than cognitive. It is through an *a priori* commitment to particular forms of language (genres, conventions, speech codes and so on) that we place boundaries around what we take to be "the real." ... In Goodman's terms, it is *description* not *cognition* that constructs the factual world.[11]

From Merton's perspective, so-called scientific knowledge is only "provisional," being that part of our knowing, which is "'clear' and non-hidden" – in other words, descriptive, in the sense as outlined by Gergen.[12] In his writings Merton introduces a far more encompassing epistemology, that of wisdom, which according to him "embraces and includes science ... [for] behind all that is unveiled and 'discovered' [through science], wisdom touches that which is still veiled and covered."[13] The critical point here is that Merton does not contrast scientific knowledge with wisdom, or what he calls sapiential knowledge (for that would be to fall into the scientific, classificatory paradigm), but says it is the hidden aspect of all things beneath their non-hidden or surface "description."[14] He also uses the verb "touches" for wisdom, thus hinting at an approach that is personal and intimate as opposed to the objective, calculating approach of science. This fits in nicely with his use of the term "sapiential," which derives from the Latin *sapere*, meaning "to taste"—sapiential knowledge is thus gained by "tasting," and is accordingly a more experiential kind of knowledge.

Merton calls scientific knowledge "provisional" for it is incomplete, not total. Wisdom is complete knowledge, known and understood in the knower in the form of a cognitive realization through direct apprehension or intuition. This kind of knowledge does not appeal to any external authority or objective standards for its credibility but rather appeals directly to the authenticity of a person's own being. This understanding of sapiential knowledge, I would argue, is what is missing from our present educational agenda and urgently needs to be built into our teaching curricula.

Merton describes his own realization of this type of sapiential knowledge in a poetic manner, which is the only way it can be described (although it is a universally shared experience), as an apprehension, in "all visible things," of an

> invisible fecundity, a dimmed light, a meek namelessness, a hidden wholeness. This mysterious Unity and Integrity is Wisdom, the Mother of all . . . There is in all things an inexhaustible sweetness and purity, a silence that is a fount of action and joy. It rises up in wordless gentleness and flows out to me from the unseen roots of all created beings . . . [15]

What this description does is to invite readers, through the agency of words, to "taste" this type of communion experience for themselves or to affirm their own experience against it. In this specific sapiential learning instance, the knower is of central importance and needs to cultivate the disposition of wholehearted attentive awareness rather than that of a detached observer as in scientific investigations. The qualities of wisdom, "inexhaustible sweetness" etc., which Merton refers to are also to be found expressed in a multitude of ways in the world's wisdom literature as the underlying truths of existence and are named in general terms as truth, love, purity and beauty. These qualities are not the romantic niceties of life as opposed to all that is harsh such as suffering and violence but represent the verities of existence that can spiritually support and comfort a person in the midst of hardship. The proof of this is in the fact of their cross-cultural acceptance and staying power and universal elevation under the title of wisdom.

They are certainly not doctrines to be learnt, thought constructions, scientific conclusions, nor the product of critical rational thought. Rather they are to be discovered built into the very spiritual fabric of existence itself, as Merton found them. To find ("taste") these qualities is to know sapientially. This knowledge does not build bridges, cure diseases nor give a definitive meaning to life; what it does give, which is essential for living, is nourishment for the soul, spiritual health, or what the poet Edward Hirsh calls "soul culture."[16]

In contrast to Merton's description of wisdom as a real presence to be experienced beneath or beyond the descriptive surface of things is the following statement by the contemporary theologian Don Cupitt, which is representative of a contemporary nominalistic attitude to language. It represents what could be described as a type of an anti-wisdom manifesto that invites readers only into an interactive world of words that point to nothing beyond themselves:

1. As both philosophy and religion have in the past taught, there is indeed an unseen intelligible world, or spirit world, about us and within us.
2. The invisible world is the world of words and other symbols.
3. The entire supernatural world of religion is a mythical representation of the world of language.
4. Through the practice of its religion, a society represents to itself, and confirms, the varied ways in which language builds its world.[17]

Here we stay firmly lodged on the page where words, now elevated as having a mind of their own, play and perhaps even misbehave without their creator's consent. In this instance words are seen as mere signs with no "invisible fecundity" illuminating them, stripped of any symbolic value and potentially revealing sapiential presence. Ironically this attitude illustrates distrust in language, in the mysterious ability of words to point to something of value beyond themselves and beyond quantitative formulations. From Cupitt's perspective words have been well and truly flung from the gates of paradise into an unconsoling exile of their own and left to amuse themselves as best they can. In Merton's eyes this would be a world devoid of poetry where wisdom is allowed no revealing presence.

Sapiential Poetry

Working out of the Christian tradition and its symbols, although analogous ideas can be found in other spiritual traditions, Merton elaborated on the unique connection of wisdom and poetic language. For Merton, not all poetry had to be connected with wisdom but as George Kilcourse affirms, poetry as an expression of a "paradise consciousness" was central to his understanding of poetic experience.[18] This understanding is illustrated, for instance, in his review of Louis Zukofsky's poetry. Here Merton describes how the reader can be given an intimation of a pristine, archetypal Edenic state, the state of the spiritual origin of all things, through the imaginative language of poetry. In a sense, for Merton, all created things contain a vestige of this primordial state, which the poet can penetrate and reveal. Merton writes that

> All really valid poetry (poetry that is fully alive and asserts its reality by its power to generate imaginative life) is a kind of recovery of paradise. Not that the poet comes up with a report that he, an unusual man, has found his own way back into Eden: but the living line and the generative association, the new sound, the music, the structure, are somehow grounded in a renewal of vision and hearing so that he who reads and understands recognizes that here is a new start, a new creation. Here the world gets another chance. Here man, here the reader discovers himself getting another start in life, in hope, in imagination, and why? Hard to say, but probably because the language itself is getting another chance, through the innocence, the teaching, the good faith, the honest senses of the workman poet.[19]

What Merton is suggesting is that for "fully alive" or sapiential poetry, of which Zukofsky is an example, "a new creation"—as he calls it—comes into being that radiates the same "wordless gentleness" that flows out from the unseen roots of all created things in nature. Poetry of this kind, in other words, provides a connection to and a communion with life's underlying depth and re-creates it in poetic terms, thus affirming its presence. This unique function of sapiential poetry is of vital importance for it directly contributes towards and maintains the spiritual health of a person – that ineffable quality of being which children generally have in abundance but which tends to become dissipated with adolescence due to lack of proper care and attention. If, however, adolescents are encouraged to cultivate an appreciation of sapiential poetry and come to understand its value as a means to "taste" the unifying wisdom that permeates all things, then they will eventually come to see that they are not just isolated psycho-physical beings left to survive in an alien landscape, but are in a certain sense "connected" with all existence. And, most significantly of all, this type of wisdom-filled poetry has the potential gradually to awaken the latent presence of wisdom that is mysteriously resident deep within themselves. Once this occurs then this experience, in turn, can be expressed poetically and celebrated by others in an act of spiritual community.

While some readers, perhaps those conditioned by scientific empiricism, may view this transformative potential of sapiential poetry with scepticism and see it only as a wishful projection of a closely held belief or desire, it is nonetheless a view that has an ancient heritage. Merton himself saw this potential as holding the key to understanding the enduring power of the psalms.[20] The Polish poet Czeslaw Milosz, with whom Merton exchanged a substantial amount of correspondence, noted that the idea of revering poetry as an expression of wisdom or divinity was found in pre-Homeric Greek culture where it was described in terms of an epiphany, that is, "an unveiling of reality":

> What in Greek was called *epiphaneia* meant the appearance, the arrival of a divinity among mortals or its recognition under a familiar shape of man or woman. Epiphany thus interrupts the everyday flow of time and events and enters as one privileged moment when we intuitively grasp a deeper more essential reality hidden in things or persons.[21]

To understand, experientially, what it means to "intuitively grasp a deeper more essential reality," which I take as being akin to Merton's idea of knowing sapientially, we need to begin with the question: What is the nature of poetic experience?

Poetic Experience

As master of novices at Gethsemani, Merton used Rainer Maria Rilke's poetry in his classes to illustrate what he meant by poetic experience.[22] He supported the view that poetic experience provided a means of nourishing a person's spiritual life and that it was analogous to religious experience – religious experience being the same kind of experience "only deeper." Indeed one of Merton's reasons for presenting poetry in his conferences was to help his students gain a deeper appreciation of religious experience.

One of the poems Merton used in his teaching was Rilke's "The Panther," which was a work that Rilke described as marking a threshold experience in his own understanding of poetry. During his teaching of poetry, Merton stressed to his students that they should firstly "get the image, get the picture," which in his view was sharpened and made all the more vivid in the imagination of the reader by the sound and rhythm of the language. A clear apprehension of the images, he argued, provided the avenue into the poetic experience of the poem, and to later reflecting clearly upon its possible meaning.

Rilke's poem begins with an image of a panther in a zoo, locked in a cage like a prisoner and pacing about a small circle, which appears to Rilke to be "like a dance of strength about a center / in which a mighty will stands stupefied."[23] The last stanza, which Merton gave most attention to, reads:

> Only sometimes when the pupil's film
> soundlessly opens . . . then one image fills
> and glides through the quiet tension of the limbs
> into the heart and ceases and is still.

The "one image" in this verse is that of Rilke whom the panther momentarily sees standing outside the cage. The movement of Rilke's image going inward and penetrating into the heart of the panther, and making contact there, was for Merton analogous to "how" and "where" a poet made an interior contact with a poetic object. At the same time, implicitly stated in the poem, the image of the panther, likewise, is passing into Rilke's heart and it is this silent and mysterious interpenetrative contact, in Merton's view, that "constitutes the poem": it was this mutual deep "contact," this spiritual encounter that awakens a new creative consciousness, which could be called poetic consciousness. Such a moment of consciousness, for instance, is the essence of the Japanese verse form, the haiku, which was adopted by many Buddhist Zen masters as a vehicle for the transmission of their wisdom teachings in which the quality of an "experience" was the real message, not just words, which were only the vehicle.[24] It can be seen aptly expressed in the following haiku by the Zen poet Basho, which attempts to capture the experience of a moment of heightened awareness, and in so doing "stretches" the reader's consciousness to grasp this same high degree of awareness as that experienced by the poet:

> In the utter silence
> Of a temple
> A cicada's voice alone
> Penetrates the rocks.[25]

According to Merton, the actual writing of a poem like Basho's haiku or Rilke's "The Panther" was through a re-creative perception of the poet's original interpenetrative contact. This re-creative perception took place within and utilized the powers of the poet's imagination. In this imaginative act the original experience became actualized aesthetically and given concrete form. The word "aesthetic," from the Greek meaning "perception by the senses, especially by feeling," nicely accords with this imaginative act.[26] The power of the imagination by which the poem was written was not, in Merton's view, a play of fantasy in which the mind passively viewed some superficial and self-generating "mental movie," but rather came out of the deep and creative function of the poet's intellect. This was something Merton learned from William Blake.[27] Accordingly, the poem produced, if it was an adequate poem, was not a description of the poetic object, nor a record of the poet's feeling on seeing the poetic object, but rather a type of union of the two. In Merton's words the poem represented a "new being."

In another of Rilke's poems, "The Merry-Go-Round,"[28] Merton further explored these ideas with his students. The poem begins:

Under the roof and the roof's shadow turns
this train of painted horses for a while
in this bright land that lingers
before it perishes. . . .

The intervening verses poetically capture the movement of the merry-go-round, the various animals on it, and the captivated children happily whirling around. It concludes with the lines:

And on the horses swiftly going by
are shining girls who have outgrown this play;
in the middle of the flight they let their eyes
glance here and there and near and far away –

and now and then a big white elephant.

And all this hurries towards the end, so fast,
Whirling futilely, evermore the same.

A flash of red, of green, of gray, goes past,
and then a little scarce-begun profile.
And oftentimes a blissful dazzling smile
vanishes in this blind and breathless game.

Reflecting upon his own poetic experience of this work Merton felt that Rilke had made interpenetrative contact with the transient yet beautiful "imaginative life of childhood." And in the poem's structure, its music, and particularly its imagery, he felt that Rilke gave beautiful aesthetic form to this contact. At the sapiential level of this poetic experience through the poetic trans-figuring of an everyday merry-go-round, Merton suggested that Rilke had imaginatively recreated Eden before the "fall" – "this bright land that lingers," the land of "blind and breathless" play, of child-like innocence and purity. In a sense, Rilke had given Eden a new "face," which could be poetically "touched" and known sapientially by the reader. "There it is, Eden, before your poetic eyes," Merton seemed to be saying to his students, "taste it, expe-rience it, know it!"

None of this makes any sense, however, if the reader cannot imaginatively recreate what the poet had initially experienced. Imaginative connection is a key idea in Merton's understanding of poetry; the reader has to experience what the poet experienced, otherwise the poem does not come alive in the consciousness of the reader. Imaginative connection is the electric charge that jumps across from one consciousness to another. For this to happen words creatively selected and placed on the page to form a poem cannot simply be read but need to be listened to so as to sense their fully revelatory potential and power. Ultimately, in Merton's view, words have been bestowed with the potential to carry the charge of divine utterance:

> Language is not merely the material or the instrument which the poet uses . . . When in the moment of inspiration the poet's creative intelligence is married with the inborn wisdom of human language (the Word of God and Human Nature – Di-vinity and Sophia) then in the very flow of new and individual intuitions, the poet utters the voice of that wonderful and mysterious world of God-manhood – it is the transfigured, spiritualized, and divinized cosmos that speaks through him, and through him utters its praise of the Creator.[29]

From this passage it is obvious why Merton saw poetry as a means for the cultivation of a person's spiritual life – "that wonderful and mysterious world of God-manhood." In his view, a person's spiritual life grew in direct proportion to that person's openness and the quality of his or her responsiveness to all of creation. And poetry, as he proposed, provided the means, a specific practice, for cultivating a profound depth of responsiveness. This, in short, was Merton's path for the gaining of wisdom in the midst of life. If a person, however, chose to withdraw from life, under the delusion that this was an efficacious spiritual practice, then in Merton's opinion they would eventually suffer a type of spiritual death, for they would be without access to life-giving wisdom. Spiritual death, it could be argued, may also ensue when the environment in which a person lives has become overly lifeless and artificial. This was another issue that Merton addressed.

Personalism

Before the word *simulacrum* was popularized by the post-modern cultural theorist Jean Baudrillard, Merton recalls his delight in finding it the Latin Vulgate. He writes that the word

> presents itself as a very suggestive one to describe an advertisement, or an over-inflated political presence, or that face on the TV screen. The word shimmers, grins, cajoles. It is a fine word for something monumentally phony. It occurs for instance in the last line of the First Epistle of John. But there it is usually translated as "idols" . . . "Little Children, watch out for the simulacra!" –watch out for the national, the regional, the institutional images!
>
> Does it occur to us that if, in fact, we live in a society which is par excellence that of the *simulacrum*, we are the champion idolaters of all history?[30]

The world of *simulacra* creates a world of simulation, what Baudrillard calls *hyperreality* and Merton, the world of idols. It is a world without any origin in or connection to reality, and therefore without access to wisdom. And without access to wisdom, as mentioned previously, spiritual "starvation" soon follows. It is a world that is not formed from a creative act but is indefinitely reproducible from "miniaturized units, from matrices, memory banks and command models."[31] It is a world signified by brand names, in which brand mystique, brand identity, brand placement, and building a brand-loyalty base amongst clients constitutes its existence.

It is a world in which the Ford car company, for instance, can buy Jaguar and pay a staggering 84% of its buying price just for the Jaguar name; it is a world in which, as one commentator observed, "Put Nike in a school playground to help tackle bullying and you begin to reach the most street-hardened kids"; it is a world in which "brands generate more [so-called] trust than any institution – government, church, [or] political [parties]"; it is a world in which "consumers want [to find] readily accessible packaged meanings" – as one brand consultant remarked, "Someone else has thought through the difficult issues, and they [the consumers] can then align themselves with that."[32] For Merton what most characterized this "phony" world was its dangerous and rampant misuse of language. As Thomas Del Prete states:

> Whether in the realms of advertising, politics, art, religion, love, or most destructively, war, the nature and use of language could mean the difference between openness, dialogue, and . . . tautology, control, and manipulation. Language which no longer conveys, or no longer is intended to convey, any semblance of truth or reality is, in Merton's eyes, "denatured," neither a means of authentic personal communication, nor a signification for or evocation of reality.[33]

Merton warned that the world of simulacra, of "denatured" language, actually infiltrates the unconscious and leaves individuals (a whole society) with a "denatured" identity and sense of self-worth – as if each was nothing more than a brand-labelled item for sale in a constantly changing brand-driven world. In his unfinished work, *The Inner Experience*, Merton called upon Freud's insights to present his notion of how an aspect of a person's "exterior self" can possibly become "unconscious." He argued that

> the exterior self is not limited to consciousness. Freud's concept of the superego as an infantile and introjected substitute for conscience fits very well my idea of the exterior and alienated self. It is at once completely exterior and yet at the same time buried in unconsciousness.[34]

This is a penetrating psychological insight and one that may help to explain why the hold of a mass-market, brand-saturated world is so powerful, for the roots of such a world, over time, bury themselves in the individual's unconscious. It perhaps also helps to explain why many people in contemporary society find themselves in a state of deadened (not heightened) sensibility from which they seek release in moments of escapist non-sense, which are explicitly marketed for them using these exact terms.

   As a direct consequence of the condition in which an individual's "exterior and alienated self" is "buried in unconsciousness," Merton argues, a "fake interiorization" occurs. Although he used this idea to talk about "false mysticism" and "pseudo-religiosity" it also helps to explain, on a more mundane level, the insidious hoax that can be spun by the world of *simulacra*: "Little children watch out for the simulacra!" or you'll be well and truly duped.

Merton's response to this type of cosmetic world was not to outwardly package Christianity as a more appealing "brand" for understanding life's meaning so that an individual can at least be offered the opportunity of "purchasing and identifying with the *right* product." It was to strongly reaffirm a vision of the unique person, made in the image of God, as distinct from the individual whose identity is always precarious, egotistically centered, and constantly in flux depending on what is "in fashion" at the time.[35] Merton explained his vision of person in the same way as he presented sapiential poetry, as "an experience and an attitude, rather than a system of thought."[36] The person, for Merton, and here his thoughts on wisdom and science are reiterated, was

> an intelligence open to the divine light, not merely to the study of objects – "observable data." The full dimension of personal fulfilment is to be sought not simply in knowledge and technical control of matter, but in contemplative wisdom which unites knowledge with love above and beyond the subject-object relationship which is characteristic of ordinary empirical observation.[37]

In Merton's view the person is not unlike the sapiential poem, for both proceed from the same source and both are formed through an act of re-creative perception of what lies at the heart of reality: the poet encountering wisdom through a particular object creates a genuine poem, while the individual encountering wisdom within his or her own being creates their own personal identity in that Image. In both the sapiential poem and the "created" person, wisdom can be found. And just as scientific knowledge in Merton's view was only a descriptive and "provisional" knowledge of reality, so too the individual's knowledge of himself or herself as a self-contained entity is only descriptive and "provisional," waiting to be completed through knowing wisely. Merton explained as much when he wrote:

> The individual matures and blossoms out in full personality only when the gift of spirit and of grace endows our natural

capacities with unique and creative powers to *make our own gift* to our world and to other[s] . . . The person is the individual not only as member of the species but as "image of God," that is to say as the *free and creative source of a gift of love and meaning* which, if it is not made and given, is irreplaceable and cannot be given by another.[38]

On this last crucial point hangs the difference between a fulfilled, creative, Christian adult life and what is not. It is a vision that deepens that presented by Postman at the beginning of this paper. The movement of the self-conscious individual into the expansive consciousness of the person as a "free and creative source of a gift of love and meaning"—"which cannot be given by another"—is a movement from adolescence into adulthood and spiritually defines adulthood. An understanding of sapiential knowledge as presented through poetry can help facilitate this transition because it reveals wisdom as inherent in life and living.

Notes

1. Neil Postman, *The End of Education: Defining the Value of Schools* (New York: Vintage Books, 1995), pp. 17-18.

2. Postman, *End of Education*, p. 65.

3. Postman, *End of Education*, p. 67.

4. Postman, *End of Education*, p. 68

5. Postman, *End of Education*, p. 74.

6. Postman, *End of Education*, p. 78.

7. Postman, *End of Education*, pp. 83-84.

8. *The Intimate Merton* eds. Patrick Hart and Jonathon Montaldo (Oxford: Lion, 1999), p. 11; David D. Cooper, *Thomas Merton's Art of Denial: The Evolution of a Radical Humanist* (Athens: University of Georgia, 1989), p. 167.

9. Fred Newman and Lois Holzman, *The End of Knowing* (London: Routledge, 1997), p. 7.

10. Phil Cousineau, *The Way Things Are: Conversations with Huston Smith on the Spiritual Life* (Berkeley: University of California, 2003), p. 10.

11. Newman and Holzman, *End of Knowing*, p. 27.

12. Thomas Merton, *Contemplation in a World of Action* (Garden City, NY: Doubleday, 1971), p. 190.

13. Merton, *Contemplation in a World of Action*, p. 190.

14. George Kilcourse, *Ace of Freedoms: Thomas Merton's Christ* (Notre Dame, Indiana: University of Notre Dame, 1993), p. 227.

15. Thomas Merton, *Hagia Sophia, The Collected Poems* (New York: New Directions, 1977), p. 363.

16. Edward Hirsch, *How to Read a Poem and Fall in Love with Poetry* (New York: Harcourt Brace, 1999), p. 8.

17. Don Cupitt, *After God: The Future of Religion* (London: Weindenfeld & Nicolson, 1997), p. xv.

18. Kilcourse, *Ace of Freedoms*, p.66.

19. *The Literary Essays of Thomas Merton*, ed. Patrick Hart (New York: New Directions, 1981), p. 128.

20. Thomas Merton, *Praying the Psalms* (Collegeville, Minnesota: Liturgical Press, 1956).

21. Czeslaw Milosz, *A Book of Luminous Things* (New York: Harcourt & Brace, 1996), p. 3.

22. Thomas Merton, *Poetry and Imagination* [cassette recording] (Kansas City: Credence Cassettes, n.d.).

23. Rainer Maria Rilke, *Selected Poems* (Berkeley: University of California, 1984), p. 65.

24. D.T. Suzuki, *Zen and Japanese Culture* (Princeton: Princeton University, 1973); Kenneth Yasuda, *The Japanese Haiku: It's Essential Nature, History and Possibilities in English* (Tokyo: Charles E. Tuttle, 1973).

25. Nobuyuki Yuasa, *The Year of My Life: A Translation of Issa's* Oraga Haru (Berkeley: University of California, 1972), p. 26.

26. *Coomaraswamy: Selected Papers Traditional Art and Symbolism* ed. Roger Lipsey (Princeton: Princeton University, 1977), p. 13.

27. Merton, *Literary Essays*, pp. 424-451.

28. Rilke, *Selected Poems*, pp. 85-86.

29. Merton, *Literary Essays*, p. 49.

30. Thomas Merton, *Faith and Violence: Christian Teaching and Christian Practice* (Notre Dame, Indiana: University of Notre Dame, 1968), p. 152.

31. Jean Baudrillard, *Simulations* (New York: Semiotext (e), Inc., 1983) p. 3.

32. Madeline Bunting, "When the Meaning Boils Down to a Brand Name," *Sydney Morning Herald* (July 14-15, 2001), p. 14.

33. Thomas Del Prete, *Thomas Merton and the Education of the Whole Person* (Birmingham, Alabama: Religious Education Press, 1990), p. 132.

34. Thomas Merton, *The Inner Experience* (San Francisco: HarperCollins, 2003), p. 25.

35. Thomas Merton, *New Seeds of Contemplation* (New York: New Directions, 1962), p. 38.

36. Kilcourse, *Ace of Freedoms*, p.130.

37. Thomas Merton, *Redeeming the Time* (London: Burns and Oates, 1966), p. 63.

38. Merton, *Redeeming the Time*, p. 59.

The Conflict Not Yet Fully Faced:
Thomas Merton as Reader in His Journals

Chris Orvin

In 1959, Thomas Merton expresses his feelings on the role of reading in the monastic life:

> Does it matter how much you read? What matters is the quality and variety of one's reading. Most monks are enclosed within too narrow limits and read too much of the same things and by losing their perspective lose their capacity to learn from what they read. I am perhaps at the other extreme now, but I really think that in almost everything I read I find new food for spiritual life, new thoughts, new *discoveries* ....
> There are a hundred things I want to get to.[1]

However, while cleaning out his office in August 1965, nearer the end of his life, he writes:

> The insane accumulation of books, notes, manuscripts, letters, papers in the novice master's room simply appalls me ... [Not reading books requested from publishers] and the anxiety which tears my gut, and the writing of letters, etc., etc. is certainly a type of a real deep conflict, one I have not yet fully faced ...
> But I know more and more, "in silence and hope shall my strength be" if I can only develop a silence of printed words, or words possessed and accumulated (mere shit). But the first step in this is to *read seriously* the good things that are there and when I do this there is an immediate change for the better ...[2]

In perhaps the most concise form possible, these quotations present two extremes of Merton's feelings about the role of reading in his life. Of course, any full analysis of Merton's reading would have to include complete study of his "reading notebooks," his novitiate conferences and all his literary writings. Therefore, this study of the journals must be seen as an initial step only. In the first quotation, Merton extols the value of a broad and varied experience in reading, often beyond the traditional boundaries of monastic literature, as rich spiritual food and a fertile ground for intellectual growth. He pleads for a more varied diet in monastic reading in order to sharpen the monk's ability to learn from his reading. However, in the latter, the "hundred things [he wanted] to get to" become overwhelming, an obstacle and detriment to contemplative life.[3] Inundated by the variety of reading he previously lauded, he longs for a "a silence of printed words," a deep interior silence, and a rededication to reading seriously the "good things" that immediately restore his spiritual balance.[4] The conflict between reading as a critical component of spiritual life and as a hindrance to the contemplative vocation, made explicit by these quotations, is truly one that he has "not yet fully faced" by 1965.[5] Moreover, this conflict is never completely resolved by Merton, as the life-long nature of these reading habits testify to this unresolved tension within him.

In academic circles, the journals are often used as evidence for other arguments being made about Merton, as in Mary Jo Weaver's "Conjectures of a Disenchanted Reader," which uses the journals to critique his handling of his relationship with his lover, 'M.' It appears that no sustained academic exploration of the journals for their own sake has been undertaken, except through the arrangement of texts as a quasi-auto-biography, *The Intimate Merton.* The present study of the modalities in which Merton engaged his reading reveals a reader who frequently shifts between a narrow focus on a passage or a broad summary of a whole text, and between an intellectual response and an emotional response. His focus could be centered on a close reading of a short text, a habit which was influenced by his monastic training with *lectio divina,* or could be involved in a broad summary reading which subsumed an entire book or many books into more general or universal applications. His response to his reading falls, typically, into either what I will call an academic/intellectual mode or a personal/emotional mode. Merton constantly oscillates between these four modes of reading throughout his lifetime, and the life-long nature of these tendencies reveals how entrenched such "conflict" was within him, one that he has "not yet fully faced," the tension between the monastic call for interior silence and his personal quest for intellectual satiation.

Lectio divina, the ancient monastic practice of reading, was a primary influence on the Merton of the monastic years, and provides a point of departure for a broader discussion on his reading in general. *Lectio divina*, as a form of reading, somehow slips out of the definitional hold of that category, and is something much more. Simply, *lectio divina*, meaning "sacred reading," is the prayerful reading of Scripture. Beyond a casual reading of Scripture, *lectio divina* gently opens up the flower of contemplation, revealing the heart of mystical life and the goal of the monastic life of prayer. Traditionally, a very short passage of Scripture (often a single verse, or even less, just a phrase) is read over and over for plain understanding. Having memorized the text, the monk explores its allegorical meaning by perhaps delving into secondary-source commentary on it, usually the Church Fathers or other saints or mystics. Absorbed in both the repetition of the phrase and its meaning to the monk allegorically, he would express his emotions in a heartfelt prayer, based on the words of the text. The final stage of *lectio divina* is the culmination of the entire practice and its full revelation: the state of contemplation, where words as vehicles for meaning break down, and one is born up to a loving, sometimes ecstatic, experience of the divine. As Jean Leclercq duly notes in a text read and respected by Merton, *The Love of Learning and the Desire for God*, learning is "necessary" in the religious quest, yet at some point the text must be "transcended and elevated" in the religious experience.[6] For the purposes here, what will be described as a mode of reading based on *lectio divina* will be characterized primarily by one or several of the following qualities: a narrow focus on a phrase or short quotation, the repetition of the phrase, prayerful rumination on it and its multivalent meanings, and finally its use as a "spring board for contemplation."[7]

Lectio Divina with Sacred Texts

Merton, a product of Trappist life, drew on a long Cistercian tradition of meditative reading, and his journals indicate he was engaged in this sort of reading with very traditional texts. Even before entering Gethsemani as a postulant, Merton was engaged in a style of reading influenced by a narrow rumination on a sacred text, in a method similar to *lectio divina*. While on retreat at Gethsemani during Holy Week in 1941, he writes in the first volume of his journal a very short verse, John 14:29 ("And now *I have told you before it comes to pass: that when it shall come to pass, you may believe*").[8] He then asks himself, "What does this sentence mean"? He ruminates on the passage, and says that it "does not have much sense if we only take it to mean that it is a sort of prophecy of the crucifixion," because then it would be "unnecessary." Chewing on the meaning of the short verse, he says "what He means is more [than] that," and goes on to explain that the disciples, in possessing Christ's parables and teaching, "possess the truth, but they do not rightly know what it is." He concludes that, allegorically, "So it is with every one of us"; even though we are told Christ's truth in words, it must "become alive in us" by "working itself out within each one of us in our crucifixion and resurrection." In this short selection, he focuses on a narrow passage from Scripture and ruminates on it, meditating on it discursively, in a state of *meditatio*. In this case, he uses an orthodox, accepted text for meditation, and tries through mental athletics to unpack the short verse's multiple meanings.

In August 1949, some eight years later, Merton still exhibits a tendency to observe closely sacred texts, but this time he focuses on whatever "happened to … [turn] up" in his reading of Ecclesiasticus. He "simply took up Ecclesiasticus where [he] left off" and kept reading. He records that he spent "an hour or so on the 32nd chapter," which, "[o]n the surface," appears as a "prosaic little chapter about table manners." But there is always deeper meaning in scripture, if one "know[s] how to read it," and he finds in this brief selection from scripture for the "first time that Ecclesiasticus is not dull." Believing in the value of *lectio divina*, he decides to push through the apparently dull text: "The fact that God is speaking ought to be enough to invest everything with an inestimable value. There are meanings within meanings and depths within depths, and I hasten to say that mere irresponsible allegory does not reveal the real meaning and the real depths."[9]

Thus Merton acknowledges the hidden richness of even the most obscure text. Deep within the passage is the Word speaking to him, and his job is to unearth that meaning. After outlining in a bullet-format a number of revelations he gleaned from this text, including new understandings about monastic life, the role of the Holy Spirit and the place of pleasure in life, Merton reflects more generally on the importance of holy scripture in his life. He writes,

> Merely to set down some of the communicable meanings that can be found in a passage of Scripture is not to exhaust the true meaning or value of that passage. Every world [*sic*] that comes from the mouth of God is nourishment that feeds the soul [...] Whether Scripture tells of David hiding from Saul in

the mountains, [...] or whether it tells about Jesus raising up the son of the widow of Nain [...] – everywhere there are doors and windows opened into the same eternity – and the most powerful communication of Scripture is the *insitum verbum* [the engrafted word], the secret and inexpressible seed of contemplation planted in the depths of our soul and awakening it with an immediate and inexpressible contact with the Living Word, that we may adore Him in Spirit and in Truth.[10]

This description of sacred reading is steeped in influence from *lectio divina*, and Merton's emphasis on the contact with Christ, the Living Word, through the text, aligns nicely with Leclercq's recognition that the "encounter [...] between God's saving word and the innermost human spirit" is an immediate "experience of Christ" through the scriptures.[11]

In Merton's journals we find that he frequently used one of the most standard texts for monastic contemplation, the Book of Psalms, and, in 1958, he directly addresses how he uses the Psalms in his daily practice. He records that on Good Friday (April 4) 1958, the psalter was "something tremendous," because the monks were allowed to meditate on the psalms by themselves for an hour.[12] He had been reading Dom Leclercq's *The Love of Learning and the Desire for God*, and uses the language of *lectio divina* to describe his experience. Repeating the psalms "over and over by heart in the depths of [his] being," he describes his experience as *meditatio*, a term in Leclercq's book. Merton admits that he had recited these psalms "scores of times before without ever seeing them," but now, through this "absolutely essential" practice of *meditatio*, he has discovered new, rich meaning deep in the scriptures. He focuses on two verses in Psalm 85, verses 12 and 13, and copies them in his journal because they were ones "[i]n particular" that he had rediscovered. Realizing the importance of this practice of *lectio divina*, he vows that he will "return more often to this kind of *meditatio*," indicating that he had neglected the practice previously and only now discovered or remembered its true value. His thoughts move to the problems of the monastery, which he claims has not only neglected the practice "totally" but also has been misinterpreting *lectio divina* as "thinking about" certain lines, instead of dwelling in the presence of God through the text. Merton's contrast of "saying them over [...] in the depths of [his] being" and the institutional misrepresentation of *lectio divina* as "thinking about" the lines show his preference for the experience of God's presence over a mere scholarly or intellectual grasp of the psalms' meanings.

Even though he focused more on the general feel of Psalms 85 and 86 and the value of deeply internalized repetition of them, he also would show a proclivity to concentrate on specific lines as loci of spiritual value. In Volume 6, he records specific lines from the Psalms that have been "driving themselves home" recently to him.[13] Thus there appears a tension in his experience with the Psalms and his *lectio* in general. In 1958 he learned or remembered the value of repetition and internalization of an entire psalm (or two!), and in this passage of 1966 he was struck by specific lines from them. In this way he was able to experience *lectio divina* both as an opportunity to reflect more generally on a longer passage, incorporating the flow of its imagery and emotions, and as an opportunity to lift specific lines or isolated phrases which could be used as sources of meditation.[14]

Lectio Divina with Non-Biblical Texts

In contrast to his ruminations on these traditional texts, Merton reveals in a number of important journal entries that his experience with *lectio divina* in its traditional context as a meditation on a passage of Scripture influenced how he read non-sacred texts. In his pre-monastic journal, he realizes "in a flash" that he may be "capable of understanding Racine," whom he had "never really seen anything in," but was willing to admit there was "something there."[15] Like his Ecclesiasticus reading, where he opens the book rather randomly to see what it will reveal, so does he happen upon the fourth act of *Berenice*, "where Titus is speaking to himself."[16] He transcribes six lines in French and proclaims them "tremendously moving in a very pure way."[17] Temporarily thinking about the play as a whole, his thinking returns to the act of transcribing brief passages:

> I wonder how much sense there is in quoting a single line of Racine: every single line, word, comma has an exact place in the whole structure, this symphonic structure. If a line of Racine is to be quoted at all, the only way is to make it fit into another structure, take it and fit it neatly into a paragraph of critical prose, giving it a setting with all kinds of syntactical properties able to support it and show it off to advantage.[18]

Even though it appears he is critiquing this selectively narrow read-ing of a non-sacred text, he is also demonstrating how such a pas-sage must be fully, deeply explored by a scholarly interpretation to plumb the entirety of its depths. Moreover, he testifies to the "moving" nature of such an exploration of a short, non-sacred text.[19]

Enriching his monastic diet of reading with other foods, in 1959, having spent some eighteen years in the cloister, Merton delves into the use of words in the poetry of Pablo Neruda and Giuseppe Ungaretti. Analyzing each author's use of words, he dismisses the lines of Neruda, saying "each line is a word, but the whole poem is only a line of uninteresting prose with the words strung down the page, one on top of the other."[20] In Ungaretti, on the other hand, "each word is a line or even a poem in itself."[21] Here Merton is expressing how a single word or a well-crafted phrase can open up worlds of interpretation. Just as Merton loved to dig into the depths of the language of the Psalms, he also adored writ-ers who could write with sufficient power to require meditative dissection word by word. His *lectio divina* on the Psalms and other sacred texts was clearly influencing how he read things in gen-eral, and shows a preference for texts which allowed him to plunge into their meditative depth.[22]

Merton had a habit of lifting an exciting sentence from a poorly written article and copying it in his journal, a practice, like *lectio divina*, which highlights a short phrase for edification. In the fourth volume of the journals, he notes on April 29, 1961 that he locates a "fine sentence in a mediocre article (part of that on the Church in *DS* [*Dictionnaire de Spiritualité*])" which concerns the edification of others.[23] He reflects on this passage and says that it addresses "the worst temptation and the most difficult," which "comes from the fact that we seem to be leading one another into a trap."[24] Superlatives like "the worst" and "the most difficult" emphasize the importance of the temptation addressed by the quotation. While ruminating on this passage, he expands its context, asking himself if God can truly "be ... behind all our official nonsense [at Gethsemani]" including all of their "laws and decrees and stat-utes and rites and observances."[25] This short sentence on edifica-tion propels him into a rumination on monastic life in general, despite the questionable quality of the article from which the quo-tation was lifted. Even though this verse is not meditated on in the traditional *lectio divina* sense, with silent appreciation of the presence of God in it, it is still informed by a reading style which characterized Merton's experience with that technique.[26]

Throughout his life, Merton struggled with contemporary texts which forced him to slow down and move line-by-line because of their density, and even though these texts were not sacred, his training in *lectio divina* narrowed his focus to short passages in order to muse on their meditative depth. As early as August 1949, eight years after entering Gethsemani as a postulant, Merton's exposure to *lectio divina* was showing signs of influencing his reading habits, as he was forced to slow his reading and focus on individual phrases. He writes that Fr. Paul Phillipe's book, *La Très Sainte Vierge et le Sacerdoce* is "short," but he has to "read slowly."[27] He "can't read more than three paragraphs of anything without stopping," and if he reads quickly he finds himself "confused," and his mind "simply ceases to grasp anything."[28] He likens a half hour spent reading too quickly to being "roughed up in a dark alley by a gang of robbers."[29] In a similar experience in 1964, he is completely "snowed under by" Rudolf Bultmann.[30] This "revelation" to Merton is "so powerful, so urgent, so important" that "every sentence" stops him and he cannot "seem to get anywhere."[31] The book is so "[f]antastically good" that Merton, in focusing on a text intently in a *lectio divina* fashion, cannot seem to progress.[32] Much like his reading of the Psalms, Job and Ezekiel, he finds in these texts deep meaning that has to be patiently exhumed because of the depth of the texts' richness.

Later in his life, he shows a growing patience in his reading style and greater comfort with the slowness of *lectio divina*. He reads Mai Mai Sze's *Tao of Painting*, a "deep and contemplative book," much more "slowly," to his "great profit."[33] This entry, on June 11, 1965, is almost exactly one year after the previous citation of Bultmann, and in this time Merton has learned, to a certain extent, to calm his mind for reading and open himself up to the richness of the text, patiently gleaning the truths it offers up. During his years in the hermitage, he spends a "whole morning" in 1966 on a "slow reading of *The Myth of Sisyphus* (Camus)."[34] He remarks that before he "shied away" from the book, but "[n]ow it is just right, just what [he needs]."[35] This slow reading may account for his greater appreciation of the book at this later date. In the same journal, about two months later that summer, he again notes that René Char's writing, which is "compact, rich, intense, full," must be read with "time and attention to absorb all that is there."[36]

Merton suggests a "long course of reading, in the full afternoons out under the trees" to digest fully Char's meaning.[37] Even though the works of Phillipe, Bultmann, Camus, Sze and Char are not traditionally accepted texts for *lectio divina*, Merton's exposure to *lectio divina* at Gethsemani and the inculcation of its premises allow him to expand the borders of acceptable texts for *lectio divina* into contemporary and even not specifically religious writers.

A Summary Reader

Even though *lectio divina* would leave a strong impression on Merton, he also utilized a very different method of reading which was exceptionally quick and cursory, and would often reduce an entire book or author's canon into a single phrase or idea. If *lectio divina* can be seen as a process of taking a short phrase and expanding it to uncover all of its meaning and richness, then this summary style reading is the same process, but in the opposite direction. Instead of writing a book on a phrase (*lectio divina*), he often writes a single phrase about an entire book (summary reading). This is not to be unexpected, especially with the volume of material Merton was covering, and his limited time for writing in his journal. In this manner of reading, he operates in three primary modes: a terse criticism of a book, the location of the central concept of a book or the reduction of an author's entire canon to a short phrase. In this way, he reduces a vast amount of material into a condensed form for easier reference in his notes.

In the first mode characteristic of this kind summary reading, he often offers a short criticism of a book, whether positive or negative, and these quick thumbnail sketches of Merton's responses are found throughout the journals. For example, in 1947 he writes that Paul Claudel's verse "bores" him, but Claudel's "poetic prose about the Orient" is "wonderful." Immediately afterwards he writes that Patrice de la Tour du Pin "writes too much"; he calls it "too glib" and "too silly." He sums up that he "[doesn't] like it" or the author's understanding of Christ. In this example he is condensing much of Claudel's verse to the word "boring" and his prose to the word "wonderful."[38] For Patrice de la Tour du Pin, Merton simply doesn't like it, saying he is "too silly" and "too glib."[39] On the other hand, he also writes short phrases about a book he may like as well, as when he calls *The Hidden Face* "remarkably revealing and intelligent," but does not offer any further explanation or rumination.[40] A single page later, he tersely calls Bruno Snell's *Discovery of the Mind* "enthralling but yet un-satisfactory."[41] Snell's treatment is "[t]oo simplified," and Merton does not comment any further.[42] The entire book, unmentioned in the journals to this point, is reduced to a single phrase and is quickly passed over.

In his comments on Lytton Strachey's *Eminent Victorians*, Merton characterizes large passages of the book with single words: Arnold's portrait is "disappointing," Manning's is a "masterpiece," while Gordon's is "perplexing and disturbing."[43] This interesting example is typical of a pattern evident in Merton's reading, the tendency to isolate texts as independent, even in a larger work. Again, in Volume 4, Merton comments quickly on Giuseppe di Lampedusa's *The Leopard*, saying it is "finely constructed" but "suddenly disintegrates." He calls it "humorous and moving," but also "dignified and sane."[44] Readers of the journals will sometimes be caught off guard with Merton's conciseness, as in his critique of *The Last of the Just*, which he praises as "tremendously moving thing" that "says a great deal," yet he does not elaborate further, except by pointing to pity as "the center" of the book's argument.[45] His high praise in a summary format occurs at other junctures, including his discussion of the *Prison Meditations of Father Delp* ("perhaps the most clear-sighted book of Christian meditations of our time"[46]) and his examination of Zaehner's *Hindu and Muslim Mysticism*, a "remarkable book."[47] In all of these examples, Merton does a kind of reverse *lectio divina*, using a phrase to capture an entire book.

If terse criticism marked this first mode of summary reading, then Merton's second tendency to summarize is distinguished by extracting the central kernel of a book and using it as a lodestone to guide him through the rest of the book. He says that "the heart of [Olivier] Clément's book [*Transfigurer les Temps*]" is that "'fallen Time'... *has no present*."[48] Merton goes on to unpack what this means, and quotes from the text to do so (at the end he transcribes one "superbly wise sentence" in a *lectio divina* style).[49] Likewise, in the same volume, Merton finds the "heart of Heschel's splen-did book—*God in Search of Man*" to be the "consistent emphasis on the importance of time, the *event* in revealed religion."[50] This emphasis on 'event' guides Merton's reflection on the entire book in a summary style; however, he does not offer a thumbnail sketch but goes into some detail in a several paragraph response to this theme of the book. While reading Han Urs von Balthasar's

Herrlichkeit, Merton says the book boils down to "this one central thing: all theology is a scientific doctrine and originates at the point where the act of faith … becomes understanding."[51] Merton calls this "extremely important," even though it "sounds trivial."[52] Thus within his counter-*lectio divina* trend of summarizing, he also, beyond offering quick criticism of a text, finds an overriding thesis or idea which drives an entire book.

In a third modality of summary reading, Merton takes the previous tendency to the next level and condenses all of the works by a particular author or the author's thesis on life itself to a single phrase or word or idea. After eight years struggling with St. Bernard of Clairvaux, Merton discovers that the "foundation of [the] whole doctrine" of St. Bernard is that "God is Truth and Christ is Truth Incarnate," and humankind's responsibility is thus to be "true to ourselves and true to Christ and true to God." It is "only when this emphasis on truth is forgotten" that Saint Bernard becomes "sentimental."[53] Thus Bernard and all his writings can be reduced to a central core, the understanding of which unlocks Bernard's truth. Similarly, when reading Sergei Bulgakov, Merton claims the Bulgakov's Sophianism is "built on" the idea that Creation was made for the sake of the Incarnation.[54] Merton is again ignoring specific texts of Bulgakov and instead surveys the entirety of his work and thought, the keystone of which is this idea.

With another Russian theologian, Nikolai Berdyaev, Merton "sympathize[s] with" or agrees with the "whole of his doctrine" in a "general way," although his agreement does not necessarily extend to "each particular fact."[55] In this case, Merton is skimming over individual details of Berdyaev's arguments and even books themselves, composing a trans-textual summation of Berdyaev's theology and agreeing with it in general (he also does this with Bultmann: see his "idea of God").[56] With the existentialist Albert Camus, Merton boldly states that the "central idea in Camus is that *revolt* is the affirmation of man in his common nature."[57] To Merton, Camus, in all the various novels, stories and essays he published, can be reduced to the idea of *revolt*. Merton correlates authors with key words, which guide all of their thought, regardless of the form it takes; for Saint Bernard it is 'truth,' for Bulgakov it is 'incarnation/creation,' for Camus it is 'revolt.' Merton here may be ignoring the entire developmental arc of these authors, with the complexity and specificity of individual books, but he also is navigating his way through a vast body of material, and needs to summarize the overriding theological or philosophical agenda of authors so he can triangulate his own position.

The Intellectual Response

Lectio divina and this summary style of reading represent two different movements within the same intellectual funnel. Whether all the ideas, complex arguments, recantations, paradoxes and contradictions are funneling downward and being reduced to a central argument, or whether a single phrase is expanded and unpacked in prayerful rumination to blossom into new revelations, other ideas, complex connections, or personal experience, Merton shows a sort of mental unsettledness in his reading. Sometimes he distills a core truth (whether in a single work or in all works) from an author he enjoys, and other times he finds a phrase which opens up a wide array of new understandings. He even will alternate these styles within a single journal entry, because his reading habits constantly were shifting around. This tension between his narrow and wide focus on his reading is complemented by a tension regarding his response to his reading. His impersonal, intellectual response to his reading, where he breaks down individual arguments, challenges assumptions and answers questions authors left unanswered opposes his more personal, emotional response, wherein his excitement at the works' spiritual resonance with him trumps any sort of intellectual distance.

A: Comparison of Arguments

One modality of his intellectual response to his reading is his tendency to compare the arguments of often very disparate authors, theologians or philosophers. He would sometimes bring relatively similar authors together, such as St. Bernard and St. John of the Cross.[58] He writes that Bernard's tenth chapter in *On the Love of God* and his sermons on the Song of Songs bring the two authors "into line together."[59] "When they reach their goal, they are together in their way of looking at things."[60] So these two Christian authors' ideas on mystical marriage with Christ can be conjoined, if their arguments are broken down and understood intellectually. St. John of the Cross, one of Merton's favorite authors, beyond having more obvious connections with other Christian writers, also surprisingly has connections to Werner Heisenberg.

Merton says the uncertainty principle is "oddly like [the theology of] St. John of the Cross" in that God "eludes the grasp of concepts" and that "in the ultimate constitution of matter there is *nothing really there*."[61] So Heisenberg and science can elucidate spiritual truths, and Merton cherishes Heisenberg's idea that materialism is "now unmasked *as a faith*" in the light of the deconstructive potency of the uncertainty principle.[62] In even less orthodox marriages, Merton conjoins Anselm of Canterbury and J.P. Sartre. Their understanding of liberty, even though "poles apart," has "a great deal in common."[63] Merton deconstructs their arguments and terminology, concluding that "[t]hus for both Sartre and Anselm, the exercise of true freedom is demanded for a being to become what it *is*."[64] Merton integrates their vocabulary in his synthesis, comparing the *"salaud* [sloven] of Sartre and the *insipiens* [fool] of Anselm."[65] Again, three months later, in late November of 1963, Merton muses innocently on the possibility that the *"tricherie* [trickery] of Sartre" may align with the *"rectitudo* of St. Anselm," and wonders if there is "any correspondence" between Chapter 11 in *De Casu Diaboli* and Sartre's *"néant* [nothingness]."[66] Merton does not extrapolate the consequence of the possible correspondence, but his imaginative mind certainly enjoys these interesting, syncretic combinations.

This tendency to compare arguments made by different authors occasionally is present when Merton compares his own, unspoken and developing theology with the philosophy of other authors. When struggling with his relationship with the hospital nurse he fell in love with and his own solitude, Merton finds that the "answer is in Camus' principle: that the absurd man is without (human at least) hope," and this hopelessness "isolates him in the pure present" and "makes him 'available' in the present."[67] Comparing Camus and his own ideas on the inability to have full knowledge, Merton writes that he can "accept what [he doesn't] know as unknown (like Camus)."[68] Only a sentence later Merton is demarcating his difference from Camus, writing that he "differ[s] from Camus in the immense, unknown hope that is [his] own aspect of the 'absurd.'"[69] Interestingly, he calls faith here the "fundamental revolt," using the vocabulary he assigned to the central idea of Camus as I have argued earlier (see p. 216). Camus and Merton are compared in this passage along lines of intellectual agreement, and their differences are defined by Merton in his application of Camus's thought to his own position. In commenting on von Balthasar, Merton vows to "read him more deeply," because he realized "to what extent [his] own theology goes along with that of Balthasar."[70] These entries show a Merton who, while able to break down other authors' ideas, would also compare their insights with his own.

Arguably the most important connections Merton drew intellectually from his reading were the contacts between Eastern and Western authors. As early as 1960, eight years before his death in Asia, Merton was distilling the implications of Kao Tzu's argument and comparing his conclusions with St. Bernard and Mencius. He writes that there could be an "interesting comparison" between these three, in regard to the "four beginnings."[71] Later in this volume, Merton's reading of Jacques Maritain's essay on Descartes "in connection with Fénelon" is "revealing in relation to Zen" and displays a flurry of comparative work.[72] The "inane Cartesian spirit" corrupted the West with a "the reification of concepts, the idolization of reflexive consciousness, the flight from being into verbalism, mathematics and rationalization," and has to be corrected with the shattering of this "fetish" Cartesian mirror by Zen.[73] Again Merton shows his preference for Eastern insights in his reading of Nishida's *The Intelligible World*, which is "like Evagrius, and yet better."[74] Reading T. R. V. Murti's "clear and sensible exposition" of Tantra while in Asia, Merton is "left musing on St. Irenaeus, St. Gregory of Nyssa, the catechesis of St. Cyril of Jerusalem, early Christian liturgy, baptism ..."[75] Only four days before his death, he compares the idea of self-contradiction in Nagarjuna and Hermann Hesse's *Steppenwolf.*[76] Merton's syncretic consciousness was quick to utilize authors, regardless of Eastern or Western labels, in his struggle with universal human problems.

B: Engagement

A second modality characteristic of Merton's intellectual engagement with material was his breaking down of arguments, so in this style he actively dissects parts of arguments in an effort to understand them. In his pre-monastic journal, Merton breaks down Thomistic and Augustinian theology in a style of reading which is a "thinking out" of various implications imbedded in the texts he was reading. This long entry explores the goals of Augustine's and Thomas's writings, their different styles, their similarities, their contrast with previous philosophical movements (Plato, Socrates, etc), and the place of the intellect in their messages.[77] Merton shows no real excitement or emotional response to this reading; it is evidence of a young convert to Catholicism who is grounded in literary criticism exploring the ideas of his new faith.[78]

An important example of this trend to break down arguments into manageable pieces is found when Merton is called out for his mistakes in an article he wrote. Merton's initially blasé attitude toward the article which went "to the great trouble of refuting something [he] must have said somewhere about contemplation" turns to an intellectual feeding-frenzy.[79] From January 22 to 26, Merton lays out in outline form the points made against him, recognizes the weak points in his article, struggles with his own ideas in light of this criticism, and ultimately returns to the *Summa theologiae* for clarification. This ends up being an "immense help" to him, and Thomas's definition of a 'state,' which Merton uses to see "how [he] had been wrong," helps him "see [his] own way much more clearly."[80] This intellectual clarification requires a systematic and sustained academic investigation to find the key ideas and hidden implications or assumptions in a cited source.[81] Like the young convert who needed to break down the arguments of the church fathers in order to prepare for the monastery, so too does the later Merton need intellectual digestion of the Eastern spiritual masters to prepare for his experiences in Asia. There he would find the physical manifestation of these ideas in living human vessels with whom he would find mutual understanding.

This proclivity to break apart an argument for clearer intellectual insight often involved a second mode of intellectual reading: laying out the text's structural components, presenting an argument in bullet-format or a list. Even though Merton never was one to demand "absolute structural perfection" from a novel or article, he did take these concerns into account.[82] In the pre-monastic journal, he lays out St. Bonaventure's points in an outline format, exploring the three categories of "the beautiful," "the pleasant" and "the wholesome."[83] The "very beautiful paragraph" in the prologue of the Saint Thomas's *Summa theologiae*, which contains "a whole discipline of study," has "three points" about the impediments obstructing the truth, and Merton writes a numbered list of these obstacles.[84] Reading Berdyaev, Merton, in a numbered list, transcribes his two views of the cosmos, an "incomplete [...] cosmos of the Old Testament" and what Berdyaev sees as the "real view" of creation.[85] Again, struggling with Gabriel Marcel, Merton lists Marcel's points on eschatological consciousness in order to understand his argument adequately.[86]   In a criticism of Roger Garaudy's article on Marxist-Catholic dialogue, Merton comments that there are "[c]lear-cut division[s] between us" and lays out the three primary "danger[s]" he sees in Christianity's alignment with a Marxist world view.[87]   In response to Rosemary Radford Ruether's *The Church Against Itself*, he feels her analysis is right (he "[trusts] her" because she is "very Barthian") that the "big problem" of the Church, which Catholicism has "refused to face," is the "distortions, the evasions, the perversion of love into power and resentment, and all the virtues of mimicry and practice."[88] Analyzing her argument, he lists her six possible solutions to the modern Church's dilemma, but he finds them somewhat unconvincing, asking her, in his journal, three questions about the implications of her solutions.[89]   Monica Furlong, in her biography of Merton, would agree with the intellectual nature of Merton's relationship with Reuther, as it was "a long and very searching intellectual discussion."[90]   Regardless, this process of segmenting movements of an author's argument allows for easier mental digestion of a point Merton was trying to assimilate.

C: Response to Question

Yet a another mode of Merton's engagement with intellectual material is his tendency to respond to questions that other authors bring up in the books he is reading. For example, when Berdyaev "overstates the contrast and 'incompatibility'" of sanctity life and genius, he makes an "over-generalized and false" contrast between the two.[91]   Yet his "statement of the problem *must* be faced."[92] Merton suggests an option to free Berdyaev and others from this bind. "The solution lies in prayer," Merton writes, and prayer, as a "creative act," reveals "the utmost mystery of our own being to God."[93]   In this situation Merton offers an intellectual escape-hatch to the problem of "sanctity and genius" through the act of "[p]rayer as creation."[94]   In a slightly less clear example, Merton responds to a "beautiful and deep idea of Abraham Heschel" by asking what determines revelation and its acceptance.[95]   Merton, or perhaps Heschel in his book, answers "love"; a "[p]erson makes himself responsible, in terms of love."[96]   In these ways, Merton actively engages with the texts he is reading from an intellectual angle, providing answers to the unresolved questions posed (or perceived as unanswered) in the text.

Personal Reflection

These three modalities of a hungry intellectual mind digesting ideas and concepts may suggest a Merton who read in a clinically detached way, with the surgical gloves of literary criticism to protect him from emotional engagement with his reading, but this portrait of him would be severely distorted. Merton did break apart arguments, register points made in his reading in an outline format, challenge biases, unearth hidden assumptions and delve into linguistic analysis, etc. But to contain Merton in this one corner of the spiritual boxing ring for his salvation would be a crippling over-simplification. Years of study at Columbia and teaching at St. Bonaventure's had given a sharp critical edge to his reading, but he also read to work out, in fear and trembling, his own salvation as a cloistered monk. His reading served another purpose beyond intellectual entertainment; it served as the food from heaven, given by God in a special kind of providence, to sustain, direct and inspire him in the quest for his spiritual destiny.

In his journals, perhaps the most ubiquitous examples of Merton responding in an emotional way is when he calls his reading "moving."[97] Even before he entered Gethsemani, Merton, in examining the *Spiritual Exercises* of Saint Ignatius, is "moved in the short meditation on venial sin."[98] His compunction comes "thanks to God" and not of any effort of his own.[99] Having completed this meditation, he feels the "full impact of the greatness and horror of mortal sin."[100] Even though this example could be seen as a state of prayer alone, his reading of the *Spiritual Exercises* certainly provides the groundwork or springboard for a great deal of personal reflection. He would be deeply affected by the journal of Raïssa, which was sent to him by her husband Jacques Maritain, the scholar and philosopher with whom Merton corresponded. He calls it a "most moving and lucid and soul-cleansing book," and enjoys the realization that he and she can "share so perfectly such things."[101] Even more exuberant excitement is found in his reading of William Faulkner's "The Bear." It too, like the *Spiritual Exercises* and the journal of Raïssa, is "[s]hattering, cleansing," but his praise brims over, calling it "a mind-changing and transforming myth that makes you stop to think about re-evaluating everything."[102] The profound revelation from this and "all great writing" for Merton is that it "makes you break through the futility and routine of ordinary life and see the greatness of existence, its seriousness, and the awfulness of wasting it."[103]

Additionally, another clear indicator of Merton responding emotionally to a text would be when he calls it the "answer to everything." His excitement and energy at such reading makes his writing glow with intensity. Finding a "Zen *mondo* in Suzuki," he writes that it is the "answer to everything."[104] In a continuing trend to see in a quotation or book the answer to "everything" he needs, he reads in the "three wonderful chapters in *the Cloud of Unknowing*" a quotation which is "everything" to him at the time.[105] Citing Romans 9-11 as "the key to everything today," he urges that the Church "enter the understanding of Scripture, the wholeness of revelation" during Vatican II, which he sees as "still short of this awareness."[106] Merton was particularly ecstatic in finding in William Faulkner the answer to many of his questions.[107] In all of these cases where Merton sees the key to "all" existence in a work of literature or scripture, he clearly does not respond with an intellectual cognition that all everything is 'contained within,' but with a personal response that the work addresses his primary questions, doubts and fears at that particular juncture of his life.

This capability for books to answer questions in his life and directly clarify his situation as a pragmatic aid is another broad trend that occurs under his experience as a sympathetic reader. He writes that in his observance of the Holy Week liturgy he is "immensely helped and stimulated by the Bouyer book" [*Le Mystère Pascal*].[108] Referring later to St. Augustine in the same volume, Merton says that Augustine's *City of God* "feeds [him], strengthens [him], knits [his] powers together in peace and tranquility."[109] He sings that the "light of God shines to [him] more serenely through the wide open windows of Augustine than through any other theologian."[110] While reading Marcel's *Homo Viator*, Merton feels that it "clarifies much of [his] present struggle and confusion" about his desire to live in further solitude in the hermitage.[111] Over a year later, his needs have changed, and instead, Berdyaev's distinction between the ethics of law and ethics of creativeness is "a very good one for [him] now."[112] In one of his last entries in this volume, he records that Hannah Arendt's *The Human Condition* "offers a solution to the complex question that has plagued [him]" about the nature of the individual in society, a theme of this period of his reading.[113] Remembering his tumultuous days in the hospital in 1966, he calls Meister Eckhart his "life-raft" during this time.[114] He cites an Eckhart quotation on surrendering selfhood as something Merton has "to get back to," because its need is "coming to the surface again."[115]   In all these cases, Merton's personal life meets his reading in an active and pragmatic dialogue which aids him in his spiritual quest.

Encountering Christ

Merton does not just receive help through other authors and their ideas; at points he hears the voice of Christ speaking to him through the texts, in a providential response to his situation. Before even entering the monastery, he is fascinated by the state Saint Theresa describes, where "one hears God calling in the words of devout people and good books."[116] He exclaims that he feels this very calling of God "in her book so much."[117] He certainly believed that books have a power to speak directly and personally to him, as from the mouth of God. Later, although in a more oblique reference, he refers to the books that "played a part" in his conversion, including books he cites in *The Seven Storey Mountain*: Aldous Huxley's *Ends and Means*, Étienne Gilson's *Spirit of Medieval Philosophy*, the poetry of William Blake, and G. F. Lahey's life of G. M. Hopkins.[118] If his conversion can be seen as a moment where he felt God's specific call in his life, then this call was also emanating from the books he was reading. Despite his previous tendency not to like Origen much, in *The Treatise on Prayer* he finds "the first thing of Origen's that [he has] really liked."[119] As he thinks longer on it, his praise builds, calling it "simple and great, ... [o]ne of the best things ever written on prayer," the product of a "tremendous mind."[120] Beyond just calling it "close to the Gospel," he proclaims that "Christ talks and speaks in it."[121] The Christ with whom he had grown close to in prayer was speaking directly to Merton, through the vehicle of Origen's *Treatise on Prayer*. Later he picks up *The Family of Man* and muses on "[h]ow scandalized some men would be if [he] said that the whole book is to [him] a picture of Christ."[122] The "fabulous pictures" are of people throughout the world in various daily activities.[123] In seeing Christ in these pictures, Merton witnesses the incarnation, Christ's entrance into human flesh to become "God-manhood" or our collective human nature "transformed in God!"[124] On another level, however, Merton is also witnessing Christ's incarnation into the book itself. In this way, Christ's incarnation takes place not only in other people, but also in the book which brings these images together. Understanding the voice of God in a sacred text is a rather fundamental idea to Christianity, yet Merton expands the number of legitimate texts which can speak this voice; he hears it in books by saints and philosophers and photographers.

Encountering Christ in his reading is only one, albeit the highest, example of Merton encountering in his reading living people with whom he feels a "interior bond," who bring him messages, or act as living personal acquaintances.[125]   At one point, Merton realizes the truth that "people like St. Thomas and St. Bonaventure and Duns Scotus should have told [him] long ago," that the quest for theological insight prepares the mind for infused wisdom and quickens the desire for it.[126]   Here he is imaginatively envisioning these long-dead authors as living people who "should have told [him something]."[127]   In his discovery of the penitential psalms, which reveal themselves as a message from God when one discovers "how much [one needs] them," he calls John Cassian a "go-between."[128]   He says that he has "found [these psalms], and they have found [him]," and Cassian acts as a mediating third-party, who led him providentially to this discovery when he most needed it.[129]   Like P. Emmanuel's *Qui est cet Homme?*, these psalms came to him "just at the moment when, [your] very life, it seems, depends on your reading [them]."[130]   When he receives a letter from Boris Pasternak, Merton writes that it "confirmed [his] intuition of the deep and fundamental understanding that exists between" them.[131]   He says that their "interior bond" is the "only basis of true peace and true community," even though he never met Pasternak personally.[132]   For Merton, Pasternak is a "basically religious writer," like Cassian, Scotus, and others, with whom he feels a strong kinship.[133]

This kinship is further elucidated in Merton's relationship with Emily Dickinson, whom he calls his "own flesh and blood."[134]   Even though she would not be understood in her own time, and would be "hidden" and refuse "herself completely to everyone who would not appreciate her," she would give "herself completely to people of other ages and places who never saw her," like Merton.[135]   He says this experience of finding the nineteenth-century New England recluse is like "hugging an angel."[136]   Just as he was "entranced" with Eckhart, a "great man," who had a way of "piercing straight to the heart of the inner life," so too did Merton find himself "attracted" to Julian of Norwich.[137]   Stunned by the mystic from the Rhineland and seduced by the fourteenth-century English anchorite, Merton had a proclivity to find living authors in his reading.   Julian of Norwich in particular becomes one of

Merton's "best friends," and he thrives on her "wise friendship."[138] In a sudden burst of imaginative insight, Merton sees himself having "long been around her, and hover[ing] at her door, know[ing] that she was one of [his] best friends."[139]

Similarly, Merton makes the 'acquaintance' of Simone Weil, whom he is "finally getting to know" through her biography, and finds he has a "great sympathy for her," even though he "cannot agree with a lot of her attitudes and ideas."[140] So not all of Merton's imagined relationships with authors were perfect match-ups. In a highly illuminating passage reminiscent of his feelings about Dickinson, Merton writes that he finds in Jacques Maritain's *Note-books* "the simplicity and probity of Jacques himself."[141] Looking at the pictures of Raïssa, Maritain's wife, and her sister Vera Oumansoff, Merton feels that "though [he] never actually met them," they are two people who "loved [him] – and whom [he has] loved."[142] He feels this friendship "through [their] writings and the warmth and closeness that has somehow bound [him] to Jacques and to them."[143] He calls it a kind of "family affection," which "reaches out" to others, like Dom Pierre (Van de Meer).[144] This "family affection" certainly reaches out, and in Merton's journals the "family" of his close friends and family he discovers in reading grows.[145] Merton admits shyly that he is having affairs with some writers like Mai Mai Sze, who "with Nora Chadwick, Eleanor Duckett [becomes] one of [his] secret loves."[146] Similarly, his "heart is with Camus," and Merton's somewhat turbulent relationship with Camus runs through the whole of Volume 6.[147] Whether he found a lover, a friend, or someone to argue with, Merton continually believed in the living presence of the authors he was reading and their deep importance in his life, as monastic life precluded having friends and family in the traditional sense.

"Book Providence"

The deepest and most radical manifestation of Merton reading on this personal level is his concept of "Book Providence," the providential arrival of a text, idea, or personal acquaintance provided for him by Christ as "a light to [his] path."[148] God speaking in St. Theresa, Cassian's help in discovering the penitential psalms, Origen speaking as Christ and the role of books in his conversion has already been touched on in this light.[149] He describes this providential arrival as "a grace" when mentioning Emmanuel Mounier's ideas on Personalism, and he calls the "book on Ikons from Bob Rambusch" a "great grace"; similarly, Aeschylus's *Prometheus Bound* is a "great grace on the feast of Saint Anthony!"[150] In a period where he was particularly devoted to the Virgin Mother, he writes that "Our Lady brought [Volume 41 of Denis the Carthusian] along yesterday as a mark of her love and to remind [Merton] that she is [his] guide in the interior life."[151]　Just as Raïssa's journal came to him "providentially," so too is Julian of Norwich a "great […] joy and gift."[152]　These books tended to come to him in his hour of need, or when his particular situation demanded external aid.　Citing a quotation from Berdyaev's *Slavery and Freedom* about the need to resist the world in order to realize one's personality, Merton writes that "this thought comes to [him] with all the power of a 'message.'"[153]　Regarding Dom Leclercq's *Otia Monastica*, Merton writes it is "just what [he has] been needing."[154]　Likewise, outside of monastic reading, in Camus Merton also finds in *The Myth of Sisyphus*, which he "shied away from before, […] just what [he needs]."[155]　Now it fits his new understanding of his "vocation to be an absurd man," or "at least *to try* to think in some such honest terms."[156]

His heartfelt belief in providence is most clearly revealed in a journal entry from his early days, where he writes that "There are times when ten pages of some book fall under your eye just at the moment when your very life, it seems, depends on your reading those ten pages."[157]　In them one finds "the answer to all your most pressing questions."　Finding this providential provision in his reading of Pierre Emmanuel's *Qui est cet homme?*, he discovers "what [he] was trying to get obscurely last month out of *Ecclesiastes.*"　As the "enemy of [his] angelism," Emmanuel has "given" Merton the word "discontinuity" and "reminded" him of what he "already found out" about "isolation being different from solitude."　This clearly shows the personification trends discussed above, and also the role of providence in his reading.

Beyond mere pulpy texts, he also believed that the providence of God made itself manifest in other people whom he meets in living encounters.　In an account that sounds similar to his description of Origen's *Treatise on Prayer*, Merton hears in the sermon of Fr. John of the Cross a preaching of "the Gospel, not words about the Gospel – or about something more or less remote from the Gospel."[158]　Fr. John of the Cross "preached Christ and not himself – or someone else who is not Christ," in a correlative way that "Christ talks and speaks in [*The Treatise on Prayer*]."[159]　In Fr.

John of the Cross, Merton hears the "words of Christ," which respond as deeply with him as his "friendship with Christ."[160] In a profound encounter eight years later, with a Sufi from Algeria named Sidi Abdesalam, a "true man of God," Merton feels that Abdesalam "came as a messenger from God," and that he "had this sense" as well.[161] Merton believes the "message" is that it would be "wrong for [them] to be kept here 'in prison,'" and that he was "supposed to go out," meaning travel.[162] Merton is content to wait until he knows if it is "clearly God's will," in which case he will "go out."[163] So even though Abdesalam comes with a message, it is perhaps an ambiguous one. However, Merton feels in this encounter, a "sense of God present."[164] In an interesting contrast, Merton, as he catches the "first sight of [the] mountains of Alaska," muses that perhaps he came to Alaska "in answer to someone's prayer."[165] For Merton, his own experiences and all of his encounters with others, whether in living moments of interaction or through the medium of books, came through the benevolent will of God.

Conclusions

With these four modes of reading, Merton changed the magnification of his spiritual microscope from a narrow focus on a short text (*lectio divina*) to a broader focus on an entire text or texts (summary reading), either for intellectual exercise or spiritual edification. Yet, as mentioned in the opening of this essay, there is a countervailing tendency to throw away reading in disgust. Reading, to him, can become a distraction, a nuisance, a lot of ideas about reality, experience or God. This tendency, which would last throughout his life, makes him hesitant and frustrated with the very task which consumed so much of his time.

From mid-June to late-October of 1948, this frustration made itself acutely present. Earlier, in October 1947, he writes that he feels he should spend "more time praying in Church," the "best thing" he can do, instead of "wasting time in books [he doesn't] need to read."[166] His time is a precious resource, and in this example time is being wasted for personal pursuits instead of being invested in the monastic life of prayer in solitude. Later he muses if "too much technical theology" is "deadening [his] interior life without [his] realizing it."[167] Reading becomes an impediment, an obstacle to spiritual attainment in this example. This disgust with his "greed for books and writing," which unduly "complicate [his] life," is seen as a personal failing; he has "eaten many books," a mark of his pride, which were read for his "own satisfaction."[168] In a strikingly confessional entry, he sees reading's role as obstacle in the interior life: "Still, what can I do but remain tranquil and resigned and keep my soul in silence, and recognize this truth, and wait upon God's will, and not confuse my inner life with too much reading and too many choices and too many desires and too many problems."[169] Here the monastic goals of simplicity and silence are disturbed and frustrated by the intellectual's grasping, explorative mind. The demon of pride is exorcised by partaking less in the pleasure of reading to expand one's personal knowledge.

The turmoil he finds himself in throughout this period is exacerbated after he reads a passage on poverty by Saint Francis. In accord with the monastic ideal of poverty, the deep spiritual poverty that would fascinate Merton, he feels the urge to get "rid of a lot of things [he doesn't] really need," presumably that would include the too much reading mentioned only two months prior.[170] He wants to "get out of so much writing and try to live more simply" by engaging in field labor, which he misses.[171] Exasperated by his reading and work and writing, he feels there is "no sense" in "all the elaborate reading [he does], all [his] fussing with architecture and poetry and all the rest of it," because that is "not what [he is] here for."[172] His true desire is to be "little and hidden and poor," not complicated by ideas and criticism and arguments found in his reading.[173] A month later, he writes that he "wasted almost the whole morning" reading in the Scriptorium.[174] He has "less and less desire to read anything about anything," because "all [he] need[s]" is a book about prayer or the Bible to give him "one sentence as a spring board for meditation," a reference to *lectio divina*.[175] In the final entry of this tumultuous period, he writes that it is "very hard for [him] to read anything"; he "watched the rain falling" and "burned with the love of God in silence and joy," and even though he "held a book in [his] hand," he "couldn't read more than a few lines."[176] This early struggle with his reading was particularly acute, yet similar struggles would continue to crop up throughout his life.

He often calls reading a waste of time, a non-edifying enterprise which distracts him from his monastic calling for silence and simplicity. He writes that he wishes he had "only spent the time on Scripture [he] wasted on Duns Scotus," an activity that was not "essentially useless," even though he "really never got around to understanding more than a tenth of what [he] read with so much labor."[177] He believes in the "[n]ecessity of the Bible," and he needs "[m]ore and more of it," instead of other distracting reading.[178] Sometimes his wasted time is seen too late, as in Morris West's *Shoes of the Fisherman*, which he "[w]asted [his] time reading."[179] In sapping his time and energy, his reading is dangerous if done on inappropriate or poorly written texts which do not edify; they become wasteful and damaging.

Moreover, he also sees this proclivity to flee into books, instead of working in silence and prayer, as a personal failing that he grapples with throughout his life. Instead of "seeking refuge in a book," he lets his soul "grind away at itself for an hour," in an effort to address the "old, old question" of "what shall [he] be?"[180] On the one hand is the painful and exhaustive process of self-examination in silence and prayer, and on the other hand is the flight into reading as a superficial balm. His tendency for the latter has to be counterbalanced by a direct assertion of the former. He writes that he is "too obsessed with the reading" he has been doing, during which he was "fruitlessly lost" most of the time.[181] His recurring "greed for books" manifests itself when in 1959 he questions what he "*really* need[s]," the first of which is to be "free from the need of [...] new books."[182] Cleaning up his office, the source of the introductory quotation to this article, makes him vow to "not forget" the "awful, automatic worried routine of piling up books, sorting papers, tearing some up, mailing them out, etc."[183] The clutter and confusion of his troubled experience with reading, his "intellectual gluttony" needs to be purged for a calmer, simpler, more silent life.[184]

An older Merton would tend to read less and less, as this conflict with reading eventually evened itself out somewhat. Even though several months at the hermitage have not settled the "great conflict in [him]," he muses over the first few months there, when he did "too much excited reading of too many things," and when his life was "grossly overstimulated" for a hermit.[185] In late October 1965, in light of this experience, he is "[r]eading slower and less."[186] He wants to "cut down on the ceaseless movement of books back and forth" in late 1965, and, two years later, is edified by reading "less and less" to combat being "intellectually overfed ... in the mornings."[187] Instead he reads "almost nothing at all in the early morning," and even though he "like[s]" the reading he is

doing, he has "to stop."[188]   Here he is addressing the problem of
overstimulation and tries to correct it by deliberately slowing himself down.   Similarly, he "couldn't read a line of [Buber's *Ten
Rungs*]," because he feels "utterly blank."[189]   Three months later
he writes that he "[doesn't] read much these days," and prefers to
spend his time with the *Ashtavakra Gita,* which is "very much what
[he] ha[s] been reading."[190]   In late May 1968, he writes that he
needs "[n]ot simply to be quiet [...] to pray, to read" but to effect a
"change and transformation" deep within himself, not through a
deliberate "special project" of "work[ing] on [himself]," but to be
content with his situation and "go for walks, live in peace, let
change come quietly and invisibly on the inside."[191]   The fever of
his earlier tortured conflict with reading had softened into an
awareness of the tension without overcompensating in either direction.   Even though he felt at points "too restless to do much
reading," he had learned to address the tension within him and
how to correct the imbalance reading could create in him.[192]   The
later Merton, learning from the torment of the early years, was
careful to balance reading and experience, and not get lost in an
obsessive commitment to the former with detrimental consequences for the latter.

The evidence assembled here sheds light on the world of
Merton as reader, a world marked by the paradox of reading as
necessity and frivolity and the tension between spiritual practice
and intellectual learning.   Compelled by an honest and burning
love for God in personal experience, he entered the monastery, yet
his intellectual curiosity, one of his greatest attributes, would prove
to be an obstacle when not carefully attended to.   This conflict,
which he had "not yet fully faced" by 1965, would not be fully
resolved before his death in 1968.[193]   Even in Asia, his self-proclaimed homeland, his reading style, mostly characterized by brief
quotations, fluctuated wildly between distant scholarly engagement with his reading and his emotional warmth for the living
texts of the Buddhists and Hindus he met.[194]   The matrix of reading styles that characterized his life presented tempting options to
better understand himself, the world, and God.   And yet the clearer
understanding he sought fueled his intellectual and spiritual wanderlust through the matrix of reading styles exposed here.   His
final resolution, if it can be so called, was not a "[settling] of the
great affair" of his struggle with reading.[195]   Instead, it was a tense
equilibrium, where reading was carefully balanced as both the in-

tellectual activity of a curious mind and the spiritual practice of a man seeking God.

Notes

1. Thomas Merton, *A Search for Solitude: Pursuing the Monk's True Life* (Journal 3: ed. Lawrence S. Cunningham, San Francisco: HarperCollins, 1996), p. 246.

2. Thomas Merton, *Dancing in the Water of Life: Seeking Peace in the Hermitage* (Journals 5: ed. Robert E. Daggy, San Francisco: HarperCollins, 1997), p. 280.

3. Journals Vol. 3, p. 246.

4. Journals Vol. 5, p. 280.

5. Journals Vol. 5, p. 280.

6. Jean Leclercq, *The Love of Learning and the Desire for God* (New York: Fordham UP, 1961), p. 65.

7. Thomas Merton, *Entering the Silence: Becoming a Monk and Writer* (Journals 2: ed. Jonathan Montaldo, San Francisco: HarperCollins, 1996), p. 239.

8. Thomas Merton, *Run to the Mountain: The Story of a Vocation* (Journals 1: ed. Patrick Hart, O.S.C.O, San Francisco: HarperCollins, 1995), p. 344. All quotations from this paragraph are drawn from this source.

9. Journals, Vol. 2, p. 348.

10. Journals Vol. 2, p. 349-50.

11. Jean Leclercq, "Lectio Divina" *Worship* 58 (May 1984), p. 240, 248.

12. Journals Vol. 3, 188. All quotations from this paragraph are drawn from this source.

13. Thomas Merton, *Learning to Love: Exploring Solitude and Freedom* (Journals Vol. 6: ed. Christine M. Bochen, San Francisco: HarperCollins, 1997), p. 170.

14. Other notable examples of the influence of *lectio divina* on Merton's reading habits can be found in his rumination on Job 12-3 on 13 September 1964 (Vol. 5, 144-5) and his reflection on Ezekiel 32 on 12 November 1965 (Vol. 5, 315), both of which exhibit a tendency to isolate a short passage and find in it personal significance.

15. Journals Vol. 1, p. 248.

16. Journals Vol. 1, p. 248.

17. Journals Vol. 1, p. 248.

18. Journals Vol. 1, p. 249.

19. Journals Vol. 1, p. 248.

20. Journals Vol. 3, p. 256.

21. Journals Vol. 3, p. 256.

22. In late September and early October 1959, Merton also transcribes brief selections from the Russian theologian Paul Evdokimov in a manner which shows signs of influence from *lectio divina* (Vol. 3, 330 and 334).

23. Thomas Merton, *Turning Toward the World: The Pivotal Years* (Journals 4: ed. Victor A. Kramer, San Francisco: HarperCollins, 1996), p. 112.

24. Journals Vol. 4, p. 113.

25. Journals Vol. 4, p. 113.

26. For other examples of Merton finding worthwhile information in otherwise poor texts, e.g., "in general magnificent!" in *Dancing in the Water of Life*, pp. 286-87; see Vol. 2: p. 69 and p. 208; Vol. 3: p. 286; Vol. 5: p. 45, p. 193 and pp. 286-7; Vol. 6: p. 154; Thomas Merton, *The Other Side of the Mountain: The End of the Journey* (Journals 7, ed. Patrick Hart, O.S.C.O. New York: HarperCollins, 1998): p. 35, p. 55 and p. 118.

27. Journals Vol. 2, p. 353.

28. Journals Vol. 2, p. 353.

29. Journals Vol. 2, p. 353.

30. Journals Vol. 5, p. 55.

31. Journals Vol. 5, p. 55.

32. Journals Vol. 5, p. 55.

33. Journals Vol. 5, p. 255.

34. Journals Vol. 6, p. 86.

35. Journals Vol. 6, p. 86.

36. Journals Vol. 6, p. 117.

37. Journals Vol. 6, p. 117.

38. Journals Vol. 2, p. 105.

39. Journals Vol. 2, p. 105.

40. Journals Vol. 3, p. 376.

41. Journals Vol. 3, p. 377.

42. Journals Vol. 3, p. 377.

43. Journals Vol. 3, p. 379.

44. Journals Vol. 4, p. 24.

45. Journals Vol. 4, p. 202.

46. Journals Vol. 4, p. 249.

47. Journals Vol. 5, p. 30.

48. Journals Vol. 4, p. 42.

49. Journals Vol. 4, p. 42.

50. Journals Vol. 4, p. 66.

51. Journals Vol. 5, p. 149.

52. Journals Vol. 5, p. 149.

53. Journals Vol. 2, p. 403.

54. Journals Vol. 3, p. 109.

55. Journals Vol. 3, p. 204.

56. Journals Vol. 5, p. 52.

57. Journals Vol. 6, p. 112.

58. Journals Vol. 2, p. 73.

59. Journals Vol. 2, p. 73.

60. Journals Vol. 2, p. 73.

61. Journals Vol. 4, p. 322.

62. Journals Vol. 4, p. 322.

63. Journals Vol. 5, p. 12.

64. Journals Vol. 5, p. 12.

65. Journals Vol. 5, p. 12.

66. Journals Vol. 5, p. 38.

67. Journals Vol. 6, p. 312.

68. Journals Vol. 6, p. 312.

69. Journals Vol. 6, p. 312.

70. Journals Vol. 6, p. 343.

71. Journals Vol. 4, p. 19.

72. Journals Vol. 4, p. 304.

73. Journals Vol. 4, p. 304.

74. Journals Vol. 6, p. 6.

75. Journals Vol. 7, p. 259.

76. Journals Vol. 7, p. 325.

77. See Journals Vol. 1, pp. 83-6.

78. This trend appears throughout Volume 1: see p. 275 and p. 328 on Bonaventure and Thomas, and p. 352 on Bernard's concept of charity.

79. Journals Vol. 2, p. 266.

80. Journals Vol. 2, p. 269-70.

81. For further examples of this trend, see Merton's dissection of Merleau-Ponty's argument in Vol. 5: p. 51, pp. 62-4, his break-down of contradiction in Nishida in Vols. 6, p. 10, and his patient untangling of the meaning of Madhyamika in Vol. 7, p. 260.

82. Journals Vol. 3, p. 216.

83. Journals Vol. 1, pp. 297-8.

84. Journals Vol. 2, p. 344.

85. Journals Vol. 3, p. 89.

86. Journals Vol. 4, pp. 343-4.

87. Journals Vol. 6, p. 31-32.

88. Journals Vol. 6, p. 194.

89. Journals Vol. 6, p. 197.

90. Monica Furlong, *Thomas Merton: A Biography* (San Francisco: Harper & Row, 1980), p. 297.

91. Journals Vol. 3, p. 94.

92. Journals Vol. 3, p. 95.

93. Journals Vol. 3, p. 95.

94. Journals Vol. 3, pp. 94-5.

95. Journals Vol. 3, p. 293.

96. Journals Vol. 3, p. 294.

97. For further examples of this trend, beyond those listed here, see Vol. 2, p. 390; Vol. 3, p. 124 and pp. 144-5.

98. Journals Vol. 1, p. 135.

99. Journals Vol. 1, p. 135.

100. Journals Vol. 1, p. 136.

101. Journals Vol. 4, p. 278.

102. Journals Vol. 6, p. 165.

103. Journals Vol. 6, p. 165.

104. Journals Vol. 3, p. 292.

105. Journals Vol. 4, p. 156.

106. Journals Vol. 5, p. 162.

107. See his praise of Faulkner's "The Bear" in Vol. 6, p. 166, and *As I Lay Dying* in Vol. 6, p. 281.

108. Journals Vol. 2, p. 195.

109. Journals Vol. 2, p. 384.

110. Journals Vol. 2, p. 384.

111. Journals Vol. 3, p. 179.

112. Journals Vol. 3, p. 288.

113. Journals Vol. 3, p. 389.

114. Journals Vol. 6, p. 92.

115. Journals Vol. 6, p. 92.

116. Journals Vol. 1, p. 98.

117. Journals Vol. 1, p. 98.

118. Journals Vol. 1, p. 455.

119. Journals Vol. 3, p. 64.

120. Journals Vol. 3, p. 64.

121. Journals Vol. 3, p. 64.

122. Journals Vol. 3, pp. 182-3.

123. Journals Vol. 3, p. 182.

124. Journals Vol. 3, p. 183.

125. Journals Vol. 3, p. 223.

126. Journals Vol. 2, p. 136.

127. Journals Vol. 2, p. 136.

128. Journals Vol. 3, p. 38.

129. Journals Vol. 3, p. 38.

130. Journals Vol. 2, p. 435.

131. Journals Vol. 3, p. 223.

132. Journals Vol. 3, p. 223.

133. Journals Vol. 3, p. 223.

134. Journals Vol. 3, p. 364.

135. Journals Vol. 3, p. 364.
136. Journals Vol. 3, p. 364.
137. Journals Vol. 4, p. 137, p. 173.
138. Journals Vol. 4, p. 189.
139. Journals Vol. 4, p. 189.
140. Journals Vol. 5, p. 212.
141. Journals Vol. 5, p. 235.
142. Journals Vol. 5, p. 235.
143. Journals Vol. 5, p. 235.
144. Journals Vol. 5, p. 235.
145. Journals Vol. 5, p. 235.
146. Journals Vol. 5, p. 255.
147. Journals Vol. 6, p. 154.
148. Journals Vol. 6, p. 185.
149. See Vol. 1, p. 98, p. 455; Vol. 3, p. 38, p. 64.
150. Journals Vol. 3, p. 71, p. 142, p. 370.
151. Journals Vol. 2, p. 220.
152. Journals Vol. 4, p. 281, p. 173.
153. Journals Vol. 3, p. 205.
154. Journals Vol. 5, p. 157.
155. Journals Vol. 6, p. 86.
156. Journals Vol. 6, p. 86.
157. Journals Vol. 2, p. 435. All quotations from this paragraph are drawn from this source.
158. Journals Vol. 3, p. 186.
159. Journals Vol. 3, p. 186, p. 64.
160. Journals Vol. 3, p. 186.
161. Journals Vol. 6, p. 152.
162. Journals Vol. 6, p. 152.
163. Journals Vol. 6, p. 153.
164. Journals Vol. 6, p. 153.
165. Journals Vol. 7, p. 182.
166. Journals Vol. 2, p. 128.
167. Journals Vol. 2, p. 162.
168. Journals Vol. 2, pp. 210-11.
169. Journals Vol. 2, p. 215.
170. Journals Vol. 2, p. 230.
171. Journals Vol. 2, p. 230.
172. Journals Vol. 2, p. 230.
173. Journals Vol. 2, p. 230.
174. Journals Vol. 2, p. 239.
175. Journals Vol. 2, p. 239.
176. Journals Vol. 2, p. 240.

177. Journals Vol. 2, p. 345.
178. Journals Vol. 3, p. 135.
179. Journals Vol. 5, p. 17.
180. Journals Vol. 3, p. 261.
181. Journals Vol. 4, p. 122.
182. Journals Vol. 2, p. 211; Vol. 3, p. 318.
183. Journals Vol. 5, p. 280.
184. Journals Vol. 5, p. 306.
185. Journals Vol. 5, p. 310.
186. Journals Vol. 5, p. 310.
187. Journals Vol. 5, p. 333; Vol. 7, p. 18.
188. Journals Vol. 7, p. 18.
189. Journals Vol. 7, p. 47.
190. Journals Vol. 7, p. 82.
191. Journals Vol. 7, p. 113.
192. Journals Vol. 7, p. 162.
193. Journals Vol. 5, p. 280.
194. Journals Vol. 7, p. 205.
195. Journals Vol. 7, p. 205.

A Monk with the Spiritual Equipment
of an Artist:
The Art of Thomas Merton

Paul M. Pearson

Introduction

Thomas Merton's artistic worldview was no doubt inherited from his parents, Owen and Ruth Merton. They had met in Paris where they were both pursuing artistic careers, Ruth was interested in interior decoration and design and Owen was a New Zealand painter who had already had a number of exhibitions. Ruth wrote that "there is no more fascinating subject in the world than the influence of surroundings on the human character" and Thomas Merton had described his father in the opening pages of *The Seven Storey Mountain* saying

> His vision of the world was sane, full of balance, full of veneration for structure, for the relations of masses and for the circumstances that impress an individual identity on each created thing. His vision was religious and clean, and therefore his paintings were without decoration or superfluous comment, since a religious man respects the power of God's creation to bear witness for itself.[1]

In speaking of Owen, Merton points to some trends in his father's art work which would later surface in Merton's photographs and drawings. Owen's work can be seen to be influenced by the work of Cezanne (with whom he in fact he shared an exhibition in London) and by a "synthetic cubism" adopting a "simplified and geometricised form."[2] This would also be true of Thomas Merton's own drawings which seem to be influenced by cubism as is seen in his use of strong, emphatic lines and a tendency to simplification, ignoring detail.

The obituary of Owen in the London *Times* described him as "a water-colour painter of distinction, who, had he lived longer, would have earned a wide reputation." It continued:

His pictures displayed a sense of design and a delicacy of colour which reflected his love of the Chinese masters, together with a strength and individuality which bore witness to the originality and power of the artists mind ... His love of landscape and his passion for painting enabled him to inspire all those who came in contact with him, and many other painters owe much to his helpful enthusiasm.[3]

It was inevitable that Thomas Merton should try his own hand at art. The earliest surviving images we have of Merton's were drawings he made to illustrate stories that he was writing in his early teens. Merton refers to these stories, and their illustrations, in his autobiography. In *The Seven Storey Mountain* Merton, already an avid reader, recalls how he and his friends at the Lycee Ingres, in Montauban in 1926, when he was only eleven, "were all furiously writing novels" and that he was "engaged in a great adventure story." Although that particular story "was never finished" he recalls that he "finished at least one other, and probably two, besides one which I wrote at St. Antonin before coming to the Lycee." These novels "scribbled in exercise books, profusely illustrated in pen and ink"[4] may sound like the poetic license of the budding author writing in later years but, recently discovered manuscripts dating back to December 1929 confirm his description. *The Haunted Castle*[5] and *The Great Voyage*, obviously imitating the recently published Winnie the Pooh stories, are "profusely illustrated in pen and ink" and another, *Ravenswell,*[6] is an adventure story filling an exercise book of one hundred and fifty-eight pages, and was written in just twelve days.[7] Throughout Merton's life he would be influenced by the current trends in art, literature and other disciplines, and in these early novels we can see the beginning of this trend.

The next known images date from Merton's time at Columbia University— cartoons published in the Jester, the humorous magazine on campus of which Merton was the Art Editor in his senior year, other artwork saved by his Columbia friend and Godfather, Ed Rice,[8] along with materials in the Columbia University archives. On Merton's "Declaration of Intention" for permanent residence in the United States, completed in 1938, his stated occupation was "cartoonist and writer."[9] Some of Merton's cartoons, as with those of other contributors for the Jester,[10] bear some resemblance to the work of Thurber or other cartoonists publishing in *The New Yorker* at this time.

Other Images from this period include a variety of female nudes—joyful, laughing images, full of life and energy, at times provocative. Again, there are other images, which I would suggest, were imitations of movements in modern art that attracted him—the surrealists, Picasso, Calder or Joan Miro—a trend that would later continue in some of his artwork from Gethsemani.[11] Other images from this time included figures made up of words appropriate to the subject, for example, reflecting the exuberance of life in the thirties and then, later in the thirties, the growing shadows of war.

After his conversion to Catholicism in November 1938 the subjects of his drawings changed and, as seen in many of the images to be found in the archives at St. Bonaventure University where Merton taught prior to his entry to the Abbey of Gethsemani in December 1941, line drawings of religious images came to dominate his artistic output, images though not as simple or stark as those he would draw in his early years in the monastery. However some images were still drawn by stringing words together now however reflecting Merton's conversion with religious images drawn using the words of prayers. This combination of the power of both images and the written word was one that would appeal to Merton for the rest of his life.

Early Gethsemani Drawings

Once at Gethsemani Merton continued to draw. As he could not stop writing prose or poetry, so he could also not stop drawing. His images from this period were traditional images of saints, prophets, angels, the cross and Christ crucified, most noticeably a large collection of groups of the crucifixion, St. John of the Cross, and female saints, in particular the Blessed Virgin Mary, St. Therese and Mary Magdalene. Besides these images there are a smaller number of still life and landscape studies. The majority of images from this period were unsigned, undated and untitled. But it is possible to see connections with, and the influence, of other religious art Merton may have been exposed to.

In the fall of 1954 Merton gave a series of conferences to the scholastics at Gethsemani. Although these conferences were not recorded his notes, entitled "Notes on Sacred Art," have been preserved. From these lectures Merton prepared a manuscript for publication entitled "Art and Worship."

As Merton was collecting images for "Art and Worship" he obviously thought he was in touch once more, with the larger art

world—possibly returning once more to the world of his childhood and youth, though this time from a deeper religious perspective. However both the images he was selecting for "Art and
Worship" and his text were criticized by potential publishers and
friends, suggesting he was out of touch with the current art world,
or at least the world of publishing art books. One "reader" wrote
"I have read Merton's manuscript three times now and it is my
best advice that you have nothing to do with it ... it is simply in-
credibly naïve" and "beyond any real salvation." Eloise Spaeth, in
her report to the prospective publisher, was equally harsh calling
it "Bad Merton" with "no vitality, even the usual stunning phrase-
ology is lacking" adding, "this is written by a man who has not
looked at a real work of art for a long time." Based on reports such
as these the book was put to one side and never finished or published in its entirety.

Merton, however, published a number of articles and essays
about art, partially based on his manuscript. The earliest of these
was a short section from his book *No Man Is An Island*, published
in *Commonweal* in March 1955 with the title: "Reality, Art and
Prayer."[12] The following year a much longer article appeared in
the journal *Jubilee* entitled "Notes on Sacred and Profane Art."[13]
As the title suggests this article was closer to notes than to an essay and, as Merton had planned with "Art and Worship" it was
illustrated by examples of the work of artists such as Cezanne,
Van Eyck, Fra Angelico and Rouault, and by an example of a carving from the Cathedral of Chartres. Three further articles on art:
"The Monk and Sacred Art,"[14] "Art and Worship"[15] and "Sacred
Art and the Spiritual Life"[16] were all published in the journal
Sponsa Regis between 1957 and 1960, with a further article, "Ab-
surdity in Sacred Decoration,"[17] attacking "the appetite for useless decoration and for illustration" in church decoration, published in the journal *Worship* in 1960.[18]

But Merton did not completely drop the idea of a book on Sacred Art and in September 1963 writes to Sister Therese Lentfoehr:

> I am trying finally to brush up the little book on Sacred Art I
> was trying to do four or five years ago. First we intended to
> publish it here. Then I saw it was going to be too complicated,
> and tried it on Farrar Straus and though they wanted it, we
> bogged down over a detail. I hope I can get it out of the way –
> though that is hardly the way to approach a book, least of all a
> book on art.[19]

In 1964 in "Seven Qualities of the Sacred,"[20] an article published in the journal *Good Work,* Merton presented a more coherent and developed presentation of his thinking first expressed in the 1956 *Jubilee* article about what is meant by sacredness in art. Each of the seven qualities Merton suggests—hieratic, traditional, living, sincere, reverent, spiritual and pure—was once again illustrated by examples of art work that Merton felt exhibited these qualities, once more reminiscent of the layout he had envisaged for "Art and Worship."

Experimental images:
Zen calligraphies, graffiti, ink-blots

Over the course of Merton's writings about art some of his thinking stayed remarkably consistent, whereas his actual practice of art changed and developed in a way that was at times radical.

In *The Seven Storey Mountain* Merton wrote that he had learned from his father "that art was contemplation, and that it involved the action of the highest faculties."[21] In his reading of *Art and Scholasticism* by Jacques Maritain, as he was working on his master's thesis on William Blake at Columbia University, Merton found a theory of art that confirmed the view he had inherited from his father. A belief that "art is the ability to see not merely what is apparent to the senses but the inner radiance of Being,"[22] a consciousness of paradise, of the creative *logos,* the creative word. This understanding of art is evident in many of the authors to whom Merton was attracted—William Blake, Boris Pasternak, Louis Zukofsky and Edwin Muir. It is expressed in Rainer Maria Rilke's concept of "inseeing" and in the "inscape" of Gerard Manley Hopkins.

In one of Merton's lectures to the monastic community at Gethsemani in the mid-sixties on Rainer Maria Rilke Merton described Rilke's "inseeing" as a deep encounter between the poet and his subject, getting right into the center of the subject, right into the heart. In one conference Merton describes the way Rilke gets into the very center of the thing he is describing. Taking a dog as an example this inseeing involves getting into

the dog's very center, the point from where it begins to be a dog, the place in which, in it, where God, as it were, would have sat down for a moment when the dog was finished in order to watch it under the influence of its first embarrassments and inspirations and to know that it was good, that nothing was lacking, that it could not have been made better.[23]

It was this same spirit that attracted Merton to the Shakers. Their architecture and their furniture were made, so they believed, as God would have made it, it could not have been made better. Merton discovered a similar spirit in the Hindu tradition of art, where "all artistic work is a form of *Yoga*" writing

> all art is Yoga, and even the act of making a table or a bed, or building a house, proceeds from the craftsman's Yoga and from his spiritual discipline of meditation.[24]

He goes on, in words reminiscent of his comments on Rainer Maria Rilke, and influenced by his reading of A. K. Coomaraswamy, to add

> in the East it is believed that the mind that has entered into meditative recollection and attained 'one pointedness' has liberated itself from domination by the accidental, the trivial and the jejune, in order to enter into the heart of being, and thus to be able to identify itself, by contemplative penetration, with any being and to know it by empathy from within.[25]

In contrast to his theory of art, Merton's practice of art changed dramatically at times. These changes, I would suggest, were consistent with other changes taking place in his life and thought, especially in the late fifties and early sixties. As Thomas Merton moved from the world-denying monk of the forties and early fifties to the world-embracing monk of the sixties he found that the language he had used previously in both his public and his personal writings was no longer adequate or appropriate. This is particularly noticeable in the metaphors he used to describe himself, especially his move from the role of an "innocent bystander" to that of a "guilty bystander." The change was clearly evident in both his prose and his poetry. The quiet voice of monasticism that many catholic readers had associated with Merton's earlier work had seemingly disappeared into the Gethsemani woods and the new Merton was disturbing and could grate on his readers sensibilities—the same could also be true of his art from this period.

Thomas Merton rarely wrote about his own attempts at art. The majority of information that we have has to be gleaned from the many pages of his personal journals and from his voluminous correspondence. From an entry contained in his personal journal for October 28, 1960 Merton records a marked change in his style of drawing. He writes: "Tried some abstract-looking art this week."[26] Just a few entries later he refers to "spending some work time on abstract drawings for a possible experimental book." Some of these drawings, which Merton would begin calling "calligraphies" were semi-representational, but the majority were completely abstract.

The one time Merton wrote at any length or in any detail was in the fall of 1964 as he was preparing for an exhibition of his drawings to be held at Catherine Spalding College in Louisville. The exhibition of twenty-six calligraphies opened in November 1964 and subsequently visited a number of other cities including New Orleans, Atlanta, Milwaukee, St. Louis, Santa Barbara and Washington, D.C. The pictures were available for purchase with the money raised to be used for a scholarship for an African-American student to study at Spalding. Sales did not go well and Merton writes to John Howard Griffin saying

> none were sold in Milwaukee where the price was a hundred and fifty dollars. Now we are down to a hundred. If you wait until we crawl out of Santa Barbara, Cal. in September they will be ten cents apiece with a sheaf of green coupons into the bargain.[27]

Subsequently the Abbey of Gethsemani funded the scholarship.

The essay Merton wrote was later published as "Signatures: Notes on the Author's Drawings" in his book *Raids on the Unspeakable*. It is an important essay as it contains Merton's only extended reflection on his own drawings, in particular on the drawings he was creating in the sixties. As such, I think it is really essential reading in attaining an understanding of what Merton was attempting to do with his drawings at this period. Merton begins by saying that the viewer is not to regard the drawings as "works of art," nor to seek in them "traces of irony" or "a conscious polemic against art." The viewer is encouraged not to judge them, or to consider themselves judged by them. Before moving on to say what the drawings are, Merton makes a comment on the titles writing:

> it would be better if these abstractions did not have titles. However, titles were provided out of the air. The viewer will hardly be aided by them, but he may imagine himself aided if he wishes.[28]

Merton then writes about his understanding of the drawings, and I will just quote here a few of the most incisive passages:

> These abstractions—one might almost call them *graffiti* rather than calligraphies—are simple signs and ciphers of energy, acts of movement intended to be propitious. Their "meaning" is not to be sought on the level of convention or of concept.

Again:

> In a world cluttered and programmed with an infinity of practical signs and consequential digits referring to business, law, government and war, one who makes such nondescript marks as these is conscious of a special vocation to be inconsequent, to be outside the sequence and to remain firmly alien to the program...they stand outside all processes of production, marketing, consumption and destruction.

Merton then adds mischievously that it "does not however mean that they cannot be bought." Words reminiscent, as is much of Merton's thinking in this essay, of some of the writings of Ad Reinhardt, the abstract artist, who once described his black paintings in similar terms:

> A free, unmanipulated, unmanipulatable, useless, unmarketable, irreducible, unphotographable, unreproducible, inexplicable icon.[29]

Thomas Merton and Ad Reinhardt

Merton and Reinhardt first met at Columbia University in the thirties. Although Reinhardt graduated shortly after Merton's arrival at the University he continued to provide illustrations for the *Jester*. Merton makes a number of references to Reinhardt in *The Seven Storey Mountain* and in *Run to the Mountain*, his personal journal from this period. After an evening with Reinhardt in January 1940 Merton calls him "possibly the best artist in America" writing

> Reinhardt's abstract art is pure and religious. It flies away from all naturalism, from all representation to pure formal and intellectual values ...Reinhardt's abstract art is completely chaste, and full of love of form and very good indeed.[30]

After Merton's entry into the Abbey of Gethsemani he sporadically stayed in touch with Reinhardt. Copies of a number of early letters from Merton to Reinhardt from 1956 to 1964 are preserved in the Smithsonian's Archives of American Art, along with some calligraphies Merton had sent him. Five letters to Merton from Reinhardt, all from the sixties, are preserved in the archives of the Thomas Merton Center at Bellarmine University.

In the mid fifties Merton asked Reinhardt to design the cover of a pamphlet to be printed by the Abbey of Gethsemani, requesting also "some small black and blue cross painting (say about a foot and a half high) for the cell in which I perch."[31] When the painting arrived Merton recorded in his journal:

> Reinhardt finally sent his "small" painting. Almost invisible cross on a black background. As though immersed in darkness and trying to emerge from it. Seen in relation to my other object the picture is meaningless—a black square "without purpose"—You have to look hard to see the cross. One must turn away from everything else and concentrate on the picture as though peering through a window into the night. The picture demands this - or is meaningless for I presume that someone might be unmoved by any such demand. I should say a very "holy" picture—helps prayer—an "image" without features to accustom the mind at once to the night of prayer—and to help one set aside trivial and useless images that wander into prayer and spoil it.[32]

Merton wrote to Reinhardt thanking him for the painting saying:

> It has the following noble feature, namely its refusal to have anything else around it, notably the furniture etc. It is a most recollected small painting. It thinks that only one thing is necessary & this is time, but this one thing is by no means apparent to one who will not take the trouble to look. It is a most religious, devout, and latreutic small painting.[33]

In May 1959 Reinhardt along with Bob Lax, another Columbia friend, visited Merton at the Abbey of Gethsemani. Other than recording the visit in his journal Merton makes no other comment about this visit. During the visit however they must have discussed Merton's plans for a book on art as a few days later Merton refers to this in a letter to Reinhardt:

> Now you come along and ask me to fall into the iconoclastic tradition. Which is admittedly something like my own (sup-

posedly my own) Cistercian background. St. Bernard threw out all the statues. They were a distraction, he said. I used to believe it. I think it is an affectation, from the religious viewpoint, to hold that statues are a distraction. Who is there to be distracted?... That which is religious and sacred in a work of art is something other than just the artistic content, or form, or excellence of the work of art. But it is not something material, it is not information, it is not propaganda, it is not doctrine. It is not 'about' anything. It is existential, it is what is in the work of art.[34]

Both Merton and Reinhardt were influenced by the apophatic mystical tradition – writers such as John of the Cross, pseudo-Dionysius and Nicholas of Cusa come to mind. Merton's references to apophatic mysticism are found in a number of his works throughout his monastic life, most notably his attempt at a theological study of St. John of the Cross, eventually published as *The Ascent to Truth* and in the more recently published book, *The Inner Experience*. Reinhardt also makes references to the apophatic mystics in his writings, for example in 1965 quoting Nicholas of Cusa:

How needful it is to enter into the darkness and to admit the coincidence of opposites
to seek the truth where impossibility meets us.[35]

Writing to an artist friend in Lexington, Victor Hammer, Merton describes Reinhardt's work in the following terms

His approach is very austere and ascetic. It is a kind of exaggerated reticence, a kind of fear of self expression. All his paintings are very formal and black. I certainly do not think he is a quack like so many others; on the contrary, he is in strong reaction against them.[36]

The influence of apophatic mysticism on Reinhardt has been referred to by critics of his work in recent years. Yve-Alain Bois suggested that what Reinhardt hoped to realize in his black paintings recalled the aspirations of negation theology, apophatic mysticism, a "method of thought employed to comprehend the Divine by indicating everything it was not."[37]

In fall 1963 Merton sent one of his calligraphies to Ad Reinhardt who reacted enthusiastically writing when all of a sudden out of the clear sky and mailbox, comes your calligraphy, your beautiful calligraphy but too small, don't you know them fellows way down East used brushes bigger than anyone's big head, a big pot of paint size of a big sink, and in bare feet, dance over a piece of paper bigger and longer than Ulfert Willkie stretched from end to end ... I like your calligraphy because its pure.

Merton replied humorously

I am again your friendly old calligrapher always small calligraphies down here, I am the grandfather of the small calligraphy because I don't have a big brush and because I no longer run about the temple barefoot in frosts. But I am amiable and the smaller they get the more mysterious they are, though in fact it is the irony of art when a calligrapher gets stuck with a whole pile of papers the same size and texture

going on to suggest

I invite you to pretend you are about to print a most exotic book and get samples of papers from distant Cathay and all over and then send them to your dusty old correspondent who is very poor and got no papers any more except toilet papers for the calligraphy.[38]

And concluding the letter "Take seriously the samples."

In January 1964 Merton records in his journal a package that had arrived from Ad Reinhardt. Following up on Merton's request he had sent Merton "all kinds of fine paper, especially some thin, almost transparent beautiful Japanese paper on which I have found a way of crudely printing abstract 'calligraphies' which in some cases turn out exciting – at least to me."[39] Taking note of Reinhardt's comments about his calligraphies Merton also sent a new calligraphy to Reinhardt titled: "slightly larger calligraphy."

In contrast to friends such as Ad Reinhardt Merton reflected on how his artist friend, Victor Hammer, would react to these drawings. Merton writes in his journal on November 4, 1964:

One thing that saddens and embarrasses me—that he [Victor Hammer] will be shocked at my exhibition of drawings or calligraphies or what you will. There is no way to explain this to him, and in a way I am on his side, on principle. And yet they have a meaning, and there is a reason for them: an unreasoned reason perhaps.

He then continues with a note of humour:

> I feel like writing to him and saying: if you heard I had taken a mistress you would be sad but you would understand. These drawings are perhaps worse than that. But regard them as a human folly. Allow me at least, like everyone else, at least one abominable vice, etc.[40]

And in a letter to Hammer Merton warns him that

> If you should hear news of my exhibiting strange blobs of ink in Louisville, ignore the information: it is not worthy of your notice. As always my feelings about it are very mixed …I think I have made it plain to all concerned that I do not regard it as "art" and that they are not supposed to either.[41]

But, having told Hammer to ignore the exhibit and that he did not regard the strange blots of ink as art, it is clear from other correspondence of Merton's and from entries in his personal journals, that it was important to him and expressed for him his art in this period when his representational work was no longer sufficient, when it no longer addressed the anguish of the age. Both Merton and Reinhardt reacted to the climate of Cold War America through their work. Although rarely in touch with each other their stand on contemporary issues was remarkably similar. Reinhardt was actively involved in political and social issues throughout his life, he participated in the anti-war movement, he protested against the war in Vietnam and also donated his work to benefits for civil rights activities—all areas in which Merton was involved through the sixties—even, as already mentioned, selling his calligraphies to fund a scholarship for African-American students.[42]

Merton had a similar experience with his poetry. He began to feel that language had become so abused, so overused, especially in the world of media and advertising, that it had become virtually meaningless. To compensate for this Merton began to use anti-poetry as a form of expression at this time.[43] Is it possible that Merton's calligraphies and drawings of this period are anti-art, like his anti-poetry, trying to express a form of art that made sense in the face of advertising and the media, and in the face of humanity's experience of the darker, shadow side so evident in the images of this period of the cold war, the bomb, racial violence, and the Vietnam War?

Merton first touched on this theme explicitly as he was working on "Art and Worship" and, in a chapter published in <u>Sponsa Regis</u> in January 1960, and also included in his book *Disputed Questions*, published later that year he wrote:

In an age of concentration camps and atomic bombs, religious and artistic sincerity will certainly exclude all "prettiness" or shallow sentimentality. Beauty, for us, cannot be a mere appeal to conventional pleasures of the imagination and senses. Nor can it be found in cold, academic perfectionism. The art of our time, sacred art included, will necessarily be characterized by a certain poverty, grimness and roughness which correspond to the violent realities of a cruel age. Sacred art cannot be cruel, but it must know how to be compassionate with the victims of cruelty: and one does not offer lollipops to a starving man in a totalitarian death-camp.

Nor does one offer him the message of a pitifully inadequate optimism. Our Christian hope is the purest of all lights that shine in darkness, but it shines in darkness, and one must enter into darkness to see it shining.[44]

As Merton saw, John of the Cross's Dark Night of the Soul, the experience of the apophatic mystics, was no longer confined to a spiritual minority. The horrors of the twentieth century, the degradation of human life, was making manifest the darkness within each and every one of us and Merton through his anti-poetry, his writings on war and violence, and through his art work of this period was trying to stand and face the darkness and encouraging others to do the same. As he wrote in his introduction to *Raids on the Unspeakable*:

Christian hope begins where every other hope stands frozen stiff before the face of the Unspeakable…The goodness of the world, stricken or not, is incontestable and definitive. If it is stricken, it is also healed in Christ. But nevertheless one of the awful facts of our age is the evidence that it is stricken indeed, stricken to the very core of its being by the presence of the Unspeakable.

Against this background Merton can speak words of hope.

Be human in this most inhuman of ages; guard the image of man for it is the image of God.[45]

Photography

Thomas Merton showed little interest in photography until the final years of his life. On a visit to Germany as a teenager he had bought his first camera, a Zeiss, which he subsequently pawned as his debts grew at Cambridge University[46] in the early thirties. In 1939 he visited an exhibit of Charles Sheeler's at the Museum of Modern Art, which he found "dull."[47] Then, from the late fifties onwards Merton had contact with some eminent North American photographers beginning with Shirley Burden. Burden had provided photographs for a postulant's guide, *Monastic Peace*, for the cover of Merton's *Selected Poems* and had undertaken a photographic study of the monks at the Abbey of Gethsemani, *God Is My Life*, for which Merton wrote the introduction. When Merton was considering a photographic study of the Shakers, it was to Burden he turned.

In 1963 John Howard Griffin, with whom Merton had already had contact in relation to Civil Rights, wrote requesting permission to "begin a photographic archive of Merton's life and activities." When Griffin visited Merton to photograph him he recalls "Tom watched with interest, wanting an explanation of the cameras—a Leica and an Alpa." According to Griffin Merton remarked on his friendship with Shirley Burden and also with Edward Rice, a friend from his days at Columbia, before stating "I don't know anything about photography, but it fascinates me."[48]

It is a little unclear when Merton began taking photographs himself at the Abbey of Gethsemani. On October 10th 1961 he records having taken "half a roll of Kodacolor at the hermitage" wondering "what earthly reason is there for taking color photographs?... or any photographs at all."[49] Yet, just a few months later in January 1962 Merton records taking photographs at Shakertown, finding there "some marvelous subjects."[50]

> Marvelous, silent, vast spaces around the old buildings. Cold, pure light, and some grand trees... How the blank side of a frame house can be so completely beautiful I cannot imagine. A completely miraculous achievement of forms.[51]

Merton was obviously pleased with his results that day as in a later journal entry he says he is planning to have enlargements made of some of his photographs of Shakertown, describing it as "very satisfying."[52]

Certainly by 22nd September 1964 Merton had regular access to a camera and records in his personal journal

Brother Ephrem has fitted me out with a camera (Kodak Instamatic) to help take pictures for a book Dom James wants done. So far I have been photographing a fascinating old cedar root I have on the porch. I am not sure what this baby can do. The lens does not look like much – but it changes the film by itself and sets the aperture, etc. Very nice.[53]

Just two days later Merton continues

After dinner I was distracted by the dream camera, and instead of seriously reading the Zen anthology I got from the Louisville Library, kept seeing curious things to shoot, especially a mad window in the old tool room of the woodshed. The whole place is full of fantastic and strange subjects – a mine of Zen photography. After that the dream camera suddenly misbehaved.[54]

and Merton records that the back of the camera would not lock shot. Two days later he writes again

Camera back. Love affair with camera. Darling camera, so glad to have you back! Monarch! XXX. It will I think be a bright day again today.[55]

In his journals Merton records occasional access to a variety of cameras belonging to his visitors—Naomi Burton Stone's Nikon,[56] John Howard Griffin's Alpa,[57] even on one occasion a "Japanese movie camera" which he described as "a beautiful thing."[58] In August 1967 Merton refers in passing to taking some pictures of roots, this time with a Rolleiflex. However in January 1968 Merton fell and thought he might have broken the Rolleiflex so that the back was letting in light. He immediately wrote to John Howard Griffin to take up an offer he had made to loan Merton a camera. In his letter Merton describes the kind of camera he would need:

Obviously I am not covering the Kentucky Derby etc. But I do like a chance at fast funny out of the way stuff too. The possibility of it in case. But as I see it I am going to be on roots, sides of barns, tall weeds, mudpuddles, and junkpiles until Kingdom come. A built-in exposure meter might be a help.[59]

In response Griffin loaned Merton a Canon F-X which he described as "fabulous" and "a joy to work with." Merton continues

> The camera is the most eager and helpful of beings, all full of happy suggestions: 'Try this! Do it that way!' Reminding me of things I have overlooked, and cooperating in the creation of new worlds. So simply. This is a Zen camera.

Generally Merton's preferred photographic medium was black and white, though a number of photographs in the collections at the Thomas Merton Center are in color. Merton never did his own developing or printing, this was generally done for him either by Griffin, his son Gregory, or by other friends. Griffin recalls that he and his son were frequently bewildered by the pictures Merton selected from contact sheets to be enlarged. "He ignored many superlative photographs while marking others" wrote Griffin,

> we thought he had not yet learned to judge photographs well enough to select consistently the best frames. We wrote and offered advice about the quality of some of the ignored frames. He went right on marking what he wanted rather than what we thought he should want. Then, more and more often, he would send a contact sheet with a certain frame marked and his excited notation: 'At last—this is what I have been aiming for.'[60]

Sadly, none of those original contact sheets have survived. They would have provided a fascinating insight into Merton's photography.

In January 1967 Thomas Merton began to develop a friendship with another local photographer, Ralph Eugene Meatyard who, through his photographs, has left us an intriguing photographic record of Merton. In his personal journal Merton recorded the visit of Jonathan Williams, Guy Davenport and Meatyard[61] and in particular his excitement at Meatyard's work:

> The one who made the greatest impression on me as artist was Gene Meatyard, the photographer – does marvelous arresting visionary things, most haunting and suggestive, mythical, photography I ever saw. I felt that here was someone really going somewhere.[62]

Later writing about Merton and Meatyard, Davenport described Meatyard as "one of the most distinguished of American photographers," part of the Lexington Camera Club with members such as Van Deren Coke, Guy Mendes, James Baker Hall and Robert C. May. Meatyard, was a professional optician, who bought his first camera to photograph his young son in 1950. In 1956 his photographs were exhibited with those of Ansel Adams, Aaron Siskind, Henry Callaghan and other modern masters. That same year he attended a photography workshop where, working with Henry Holmes Smith and Minor White, he became interested in Zen. Davenport describes Meatyard's work as "primarily an intricate symmetry of light and shadow. He liked deep shadows of considerable weight, and he liked light that was decisive and clean."[63] Words equally applicable to many of Merton's photographs.

From their meeting in January 1967 until Merton's death the following year Merton met Gene Meatyard numerous times and exchanged a brief but steady correspondence of over sixteen letters. During this time Meatyard took over one hundred photographs of Merton, some of the most enigmatic taken. These photographs capture both the paradox of Merton and Meatyard's surrealistic vision—Meatyard realized with Merton that he was

> photographing a Kierkegaard who was a fan of *Mad*; a Zen adept and hermit who drooled over hospital nurses with a cute behind ...a man of accomplished self-discipline who sometimes acted like a ten-year-old with an unlimited charge account at a candy store.[64]

For Merton his photography, as his writing, became a way for him to explore and express his relationship with the world. In a journal entry from December 1963 Merton reflects on a saying of Merleau-Ponty: "I am myself as I exist in the world."[65] This leads him to question the position he had been taking, of being himself by withdrawing from the world, and stating that he agrees profoundly with Merleau-Ponty providing that the world he is referring to is not one of "delusions and clichés." He writes that "to withdraw from where I am in order to be totally outside all that situates me—this is real delusion." Merton's description of his camera as a "Zen camera" fits very well with the Zen koan-like nature of this insight.

In Darjeeling, just a couple of weeks before his death, Merton struggled with the Mountain Kanchenjunga. In Kanchenjunga, Merton saw an answer to his questions, the mountain holds paradoxes together. It has a side that is seen and a side that is not seen, it is a "palace of opposites in unity," "impermanence and patience, solidity and nonbeing, existence and wisdom." Developing his reflection on the mountain Merton added:

> The full beauty of the mountain is not seen until you too consent to the impossible paradox: it is and is not. When nothing more needs to be said, the smoke of ideas clears, the mountain is SEEN.[66]

This is similar to Merton's vision of photography and, as he tries to capture images of the mountain with his camera, Merton writes:

> The camera does not know what it takes: it captures materials with which you reconstruct not so much what you saw as what you thought you saw. Hence the best photography is aware, mindful, of illusion and uses illusion, permitting and encouraging it—especially unconscious and powerful illusions that are not normally admitted on the scene.[67]

This is reminiscent of Meatyard's understanding of Zen and his way of dealing with illusion by his frequent use of masks in his photographs, most noticeably in his collection *The Family Album of Lucybelle Crater*. In *A Hidden Wholeness* Griffin describes Merton's vision of photography:

> His vision was more often attracted to the movement of wheat in the wind, the textures of snow, paint-spattered cans, stone, crocuses blossoming through weeds—or again, the woods in all their hours, from the first fog or morning, though noonday stillness, to evening quiet.
>
> In his photography, he focused on the images of his contemplation, as they were and not as he wanted them to be. He took his camera on his walks and, with his special way of seeing, photographed what moved or excited him—whatsoever responded to that inner orientation.
>
> His concept of aesthetic beauty differed from that of most men. Most would pass by dead tree roots in search of a rose. Merton photographed the dead tree root or the texture of wood or whatever crossed his path. In these works, he photographed the natural, unarranged, unpossessed objects of his contemplation, seeking not to alter their life but to preserve it in his emulsions.

In a certain sense, then, these photographs do not need to be studied, they need to be contemplated if they are to carry their full impact.[68]

From these comments by Griffin, and through looking at Merton's photographs it is clear that Thomas Merton used his camera as a contemplative instrument and he photographed the things he contemplated.

Conclusion

Thomas Merton's art parallels his spiritual journey. Moving from childhood drawings, through his Columbia cartoons, to devout, strong and simple images, to his experiments with Zen calligraphies and graffiti along with his use of a Zen camera expressing his mature relationship with God, the world and his own self. Merton's mature drawings and his photography serve as question marks, asking us to pause and to reflect on what we are seeing. The words of his poem "In Silence," with which I will conclude, serve to illustrate this well:

Be still
Listen to the stones of the wall.
Be silent, they try
To speak your

Name.
Listen to the living walls.
Who are you?
Who
Are you? Whose
Silence are you?

Who (be quiet)
Are you (as these stones
Are Quiet). Do not
Think of what you are
Still less of
What you may one day be.
Rather
Be what you are (but who?) be
The unthinkable one
You do not know.

O be still, while
You are still alive,
And all things live around you
Speaking (I do not hear)
To your own being,
Speaking by the Unknown
That is in you and in themselves.

"I will try, like them
To be my own silence:
And this is difficult. The whole
World is secretly on fire. The stones
Burn, even the stones
They burn me. How can a man be still or
Listen to all things burning? How can he dare
To sit with them when
All their silence
Is on fire?"[69]

Notes

1. Thomas Merton, *The Seven Storey Mountain* (London: Sheldon Press, 1975), p. 3.

2. Katarzyna Bruzda, "Thomas Merton—An Artist." *Studia Mertoniana 2: Collected Papers of the First Merton Conference in Poland, Lublin, Oct. 24-27, 2002* edited by Krzysztof Bielawski. (Kraków: Homini, 2003): 179.

3. *The Times*, (Wednesday, January 21, 1931), p. 10.

4. Merton, *Seven Storey Mountain* (London: Sheldon Press, 1975), p. 52.

5. Thomas Merton, "The Haunted Castle," *The Merton Seasonal* 19 (Winter 1994), pp. 7-10, is the earliest of these manuscripts and dates back to Christmas 1929.

6. "Ravenswell." Unpublished Manuscript. April 1929. [photocopy]. All unpublished materials referred to in this paper, unless indicated otherwise, are available at the Thomas Merton Center, Bellarmine University, Louisville, Kentucky.

7. These manuscripts were discovered in December 1993 by the present writer and Robert E. Daggy in the possession of Frank Merton Trier, a first cousin, with whom Merton spent some school holidays until the summer of 1930. The style of the author's handwriting, the content of the stories, and Mr. Trier's testimony, verified their authenticity. The manuscripts remain in Mr. Trier's possession with photocopies held on file at the Merton Center.

8. These drawings were acquired by Georgetown University in Washington.

9. Thomas Merton Center Collections, Bellarmine University.

10. Merton served for a while as art editor of *The Jester*.

11. See for example his Geometric Cross from around the early fifties which could be compared to French Concrete Art.

12. *Commonweal* 61.25 (March 25, 1955), pp. 658-659.

13. *Jubilee* 4.7 (November 1956), pp. 25-32.

14. Sponsa Regis 28.9 (May 1957), pp. 231-234.

15. Sponsa Regis 31.4 (December 1959), pp. 114-117.

16. Sponsa Regis 31.5 (January 1960), pp. 133-140. Republished in *Disputed Questions*.

17. Thomas Merton, *Disputed Questions* (New York: Harcourt Brace, 1960), pp. 264-273.

18. *The Road to Worship*, 34.5 (April 1960), pp. 248-255. Republished in *Disputed Questions*.

19. Thomas Merton, *The Road to Joy: The Letters of Thomas Merton to New and Old Friends* (New York, Farrar, Straus, Giroux, 1989), p. 246.

20. *Good Work* 27.1 (Winter 1964), pp. 15-20.

21. Merton, *Seven Storey Mountain*, p. 203.

22. Christine M. Bochen, Patrick F. O'Connell and William H. Shannon, eds., *The Thomas Merton Encyclopedia* (Maryknoll, N.Y.: Orbis Books, 2002), p. 9.

23. Thomas Merton. *Natural Contemplation* (Kansas City: Credence Cassettes, 1987). Transcribed by the current author.

24. "Sacred and Profane." *Stained Glass* 69.4 (Winter 1975), p. 82.

25. *"Sacred and Profane,"* p. 83.

26. Thomas Merton, *Turning Toward the World: The Pivotal Years* (San Francisco: Harper Collins, 1996), p. 60.

27. Merton, *The Road to Joy*, p. 133.

28. Thomas Merton, *Raids on the Unspeakable* (New York: New Directions, 1966), p. 180.

29.http://www.guggenheimcollection.org/site/date_work_md_133A1.html [Accessed 23rd January, 2004.]

30. Thomas Merton, *Run to the Mountain: The Story of a Vocation* (San Francisco: Harper Collins, 1995), pp. 128-29.

31. Thomas Merton to Ad Reinhardt, July 3, 1956. Unpublished letter. Archives of the Thomas Merton Center, Bellarmine University, Louisville, Kentucky.

32. Thomas Merton, *A Search for Solitude: Pursuing the Monk's True Life* (San Francisco: Harper Collins, 1996), pp. 139-40.

33. Joseph Masheck, "Five Unpublished Letters From Ad Reinhardt to Thomas Merton and Two in Return." *Artforum* 17 (December 1978), p. 24.

34. *"Five Unpublished Letters..."* p. 24.

35. *"Five Unpublished Letters..."* p. 24.

36. Thomas Merton, *Witness to Freedom: The Letters of Thomas Merton in Times of Crisis* (New York: Farrar, Straus, Giroux, 1994), p. 5. In another letter to Victor Hammer Merton suggests that both Hammer and Reinhardt would be "in fundamental agreement" and regrets the fact that they have not had the opportunity to meet. Merton, *Witness to Freedom*, p. 6.

37. Quoted at http://www.guggenheimcollection.org/site/date_work_md_133A1.html [Accessed 23rd January, 2004.]

38. Thomas Merton to Ad Reinhardt, October 31, 1963. Merton, *The Road to Joy*, p. 281.

39. Thomas Merton, *Dancing in the Water of Life: Seeking Peace in the Hermitage* (San Francisco: Harper Collins, 1997), p. 58.

40. Merton, *Dancing in the Water of Life*, p. 162.

41. Merton, *Witness to Freedom*, p. 10.

42. As Merton was attempting to find other galleries to host the exhibit of his calligraphies he wrote to Shirley Burden in California requesting his help. In Burden's reply to Merton he also noted that royalties from his book *I Wonder Why* had been earmarked for scholarships for African-American students. Burden to Merton, March 29, 1965.

43. Elsewhere I have argued that Merton's development of anti-poetry developed at the same time as that of Parra in Chile, that his anti-poetry was not copied from Parra, and that in a relatively short period of time it matured in ways that Parra's never did. See "Poetry of the Sneeze: Thomas Merton and Nicanor Parra." *The Merton Journal* 8.2 (Advent 2002), pp. 3-20.

44. Merton, *Disputed Questions*, p. 164.

45. Merton, *Raids on the Unspeakable*, pp. 5-6.

46. Michael Mott, *The Seven Mountains of Thomas Merton* (Boston: Houghton Mifflin, 1984), p. 83.

47. *Run to the Mountain*, p. 68.

48. John Howard Griffin, *A Hidden Wholeness: The Visual World of Thomas Merton* (Boston: Houghton Mifflin, 1970), p. 37.

49. Merton, *Turning Toward the World*, p. 169.

50. Merton, *Turning Toward the World*, p. 194.

51. Merton, *Turning Toward the World*, p. 194.

52. Merton, *Dancing in the Water of Life*, p. 23.

53. Merton, *Dancing in the Water of Life*, p. 147.

54. Merton, *Dancing in the Water of Life*, p. 147.

55. Merton, *Dancing in the Water of Life*, p. 149.

56. Thomas Merton, *Learning to Love: Exploring Solitude and Freedom* (San Francisco: Harper Collins, 1997), p. 221.

57. Griffin, *A Hidden Wholeness*, p. 37.

58. Thomas Merton, *The Other Side of the Mountain: The End of the Journey* (San Francisco: Harper Collins, 1998), p. 286.

59. Merton, *A Road to Joy*, p. 140.

60. Merton, *The Other Side of the Mountain*, p. 90.

61. Writing to Bob Lax he referred to them as "three Kings from Lexington."

62. Ralph Eugene Meatyard, *Father Louie: Photographs of Thomas Merton* (New York: Timken, 1991), pp. 34-35.

63. *Father Louie: Photographs of Thomas Merton by Ralph Eugene Meatyard*, p. 34.

64. *Father Louie: Photographs of Thomas Merton by Ralph Eugene Meatyard*, p.35.

65. Merton, *Dancing in the Water of Life*, p. 48.

66. Merton, *The Other Side of the Mountain*, p. 286.

67. Merton, *The Other Side of the Mountain*, p. 284.

68. Thomas Merton, *The Collected Poems of Thomas Merton* (New York: New Directions, 1978), pp. 280-281.

69. Merton, *The Collected Poems of Thomas Merton*, pp. 280-281.

Do I want a small painting?

The Correspondence of Thomas Merton and Ad Reinhardt: An Introduction and Commentary

Roger Lipsey

Thomas Merton and Ad Reinhardt met as undergraduates at Columbia University (respectively, Class of 1937 and 1935) and formed a lifelong friendship. Although from wholly different backgrounds, in some ways they were uncannily alike. With their friend, the poet and sage Robert Lax (Class of 1938), and a second friend, the multi-talented editor, writer, and photographer Edward Rice (Class of 1940), they were seekers of truth who never lost touch with one another, however great the geographical distance separating them. Close readers of Thomas Merton have known for years of the Merton-Reinhardt correspondence, published in part and cited where useful to other purposes in the large Merton literature. It has never appeared as a whole, and several brilliant letters have remained unpublished. Further, in the absence of context, certain published passages were enigmatic—one had to guess their meaning, and it was more sensible not to guess at all.

The extant correspondence is just 20 letters, spanning the years 1956 to 1964. This is conceivably the entire correspondence, but that seems unlikely; there are evident gaps and it ends too soon. The first, Reinhardt to Merton, is a catch-up letter—Reinhardt tells Merton what he has been doing in recent years—but it also responds to a request, relayed from Merton through Lax, for a cover design that would suit an instructional pamphlet or series of pamphlets which Merton was preparing for the novices at the Abbey of Gethsemani. Reinhardt's first letter could be the beginning of the correspondence, but it could also be the resumption after a gap of some years. The last letter, Merton to Reinhardt in early 1964, is in full motion; there is no sense of a stop, no sign that the friends would fail to continue their exchanges, which had intensified in recent years. Since late 1960, Merton had been practicing a visual art—at first brush-drawn ink calligraphy on paper, later a rudimentary but effective form of printmaking—and in the course of 1964 he achieved his impressive maturity as a visual artist. That was hardly an opportune moment to break off communications with Reinhardt, a well-known artist and peer of Jackson Pollock, Mark Rothko, Willem de Kooning, and other participants in the so-called New York School. Reinhardt had served as a mentor in art, though distant; he had provided fine paper for Merton's use; and the correspondence has the verve of a going concern.

How often did Merton and Reinhardt actually meet? Like so many of Merton's relationships, this one was conducted largely by correspondence. Reinhardt and Lax called together on Merton at Gethsemani in the spring of 1959. Although Reinhardt and Merton had ambitions to meet more frequently, this was Reinhardt's only visit; Lax visited more often. Apart from that meeting, correspondence was the link. But the common word "correspondence" doesn't reflect the place of letters dispatched and received in Merton's inner life. Though he was voluntarily cloistered in rural Kentucky and scarcely traveled until the last year of his life, some magical ether linked Merton to friends and correspondents worldwide. He seemed to experience his correspondents as nearby, as engaged with him in shared concerns and tasks that undid distance.

Ad Reinhardt (1913-1967) was an artist of unique mind and temperament. As noted earlier, Merton and he met at Columbia, where they both provided creative leadership for student publications. At the time, Reinhardt was studying art history with the great Meyer Schapiro, while Merton was studying literature with the great Mark Van Doren—those were especially good years at Columbia. Though Reinhardt's art would evolve through many stages in later decades and become a profound and profoundly sophisticated offering, the young Reinhardt described by the young Merton is surprisingly consistent with Reinhardt in his maturity. "The other evening I was to Ad Reinhardt's," Merton wrote in his journal at the beginning of 1940.

I think Ad Reinhardt is possibly the best artist in America. Anyway the best whose work I've seen.... Reinhardt still sticks with the communists. Certainly understandable: a religious activity. He believes, as an article of faith, that "society ought to be better," that the world ought to be somehow changed

and redeemed.... In such a state artists would be free to paint
what they were really impelled to paint by a kind of inner necessity, or by the light of grace....

Reinhardt's abstract art is pure and religious. It flies away
from all naturalism, from all representation to pure formal and
intellectual values.... Reinhardt's abstract art is completely
chaste, and full of love of form and very good indeed.... He'd
make a pretty good priest....[1]

So much of Reinhardt is already recognizable: religious intensity
after his own manner, the detectable presence of some inner necessity that would shape his art in later years, an art that is chaste
and avoids mixing, intellectuality ceaselessly cultivated and used
to good purpose.

Ad Reinhardt came of age as an artist in the same rough cradle
as many of his American peers. The son of immigrant parents
from Lithuania who brought with them their Socialist beliefs, he
was drawn to Communism in the 1930s—hence Merton's recur-
rent teasing comments in the correspondence about Moscow—but
gradually withdrew from politics while retaining a wounded, easily angered idealism to the end of his life, at least where art was
concerned. In the mid 1930s, like many of his peers, he joined the
American Abstract Artists group and derived a modest living from
1936 to 1941 in a Depression-era federal program that employed
artists. He served in the US Navy in the last two years of World
War II as a photographer and after the war, on the GI Bill, studied
art history with a distinguished scholar of Asian art, Alfred
Salmony. His work with Salmony and extensive travel in the
Middle East, North Africa, and Asia as the years went by prepared
him to teach college-level art history at various institutions, and
until quite late in life his teaching career afforded him the living
wage that his art—little valued at the time—did not offer through
gallery sales. Today he is recognized as a major artist.

Reinhardt shared with Merton a taste for cartooning, and
Reinhardt's hilarious, edgy, sometimes bitter cartoons about the
art world of his time and its public in the 1940s and '50s remain
key documents of their era, both funny and wise.[2] An early par-
ticipant in the New York School and a familiar presence at artists'
gatherings from the 1930s forward, Reinhardt was nonetheless also
an outsider increasingly at odds with his peers, uncomfortable with
the impact of material success on his artist friends when at last
they were materially successful. He was pure in an impure world,

demanding in a world that he regarded as compromised. Reinhardt's art became simpler and simpler, more and more still, darker and darker, until in 1954 he found his way to what became known as his Black Paintings, astonishing works. In their developed form, they were unchangeably the same in many respects: a five-foot by five-foot canvas, with a cross-shaped pattern, painted in subtly differing shades of matte black. Precursors of what would be called Minimalism in the next decade, these are works that one has to learn to see: they confront the observer ruthlessly with his or her own act of observation, the waywardness or steadiness of attention, the act of seeing as a discipline of mind, an exercise of patience. As one stands, of necessity quietly, before a Black Painting, one's first impression of a black canvas of no interest gradually resolves into a perceptual experience—and potentially a spiritual experience—of surprising richness. The cruciform pattern emerges, the extreme subtlety of differing shades of black emerges (plum black, orange black, blue black—wonderful kinds of black). Some observers bring to this experience their appreciation of the last moments of twilight, when the sky is a tinted black; others may bring their appreciation of phases of Christian and Buddhist literature with which Reinhardt himself was familiar, from St. John of the Cross on the Dark Night of the Soul to the Buddhist concept of Emptiness.

Many, in Reinhardt's lifetime, bought nothing at all and found nothing in his art. Reinhardt became known in art circles as the Black Monk—an irony not lost on his friend, Thomas Merton. Until the last year of his life, in late 1966 to early 1967, when he had a major retrospective at The Jewish Museum in New York and was featured in an article in *Life* magazine,[3] Reinhardt had to make do with the esteem of few peers and still fewer art critics. When well-deserved attention at last came his way, it came so late that it, too, was received with irony.

Like some earlier embattled artists of the twentieth century with a gift for the written word, Reinhardt wrote quite extensively and published just some of his writings in art journals, not precisely to explain his art—he did not respect explanations—but to surround it with the nutrient ideas and poetic-religious images from which it drew. Just as his art coalesced into a single form subject to slight but eloquent variations, his writings coalesced into what he willingly called "dogma," a chant-like, compressed style of statement reminiscent of some Buddhist scripture.[4] In homage to his late friend, Merton published an excerpt from a writing of this kind in *Monks Pond*, the literary journal which it was Merton's delight—and burden—to publish in four issues in the course of 1968. Reinhardt's unique voice perfectly matched his unique paintings:

> The one object of fifty years of abstract art is to present art-as-art and as nothing else, to make it into the one thing it is only, separating and defining it more and more, making it purer and emptier, more absolute and more exclusive—non-objective, non-representational, non-figurative, non-imagist, non-expressionist, non-subjective. The only and one way to say what abstract art or art-as-art is, is to say what it is not.[5]

There is much more to say about Reinhardt himself and about the dynamic friendship between Merton and Reinhardt. At this point, however, we can ask their correspondence to lead us and suggest themes for further exploration. It seems best to present the correspondence without interruption. Commentary, on each letter in turn, resumes after this middle section in which the friends speak.

1: Reinhardt to Merton, Thomas Merton Papers, Rare Book and Manuscript Library, Columbia University

June, 1956

Dear Rev.? Louis? Merton?: Is that your joke Lax is telling, from Avenue A to Albany, about the herring to the whale, "Am I my blubber's kipper?" Did you ask, in a letter to Lax, was I still straddling a fence? Whether to choose Rome or Moscow? Is that a choice between Togliatti and Sergius? Please answer. The summer's stupor's in and four months now of nothing, just sitting in my studio, working when I work, painting Greek crosses, my black and blue period. I almost came to visit you for a day this June and I will next time I get a ride to Ohio or Kentucky. You know one side of me is on the side of the angels, and part of me is part of things, half of me is tied to an ivory tower, two-thirds to a family (new), two-fifths of me is tied to a job which I thought would be like the monastic life (that it grew from) (but university teaching is the life of the advertising-agency and entertainment-business) (But I do teach Chinese and Indian painting and sculpture, art history, art theory, etc., for Western novices), the rest of the parts of me is free. But little time for either yogi or commissar activity. Must I choose? What could I do for you? I do things and I thought these things might parallel some things you say. Lax gave me the book of instructions (and my only background is Tillich, Buber, Maritain, Suzuki, Coomaraswamy and Bishop Berkeley) which I read, and I see only abstract forms, concrete, but not as specific and particularized as your images and symbols, the vertical and horizontal, the Greek cross, transcendent color, all right, but I don't know what to do with your Christian words, and I'm not a good illustrator, I understand the invisible, unseen but not the unspoken, so what could I do? Outside of my own process, vision, work? What do you suppose I could do, say for *Pax*? For *Jubilee*?

Love, Ad

2: Merton to Reinhardt, The Archives of American Art[6]

July 3, 1956

Dear Ad,

Deep calls unto deep and salt mine unto salt mine. From tunnel to tunnel, how are you these days? First the statements and later the questions, as for the choices, the answer is choose everything. As for me, neither Togliatti nor Sergius are characters in the operas of these here deeps in which I find myself my brother's scraper. Who are they? Baseball players? (Important dissident clergy I profoundly suspect)

First then about the pamphlets which I have carved out for my young. The words of the pamphlets are chosen and selected according to the pictures in the mind thereof. With which the cover has nothing necessarily to do. All I can say is I can think of no better cover than crosses within crosses black upon black, brown, blue, grey, what have you (two colors at the most though for the pennies' sake). If the words in the pamphlet are more specific than make me generally comfortable in my own private conclusions the cover need say no more than the general darkness which lies beyond the conclusions and in which the realities are grasped which the words fail to signify as much as they pretend to. The mandala, now, while interesting, would fail to make an appropriate cover. (A sort of general abstract mandala maybe, why not? We can think about it)

The only thing I would say nothing negatively specific should be in there, such as various masonic insignia, hammer and sickle, etc etc.

The very name of Suzuki produces in me electric currents from head to foot. If you come here you will have to answer such questions as "Why did Bodhidharma come from the west?" You will be given a cell in which to meditate on Joshu's Mu. Etc etc.

My favorite answer to all questions is "The wooden man sits at the loom and the stone man at night throws in the shuttle."

My favorite character—Hui Neng, the 6th patriarch.

My roots: Wu-chu, which is to say not abiding anywhere.

My philosophy: Wu nien, or in plain English, "leave them all be: they are okay the way they are."

(Whose character, whose roots, whose philosophy? The blue man sits on the dome and the other one draws forth stars from his pockets.)

I guess I better tell you more about the pamphlet. It is printed in Janson or will be, if that means anything. The size of the thing is 6 by 9. Any kind of a cover will do, so long as it is decent and does not look anything like the usual cover on those things.

Lax kept assuring me that you and he would come down here in the fall, and that would be a fine idea. If you suddenly get a ride any time, that is fine too, only let me know beforehand. End of July and early August will be no good for me as during that time I shall be in jail for two weeks for subversive activities. I can hardly think of anything better for a person of quality in polite society to do than teach Chinese and Japanese painting. Do you think there is any hope of anyone really learning what is behind all that and what has been so largely forgotten by everyone? I conclude with a lyric which come to me on a sudden whilst I was climbing palm trees:

The lyric is called "Wisdom." The English version is as follows:

I studied it and it taught me nothing
I learned it and soon forgot everything else:

Having forgotten, I was burdened with knowledge
—The insupportable knowledge of nothing.

How sweet my life would be if I were wise!
Wisdom is well known
When it is no longer seen or thought of.
Only then is understanding bearable.

As for the insides of this particular existence here, it is most simple although everyone tries to make it most complicated. In all directions people run as fast as they can from themselves, even when they are religious, because they want to appear to themselves as gods and the effort is exhausting. After having run in all directions at once, a person decides through no fault of his own that he has to stop running and finds himself in the center of everything, having everything knowing everything because they have and know nothing and realize that this is the way it should be. This, as I say, comes about against all our own plans and best intentions, and the less said about it the better.

    With hymns and canticles I return into the cellar of darkness. I shall hold off from becoming an Arhat until after you have been here, but after that—Pfft!

    For *Pax* and *Jubilee* you should do just what you actually do, no? Why something else?

Love, blessings,
in Christ
Tom

PS If you wouldn't be doing a cover say within a couple weeks, or if it still perplexes you, let me know real quick and I will cook up something with letter-spaced Janson. Have you some small black and blue cross painting (say about a foot and a half high) for the cell in which I perch? But Lax says everything you do is now the size of a building.

I think the Yhung Mandala covers just about everything!

3: Merton to Reinhardt, The Archives of American Art

July 9 1956

Dear Ad

Make out this letter so terse and excited is really a telegram. Hurry hurry to the post offices with the files of emergency decisions. Paste them on to the wires and zip! Here goes telegrams for Ad Reinhardt New Yorks New Yorks. Psst! Reinhardt! Are you listening to the files slipping up and down the cables?

Practical Lax as usual horrible mistake stop all newyork in uproar over Lax's mistake stop stop stop. Lax in jail. Stop. Told you and Rice at same time design pious pamphlets of Chinese Merton in Kentucky cookie factory (joke some other time) stop.

Seems Rice had designed pamphlets stop, one to ten new pamphlets he has designed same time taking over print shop of Margrave or Marbrigge with guerilla hostiles stop. Printing pamphlets badly in dusk beyond Varick Street while cops all lie drugged in dopedens Stop. Alas, what about your designs. Don't stop.

You Reinhardt don't stop also designing Chinese pamphlet I got great idea stop continue stop no, continue. I got wizard idea, I return Chinese cookie factory and write out marvelous new secret fortunes each night with stolen pencils braving guerilla hostiles and all others with Zen fury cloaked in my swift overcoats. Stop. I drum up fifty select pages very small sharp koans break heads of all modern western stupids with tricky oriental koans and you illustrate wow, how you like question mark stop. Wham. Solution to all problems found in lightning flash stop start stop no start right away. Just wait until I get a pencil sharpened. Get Lax out of jail quick feed with vitamins embrace and forgive. Am I my buzzard's flipper?

Meanwhile New York is so full of new pamphlets by me that nobody can hear themselves think. I go hide immediately.

Lv, blessings, woe to Moscow.

Tom

4: Reinhardt to Merton, Thomas Merton Papers, Rare Book and Manuscript Library, Columbia University

[July 10,] 1956

Dear Tom: I was going to try a cover but I'm afraid what exactly I get in a painting (plattdeutsch) is exactly what gets lost in a photography, reproduction or in a designing for something else—I'll send you a small painting in the fall, or bring it, after my show (I wonder why I still show, and act as if my painting were a public thing, and sometimes even expect some response, even fame & fortune—but I guess I don't—only money, security, bellyful, car, house—of these things, all I seem to have is security, maybe a pension in twenty-five years)

I guess I could tell you more in some words than I can by some diagram like this?

[here Reinhardt offers a simple rectilinear sketch of a proposed cover design]

(Thomas Merton in letter spaced Janson, of course)

Words like black & blue crosses, vertical & horizontal equal bands, bars & squares, dark colors, deep but not heavy—like Amida-Buddhist ceilings, Russian icons, Irish stones, Jain prayer cards, Persian rugs, Carolingian reliefs, Maya temples, 13th century Italian crosses, Koran covers, Chinese landscapes, Greek church floor plans, Neolithic columns, Japanese girders, Gothic window glass, Peruvian textiles, Amerindian adobe houses, Early Christian manuscripts, etc.—all these words are a little better than my design above, attached enclosed

A painting has the possibility of becoming a serious object of contemplation, but how long can you look at a design? My design, above, would look like nothing to a publisher, not even like a cross (because of the color)

I haven't read much about Zen or Suzuki, more on early Ch'an and Dhyani Buddhism, the Chinese and Indian being less handcrafty to me, than the Japanese.

Lax says maybe you don't know who Togliatti of Rome and Sergius of Moscow are? Commissar of Italy and Metropolitan of Russian-Greek Orthodoxy! You don't read newspapers? Or see television? All kinds of gag cartoons have monks in them now, do you know? You know about movies? Lax says Don Ameche wants to play your movie life.

I like that "wisdom" piece. Did Lax tell you how much I thought about your "tower of babel"? Rice and Breughel did a good job of illustrating it for you.

My daughter (2 1/2 yrs.) calls Lax "cracker" something to do with fourth of July, I think, and not "Georgia" or "wise."

My ex-stepson (18 yrs.) (Pat's son) is a sophomore at Middlebury College in Vermont

The "jhs" at the top of your letter, Lax says, is not the New York lawyer, John Hampton Slate?

I haven't seen many of your books or pamphlets except the first and last, I think—an advertisement of one of them, a design, a chalice, mosaic-like, was pretty nice—

Here's some more designs, free—

[*Reinhardt includes additional sketched cover designs*]

Do you know who Elvis Presley and Erwin Panofsky are? Do you know what Fulbright and Ford Fellows are? I tried to get a Fulbright to Ceylon and a Ford to Iran and India but was not successful—I'm not liked in a lot of quarters and circles, and quadrants and squares—May I have some sympathy for my wanderlust?—Do you know anything about the Caves of the Thousand Buddhas in Central Asia at Tun Huang? The equivalent in the East of the ceiling Chapel Sistine, which I saw several times, passing through the Vatican Museum. Ever been there? Love, Ad

5: Merton to Reinhardt, The Archives of American Art

Jul 19, 1956

Dear Ad:

Telegrams from Rice say Lax lies dismembered in Union Square.

Your suggestion on page one of the last missive from Chinese Cookie function is very fine, but have you all got mad and dropped the pamphlet singly and severally I hope not. Only question about your design is if it is in three colors maybe it would cost more than we could pay if (as happens) the monastery is printing the pamphlet. But I like it so much I would like to save it for say a bigger book to be printed by Farrar Straus—we could try it out on Giroux. What I have coming out next (I mean next after what is already bought) is a thing called Thirty Seven Meditations of which Lax has the manuscript. Get him to give it to you.

All the words you mention are for me like letters from home viz covers, stones, prayer cards, ceilings, icons, beams, reliefs, crosses, columns, neolithic, Jain, Amida, Peruvian, Amerindian (not so much) etc. Anything you got.

My real idea is that I write a book of proverbs and you maybe fill in with beams, girders, textiles, and korans.

Seriously what you know about Cistercian architecture? Like Fontenay cloister on end sheets of my book *Waters of Siloe* which if you not got I send. Ought to see a big album on a place called Senanque photos by Jahan, published by Editions du Cerf Paris. Monk friends of mine in France put out three marvelous books on Romanesque churches in 1) Burgundy, 2) Auvergne 3) Loire Valley. I'm talling you supoib. Lax got one anyway. He can show it to you.

Got to quit now to go to the Elks' convention in Seattle. I seen a picture of Sergius and I don't trust him. Lv—and don't forget to come in Sept.

Tom

6: Merton to Reinhardt, The Archives of American Art

Aug 22, 1956

Dear Ad.

Split second flash speed note. Business efficiency bubbles all around. We are delighted with yours of the inst. Ours of the ult. will follow by return of press.

We have all the characters on your graph present here in this domicile. The whole is resplendent, each part is a gem. Jack frost hath nipped the toes of the dandies. The Late neo classicists are among my favorite crystal. Each snowflake spells mysterious russian pax. Flying machines are fastest ever. Clowns hoopla, even the devils truly dandy.

How would it be to take a few of them and put them all over the cover like a pattern, if I make myself obscure. One I like a lot is a cross as follows: [*here Merton puts a simple drawing*] This could be a big one by itself in the middle of the cover. Or this. Or the star. [*further drawings*] Or some form of Pax which I would be swiping I presume from Lax? He is rich in Paxes and would not care, the rich millionaire.

Or has Rice designed a cover of his own with celtic wit? I must stop now or the supper will spoil. The Georgia Cracker cleric in person waits to be seen. Where is my pipe and my bowl and my fiddlers three? How I wish I could spell. I close with my devotions. I bow to everyone and I vanish.

In the Spirit.

Tom

I know a man who consulted a shaman about a siberian tiger which he missed. The shaman said one day he would hit. He is waiting.

7: Merton to Reinhardt, The Archives of American Art

Oct. 29, 1957

Dear Ad:

Do I want a small painting? You inquire if I want a small painting. What you wish to know: do I desire a small painting.

Do I desire a small painting? Well, it is clear at least to me that I desire a small painting since I am in point of fact crazy mad for a small painting. They have to keep me chained to the wall day and night and a gag in my mouth because I roar continuously that I am dying for lack of a small painting. I have already started on a campaign of actively destroying every large painting that I can lay hands on because I am totally consecrated in life and in death to the cause of small paintings, for this reason that I am consumed with a most ardent thirst for a small painting. So much so that if I do not have a small painting in my hands by Christmas I am like to destroy the entire building and all the monks in it, for when I love something I love it very aggressively and thus hate the opposite. Now the monastery is very large. Thus, if I do not very soon get a small painting, I will destroy the large monastery which, by contrast, reminds me of my lack of a small painting, and this is torment. Therefore it is clear that I want a small painting. I dream at night of getting one tomorrow, and tomorrow turns into today and brings no small painting. This is to me an ever increasing source of consternation which has by

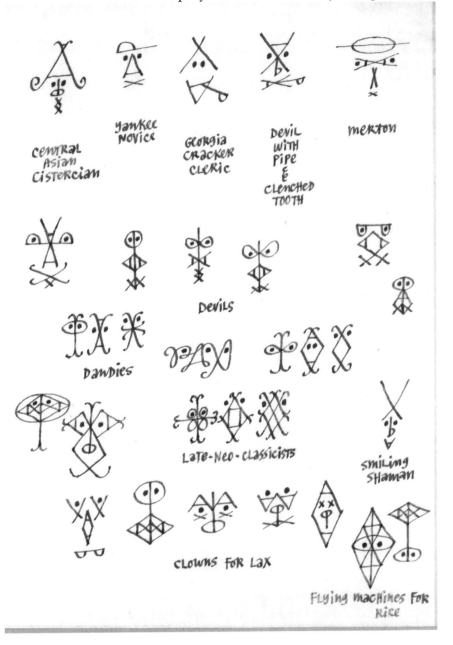

Fig. 1: Ad Reinhardt, Entertaining Sketches for Thomas Merton, 1956 (mentioned in Merton's letter of August 22, 1956)

now turned into a river of consternation, and I have to be re-strained by force from rushing headlong to the paint brush and painting for myself a small painting which would clearly be a disaster. Therefore the only solution to this problem which sears and burns the inner man, is for you to send in all haste, carefully packed, mounted upon lamas, the small painting of which you speak. I will have my scouts wait for the small painting upon the summit of the Alleghany mountains and escort it with fifes from thence to hence.

After the arrival of the small painting there will be here a week of sabbaths or a sabbath of weeks. The small painting will be honored by deacons and acolytes. The small painting will be taken in procession from the larvas to the basilicas. The small painting will be laid in reverence upon the altar of Saint Panteleimon. The small painting will be removed thence with lights and incense to the altar of Sts Boris and Bleb or is it Greb (Gleb)? The small painting will be set up on the iconostasis. It will be viewed by all during the mysteries. It will elevate the hearts and minds of all to participate in the mysteries. It will bring to the artist the Holy Spirit. It will cause all things to be transfigured. It will hasten the day of glory.

As the hart thirsteth for the waterbrooks I thirst for the small painting.

The sickness of Lax, as I know for certain, was caused by malevolent pixies. But good comes out of evil and Lax has gone to Connecticut to stay with holy people, and this I know through the thought waves. Lax's auric colors, as I view them here from a distance, are growing more healthful.

Beware of wines, love healthful meats, tropical fruits are good. Painters should ea[t] much egg, for the sake of pigment. Beers you may tolerate. Do evil to no man. Fly bank robbers. Let your conversation be only with honest men. Do not believe everything you read or hear. Watch out for the Asiatic scurvy. Collect stamps in your spare time, one day you will not regret it. Every man ought to have one or two dogs in the house, as a mortification. Once a sage sat in a barrel and looked for an honest man. What did he find? I often wonder.

After this advice every word of which is solidly impracti-cal, I return to my hymns and spiritual exercises. May you enjoy a holy and solitary Martinmas, in the caves.

Remember the small painting.

Harps sound as we withdraw. Benisons.

Folio

8: Merton to Reinhardt, The Archives of American Art

Nov 23, 1957

Dear Ad.

Your letter found me, as I hope this does not find you, in the hospital.

The small painting arrived just before I was removed from my haunts and it enabled me to bear up against despair in the wilderness in which I have since found myself.

They have rushed upon me from all sides, singing their abominable hillbilly anthems, wrenching my teeth from my head and at the same time submitting my person to every indignity in order to remove, as they jestingly asserted, piles. Nay rather they have made off with an entire bowel. From bitter experience I will send this message to any man who has piles. To such a one I will say: "Brother, keep your piles and with them your honor."

It would not have been so bad if I had not foolishly decided this was the best time to get an impacted molar dug out too.

With this darkness and chaos there comes filtering from time to time the distant memory of your small painting so soon lost after having been looked at! When shall I return to this mysterious small painting? When shall I once again console myself with the mystical abyss of the small painting? It has the following noble features, namely its refusal to have anything to do with anything else around it, notably the furniture etc. It is a most recollected small painting. It thinks that only one thing is necessary and this is true, but this one thing is by no means apparent to one who will not take the trouble to look. It is a most religious, devout, and latreutic small painting. For it I award you the Molotov-Zhukhov-Malenkov prize for the painter of the year who has gone absolutely the farthest from Socialist realism. The small painting is a landmark in the history of Kentucky. The state, having within it such a painting, can now raise its head and brush its hair and talk English. I will write more when I am back in one piece. Love to all— in Xt

Tom

9: Reinhardt to Merton, Thomas Merton Papers, Rare Book and Manuscript Library, Columbia University

[May 6] 1959

Dear Tom: Bread and cheese letter? I forgot to pick up some Trappist bread and cheese in my last minute rush into that Cadillac that took me right to the airport, fellow name of Steptoe or Tiptoe, five fellows, Catholics, I assumed, politicos of Louisville, wanted me to tell them all about you. So I did. You don't mind?

It was good to see you and you look great. I expected you to look old, sick, holier. I had a good time but I ate too much, gained three pounds. It was a real "retreat" for me, things here have been a pain in the spine for some time, during the boom, everybody being prosperous, fat.

I expected more caves, more eleventh and twelfth century stones and places, more seductively "contemplative" niches. Your Romanesque garments and singing were not disappointing in any way. I needed more time to find more things to point my camera at. There's never anything out there always, theoretically, for me, anywhere in the world, but some places take longer to put something there. A place like the Acropolis, Athens, insists on its every stone, corner, inch being photographed, photographed in every way and manner it always has been photographed since the invention of the photograph. I'll send you your picture in color.

Next time I come I'll bring a projector, and project for you the wonders of the world.

I wrote to Ulfert Wilke, art dept., University of Louisville, who spent a couple of months in a Zen Buddhist temple and study center in Kyoto, where I found him last summer and made a tourist out of him for a couple days. He was "ink painting" like any eccentric monk, and not seeing any sights, like in the museums.

I told him to invite you to his next Kentucky cocktail party or university tea, probably around Derby time. I don't know whether he plays the horses. He just won a Guggenheim to study in Braunschweig, Germany (where my wife was born) (He was born in Munich, I think.)

Next time I'll send the writings I write, not necessarily cross-legged. An artist need not sit cross-legged, I feel, which puts me outside the dhyana, ch'an and Zen main line. I always wanted to ask someone if "Zen" from the Japanese "za-zen" was any relation to the German "zit-zen"? Joke.

Let's argue about art and religion some more. If you're doing a book on it, and you have a world-wide audience, can I help you say what's right, instead of saying things people want to hear and agree with? You just make people happy if you don't say what's right, true. (beautiful?)

Write,
Ad

˙ǝɯ s,ʇɐɥʇ ʞuᴉɥʇ I „'sʇsᴉʇǝᴉnb„ ʞɔɐʇʇɐ noʎ ǝɯᴉʇʎɹǝʌƎ

Thanks for the weekend

10: Merton to Reinhardt, The Archives of American Art

May 9, 1959

Dear Ad,

This I write flash fast in two minutes got to get out to the woods and think. First if Wilke of Louisville wrote I never got it, but tell him maybe I'll be able to look him up in town if I ever happen to get in there before he goes to study the Guggenheim at Brunswicks. I like to see him.

About the art argument, I am not clear where it was getting and I am not clear in what way I was writing just what will please readers because a lot of what I have written about art will make them mad. The first thing to make clear about the art book is this however: it is expressly designed for people who, as priests or laymen, need to know what the Church thinks about art. Has thought about art, done about it, etc. Hence I am limited to a traditional approach, designedly. It is that kind of a book. But there is every obligation for one who follows tradition to be alive and original, and not simply to follow convention. Now you come along and ask me to fall into the iconoclast tradition. Which is admittedly something like my own (supposedly my own) Cistercian background. St. Bernard threw out all the statues. They were a distraction, he said. I used to believe it. I think it is an affectation, from the religious viewpoint, to hold that statues are a distraction. Nothing is a distraction or everything is a distraction. Who is there to be distracted?

A lot of the background of this book is the Mount Athos tradition that an ikon is so alive that if you cut it it will bleed. Idolatry, hah? And yet being a sophisticated monk I am not really interested in that idea the way they (unsophisticated) are. I am interested in it as a pattern.

That which is religious and sacred in a work of art is something other than just the artistic content, or form, or excellence of the work of art. But it is not something material, it is not information, it is not propaganda, it is not doctrine. It is not "about" anything. It is existential, it is what *is* in the work of art.

Quietist? Neither here nor there. Quietist as an insult is restricted to a peculiarly baroque sphere of spiritual reference. How could you be superficial enough to be a quietist? I think that your use of the label, which is a sophisticated use, is elegant and effective. Like the dead black paint rather than the lively which the other ones choose.

You tell me, then, what it is that makes Giotto different from Carlo Crivelli. The date? The example is badly chosen. The spirituality of Giotto is part and parcel of his time, I suppose. But as I write these things I wonder how one can make sense arguing about them.

If it is about the book, you should have the proofs of the book and pick out the points and say what you say. I wish you would. But wait until there are proofs, which will be a little while yet. Meanwhile, how about letting me have some Asiatic non-Christian religious art, if you can reduce your disbelief in this category into a practical discrimination.

Got to get out of here. Lawnmowers all around like divebombers. More later. Yes, come back with projectors and the wonders of the world.

To all a great salute.

In Christ,
Tom

11: Reinhardt to Merton, The Thomas Merton Center

[June] 1959

Dear Tom:

Thanks for the bread and cheese. I gave some to the starving Lax, who's so ready to come visit again, you watch out, he'll be there full time, visiting, eating all your bread and cheese, or rather, eating you all out of your bread and cheese. Enclosed find seven images I made with my magic box. What's to prevent me from making your image into postcards and cleaning up everywhere there's Catholics? And Thomas-Merton-fan-clubs?

I think I've got it in for celebrities these days. I read a book called "The Power Elite" and it seems that celebrities everywhere nowadays are used as "distractions," celebrities and their doings are the "opium of the people." "Who is there to be distracted?" You ask of statues? People. Distracted from "reality." People don't face reality, I guess. Nobody knows what's real. In art, we know that realism (according to the Hindu?) is one of the fifty-seven varieties of decoration.

Latest idea is, what is religious and sacred in a work of art is its pattern, form, artistic content, which is not anything you can pin down, as excellence or specific quality, or etc. or anything like that. Latest idea among theologians on art? This is an old "puritanical," Moslem, and Zen idea? Jewish too? Not Negro, I bet. Or Porto Rican.

I'll probably give a slide-lecture at the Dayton Art Institute on "Moslem vs. Hindu Art" (I make it sound like a war in the title to attract crowds) this fall, when Lax and I may come by again. I'll have projectors, etc.

I'll dig up what I feel is the great "Asiatic art," though your asking me for "some" of it is like asking, like some non-Christian asking, how about a little "Christian art"? Some great Christian art?

Classic "Buddhas," Indian, Chinese, Cambodian, Japanese, Javanese, Singhalese. And "mandalas," Indian, Central Asian, Japanese (mandaras), Tibetan, etc. I'll send photographs or bring them. You can parallel everything "east" in "west," celestial ceilings, paradise scenes, infernos, temptations, diagrams, icons, etc.

See you soon,
Ad

12: Reinhardt to Merton, The Thomas Merton Center

1960

Dear Tom:

Merton, Thomas, 1937 .... unknown*
Robinson, Leonard, W., 1935 .... unknown
Reinhardt, Adolph, F., 1935 .... 732 Broadway, N.Y.

From a new book of the old Sachems. Did you know we belonged to the same lodge, same tribe? I saw you summer of 1958, last spring 1960 I saw Leonard Robinson at our 25 reunion. Shall I report you two as not unknown? To me?

There's too much to say about a reunion, particularly one's history, remembrance. I got angry at an article on the middle thirties by James Wechsler (1935) and several years ago by Herman Wouk (1934). Too much trouble to write my history to kill their history. As the old Sachems have it: "By your words and not by your deeds shall you be known." Old Indian saying, some people "unknown"* no matter how many best sellers.

I don't have to apologize for that remark? Lax says your best seller book on art is out? Some day I'll make a book on art.

I was in Paris, London in June, also finished my "Arab tour" in Andalusia (Seville, Cordoba, Granada) which I started in India, Persia, Egypt in 1958. Now I'm tired of traveling, especially by jets. Next trips, slow boats. No reasons to get anywhere that fast any more.

I'm working, not teaching next year, planning a painting retrospective show, 25 years of abstract art, like 1935-1960 (Columbia), next reunion and survey or show like this 1985. See you before then. What's up? Ad.

13: Merton to Reinhardt, The Archives of American Art

Aug. 8, 1960

Dear Fellow Sachem:

Little do you realize that we "unknowns" are in all actual fact the very heart and marrow of our sacred and venerable organization. Yes, we are indeed the powers behind the tom tom. I authorize you to inform them that I am deceased. I estimate that the twenty-fifth reunion of my class will be in 1962. But tell me, WHO ARE THOSE PEOPLE? Those NAMES. Those guys claim they are sachems. They have substituted themselves for the genuine sachems of twenty-five years ago. This is a national nay world wide scandal that has been hushed up by the daughters of Pocohontas, a Barnard Jewish cell of the Fathers of the American Revolution. Wait til I get that Pocohontas. Meanwhile I would like to state that those guys are entirely unknown. Their homes are false props and vacant lots. Their addresses are the back doors of bars and alleys. Their claims are egregious. Everybody knows that Lax was always the president of sachems. Where is he on the list? And if the truth be told, *I was a member of Nacoms.* Tell them to put that in their pipe and smoke it. Yeah, tell them the next time that list comes out they got to put after my name "deceased member of nacoms."

I went to one dinner of sachems in my life and it was so dark that it was utterly impossible to discern anybody else present. The entire organization is unknown and always has been. I am waiting for the twenty-fifth annual reunion of the 1848 society in order to make this fact public. This society is a horse of a different hue, I can tell you that. Its members were selected purely by divine Providence. When the cameraman came to take the picture of the 1848 society for the Yearbook we went out into the hallway and pulled in everybody who happened to be walking about at that precise moment. Thus we got Lax, Syd Luckman, and many other people too notable to mention. And we despised dinners, dark or light. We just lived for that photograph.

It is absurd and preposterous to state that the Art book by me is out. It is impossible for an Art book by me to come out in anything under ninety years. I am now waiting in complete docility and torpor for a woman to tell me what to put in about modern sacred art. That is, to send me pictures. Why don't you enter into competition with this female and send me some pictures black and white glossy fit to arouse a spark of enthusiasm in the breast of a neglected author. Above all, serious, can you send me some good buddhas and hindu things and some Islam architecture of which you are so replete? I need a section of pix on non-Christian sacred art, if that makes meanings to you.

Above all when you come down here not on jets but on slowpoke trams? You are invited to come here in Sept or Oct, with or without Lax, bad time to come is middle of Oct, then I am deluged with academicians.

You are invited to come here for the twenty-fifth reunion of the unknowns.

Twenty-fifth reunion of the unknowns can easily be held on Labor Day weekend and thence, no wait, not that Sunday so much, but Labor Day and after. If you was to arrive [by] swans in the evening of Sunday before Labor Day and there would be no labor the following day but only a reunion of unknowns. What you think about that. Tell me what you think about that. Now I fade.

> With extreme reserve and cordial invisibility
> Tom

14: Reinhardt to Merton, The Thomas Merton Center

> 1962 [before February 20]

Dear Tom:

Sometimes we see jolly old friends only at sad funerals, dear relatives and classmates only at tragedies, communicate only at crises. When everything is all right, everything is all right. The other day I received in my mail, a mailing piece and a blurb... I couldn't believe my eyes when I saw....

Why shouldn't you be human after all and to err is human, we all know, but why should I be forgiving? And you forgiven? It seems that all my favorite religious writers, one day, like Coomaraswamy and Suzuki, who were all right until... Then Tillich had to be abandoned because of his introduction to the Museum of Modern Art's catalogue of "The New Images of Man," now Maritain and you... Is Buber still all right? He sympathizes with the Arabs... Can you understand why I became a white Muslim two summers ago?

Do you know I was in Jerusalem-Jordan (7th century), Damascus (8th), Cordoba (8th, 9th), Cairo (9-14th), Seville and Granada (13-15th), Konya (12-14), Istanbul (16-19), the last few summers, fellow-Sachem? And before that in Delhi and Agra (14-18) and

Isfahan (16-18)? The dates are the dates of the mosques I saw. Do you know that I give a survey course in Islamic, and Coptic, art at Hunter and Brooklyn Colleges in the City University of New York? It's proper maybe, I should find myself among anti-imagists, anti-idolatrists, pro-iconoclasts, and nonobjectivists?

Imagine you after all these years.... Have you given up hope? Have you no respect for sacredness and art? Reality-schmearality, as long as you're sound of body? Are you throwing in the trowel at long last? Can't you tell your impasto from a holy ground? Any more? Is the scum of its pots greater than the holy? Just pack up your scribbles in your old kitch bag and smile, smile, smile, hey? Is the potchy calling the whole kittle-kaboodle back? With all the scumble-bumpkins and Mac the Palette-Knifers storming the gates of all the four quarters, Lax and I have been meeting to discuss means... We'll send help, hold on, old man.

Your old friend,
Ad

15: Merton to Reinhardt, The Archives of American Art

March 3, 1962

Dear Ad:

Once, twice, often, repeatedly, I have reached out for your letter and for the typewriter. Choked with sobs, or rather more often carried away by the futilities of life, I have desisted. Dear relatives and classmates at tragedies. Ah yes, how true. As life goes on, as we descend more and more into the hebetude of middle age, as the brain coagulates, as the members lose their spring, as the spirit fades, as the mind dims, we come together face to face with one another and with our lamentable errors.

Our lamentable errors. My lamentable errors.

Truly immersed in the five skandhas and plunged in avidya, I have taken the shell for the nut and the nut for the nugget and the nugget for the essence and the essence for the suchness. Form is emptiness and emptiness is form.

You throw the centuries at me and you are right. Throw them all. Kneeling, I receive the centuries in a shower cascading all over my head. Weeping and penitent I receive upon the back of the head Jordan (8th cent.) and Damascus (8th cent.). You do not mention Isphahan, or the place where the Blue Dome is and where some Imam whose name I forget is venerated (9th cent?). These are the centuries, indeed they are the centuries. And I, as I look at myself with increasing horror, I remark that I have become a boy of the twenty-first century. Throw then your centuries at me, you are right, the centuries are right, and the twenty-first century has very slim chances of ever existing.

Going further down I see you do mention Isphahan after all but you spell it with an F. Go on throw it, I deserve it with an F also.

I have embraced a bucket of schmaltz. I have accepted the mish mash of kitsch. I have been made public with a mitre of marshmallows upon my dumkopf. This is the price of folly and the wages of middle aged perversity. I thought my friends would never know.

Victor Hammer is coming today. He does not know. If he has come to know about this disgrace, I shall efface myself in a barn someplace and become a sheep. I shall weave rugs out of cornsilk, equivalent in substance to my artistic judgments which I eternally regret.

My artistic judgment has contacted the measels. My love of kunst has become mumped. My appreciation of the sacreds hath a great whoreson pox and is reproved by all with good tastings and holy lauds. What would it be if he knew, the Imam? If he knew? Under his blue dome? He would stir, he would stir.

You are pro-iconoclast and you are right. You are quietists and you are right. You are non-objectivist and you are right. Down with object. Down with damn subject. Down with matter and form. Down with nanarupa. I mean namarupa. Sometimes get my terms wrong. Terms in general have the weasels.

Now the thing is, I am up to my neck. I am in the wash. I am under the mangle. I am publicly identified with all the idols. I am the byword of critics and galleries. I am eaten alive by the art racket. I am threatened with publication of a great book of horrors which I have despised and do recant. Bring the bell book and candle and have me shriven. Lift the ban, dissolve the excommunication, release the golden doves from the high dome, let the bells ring and let me be reconciled with the Moslem Synagogue. Help, help, rescue your old fellow sachem from way back in 1937 or whenever there was sachems. Tell Lax, help, help, help.

Tom

16: Merton to Reinhardt, The Archives of American Art

Sept 28, 1963

Dear Ad.

Ulfert Wilke was here, and before that I was doing calligraphy – but since I have done more. As this is the most rapid form of art production I have now thousands of calligraphies and the only reason I don't have millions is that I have been in the hospital with a cervical disc.

Let's hear from you some time.

All the best.
Tom

17: Reinhardt to Merton, The Thomas Merton Center

October [3], 1963

Dear Tom:

Talk about telepathy, extra-sensory-stuff or what you would call it. I was about to sit right down and write you a letter or post card, a pleasant one maybe, or one chewing you up or down for the Billy-Congdon-business, digging up old sores, dead horses, sleeping dogs, telling you about how I was on that March-on-Washington, only saw two other artists, saw no Catholic poets, especially neither Lax nor [Ned] O'Gorman, their being on Greek or Manhattan islands being no excuse at all, tomorrow I write them chewing them up about it, when all of a sudden out of the clear sky and mailbox, comes your calligraphy, your beautiful calligraphy but too small, don't you know them fellows way down East used brushes bigger than anyone's big head, a big pot of paint size of a big sink, and in bare feet, dance over a piece of paper bigger and longer than

Ulfert Wilke stretched from end to end, rack-like, didn't Wilke tell you and how I found him in a Kyoto temple sitting on the floor with his ink and paper, and I grabbed him and made a Western tourist out of him again, showed him the sites and sights, museums, made him take his camera out and shoot whatever you see in the books and histories of art, whacking him on the head whenever he thought about going back to the meditations, and cross-legged sitting he was doing?

The old-time, big, choreographic calligraphy was too physical, too poetic (they called their marks "Dog Baying at Moon" or "Tiger in the Marches" or "Dragon in the Lilies")—I like your calligraphy because its pure and to me. I'm as pure as ever, people say he thinks he's "holier than thou" about other artists still. I title my written works "Art-as-art Dogma" now (I used to make sentences out of words as a joke and after I kept repeating the same jokes over and over again, they suddenly turned into dogma, a sort of absolute truth, more or less). I had a show in Paris that sounded mystical again, "Les forces immobiles" (not my idea), lectured in Oregon "Against Things" in July (show in Paris in June), and marched one day in August and that's this summer.

Have I sent you the Museum of Modern Art catalogue of "Americans, 1963"? The officialdom finally proclaimed my existence, stuck me into a "Pop-"Art" and "Young Talent" show (about 15 years after my age-group graduated into the museum). Well, "That's life" (everyone says, when I call it corruption, injustice, vanity, misery, success, failure, karma, sellout, fall-out, money-grubbing, imperialist, colonialist, profiteerist, etc.).

Well, I wrote this at "one throw," just like that, all at once, the way the calligraphy's supposed to go, hit or miss, all the way to the bottom of the sheet, only one or two under the belt, Spanish brandy. Propaganda will follow, next mail. you write.

18: Merton to Reinhardt, The Archives of American Art

Oct 31, 1963

Dear Ad:

Well, October has thirty one and here I am again your friendly old calligrapher always small calligraphies down here, I am the grandfather of the small calligraphy because I don't have a big brush and because I no longer run about the temple bare-foot in the frosts. But I am amiable and the smaller they get the more mysterious they are, though in fact it is the irony of art when a calligrapher gets stuck with a whole pile of papers the same size and texture, why don't friends from New York who received all kinds expensive samples of paper send me samples of exotic and costly materials I invite you to pretend you are about to print a most exotic book and get samples of papers from distant Cathay and all over and then send them to your dusty old correspondent who is very poor and got no papers any more except toilet papers for the calligraphy.

I mean it about the samples. Or scraps that are left over from your large calligraphies (come on, I know you are mak-ing large calligraphies in secret and that corners of the huge papyrus are lying around and fed to the mice they should rather be sent down here and to be made into calligraphic minus-cules of which I am the grandfather.)

Here are some more calligraphic hats for New Years.

And now a jocular thrust: history has sure made your face red, yes? when all the time who was at the parade but Ned O'Gorman the Catholic Poet and you having surveyed a small sea of only two thousand faces mostly non-Catholic have cyni-cally asserted that there was no Catholic poets present, well history gave you the lie because there it was in *Jubilee* not only Catholic poets but also Catholic babes, extremely well fed and furnished by nature with unusual great wads of insulation fit for the pencil of a Rubens. Oh for the pencils of a Rubens. (You don't get the classical reference of this quip it is an 1840 book by some Lord Curzon or other who was in the Greek monasteries and mocked at the monks and when some staretz would creep out of a grotto with a beard this Limey would mock out loud: "Oh for the pencils of a Rembrandt.") Well now I a boy of the twentieth century exclaim for the pencils of a Rubens at all the well baptized flesh that was in that parade and you had no eyes for any of it, you were in one of your trances, you were getting into one of those dervish moods of yours, you were hobnobbing with the Muslims and not pay-ing any attention to the delights of Christianity, it is pretty easy to see you are no Rubens you big quietist wait till the Jesuits get after you but this is only a jest and not a threat you go ahead be a quietist I am right with you I am a Jansenist also and a Sufi, I am the biggest Sufi in Kentucky though I admit there is not much competition. Anyhow it is when I dance that I make the calligraph.

Lax was very piqued with all your nasty stabs about the parade and he has written me since then fifteen letters about the parades he has been in that you were not in I have no doubt he has treated you to the same.

What else I do is make the snapshot of old distilleries. And now enough of art. Take seriously the samples.

Tom

19: Reinhardt to Merton, The Thomas Merton Center

[Jan 1,] 1964

Tom: Rev. M Louis Merton, O.C.S.O.—is that still your title, rank, status, position, do you get promoted inside there in the monastery as everyone does outside? If one endures long enough in our art world, one becomes a "dean." I'll be the "dean of abstract art" when a few of the older men are no longer alive. Stuart Davis used to be "dean" but now he's only "dean of regional art" or is second in line after Hopper, "dean of American Scene art." Josef Albers, I guess, is "dean of squares." Robert Lax is "dean of the American Catholic poets in the Orthodox islands." Did you ever see Lax and O'Gorman on the telly (TV) reading their stuff? I'm sure you're the dean of something besides small calligraphy.

That "T" above, its stem, is a sample of the best paper I could find to send you. I had to fold it "eightfold" wise to fit it in an envelope so please forgive the creases. I put in two other mailings some fine-Italian-hand-paper and some non-yellowing-fine-Japanese-paper. I couldn't find any fine, clean, efficient, German papier, old Nazi stock, parchment, but enough of Fascist business. I'll look up some 100% American stock. You want a big brush? Happy New Year,

Ad

om: Rev. m Louis merton, o.c.s.o. — is that still your title, rank, status, position, do you get promoted inside there in the monastery as everyone does outside? If one endures long enough in our art world, one becomes a "Dean". I'll be the "Dean of Abstract Art" when a few of the older men are no longer alive. Stuart Davis used to be "Dean" but now he's only "Dean of Regional Art" or is second in line after Hopper, "Dean of American Scene Art". Josef Albers, I guess, is "Dean of Squares". Robert Lax is "Dean of the American Catholic Poets in the Orthodox Islands". Did you ever see Lax and O'Gorman on the Telly (TV) reading their stuff? I'm sure you're the Dean of something besides small caligraphy.

↑ That "T" above, its stem, is a sample of the best paper I could find to send you. I had to fold it "eightfold" wise to fit it in an envelope so please forgive the creases. I put in two other mailings some fine-italian-hand-paper and some non-yellowing-fine-japanese-paper. I couldn't find any fine, clean, efficient, german papier, old nazi stock, parchment, but enough of fascist business. I'll look up some 100% American stock. You want a big brush? Happy new year, Ad

Fig. 2: Ad Reinhardt to Thomas Merton, [January 1,] 1964

*Reproduced with the kind permission of Anna Reinhardt
for the Estate of Ad Reinhardt and the Merton Legacy Trust*

20: Merton to Reinhardt, The Archives of American Art

Jan 12, 1964

Dear Dean:

Yes, as one dean to another, I am frequently promoted as dean, usually by myself as I get little cooperation in this matter from others. However, it is true that with your encouragement and assistance I am already the dean of the small abstract calligraphy. As to the title of Louis which I share with too many bartenders and taxi drivers, I am detached from it and as to OCSO after the Louis I am in a state of torpor with regard to this. Not unappreciative, just torpid as to letters after names which are a Jesuitical trope. I am through with all tropes. I am begun to be nothing but a dean. I want all the letters in front of the name only, and after the name just a lot of room to get out of the way when they throw things, not to have to stumble around with any OCSO. Promotion is what I despise, except promotion once in a while as dean.

Now as to your papers you have been most generous with the papers and if I send you some of the small abstract calligraphies it is not in order to plague you and clutter up your flat, but to show you whereof I am the dean, and you should send back whatever would otherwise just clutter up the flat as I intend to get through to the millionaires like all the other deans. But for you I have signed the small abstract clalligropos which I take to be the most lively, for the Dragon Year as a new year card and stay away from feminine dragons in this year especially.

The big fine Italian hand paper I have not yet got to with my fine Italian hand.

Now what do you think of the printing method I have devised as dean in my specialty? I think it makes for very nice small obscure calligraphies and comes out more fine than the great brush. I am nuts about my method, like all the other deans. While you have a free moment from being Dean of Regionals and Folk Art and Dean of the Great Quiet, maybe you tell me which is the most lively methods and second how I get to the millionaires with the minimum of delay. No this about the millionaires is joshing, but if you think they would be good for calendars or Antonucci children books or other such, tell me what you think. In any case this pictures is for pleasures of contemplation and if it has this effect I go back content to my deanery and make a lot more, however not threatening to send you the whole tidal wave which is soon to break.

What is your mind about the great brush? It seems to me that with the great brush goes also a huge pot, as I cannot get the great brush into the small bottle of India ink, it seems to me I should experiment with a slightly larger brush which I have and make prints and see what happens, but all large brushes drink up the whole bottle of ink in one gulp then where are you, I ask myself? What is your counsel in this grave matter? Maybe there is some funny way of making the ink bottle go a long way like putting i[n] half water or something mean like that.

Lax has got out of being dean of Greek Islands for a while. It is he that start all the wars in Cyprus. You wait, it will all come out.

I hide my head from the American hubris that starts and will start wars and violence all over the place, I go back to be dean of the small silent calligraphy and weep for the peace race. Now its flags in Panama, and I got a friend just through telling me of peaceful Indians on islands around there etc. Bah. Fooey on the pale faces.

Coda: Merton to Robert Lax, on the death of Ad Reinhardt[7]

Sept 5 67

O Lax:

Do you know the great sorrows? Just heard today by clipping from Schwester Therese about Reinhardt. Reinhardt he daid. Reinhardt done in. He die. Last Wednesday he die with the sorrows in the studio. Just said he died in a black picture he daid. The sorrows have said that he has gone into the black picture for he is dead. All I read was the clip. Very small clip. Say Reinhardt was black monk of the pix and he daid. Spell his name wrong and everything. Dead none the less. Tried at first to figure it because the name was wrong maybe it was not Ad Reinhardt who was dead. But all the statements was there to state it. Black monk of pix. Was cartoons in PM now defunct. The sorrows is true, the surmises is no evade. It is too true the sorrows. Reinhardt he dead. Don't say in the clips how he died, maybe just sat down and give up in front of the black picture. Impossible to believe.

Maybe if Reinhardt had the sense to die quietly in quietist studio it is becoming soon the long procession of big woes and he seen it come.

Maybe the sorrows is coming to roost and to lay the biggest egg you ever did see and he seen the sorrow coming with the egg to lay and he walked off into his picture.

Impossible to believe but is truth nevertheless too much sorrows.

How to grasp with the grapple sorrows? How to understand the excellence of the great squares of black now done in? Glad he was to become the Jews exhibit this year for final success and laurels before the departure. He have this satisfaction how he was in *Life* think of the satisfaction probably so much it caused death. For to appear in *Life* is too often the cause of death.

Tomorrow the solemns. The requiems alone in the hermit hatch. Before the ikons the offering. The oblations. The clean oblations all round thunder quiet silence black picture oblations. Make Mass beautiful silence like big black picture speaking requiem. Tears in the shadows of hermit hatch requiems blue black tone. Sorrows for Ad in the oblation quiet peace request rest. Tomorrow is solemns in the hermit hatch for the old lutheran reinhardt commie paintblack. Tomorrow is the eternal solemns fending off the purge-fire place non catch old skipper reinhardt safely by into the heavens. Tomorrow is the solemns and the barefoots and the ashes and the masses, oldstyle liturgy masses without the colonels and without the sargeants yelling sit down. Just old black quiet requiems in hermit hatch with decent sorrows good bye college chum.

It is all solemns and sads all over beginning to fade out people in process before comes the march of ogres and djinns. Well out of the way is safe Reinhardt in his simple black painting the final statement includes all.

Next thing you know the procession of weevils and the big germ. Pardon the Big Germ in capitals. It is now waking in the labor-blossoms a big pardon Big Germ. Ad is well out of sight in his blacks. It is likely too true the bad fortunes and the sorrows. Gypsy Rose Lee look in her crystal ball and see no more jokes and no more funnies it is not any more like thirty-seven college chums. I must therefore cease and sit in the sorrows. I was not write before because I was in the dump with a sickness. Nothing bad. But you can only daid oncet. Like said uncle arthur in the aforesaid. Well is all silence in the den of glooms. Look around at some cheerful flower.

Lv.

Commentary on the Correspondence

1

Merton, Reinhardt, and Lax acquired as young men a taste for punning language which they retained ever after. The immediate inspiration must have been James Joyce's *Finnegans Wake* (1939). In the Merton-Lax correspondence (see endnote 7 for details), Joycean complexity and playfulness dominate to the point that one sometimes puts the published letters aside with an exasperated sigh; they could write in wholly impenetrable code to one another. The Merton-Reinhardt correspondence has sallies and sorties of this kind ("Am I my blubber's kipper?"), but it never goes over the top.

At the time of this opening letter, mid 1956, Merton must have been unsure about Reinhardt's political and religious convictions. Hence the inquiry, relayed by Lax to Reinhardt, about Rome or Moscow, Togliatti or Sergius. This is tightly wound—these witty men delighted in puzzling each other—but the meanings are clear enough. The choice between Rome and Moscow suggests Catholicism on the one hand and Communism on the other, while the choice between Togliatti and Sergius reverses the proposition for the fun of it: Palmiro Togliatti was the crusading leader of the Italian Communist party, while St. Sergius of Radonezh was a fourteenth-century Russian saint, still widely venerated.

The mid-section of this letter, Reinhardt's inspired riff on his many parts, ties, and bondages, is altogether memorable. "Part of me is part of things"—few could say this so cleanly and well. The wacky cumulative arithmetic is just one delicious element among others in this classic Reinhardt self-assessment.

With some reserve, Reinhardt offers to design the cover for a pamphlet or perhaps a series of pamphlets Merton has prepared for the novices at Gethsemani, whom he was serving at the time as Master of Novices, their principal instructor in monastic knowledge and customs. He questions whether his art is fully suited to the purpose. Beyond that, he questions whether his sensibility is attuned to Merton's world: "I don't know what to do with your Christian words... I understand the invisible, unseen but not the unspoken...." And finally, on a quite separate topic, he asks Merton what sort of contribution he might make to two Catholic journals, *Pax* and *Jubilee*, with which their friends Robert Lax and Edward Rice were associated.

No instructional materials were ultimately published at Gethsemani with a cover by Ad Reinhardt.

2

Merton responded promptly to Reinhardt with much the same playfulness and sudden rushes of seriousness. "...As for the choices, the answer is choose everything." These few words, seemingly tossed off in the course of a playful opening, are rooted in Merton's engagement with Zen Buddhism, still quite new in 1956. They reflect the intensity of his engagement but also something that was his before he encountered Zen. Call it the need to say yes to life, to love fully. In the mid 1960s he wrote, very beautifully, "My whole being must be a yes and an amen...."[8]

In his discussion of the pamphlets being readied for the novices, Merton refers to the distance that had appeared over the years between what he is expected by monastic authority to teach and what he privately feels and thinks. The stark cover design he hopes to receive from Reinhardt will wordlessly convey his deeper view: "...the cover need say no more than the general darkness which lies beyond the conclusions and in which the realities are grasped which the words fail to signify as much as they pretend to." The year is 1956, many years still lie ahead. Merton was not yet pressing hard against the bounds set for him by Cistercian tradition and his Father Abbot, but the signs that he would need to do so, for the sake of his maturing religious vocation and his gifts and concerns as a writer, are already evident.

Merton's allusions to Zen Buddhism are wonderfully revealing. More than a year earlier, he had written to his friend and publisher, Jay Laughlin of New Directions Books, to request whatever books Laughlin could send by D.T. Suzuki, the sage and scholar who had almost single-handedly introduced Zen to the

West.[9]   The impact of the books he received is evident: "The very name of Suzuki produces in me electric currents from head to foot." The lines that follow in the letter show how very much Merton had absorbed from Suzuki's writings. We can be certain of at least one book he was reading, *The Zen Doctrine of No Mind* (1949), in which Dr. Suzuki explored in depth the teachings of the Sixth Patriarch of Zen, Hui-Neng, who organized much of his teaching around the concept of *wu-nien*, translated by Suzuki as "no-thought" or "no-mind." Where Merton offers in the letter his own vernacular gloss on this ancient concept ("Leave them all be: they are okay the way they are"), we witness a very early stage of his adoption of Zen thinking and impulse to naturalize it, to make it his own.

Even with generous help from within the American Zen community, I've been unable to track down the specific source of Merton's cited line about the wooden man and the stone man. In Zen literature as a whole, the images refer to the Zen adept who is no longer enslaved by life experience happy or sad: he or she (the stone woman shows up in Zen literature) is unshakably serene.[10]

Merton's reference to jail for subversive activities signals that he expects to attend a mid-summer conference away from the monastery. It was to be one of his rare sorties beyond the walls, and he speaks of it lightly. Not light at all in the same paragraph is his question about Reinhardt's college courses in the history of Far Eastern painting. "Do you think," asks Merton, "there is any hope of anyone really learning what is behind all that and what has been so largely forgotten by everyone?" This perception of forgotten wisdom—of a Church that has forgotten its own contemplative traditions, and here of a distant world of art that could teach great things, if only we could learn great things—was much with Merton in these years and in years to come. He longed to retrieve lost wisdom at the conceptual level and wise practices at the level of daily life. The poem, "Wisdom," with which he brought these thoughts to a close, must have been very new at the time Merton wrote this note to Reinhardt. It was published in the following year in his book, *The Strange Islands*.[11]

Merton's closing remarks about "the insides of this particular existence" return to the theme of his restless, increasingly disillusioned experience of monastic life, already evident paragraphs earlier where he refers to the difference between his private views and those he felt obliged to offer in the novice pamphlets. Again

Zen Buddhism throws much of the light and offers much of the language:

> In all directions people run as fast as they can from themselves, even when they are religious, because they want to appear to themselves as gods and the effort is exhausting. After having run in all directions at once, a person decides through no fault of his own that he has to stop running and finds himself in the center of everything, having everything knowing everything because they have and know nothing and realize that this is the way it should be. This, as I say, comes about against all our own plans and best intentions, and the less said about it the better.

The overall vision owes much to Zen, although at the end the Christian notion of grace unmerited, freely offered by the Lord and wholly redemptive, makes itself felt. In these years, Merton had begun working toward the integration of Christian faith with the stark psychological realism and practice of awareness here and now, which he had discovered in Zen.

Always ready in these years to spring free of solemnity so as not to be snared by pride and prudery and who knows what else, Merton writes with good humor that he would resist becoming an Arhat until after a visit from Reinhardt. Well versed in Buddhist thought, Reinhardt would have recognized at once Merton's reference to the early Buddhist Arhats, enlightened disciples of the Buddha, represented particularly in Chinese art as majestic, sometimes marvelously eccentric elders.

At the very end of his letter, Merton expresses his appreciation for one of Reinhardt's wittiest cartoon art commentaries, "A Portend of the Artist as a Yhung Mandala," which Reinhardt must have sent him.[12] The play on words, multiple, takes in the title of a famed book by James Joyce, the mandala studies of C.G. Jung, and the typical look and feel of Tibetan in English transcription.

You will notice in Merton's postscript that he requested a small painting from Reinhardt. From this request, much good would come.

An admission of defeat: who are the "blue man" who "sits on the dome and the other one [who] draws forth stars from his pockets"? Merton's references to the Blue Dome in letter 15 yield to inquiry: he is thinking of a shrine complex in Iran where the Imam Ali ibn Musa-ar-Reza has his resting place, surmounted by an el-

egant turquoise-blue dome. Merton had much appreciated a textile from that shrine, preserved in the Cincinnati Art Museum.[13]
As well, he translated verse inscribed on the textile in his poem,
"Tomb Cover of Imam Riza."[14] But I have no idea what Merton
means by the blue man and the one with stars, images distantly
reminiscent of the Revelations of St. John, but for the moment un-
moored.

3

Written only six days after the preceding, this letter is all fun and
mostly self-explanatory. Merton seems to have been tripping over
himself—his friend Ed Rice, an editor and capable designer, must
also have been asked to design the novice pamphlets and had gotten out ahead of Reinhardt. Merton nonetheless encourages
Reinhardt to continue his design effort and already has a new,
ambitious idea to offer: Merton would write (or adapt) a series of
50 "small sharp koans," the enigmatic teaching tales of Zen tradition, and Reinhardt would illustrate the book. "…wow, how you
like question mark stop." This "wizard idea" didn't come to fruition, but as it breezes by we catch a glimpse of Merton's tireless
creativity.

4

Reinhardt's response to Merton about the novice pamphlets must
have crossed the preceding letter in the mail—the dates are tight
and Reinhardt doesn't realize that Merton's plans were changing.
Reinhardt offers quite a thorough study of potential cover designs,
complete with two sets of sketches. He plunges in his letter from
a proper artist-client discussion into the intricately furnished world
of his own creative life as he deploys the long list of works of art
that his design will somehow evoke. "Amida-Buddhist ceilings,
Russian icons, Irish stones, Jain prayer cards, Persian rugs,
Carolingian reliefs…," and so on through many more reference
points in the history of art. Reinhardt's knowing love of these
things is evident, and his impulse to create litanies or chants, as in
his published writings, is also audible.

   A few references in the balance of the letter may be unclear.
Reinhardt had read and liked an early poem by Merton, "Tower
of Babel," published by Ed Rice in the Catholic journal, *Jubilee* (3:6,
October, 1955),[15] where it was accompanied by a reproduction of
the famous painting on the same theme by Pieter Breughel.

Reinhardt's inquiry about the initial "jhs," which Merton almost always inscribed at the top of his correspondence, is a teasing joke about a Columbia classmate, John Hampton Slate, strictly speaking an aviation lawyer who at Merton's request turned his skills to providing an initial structure for the Merton Legacy Trust. The initials are a beautifully solemn Christian remembrance, more familiar in the form IHS, a monogram for the name of Jesus derived from Greek.

Reinhardt's last paragraph is a funny and sad, slightly exasperated tease targeting Merton's presumed ignorance because he lives the cloistered life. A few paragraphs earlier he had launched the theme: "You don't read newspapers? Or see television?" And now he continues: "Do you know who Elvis Presley and Erwin Panofsky are?" This is a droll juxtaposition—the pop culture idol and the distinguished art historian, whose writings Reinhardt would have encountered as a graduate student of art history. A sophisticated New Yorker, Reinhardt is not about to wax sentimental over Merton's status as a monk. Yet Reinhardt was a seeker, no less severe and impelled from within than his friend.

5

A lighthearted letter from Merton to Reinhardt, it has few points that call for added context. Merton's mention of a forthcoming book, *Thirty-Seven Meditations*, refers to the book actually published in 1958 as *Thoughts in Solitude*.[16] The paragraph about Cistercian architecture mentions the marvelous series of books on Romanesque art and architecture edited and published by French Benedictine monks under the name Editions Zodiaque.

Apart from these matters of detail, there is one strong pulse in the letter: Merton's response to the litany of arts in Reinhardt's previous letter. "All the words you mention are for me like letters from home, viz. covers, stones, prayer cards, ceilings, beams...," and so on. In mid 1956, when Merton wrote these words, he was not yet seriously practicing a visual art, although he is likely to have been doing brush drawings on simple, repeated themes— above all, the Blessed Virgin and the portrait of a tonsured, bearded monk with wistful eyes. But the immediacy and power of his response to Reinhardt's inventory of kinds and times of art suggest that Merton could himself become a working artist.

6

Between Merton's letters dated July 19 and August 22, 1956 (nos. 5 and 6), Reinhardt sent his friend a wonderfully droll collection of line portraits (fig. 1), ranging in theme from a "Central Asian Cistercian" with a peaked Tibetan hat to various glowering devils and an assortment of "Clowns for Lax." Their friend Robert Lax had followed a circus troupe in 1949, and in 1959 would publish a book of poems, *Circus of the Sun*, inspired by his experiences in and around the circus. Reinhardt and Merton must have known that the book was on its way.

In the Thomas Merton Papers, Columbia University, there is what appears to be a draft of the sketches in fig. 1; the images are much the same, though fewer in number and lacking captions. This is not the last time we will see Reinhardt making a draft of something he wished to convey to Merton. The sketches in fig. 1 float free of any specific letter. There may be a gap at this point in the preserved correspondence, as it seems doubtful that Reinhardt would have sent the sketches with no accompanying note.

Merton immediately applies Reinhardt's intriguing human comedy to his own life and circumstances. "We have all the characters on your graph present here in this domicile," he writes. Looking around him among his monastic brothers, he finds the same cast of characters as in Reinhardt's collection of "snowflakes," as Merton puts it.

The "Georgia Cracker Cleric" is one of Reinhardt's sketches, and we know from a prior letter that this is a joking reference to Lax. Merton writes that Lax is visiting the monastery just then, and he needs to join him for supper. The word play about pax refers to the Catholic journal, *Pax*, to which Lax and other friends contributed. Getting Russia into it—the "mysterious russian pax"—must be yet another tease targeting Reinhardt's involvement with Communism when both men were young.

7

Every reader will quickly recognize that Merton's letter to Reinhardt of October 29, 1957, is one of the gems of this correspondence. It is perfect Merton.

In an earlier letter (no. 2) Merton had asked Reinhardt whether he could spare a small painting "for the cell in which I perch." Reinhardt rather promptly promised to do so: "I'll send you a small painting in the fall, or bring it...." But well more than a year has now passed, and Merton again raises the topic, this time with superb humor and mock pathos—beneath which one senses a very real pathos and need. There is again likely to be a gap at this point in the sequence of letters. The extant correspondence doesn't reveal why Merton would return just now to the topic of his wish for a small painting.

Apart from a few details—for example, the custom Merton shared with Lax of signing letters in some original, obscure way, here "Folio" or perhaps "Folie"—the letter needs no commentary. But one larger point might easily escape us. Merton had never seen an original Black Painting. He had almost certainly seen illustrations, and if not illustrations then he must have heard enough to know roughly what a Black Painting was. But unlike many of us now reading this correspondence, who have seen Reinhardt's mature work in museums and galleries, Merton could not at the time have fully known what he was asking for. This explains, in part, the truly touching letter that follows, in which Merton conveys to Reinhardt his initial responses to the small painting that did, indeed, reach him at Gethsemani.

It is difficult today to imagine the experience of seeing a Reinhardt Black Painting for the first time. The next letter restores that experience to us.

8

Merton's acknowledgment of Reinhardt's gift[17] is in a letter dated November 23, 1957. An earlier journal entry, for November 17, 1957, records in perceptual flashes Merton's first responses to the Black Painting:

> Reinhardt finally sent his "small" painting. Almost invisible cross on a black background. As though immersed in darkness and trying to emerge from it. Seen in relation to my other object[s], the picture is meaningless—a black square "without purpose." You have to look hard to see the cross. One must turn away from everything else and concentrate on the picture as though peering through a window into the night. The picture demands this—or is meaningless for I presume that someone might be unmoved by any such demand. I should say a very "holy" picture—helps prayer—an "image" without features to accustom the mind at once to the night of prayer—

and to help one set aside trivial and useless images that wander into prayer and spoil it.

He deserves the Molotov-Zhukhov medal as the artist who has gone farthest from "socialist realism."[18]

This entry and his letter show vividly that Merton was far better prepared to appreciate a Reinhardt Black Painting than the New York critics and collectors who at the time were still treating Reinhardt with indifference or contempt—Reinhardt's breakthrough to fame and recognition in 1967, the last year of his life, was quite far ahead.Merton's practice of contemplative prayer, under the inspiration of St. John of the Cross and other Catholic teachers of the "night of prayer," and his avid study of Zen Buddhism, still at an early stage in 1957, provided him with all of the concepts and intuitive recognitions he needed to embrace Reinhardt's painting in a way that must have been enormously touching to Reinhardt himself.

Merton's thought that the painting is "a black square without purpose" draws from Zen. A few years later, when Merton was first beginning to spend time at the hermitage that had recently been built with him in mind, he returned to the notion of purposelessness in a way that shows us what he meant—not aimlessness, not triviality, but something more like transcendent freedom. Speaking of his life at the hermitage, he wrote:

Afternoons are for nothing.

For cutting away all that is practical.
Learn to wash your cup and give rise to nothing.
What house? No house could possibly make a difference.
It is a house for nothing. It has no purpose. Do not give it one, and the whole universe will be thankful.[19]

One further point in this letter needs clarification. At the heart of Merton's memorable praise of the painting is an antique word. "It is a most religious, devout, and latreutic small painting," he wrote. I cannot imagine that the marvelously Latinate word "latreutic" was common, even at Gethsemani, even in 1957, well before Vatican II and its introduction of the vernacular Mass, which signaled the retreat of Latin. Referring to the worship of God, "latreutic" fits into a triad of terms, *latria, hyperdulia, dulia,* by which the Church designates worship of God, the Blessed Virgin, and the Saints.[20]

The swinging freedom of Merton's description of Reinhardt's painting alerts us that when he wrote privately about art in these years he used the full resources of his keen eyes and creative imagination. It was otherwise when he wrote of art for the public. He would soon be struggling to complete a book on sacred art, under the title *Art and Worship,* which started as a joyful project and became, by 1960, a thorn in his side. The book was ultimately never published.[21] He would need to dare to release his perceptions of art, rich and true, from a preachy, constricted view that he had perhaps unknowingly absorbed in the course of his monastic experience. He was repelled by the sentimental, realistic Catholic art of holy cards and standard statuary of the saints. But in 1957 he had not yet found a whole and truly individual view of art. He had only bits and pieces. The utter simplicity and sobriety of Reinhardt's canvas skipped over all that and spoke to him in depth. Strange to say, Merton was one of the first to understand Reinhardt's art.

The letter includes the customary dig at Reinhardt for his youthful Communistic leanings. In this case, Merton conjures up a prize for the painting *least like* the prescribed Socialist Realism of the Soviet Union.

9

This letter, Reinhardt to Merton, was written just after Reinhardt in the company of Robert Lax had visited Merton at Gethsemani. Vividly descriptive, it is one of the many treasures of the correspondence. Among other things, it reflects Reinhardt's love-hate relationship with formal religious discipline. On the one hand, Reinhardt writes with perfect Zen pitch about his photographic venture at the monastery: "I needed more time to find more things to point my camera at. There's never anything out there always, theoretically, for me, anywhere in the world, but some places take longer to put something there...." This is indeed perfect Zen pitch, paradoxical, playful, aware of the Buddhist concept of *sunyata*— the unutterable, infinitely alive emptiness at the core of things. On the other hand, toward the end of the letter Reinhardt produces a coarse joke about Zen, asking whether *zazen*, the practice of sitting meditation, bears any relation to German *Zitzen*, meaning teats. Like us all, Reinhardt was trying to find his way: he was allergic to pretentiousness, including religious pretension; he avoided organizations and adopted the role of gadfly when near them; and yet he learned in depth from the written texts and art of religious and spiritual traditions, virtually all of which developed within the shelter of ordered communities, as he well knew.

Reinhardt's mention of Ulfert Wilke, professor of studio art at the University of Louisville, is a sign of future meetings and meanings. In the spring of 1959 when this letter was written, Merton had not yet begun to explore with brush and ink and paper the world of calligraphic marks and signs—that would come later, in the fall of 1960, and Wilke would prove to be a friend to that enterprise. Wilke and Merton met only some years later, in fall 1963.

At the end of the letter, Reinhardt expresses the hope that he and Merton can "argue about art and religion some more." They must have done a good deal of that when they had been together. Merton would have asked Reinhardt for insights that could enrich his planned book on sacred art, and Reinhardt's remarks in this letter betray a certain impatience, as if he is unsure whether Merton had been listening well. "…Can I help you say what's right, instead of saying things people want to hear and agree with?" Merton's response to this letter, nearly immediate, betrays some irritation in return.

10

"I am not clear," writes Merton, "in what way I was writing just what will please readers because a lot of what I have written about art will make them mad." And so he joins battle, with just a trace of rancor, against Reinhardt's assertion. Other elements in the letter clearly continue discussions begun when they were together at Gethsemani—for example, the topic of iconoclasm. As Merton notes, threads from the Byzantine quarrel over the validity of sacred images found their way into the Cistercian Order. Its founder, St. Bernard of Clairvaux, was indifferent to art. Merton's critique of Bernard's attitude—"Who is there to be distracted?"—draws on the Zen inquiry into human identity to make its point. Reinhardt himself, advocate of the most extreme and radical abstraction in art, was a born iconoclast. From his perspective all descriptive images were anecdotal and ultimately trivial.

Reinhardt had expressed in the previous letter a concern that Merton viewed him as a "quietist," not a word of praise in the traditional Catholic lexicon. A current Catholic encyclopedia defines it, in part, as "the doctrine which declares that man's highest perfection consists in a sort of psychical self-annihilation and a consequent absorption of the soul into the Divine Essence even during the present life.... Quietism is thus generally speaking a sort of false or exaggerated mysticism."[22]   Merton now assures Reinhardt of his admiration for Reinhardt's "elegant and effective" approach to issues of importance to Merton also: the emptying out of all personal nonsense so as to be open to something other and incommensurably greater. For Reinhardt the locus of this drama was the work of art; for Merton it was the living person.

There is a further point about art that the reader may find puzzling. Merton's deepest preference in art was for Byzantine and Russian Orthodox icons, which he glosses here as "the Mount Athos tradition." His hermitage chapel in later years would have images of this kind. Some were precious antiques offered by friends, others were reproductions which he valued just as much owing to their religiously powerful imagery. Readers will find in his essay, "Mount Athos," in *Disputed Questions* (1960), Merton's sweet praise of the Holy Mountain's religious attitudes, way of life, and art. In the journals and other correspondence occur passages recording his love of the icon tradition—as for example these words from a letter written toward the end of his life:

> The Christ of the ikons represents a traditional *experience* formulated in a theology of light, the ikon being a kind of sacramental medium for the illumination and awareness of the glory of Christ within us (in faith). The hieratic rules for ikon painting are not just rigid and formal, they are the guarantee of an authentic transmission of the possibility of this experience, provided the ikon painter was also himself a man of prayer (like Roublev).[23]

Toward the end of the letter, Merton's contrast of the 14th-century Florentine painter, Giotto, with the 15th-century Venetian painter, Carlo Crivelli, sets up but retreats from a discussion of pictorial style in relation to the religious moment. Crivelli was an elegant painter within a tradition that had already found its stylistic fundamentals, while Giotto was the artist of genius who first discovered and displayed those fundamentals. Merton seems to intuit behind Giotto's greatness another greatness in the religious sensibility of his time.

11

Reinhardt's letter of June, 1959, still moves in the enriched wake of his May visit to Gethsemani. The seven photographs Reinhardt sent of that occasion have not come to light, but they may yet be found.[24] Central to this letter is Reinhardt's continued questioning of Merton's views on art. Merton may well be a famous author read by millions but Reinhardt, who served all by doubting and probing, did not neglect to doubt and probe here, too.

Merton had written his Zen-like pronouncement: "Who is there to be distracted?" It doesn't suit Reinhardt, who takes a more earthy approach. He asks Merton whether he is speaking of statues—they can't be distracted. But real people are easily distracted, and in that lies a certain tragedy: "Nobody knows what's real." This is not the end of Reinhardt's uneasiness with Merton's thinking. Responding to Merton's thoughts in the previous letter about "that which is religious and sacred in a work of art," Reinhardt cuts him no slack. He describes Merton's views as perhaps new to theologians on art, by which Reinhardt means nothing very complimentary, but out of touch with the reality of the art object. Reinhardt is emerging as Merton's loyal adversary, where questions of art are concerned.

12

Because Merton and Reinhardt belonged to different classes at Columbia University (respectively, 1937 and 1935), they must have been unaware that each had been a member of the same final-year honor society, the Senior Society of Sachems, founded in 1915. This letter is newsy, although not quite serene in every line. Among other things, Reinhardt conveys his edgy attitude toward fame ("I don't have to apologize for that remark?").

As Merton clarifies in the next letter, Reinhardt had been misinformed about the appearance of an art book by Merton; nothing had as yet been published.

13

Merton to Reinhardt in response is mostly fun. Nacoms was another Columbia institution, a senior honor society, apparently a rival to the Sachems.[25] Later Merton refers not kindly to Eloise Spaeth, the young art historian who had been asked by Robert Giroux, Merton's friend and publisher, to help Merton solve the difficulties that had been preventing progress on his projected book, *Art and Worship*.

Merton's longing to see Reinhardt again at Gethsemani, restated in letter after letter, is the poignant note here. Reinhardt brought to him the warmth of old friendship and a keen, demanding knowledge of art which Merton clearly respected.

14

Letters 14 and 15 enact a drama that proved to be a turning point for Merton. The letters do not simply reflect that drama, as if they were reports after the fact. They are the drama itself, direct vehicles of transformation. However, background information is needed to understand the exchange.

Since the later 1950s, Merton had been struggling to write *Art and Worship* and, as we have seen, recruited Reinhardt to help him illustrate the section on sacred art in Asia. Robert Giroux had introduced Eloise Spaeth into the project in order to bring an art historian's experience and judgment to bear, especially in the field of modern sacred art where Merton had run short of ideas. Merton had nurtured for some time the thought that the language of Abstract Expressionism, the art of his own time and place, could lend itself richly to the themes of Christian art. However, it was not until he encountered the art of a devout Catholic convert, William Congdon, who painted classic images of Catholic spirituality in an Abstract Expressionist style, that Merton felt justified in his original surmise. Eloise Spaeth shared his enthusiasm for Congdon's work. Together they felt that they had discovered a great and specifically Catholic modern master. Merton invited Congdon to visit him at Gethsemani, but even before that meeting occurred he wrote a statement in praise of Congdon's art that appeared as a lengthy endorsement on the back of a substantial art book: *In My Disc of Gold: Itinerary to Christ of William Congdon* (ca. 1962). What Merton wrote could be described, not unfairly, as purple prose:

> There is in the recent painting of William Congdon an air of theophany that imposes silence.... Here we see a completely extraordinary breakthrough of genuine spiritual light in the art of an abstract expressionist.... Here we see a rare instance in which the latent spiritual *logos* of abstract art has been completely set free. The inner dynamism which so often remains

pent up and chokes to death in inarticulate, frustrated mannerism, is here let loose with all its power. How has this been
possible? Here the dynamism of abstraction has been set free
from its compulsive, Dionysian and potentially orgiastic self-
frustration and raised to the level of spirituality....

To Merton's good fortune and misfortune, Reinhardt received this
effusion as a mailing piece and fired off the letter reproduced here,
no. 14 in the series. "Fired off" is the right expression as to general
mood and impact, but in point of fact the Archives of American
Art has on microfilm the draft of a key portion of the letter—and
so we know that Reinhardt took aim before he fired.

On February 20, 1962, Merton recorded in his journal an initial
reaction to Reinhardt's letter: "A very funny and also serious letter from Ad Reinhardt, mocking and reproving me for the piece I
wrote about Congdon and which is splashed all over the back of
his big book. Ad is perfectly right. Congdon not yet here."[26] But
that was hardly the end of the matter. Two weeks later, he sat
down to write Reinhardt from within the shock and turmoil that
his friend's letter had caused. That response follows here as the
15th letter.

There is one further movement across this map that readers
would wish to know. Since late 1960, Merton had been experi-
menting with brush-drawn calligraphy on paper, probably in the
quiet remoteness of the newly built hermitage at Gethsemani. He
was not yet living there full time—that would take some years
more—but the hermitage quickly became his second home, the
center and solace of his life in the 1960s and, among other things,
an improvised art studio. Merton's experiments as a visual artist
began with images that had debts of studentship to Ad Reinhardt
and to the late period of Paul Klee, the twentieth-century artist he
most deeply admired, but he was moving steadily toward his own
ground, midway between Abstract Expressionism and the Zen
calligraphy he so appreciated in the work of the eighteenth-cen-
tury priest and artist, Sengai.[27] Although in 1962 Merton's own
art had not yet matured—he was still finding his way, unsure but
advancing—he was nonetheless now writing to the artist Ad
Reinhardt as the artist Thomas Merton.

15

The high point of Merton's side of the correspondence in terms of imaginative ingenuity and biographical importance, this letter needs surprisingly little commentary. Merton's anguish is real. He plays with it, makes it utterly funny, mocks himself in ways hilarious, philosophical, and sad, but throughout he is asking forgiveness. For what, really? For so wanting a baptized, Catholic, at least marginally traditional solution to the difficulties surrounding contemporary sacred art that he had turned his back on the world to which Ad Reinhardt and his peers belonged. He had described Congdon's art as transcending and legitimizing a darker realm of art in which, Merton had written, there was little more than "inarticulate, frustrated mannerism…, compulsive, Dionysian and potentially orgiastic self-frustration…." Reading these words, Reinhardt could only have felt that his friend had slipped into attitudes—judgmental, oddly frantic—from which there was perhaps no return. It was a great kindness on Reinhardt's part, and a sign of his underlying confidence in Merton, that he wrote at all.

Merton had broken faith not only with the formidably rich quest of artists of his own time; he had also broken faith with himself. His own tentative explorations with ink, brush, and paper drew from Abstract Expressionism and shared with the artists of that generation—his own generation, precisely—a deep interest in Far Eastern calligraphy and the expressive power of abstraction. In his impromptu hermitage studio he was not exploring traditional Christian imagery. He was learning to float in the wild seas of unconstrained visual imagination, learning to let the brush lead, learning to discover rather than impose. He was learning as a visual artist lessons long since learned as a poet.

There was a debate in Merton's mind and heart at this time between the old and the new, the contained and the released, the known and the wholly uncertain. Close readers of Merton will know that this debate was occurring not only where art was concerned, but also in his approach to issues of war and peace, racial justice, and the religious life itself. Merton's eventual resolve to explore as a visual artist the forms and methods of his own time parallels his resolve to participate fearlessly in what he perceived as the great issues of his time in the world at large.

After this letter, Merton accepted the art of his time as his own. His friend, Reinhardt, who had not ceased helping him, could now be still more helpful.

16

Some 18 months after the preceding exchange, Merton briefly reports to Reinhardt that he is working with great intensity on brush-drawn calligraphy and has received the visit of Reinhardt's friend, the artist Ulfert Wilke.[28] An artist of very real sophistication, born and educated in Europe with a wide circle of artist friends ranging from Ad Reinhardt to Mark Tobey and Robert Motherwell, Wilke had studied brush calligraphy in Kyoto. Sent by Reinhardt, he was the ideal partner and mentor for Merton at this point in Merton's development as a visual artist.

It appears that soon after Wilke's first visit—there were further meetings in the following year—Merton began to explore a very simple but effective approach to printmaking, based on transferring marks from one sheet of paper to another by hand pressure. Merton's art at this point is akin to Wilke's calligraphic art of somewhat earlier date, which Wilke had shown him. The topic of Merton's printmaking is too complex for discussion here, but readers will find a full discussion and examples in *Angelic Mistakes: The Art of Thomas Merton.*

17

Reinhardt's immediate response to Merton's previous letter is rich in content. Reinhardt tells briefly about his participation in the celebrated March on Washington for civil rights, August 1963, at which Martin Luther King, Jr. gave his great speech, "I have a dream," to a peaceful assembly of some 250,000 people. Reinhardt had expected to see Robert Lax and the gifted Catholic poet, Ned O'Gorman, at the March, but in the huge crowd failed to spot them.

Reinhardt responds with marvelous warmth to Merton's gift of representative examples of his brush-drawn calligraphy (the first of three such gifts in the coming months). There is likely to be a gap in the preserved correspondence at this point—if Merton wrote a cover letter with the gift of calligraphy, it has not yet come to light. This letter sets up a witty exchange about the size of Merton's calligraphy, too small in Reinhardt's view. Merton replies archly and with good humor in the next letter.

Reinhardt's bitterness over his treatment by the New York art establishment is poignantly evident toward the end of this letter, where he refers to his inclusion in a prominent exhibition of much younger artists among whom he felt out of place.[29] His gloss on the stock phrase "that's life" is classic Reinhardt.

18

Merton responds with little delay to Reinhardt's most recent letter and sends a further batch of calligraphic drawings with a plea for fine paper—"your dusty old correspondent who is very poor...got no papers any more...." By now, in late 1963, Merton was fully engaged in the exploration of visual art and kinds of meaning that have nothing, or nearly nothing, to do with words. The realm of images had opened.

Readers who are aware of Merton's interest in photography, growing ever stronger in the course of the 1960s, will note his glancing reference here: "What else I do is make the snapshot of old distilleries."

19

Two months after receiving Merton's request for fine paper, Reinhardt sends three types of paper, including the "non-yellowing-fine-Japanese-paper" that Merton would come to prefer. Some of his most beautiful calligraphies and prints are on this paper. Apart from this generous offering, Reinhardt sets up the premise for the next extended round of humor, this time focused on the concept of being designated a "dean."

20

As noted at the beginning of this exploration, this last preserved letter of January 12, 1964, is unlikely to be the last exchanged. They are both in motion and have more topics than ever of shared interest. Merton includes a third batch of calligraphy in this mailing, works now part of a generous donation to the Thomas Merton Center by the Reinhardt family.

Merton is engaged by now in printmaking on the basis of brushed calligraphic marks, to which he was learning to add found objects such as grass stems from the fields surrounding the hermitage. Helped by Ulfert Wilke toward the end of the year, he would by then be sufficiently confident to accept the invitation of a local Catholic college to mount an exhibition of his ink drawings and prints.

Merton collaborated with Emil Antonucci, artist and graphic designer, to produce an anti-war book in 1962, *Original Child Bomb*. Antonucci's heavily inked, calligraphic illustrations for the book must relate in some way to the development of Merton's own calligraphic art, but it has so far proved difficult to document and specify this connection.

Readers interested in Merton's changing relations with his Church, his Order, and the monastery will not miss the poignant humor of his discussion of the initials OCSO, denoting the Order of the Cistercians of the Strict Observance, to which he belonged as monk and priest. Through the 1960s he became more and more informal, with the exception of his conduct of the Mass, his enduring love of the traditional Latin of the Church, and careful service to his community as Master of Novices (until 1965). Informal though he now was in some respects, he was also one of the most strictly observant Cistercians of all: observing himself and his friends and the troubled life of society with keen vigilance, ever-increasing compassion, and faith in the workings of the Lord.

Coda

Thomas Merton outlived Ad Reinhardt by some 16 months. His letter to Robert Lax, conveying and mourning Reinhardt's death, is the natural coda to this vital exchange of letters. The letter reads easily without added commentary, although it is partially written in the Joycean, fluidly transforming language that Merton and Lax had enjoyed with one another for years.

A few points of information may interest the reader. Schwester Therese refers to Sister Thérèse Lentfoehr, of the Congregation of the Sisters of the Divine Savior, a Merton friend and correspondent who was one of the earliest and most thorough collectors of Merton memorabilia—correspondence, manuscript, and much else. Her collection, now in the Columbia University Rare Book and Manuscript Library, is an important resource for Merton scholars.

The "Jews exhibit" is not an attractive expression but without anti-Semitic intent (it is simply another example of contracted Joyce-speak). Merton is referring to the 1967 exhibition of Reinhardt's art at The Jewish Museum in New York City, the art-world event that at last paid him well-deserved homage as an artist. Merton also mentions the article on Reinhardt in *Life* magazine, cited in earlier pages (and offering some of the most compelling photographs of Reinhardt ever made). He speculates that all of the attention was too much for his friend to bear, too unfamiliar. The thought that Reinhardt "walked off into his picture" echoes an old Chinese tale recounted in the writings of Ananda K. Coomaraswamy, whom Merton read with particular care over the years.

What is "the Big Germ"? Earlier in the year, U.S. Army efforts to develop biological weapons had been in the news. That must have stuck in Merton's mind as a further dreadful feature of the violence and threats in society at large, of which he was acutely aware through these years.

In the first issue of his literary journal, *Monks Pond*, Merton wrote a brief biographical entry for his late friend. Using the slightly formal language suited to the task, he acknowledged his friend in terms of his own values as a religious seeker. Reinhardt was "a rigorous contemplative." He was "prophetic." He was the black monk. Merton saluted not just a friend but a companion on the way.

> Ad Reinhardt was an abstract painter who died in August 1967 at the height of his powers, soon after an exhibition of all his most important work at the Jewish Museum in New York. Though he had made common cause with abstract expressionists like Pollock and De Kooning in the fifties, he differed entirely from them. A classicist and a rigorous contemplative, he was only just beginning to be recognized as prophetic by a new generation. He was called the "black monk" of abstract art, a purist who made Mondrian look problematic, who referred to himself as a "quietist" and said: "I'm just making the last paintings which anyone can make."[30]

Notes

This article supplements my forthcoming book, *Angelic Mistakes: The Art of Thomas Merton* (Boston and London: New Seeds/Shambhala Publications, 2006). I wish to extend sincere thanks to Dr. Paul M. Pearson, Director of the Thomas Merton Center, Bellarmine University, for his extraordinarily generous help; to the Merton Legacy Trust, for permission to print the Merton side of this correspondence; to Anna Reinhardt for the Estate of Ad Reinhardt, for granting permission to print the Reinhardt correspondence and two illustrations; to The Archives of American Art, for permission to publish the parts of the correspondence on microfilm in its care; to the Rare Book and Manuscript Library, Columbia University, for permission to publish correspondence in its collection; to Marcia

Kelly for the Estate of Robert Lax and the University Press of Kentucky, for permission to publish Merton's letter to Robert Lax; to Farrar, Straus & Giroux for permission to reprint three letters first published in Thomas Merton, *The Road to Joy: The Letters of Thomas Merton to New and Old Friends* (ed. Robert E. Daggy; New York: Farrar, Straus & Giroux, 1989), pp. 279-83; to Bonnie Myotai Treace, for her help in exploring the Zen background of certain letters; to Victor A. Kramer for his kind offer to write for *The Merton Annual*; and to Glenn Crider for his able project management. I first learned of this correspondence through the pioneering article by Joseph Masheck, "Five Unpublished Letters from Ad Reinhardt to Thomas Merton and Two in Return," *Artforum*, December 1978, pp. 23-27. See also "Two Sorts of Monk: Reinhardt and Merton," in Joseph Masheck, *Historical Present: Essays of the 1970s* (Ann Arbor: UMI Research Press, 1984), pp. 91-96.

1. Thomas Merton, *Run to the Mountain: The Story of a Vocation. The Journals of Thomas Merton, Volume One, 1939-1942* (ed. Patrick Hart; San Francisco: HarperSanFrancisco, 1995), pp. 128-29.

2. See Thomas B. Hess, *The Art Comics and Satires of Ad Reinhardt*, Düsseldorf : Kunsthalle; Rome: Marlborough, 1975.

3. David Bourdon, "Master of the Minimal," *Life*, February 3, 1967, pp. 45-52; *Ad Reinhardt Paintings*, New York: The Jewish Museum, 1966 (exhibition dates Nov. 23, 1966 – January 15, 1967).

4. See Barbara Rose, ed., *Art-as-Art: The Selected Writings of Ad Reinhardt* (New York: Viking, 1975). The classic study of Ad Reinhardt's art is Lucy R. Lippard, *Ad Reinhardt* (New York: Abrams, 1981).

5. Robert E. Daggy, ed., *Monks Pond: Thomas Merton's Little Magazine* (Lexington, KY: University Press of Kentucky, 1968), pp. 6-8.

6. The Archives of American Art has microfilm of all letters attributed to that collection. The originals remain with the Reinhardt family.

7. Arthur W. Biddle, ed., *When Prophecy Still Had a Voice: The Letters of Thomas Merton and Robert Lax* (Lexington, KY: University Press of Kentucky, 2001), pp. 368-69.

8. Thomas Merton, *The Courage for Truth: The Letters of Thomas Merton to Writers* (Christine M. Bochen, ed., New York: Farrar, Straus & Giroux, 1993), p. 225.

9. See David D. Cooper, ed., *Thomas Merton and James Laughlin: Selected Letters*, New York and London: Norton, 1997, p. 108.

10. See, for example, Victor Sogen Hori, *Zen Sand: The Book of Capping Phrases from Koan Practice*, Honolulu: University of Hawaii Press, 2003, indexed references.

11. Thomas Merton, *The Collected Poems of Thomas Merton* (New York: New Directions, 1977), p. 279

12. See note 2.

13. Thomas Merton, *Turning Toward the World: The Journals of Thomas Merton, Volume Four, 1960-1963* (ed. Victor A. Kramer; San Francisco: HarperSanFrancisco, 1996), pp. 60-61.

14. Merton, *Collected Poems*, p. 985.

15. Merton, *Collected Poems*, pp. 21-22.

16. Thanking Dr. Paul Pearson for this information.

17. For an illustration of the Black Painting given by Reinhardt to Merton, see Joseph Masheck, "Five Unpublished Letters...," p. 23.

18. Thomas Merton, *A Search for Solitude: The Journals of Thomas Merton, Volume Three, 1952-1960,* (ed. Lawrence S. Cunningham; San Francisco: HarperSanFrancisco, 1996), pp. 139-40.

19. Merton, *Turning Toward the World*, p. 100.

20. Thanking Joseph Masheck for clarifying this triad of terms.

21. On the troubled manuscript *Art and Worship*, see David D. Cooper, *Thomas Merton's Art of Denial: The Evolution of a Radical Humanist* (Athens (GA) and London: The University of Georgia Press, 1989), chapter 4, and scattered references in Lipsey, *Angelic Mistakes*.

22. See www.newadvent.org/cathen/12608c.htm.

23. Thomas Merton, *The Hidden Ground of Love: The Letters of Thomas Merton on Religious Experience and Social Concerns* (ed. William H. Shannon; New York: Farrar, Straus & Giroux, 1985), p. 642.

24. In a letter to Sr. Thérèse Lentfoehr, 11 December 1959, Merton refers to photographs of himself, Lax, and Reinhardt, which he is sending as a Christmas present to some friends; this argues for the eventual recovery of the photographs. Merton, *The Road to Joy*, p. 235. Thanks to Dr. Paul Pearson for this reference.

25. Thanking Joseph Masheck, a Columbia graduate, for information about honor societies.

26. Merton, *Turning Toward the World*, p. 204.

27. See Lipsey, *Angelic Mistakes*, s.v. "Kyoto" and "D. T. Suzuki." A primary source for Sengai, assembled as a book in part from materials Merton had seen and valued, is D.T. Suzuki, *Sengai: The Zen Master* (London: Faber and Faber, 1971).

28. For a fuller account, including correspondence between Merton and Wilke, see Roger Lipsey, "Thomas Merton and Ulfert Wilke: The Friendship of Artists," *The Merton Seasonal* 30.2 (Summer 2005), pp. 3-12.

29. Dorothy Miller, ed., *Americans 1963* (New York: Museum of Modern Art, 1963).

30. Merton, *Monks Pond*, p. 62.

Art in *The Merton Annual*, Volumes 1–5

A Bibliographical Note and Compilation
by Glenn Crider and Paul M. Pearson

When *The Merton Annual* was originally planned, Robert E. Daggy, as one of the four editors and Curator of The Thomas Merton Center, elected to include drawings by Merton within the first volumes as dividers between groups of articles. These selections were first used in Volume one as a means of emphasizing groups of articles which were thematically united.

A similar procedure was used with inclusion of photographs in Volume two. In Volume three, Daggy provided a short note about these art works.

The cover images were selected, volume by volume, as appropriate for transfer to the front of the hardback volumes. Brother Patrick Hart, one of the editors, made the initial decisions for each of these five drawings.

In subsequent volumes, additional images by Merton were also reproduced. In the listing which follows, the catalogue numbers at The Thomas Merton Center at Bellarmine University, where these images are archived, are provided so that identification is clear. Also, if the subject or the specific place where a photograph was taken is known, that information is provided.

This new listing should be of value for future scholars.

Volume 1

Calligraphies and drawings from the Thomas Merton Center at Bellarmine University. Generally later images except for # 0010f and # 0321.

# 0459	Cover	Unsigned.
# 0585f	p. 1	Signed.
# 0443	p. 33	Unsigned.
# 0010f	p. 77	Unsigned.
# 0556	p. 115	Unsigned. "Paradise."
# 0375f	p. 148	Unsigned.

# 0573f	p. 213	Initialed. "Considerable Dance."
# 0321	p. 247	Unsigned.
# 0348	p. 319	Unsigned.
# 0337	p. 339	Unsigned.

Volume 2

Photographs from the Thomas Merton Center at Bellarmine University.

# 0356	Cover	Unsigned.
# 0565	p. 1	Christ in the Desert, New Mexico.
# 0648	p. 29	Redwoods, California.
# 0829	p. 57	Banner with Icon, Orthodox Church, Alaska.
# 0344c	p. 114	Triptych icon in Merton's hermitage; gift of Marco Pallis.
# Griffin, *Hidden Wholeness*, 116/7		
	p. 119.	Track in sand/snow.
# 0124	p. 143	Water, near Abbey of Gethsemani.
$ 0242	p. 191	Stone wall, Kentucky.
$ 0548	p. 239	Christ in the Desert, New Mexico.
# 0615	p. 289	Typewriter, Alaska.
# 0873	p. 309	View, Himalayas.

Volume 3

Drawings from the Thomas Merton Center at Bellarmine University. Generally earlier images except for # 0363.

# 0448	Cover	Unsigned.
# 0191	p. 1	Unsigned.
# 0028	p. 45	Unsigned.
# 0100	p. 91	Unsigned.
# 0047	p. 119	Unsigned.
# 0034	p. 173	Unsigned. "St. John the Baptist."
# 0019	p. 201	Unsigned.
# 0104	p. 231	Unsigned.
# 0363	p. 275	Unsigned.
# 0161	p. 291	Unsigned.

Photographs accompanying an article by David Kocka about Merton's Hermitage.

# 0150	p. 253	Photograph of Hermitage.
# D97	p. 259	View from within the Hermitage.
# D77	p. 265	Hermitage fireplace.
# 1315	p. 271	The Hermitage Cross.

Volume 4

Photographs and drawings from the Thomas Merton Center at Bellarmine University.

| # 0377af | Cover | Initialed. |

Drawings:

# 0116	p. 75	Unsigned.
# 0313	p. 221	Unsigned. Abbey of Gethsemani.
# 0370	p. 257	Unsigned.
# 0388	p. 273	Unsigned. Geometric Cross.

Photographs:

# D21	p. 41	Abbey of Gethsemani.
# 0939	p. 111	Thomas Merton and Amiya Chakravarty. October 1968, Calcutta.
# 0496	p. 153	Crucifix in window, Christ in the Desert, New Mexico, 1968.
# 0956	p. 203	W.H. "Ping" Ferry, California, 1968.

Volume 5

Calligraphies and drawings from the Thomas Merton Center at Bellarmine University.

# 0333f	Cover	Unsigned.
# 0459	p. 1	Unsigned.
# 0356	p. 63	Unsigned.
# 0448	p. 131	Unsigned.
# 0377af	p. 187	Initialed.
# 0333f	p. 355	Unsigned.

Reading Merton from the (Polish) Margin: 2004 Bibliographic Survey

Malgorzata Poks

In 1958 Merton was reading Czeslaw Milosz's *The Captive Mind*, a book that opened many Western eyes to the brainwashing rituals of the New Faith practiced behind the Iron Curtain, on the far-away rim of the Western world, and to the desperate struggle of Eastern intellectuals to adjust to the new reality without compromising at least some of the values they deemed crucial to their artistic integrity. Deeply touched by what he had read, Merton decided: "I have got to write stuff that will be *worthy* of the public in Poland, Hungary, Czechoslovakia, Russia, even though it never reaches them."[1] As a Pole, I am struck by the extent to which Merton's wish has come true. Actually, his ardent desire to write for the willing and not-so-willing converts to Dialectical Materialism to provide us with glimpses of the spiritual reality for which we hungered, albeit half-consciously, had been fulfilled even before Merton managed to verbalize it.

As early as 1949 the Polish Catholic monthly *Znak* published an anonymous article on Merton entitled "A Popular Trappist."[2] Although, possibly in order to satisfy the censors, the author of the article attributed much of the American popularity of Merton's ascetic religiosity to the American love of the exotic, supposedly characteristic of the shallow, consumerist societies of the West, he recognized Merton's books, *The Seven Storey Mountain* and *Seeds of Contemplation*, as religious classics. Two years later the Catholic socio-cultural weekly *Tygodnik Powszechny*, providing a—monitored, to be sure—forum for the Catholic intelligentsia in Stalinist Poland, published a laudatory discussion of Merton's autobiography. Fragments of Merton's poetry and prose started to appear in Catholic periodicals. Since then interest in Merton has been steadily growing. When *No Man is an Island* was published in 1960, the whole edition of several thousand copies was sold almost immediately. Theologian and philosopher, Archbishop Jozef Zycinski, then a seminarian, recalls that one female reader was so fascinated by Merton's book that she stayed at work after hours to typewrite it in several copies. "The book," claims Zycinski, "with its profound analysis of spiritual resources, then unnoticed in official philosophy, was a tremendous success."[3]

Also other countries from the Soviet block started to recognize the authenticity of Merton's religious experience in a progressively more and more confusing, post-Christian age. In the Fall 2001 issue of *The Merton Seasonal* we can find short information, based on Margot Patterson's article from the *National Catholic Reporter*,[4] on how Merton's works, secretly translated into Czech and read in defiance of the reigning, militantly atheistic ideology of communist Czechoslovakia, allowed their Czech readers to rediscover the contemplative dimension of prayer, and eventually, in 2002, helped to reintroduce Cistercian monastic life to the Czech Republic. Lately Merton has been gaining readership in Russia, with the translation of Jim Forest's biography *Living with Wisdom* (2000) and of fragments of prose and poems by Merton himself. In 2003 a translation of *Thoughts in Solitude* was brought out by the Franciscan Publishing House in Moscow. A glance at the running Merton bibliography in *The Merton Seasonal*, however, suffices to conclude that in the so-called Eastern part of Europe it is Poland that continues to evidence the greatest activity in publishing *Mertoniana*.

Digression: Problematizing the Margin

Wedged between the "civilized" West and the East represented by the powerful Russian empire, our eastern frontier raided by savage infidels (Turks and Tartars), 17th century Poland turned vices into virtues and prided itself on being a rampart of (Western) Christianity, a perception only testifying to our unredeemed sense of inferiority resulting from geographical and cultural marginality. The paradigm of marginality has been confirmed ever since. Even as I am writing these words, I am conscious of the marginal position of this country, which along with several other countries from the former Eastern block has only recently been admitted to the European Union. Prior to 2004 we had not even been "in" Europe, now we are the continent's (somewhat problematic) periphery, a new arrival to the wealthy economic empire, and as it happens with recent arrivals, advised to keep silent. Interestingly, the geographical map of Europe, if consulted, will tell quite a different story. It will reveal that the geographical middle of the continent is situated somewhere in the north-eastern Poland (or south-western Lithuania): the center literally *is* in the margin. I am sure Merton would have savored the irony of this and he would have been quick to point out the blessings this privileged marginality—if I am allowed to resort to an oxymoron—is likely to bestow on us. In Merton's language marginality was the proper sphere of the monk, whether of the professed or unprofessed, right-side-out or inside-out kind, and that category included every person who would listen to a drummer other than the technological-commercial one. While some must struggle hard to attain to this position, in our part of Europe marginality has been a birthright. Is this another reason why Merton appeals to us so strongly?

In my bibliographic essay I intend to read the recent publications by and about Merton from a marginal vantage point. Starting with the Eastern outskirts of Europe, where Merton Studies have been instituted only recently, I shall work my way through to their well-established, Anglo-American center, hoping to redraw the Merton map and to redefine marginality as a process, rather than a fixed position.

Merton's Presence in the Polish Margin

Looking at the Merton bibliography in Polish, one notices certain regularities. The earliest Merton works to be published in Poland relate to areas of experience discredited, even actively discouraged by the New Faith: spirituality and contemplation (*No Man is an Island* [1960], *The Sign of Jonas* [1962], *The Seven Storey Mountain* [1971 and 1972], *Seeds of Contemplation* [1973]; substantial fragments of those books had first appeared in periodicals). While this has proved to be a seminal field of interest, in the late 1980s we turned to Merton for more adventurous nourishment. The publication of *Zen and the Birds of Appetite* (1988) seems to have responded to the growing attraction of Oriental spiritualities in certain circles dissatisfied with the "safe," and therefore spiritually uninspiring, religious experience offered by the institutional Church. Recently, in his preface to the Polish edition of Merton's *Thoughts on the East* (2003), Maciej St. Zieba, lecturer in Oriental religions at the Catholic University of Lublin, remembers reading Merton's "The Transcendental Experience," a fragment of *Zen and the Birds of Appetite*, published in *Znak* in 1979. He reminisces how that essay influenced members of his generation, Poles born in the second half of the 1950s, who started to perceive Merton as a bridge-builder between the West and the East and a guru of the flower-power movement along with such New Age mystics as Alan Watts, Fritjof Capra, Philip Kapleau, and Edward Conze. Such was at least their initial impression of Merton in the face of the postmodern confusion of values. Like Bede Griffiths, another important bridge-builder, Merton approached other cultures through the "transcendental experience" of the essay's title. "Here was a proof"—or at least so it seemed to the Zieba generation—"that the Catholic Church was . . . opening itself to the spiritual heritage of the whole humankind."[5] That this was a premature conclusion soon became apparent, eventually, however, a close reading of Merton allowed them to rediscover authentic Christian spirituality and remain with it, rather than yield to the facile syncretism of New Age.

Zieba's essay, which obviously captures something of the experience of Merton *aficionados* across generational or geographical borders, discreetly addresses the doubts of the numerous critics of Merton's engagement with Asia and, by implication, rebuts the arguments of sensation-seeking, tendentious novelists like Huorihan[6]: the risk of living faith must be taken in order to demystify the "little securities" of the Law as idols, false gods that obscure the Law's spirit.[7] Zieba's preface is a confirmation of the experience of many Christians who have discovered that an attentive reading of Merton will eventually return them to the God of Abraham, Israel, and Jacob, even if they initially come to Merton with different expectations. If I devoted much space to the issue that is far from new, it is because the perception of Merton as somehow "dangerous" persists to haunt Merton studies and there is never enough stressing how groundless and absurd it is.[8]

The 1990s and the first years of the new millennium have yielded an especially ample harvest of *Mertoniana* in Poland. The year 2004 alone saw the publication of five books by Merton,[9] a personal anthology of Merton texts,[10] a variety of reviews and short essays, and even a curious anthology of texts on charity translated *en block* from Italian, which includes Thomas Merton's essay "The Climate of Mercy."[11] As far as the current boom on the Merton market is concerned, we owe much to Krzysztof Bielawski, the editor-in-chief of the Homini publishing house dedicated to popularizing the message of the Gethsemani monk through translations, book-launching events, Merton conferences, and the publication of the periodical *Studia Mertonana*, of which two issues have appeared so far. It is only to be regretted that the Polish Merton Society, officially launched during the First International Merton Conference in Poland in 2002, has mysteriously fallen silent after the initial period of enthusiastic planning and organizing. In 2004 work had been in progress to prepare a two-day Merton conference, alas the event did not take place and not even a note was issued to explain why, or even THAT, it would not. I want to believe these are only temporary difficulties and that the Society will shortly resume its activities in a more reliable manner.

Obviously, the high point of Merton Studies in Poland was the above mentioned international conference, the proceedings of which have been published in a bilingual edition of *Studia Mertoniana 2*. Paul M. Pearson has already written about "a wonderful variety and diversity" of scholarship to be found in that volume.[12] Considering that it came out at the very end of 2003 and has not been reviewed at length, I feel it falls into the temporal range of this bibliographic essay and will include it in later discussion. First, however, I wish to conclude this brief overview of Merton's reception in Poland by referring to my personal experience as lecturer in American Literature and member of the Polish Association for American Studies (PAAS). Over more than a decade I have heard only two scholars (other than me) giving papers on Merton at our annual American Studies conferences or other literary conferences in the English language for that matter. Unfortunately, in the academic life outside the confines of theological and spiritual studies' departments, Merton is a marginal presence at best, a significant absence at worst.

Pitfalls of Merton-Centricity

This brings me to the ambiguities of Merton's canonical status and his reputation as a poet in particular. Although the Gethsemani monk treated poetry as his most authentic and probably most important means of expression, judging by publications about Merton from the serialized bibliography in *The Merton Seasonal*, only a narrow margin of Merton scholars have recognized this, while the larger critical establishment remains totally oblivious to the merits of his verse, or even to its existence. Are we, Merton readers and scholars, aware of this fact, or is our perception distorted by the gravitational pull of our sympathy for and professional interest in Merton? Recently, when reading Krzysztof Bielawski's short introduction to a section on literature and art in the Merton anthology in Polish, *Aby odnalezc Boga* (To find God), it dawned on me how easily, how willingly in fact, we all fall into the trap of

Merton-centricity. Bielawski claims that Merton considered himself a poet, which is true, and that he is perceived as such in the Anglo-Saxon cultural context, which is already a wish projection of a dedicated Merton reader, I am afraid. It is sufficient to leaf through a couple of recent anthologies of American poetry (other than spiritual or religious poetry) to realize that Merton is not included at all.[13] David Perkins' classical two-volume study *A History of Modern Poetry* mentions Merton only in passing, as a representative of the neo-Metaphysical mode of the 1940s and 1950s. Perkins writes:

> Merton, a Trappist monk, was better known for his prose writings than for his poetry. Though his verse is rather conventional, some lines are memorable, as, for example, when he observes that Greek women "Walk like reeds and talk like rivers." In the 1960s Merton's verse engaged social issues, and became satiric and declamatory.[14]

And that is all.

While this comment, free from the bias of Merton-centricity, may dispel some of our deeply cherished illusions and help us regain a healthier perspective on Merton, it also makes us realize how much serious research is still needed to bring the readers' and critics' attention to such late poems as *Cables to the Ace* and *The Geography of Lograire*, which remain less known then they deserve to be.[15] Their full appreciation might turn the tables of critical opinion in Merton's favor, as these poems register the challenges of late modernity and contain insights the contemporary reader can well relate to, regardless of his or her religious affiliation. Sadly, Merton's late poetry is practically unknown in Poland. The only Polish collection of Merton's selected poems, published in 1986,[16] contains about seventy pieces, including eight fragments from *The Geography of Lograire*, and almost no other late verses.

Free-Floating Existence under the State of Risk: Collected Papers of the First Merton Conference in Poland

Among the contributors to the bilingual post-conference volume *Studia Mertoniana 2*, the English and American scholars need no introduction. Most of the Polish names, however, are not so easily recognizable to an English speaking reader, though they deserve to be. The essays presented in the collection can be grouped into several categories: some examine Merton's contemplative experience, others discuss his, broadly understood, witness to life, still others deal with the monk's art and poetry, as well as the Milosz connection. Regretting that I cannot discuss them all in detail, since they are all stimulating, I intend to devote more attention to those pieces that offer intriguing arguments and open fresh vistas on Merton Studies.

Jozef Zycinski's "The Crisis of Scientific-Technical Civilisation and the World of Spiritual Values in the Reflections of Thomas Merton" leads off the volume, presenting Merton as a guide in the axiological deserts of the third millennium and providing a frame of reference for the essays to follow. The author starts with an overview of the postmodern condition, tracing its roots to the post-Enlightenment disillusionment with the rhetoric of progress and the unfulfilled promise of science to usher in a world of universal peace and happiness. Zycinski shows how the de-centering process initiated with Nietzsche's radical critique of the metaphysic of presence resulted in the subsequent revisions of such concepts as truth, sense, and the human person. Small narratives of weak thought, with no aspiration to understand existence in its totality, have replaced the discredited metanarratives. Consequently, *homo postmodernus* is a tragic nomad wandering aimlessly in a disorientated territory which resembles a rhizome. Such a person becomes easily seduced by New Age ideologies offering a substitute of authentic mystical experience along with a makeshift of sense in an otherwise absurd reality. Here the author draws an arresting analogy between New Age, kitsch, and belief in the UFOs, the three being identified as extreme examples of pathologies in the realms of religion, art, and science respectively. Shown against this background, Merton's religious quest, solidly grounded in the mystical tradition of the West enriched and complemented by Eastern contemplative spiritualities, a quest that stresses personal effort rather than passive obedience to necessary laws, becomes an attractive option in the open society of late *modernitas*. The essays that follow explore aspects of this intriguing attractiveness.

Patrick Hart, OCSO, concentrates on Merton's contribution to monastic renewal as an important aspect of Merton's witness to life. Insisting that the monastic charism is a charism of freedom, Merton specified that in order to exercise it in a prophetic spirit, monks must be liberated from the confusions of the "worldly" existence. In other words, they must be marginal and deliberately irrelevant to the world, which in turn aligns them with such marginal persons as poets or hippies. The paper introduces the theme of marginality, which comes under close scrutiny in another essay presented in the volume. Maciej Bielawski, OSB, professor of theology at St. Anselm University in Rome, Italy, looks at "Merton's Margin" from socio-historical, existential, theological, and symbolic perspectives, performing some dazzling verbal acrobatics to expose the paradoxes and ambiguities of marginality. First, since what passes for the center of life in the *polis*, proves to be a center-less world, a world without God, the monk must move away "to the margins of civilization, Church, monasticism, and himself," although he never leaves those dimensions completely.[17] Next, in his search for meaning and authenticity, he discovers a new center in the margin, which discovery makes the ex-center circulate around the new one, thus depriving the anti-center "of its lethal power."[18] On the other hand, viewed from the theological perspective, the monk arrives "to the margin of the world with faith," and, having discovered doubt in its margin, he goes "to the margin of faith" in order to purify faith itself. Bielawski adds that in the act of creation God decentralized himself to allow the world to exist in the center. Our task as believers, therefore, is to discover the centrality of this self-marginalized God.[19] In our search for this true center we are aided by marginal persons, among whom Bielawski enumerates Kafka and his protagonists, Pinocchio, characters created by Hans Christian Andersen, Dostoyevsky and his Prince Myshkin, Kierkegaard, Lao Tzu, Seneca, Marcus Aurelius, and such Polish poets as Cyprian Kamil Norwid and Czeslaw Milosz. "It is good to ... place [Merton] in this specific company," says the author.[20]

Czeslaw Milosz is another contributor to *Studia Mertoniana*. His short essay,[21] one of the last things he wrote before his death last year at the age of 93, is a tribute one marginal person paid to another. The Nobel laureate places Merton among such heroes of the troubled 20th century as Simone Weil and Albert Camus, "whose creative thought may tip the scales of victory of good over evil."[22] This comment is a lucid proof that Milosz finally succeeded in freeing himself from the limitations of the Eastern European perspective that for a long time had been influencing his view of the Gethsemani monk.

The burden of history resulting in misapprehensions and mutual misreadings is carefully analyzed in the essay entitled "Merton and Milosz in the Face of Totalitarianisms." Elzbieta Kislak, a literary scholar, finds it ironical that Milosz should have misread the author of "Letters to an American Liberal" as a liberal, while Merton misread the Polish émigré poet, who happened to have written the tremendously influential *Captive Mind*, as a political writer, apparently undervaluing his poetry. The whole essay seems to circle around the insidious traps of perspectivism which distorts ideas in the process of, literally, getting them across. On the other hand, such misapprehensions can become a *felix culpa*, a broadening of horizons inescapably limited by one's unique and always fragmentary experience. And thus, for instance, in consonance with his understanding of resistance to the totalitarianism of commercial culture (which found its expression in his practice of anti-poetry), Merton (mis)read Milosz's Ketman[23] as a paradoxical affirmation of one's identity through a dialectical game with the regime, while, protests Kislak, "independence and inner freedom weren't at stake, they constituted the cost."[24] At the same time, however, Merton's broad understanding of totalitarianism made his reading of *The Captive Mind* "innovative and profound,"[25] anticipating the development of Milosz's own thinking on the subject as expressed in *The Year of the Hunter*.[26] All in all, it is the spiritual kinship of the two "monks," rather than divergences between them, that emerges with clarity in the Polish poet's later work (*The Land of Urlo, Hymn to the Pearl,* and *Another Space*).

"Thomas Merton—an Artist" is the title of Katarzyna Bruzda's engaging study. Herself an artist, Bruzda discusses four categories of Merton's artistic work: 1) early drawings, caricatures, and sketches; 2) the cycle of female portraits; 3) photography; 4) calligraphies, specifying that the subject calls for a more detailed analysis. Her essay is informative, entertaining, lucidly argued, and quite exhaustive, considering the limited range of its twenty pages.

Waclaw Hryniewicz, OMI, head of the Faculty of Orthodox Theology at the Ecumenical Institute of the Catholic University of Lublin, compares the visions of universal salvation in the mystical experience of Thomas Merton and Julian of Norwich.[27] In his essay Hryniewicz argues that mystics are crucial to our times, since the difficult task of rethinking the mysteries of Christian faith in order to bring out Christianity's most daring and thought-provoking aspects cannot be realized in a purely discursive way. Mystics are on the side of mercy, concludes the author, they cannot accept eternal damnation, they preach hope and build bridges of understanding between religions. That is why Merton and Lady Julian are so close to his heart.

Theresa Sandok, OSM, brings her philosophical expertise to a study of Merton's evolving views on contemplation ("Thomas Merton's Contemplative Vision"). She argues that Merton's understanding of God as pure Being "helped him avoid saying foolish things about God and the spiritual life"[28] and ultimately grounded his interreligious dialogue. Merton knew that contemplation is a theological grace, rather than a technique that can be taught. What enables us to receive it is *Gelassenheit*, a resolve to open ourselves to Being.

Openness is a key term in Krzysztof Bielawski's empathic reading of Merton's *Midsummer Diary*. Accidentally, his essay may provide a counterpoint to the disenchanted (I would say ill-disposed) readers who feel irked by Merton's supposed dismissal of his affair with M. as "incredible stupidity."[29] At this point I feel tempted to benefit from the opportunity provided me by this essay and express my personal conviction that, when placed within the whole context of Merton's life and vocation, it becomes clear that what the monk dismisses is not the seriousness of his engagement, but the ensuing entanglement in illusion and sentimentality. Having married compassion, Merton discovered that his vocation to universal love was incompatible with the commitment and exclusivity required by passionate love. A careful reading of his journal entries and the diary he wrote for the student nurse suggests that Merton found himself in a state resembling anomie, a condition in which norms of conduct are unclear or contradictory. Introduced by sociologist Emile Durkheim in his classical study on suicide, anomie can be defined as "rootlessness bordering on self-annihilation that occurs when human desires are raised beyond their realistic life expectations."[30] It seems to me that what Merton termed "incredible stupidity" was his recklessness in pursuing unrealistic desires and the self-division this recklessness fostered.

The remaining essays in *Studia Mertoniana* exercise familiar themes. A literary scholar, Zofia Zarebianka, interprets the monk's verses in terms of a personal spiritual diary ("Meditative Experience in the Poetry of Thomas Merton"). Konrad Bereza, OSB, comments on "Thomas Merton's Theology of Self," while another Cistercian scholar, Konrad Malys, analyses Merton's reading of St. Bernard. Basil Pennington, an American member of the Cistercian community, in his essay "Thomas Merton and Centering Prayer," develops the insights introduced earlier in his book *Thomas Merton: Brother Monk.* Two other interesting contributions complete the collection: Paul M. Pearson's 'Thomas Merton, Archivist" and the Polish Jesuit Stanislaw Obirek's "Second Round of Merton's Beer or Mysticism Incarnate." Since both had already been published in other periodicals, I assume they are familiar to the interested English reader.[31]

Unfortunately, the English reader will not always get the full flavor of the papers which were originally written in Polish, as the translations are of uneven quality. Thus, for example, the compact, erudite text by Zycinski, sprinkled with philosophical and scientific terminology, suffers in translation from stylistic awkwardness and sometimes it is hard to get the gist of his argument without referring to the original. Surprisingly, there are some rather serious linguistic mistakes in it, too. But the essay by Katarzyna Bruzda seems to suffer the most. The translation is simply negligent: it loses articles and prepositions, whole phrases or even sentences are missing, adjectives are used as nouns, meanings are distorted. Occasionally, one has the impression of listening to a learner of English.[32] Additionally, the publisher did not always remember to set longer quotations apart from the text or, when they are indented, they get mixed up with the (also indented) commentary. I really see no justification for allowing so many mistakes and mistranslations slip into a volume that was to be a milestone in the history of Merton Studies in Poland.

Translation and Stereoscopic Vision

The literal sense of translation is to bear across. What can be borne across, however, are not only words or ideas, but people, too. "Having been borne across the world, we are translated men [and women]," says a contemporary writer.[33] It strikes me that Merton can bee seen as a typical translated person, son of translated parents, and that his life exemplifies all the attendant risks and hard-won gains of the translating process.

Czeslaw Milosz described his correspondence with Merton as "an interesting clash of American and European minds."[34] There is, obviously, much truth in it, but while Milosz was attracted to Manichean dualities, Merton struggled to transcend dichotomies, and this is part of his abiding attractiveness. Born in France of a New Zealand father and an American mother, and educated in French and English schools, he accepted American citizenship as late as 1951, though even then he was far from settling his ongoing argument with America. That it was the old continent that had actually had a formative influence on the young Thomas Merton was once again brought to our attention by a recent article, "A New Zealand Painter in Medieval France," published by Roger Collins, a specialist in Owen Merton and the curator of an exhibition of his drawings and paintings entitled "Owen Merton—Expatriate Painter," held in 2004 at the Christchurch Art Gallery in New Zealand. In an interesting earlier essay Collins had already pointed out the paradoxical geographical trajectory of Owen Merton's life, which, from hindsight, seems to anticipate his son's ambiguous relation to the dialectics of margin and center. In 1916, when Owen with his wife Ruth and their one-year-old son Tom were leaving France for New York, Owen was an expatriate who twelve years earlier "had traveled form his colonial periphery to the center (first London, then Paris)" and subsequently retreated "to the isolation of the French provinces." Now, continues the author, he "was once again moving to a metropolitan center."[35] The constant shuttling between periphery and center, between continents and cultures, entails both losses and gains. It seems that the greatest gain, as well as the most precious gift the translated person can offer the world, is a sort of "stereoscopic vision."[36] The problematic attitude to the "nationality" category in passport, manifested by the narrator of Thomas Merton's early semi-autobiographical novel *My Argument with the Gestapo*, becomes paradigmatic of the loss of sharp outlines and the blurring of borders in the process of being "borne across."

Roger Collins' primary interest in "A New Zealand Painter in Medieval France" is to detail Owen Merton's discovery of French landscapes, art, and architecture, to document his sensitivity to color and the effects of light, and how these influences enhanced his art. The artist's letters to his mother and the pictures he painted while in France prove that France made Owen aware of Europe's medieval heritage.[37] Owen first visited France in 1905 or 1906. He came back in 1910 to attend a sketching school in Brittany and to travel in the country. It was only then that he started to absorb the medieval atmosphere of southern townscapes which he was contemplating with a painter's eye. Poitiers, the site of the great battle of 1356, in which the king of France was defeated by England's Black Prince, and Chinon, suggestive of Joan of Arc and François Rabelais, made him aware of the historical dimension of the present moment; they spoke of continuity rather than break with the past. Roger Collins identifies an important epiphany Owen experienced during his stay in Chinon. Becoming tired of the merely picturesque, he understood the value of structure and of the arrangement of details within a picture as crucial aspects of beauty and art itself. Significant details—all those "small things"—claims Collins, continued to delight the painter throughout his life. Such details also dominate the artist's epistolary descriptions of his travels in France, aligning his letter-writing with the painting technique he adopted.

Infatuated with France, Merton decided to settle in Paris, where he was exposed to some more medieval architecture. Although Owen Merton "cannot be acclaimed as an exemplary pioneering New Zealand medievalist,"[38] says Collins, he did appreciate the beauty of French cathedrals, was discovering organ music and Gregorian chants, and delighted in his visits to Chartres and Carcassonne. In 1913, the beauty of Chartres Cathedral and the color of Provance made Owen confess in a letter to his mother, Gertrude Merton: "I cannot bring myself to contemplate the possibility of life anywhere but in France."[39] He managed to communicate some of this fascination with France and its medieval heritage to his son, Tom, born in Prades, a town permeated with medieval atmosphere. In his autobiography *The Seven Storey Mountain* Thomas Merton remembers his passion for "those cathedrals and ancient abbeys and those castles and towns and monuments of culture"[40] he first studied as a boy in a richly illustrated book *Le Pays de France*. Roger Collins' article, documenting an important period in the life of an unjustly undervalued artist, whom John Simpson calls "a shadowy figure mostly remembered as being the father of Thomas Merton,"[41] throws an interesting light on the importance of the European heritage in the life of Owen's celebrated son. Thomas Merton was to remain faithful to this early awakened passion for the Middle Ages and gothic architecture and would eventually become member of a religious order which had originated in twelfth-century France.

A Polish Cistercian scholar has recently presented Thomas Merton as a person captivated by St. Bernard's "youthful Europe," with its simplicity, vigor, universality, and magnanimity. In his introduction to the Polish edition of Merton's *The Last of the Fathers*,[42] Michal Ziolo, OCSO, presents the American monk as a spiritual seeker able to perceive God's presence in the most profane dimension of life, an artist gifted with a capacity for wonder, an intellectual endowed with brilliant intuitions, and a man of creative restlessness intrigued by the dynamics and daring of early Cistercians in their confrontation with seemingly hopeless situations. Cistercian spirituality is thoroughly rooted in the here and now and attentive to quotidian reality, so that the most prosaic object or event may trigger an illuminative experience, explains the author. Interestingly, his comments imply a continuity of experience between Owen Merton's appreciativeness of details, which Roger Collins attributed to the influence of France, and the Cistercian spirituality embraced by his son. The Cistercian ecstatic but always realistic optimism[43] points to the indebtedness of Thomas Merton's hopeful disposition to an original European tradition, rather than being derived solely from the optimistic legacy of Emerson and Whitman.[44]

Merton left evidence of his contemplative attention to and deep respect for the immediate reality in numerous spiritual and poetic works, as well as in his calligraphies and photographs. *A Hidden Wholeness: The Zen Photography of Thomas Merton* edited by Paul M. Pearson is a slim but important publication that continues to introduce us to the monk's photographs collected in the archives of the Thomas Merton Center at Bellarmine University. Like the 2003 booklet, *The Paradox of Place: Thomas Merton's Photography*, it is a catalog of an exhibition, held at the McGrath Art Gallery, Bellarmine University, Louisville, Kentucky from November 19th 2004 to January 5th 2005. In addition to reproductions of some of the photographs, accompanied by a list of all the thirty-five exhibits paired with carefully selected quotations from Merton's prose and poetry, *A Hidden Wholeness* consists of three essays that explore various aspects of Merton's photographic art in terms of the artist's Zen way of seeing. These are: "Thomas Merton: Photographer" by Paul M. Pearson, "Through a Glass Purely" by Deba P. Patnaik, and "'One Aesthetic Illumination:' Thomas Merton and Buddhism" by Bonnie B. Thurston.

In his documentation of Merton's fascination with the camera, Paul M. Pearson brings out the monk's growing awareness of the captivating beauty of the "unpoetic." In 1962 Merton was taking photographs in Shakertown and wondering: "How the blank side of a frame house can be so completely beautiful I cannot imagine."[45] Another important self-revelation that Merton registered with his camera concerned his position vis-à-vis the world. In the best of his photographs what we see is not an "objective" world existing independently of the observer, but a world the observer is a part of, though s/he never "possesses" or controls it. In 1963 Merton meditates on Merleau-Ponty's dictum: "I am myself as I exist in the world." Pearson comments:

> This leads him to question the position he had been taking, of being himself by withdrawing from the world, and stating that he agrees profoundly with Merleau-Ponty providing that the world he is referring to is not one of "delusions and clichés." He writes that "to withdraw from where I am in order to be totally outside all that situates me—this is real delusion."[46]

This moment is highly significant not only for situating Merton within the optics of Zen-consciousness, with its annulment of the subject / object split and the recovery of the sense of oneness with all creation, but also within the vitally important tradition of object-based poetics, itself influenced by the Zen-inspired Anglo-American imagist movement of the 1910s. Although Pearson's focus is obviously different, he manages to smuggle in a reference to Merton's use of the camera to produce "images which had the same effect as his later drawings and antipoetry." [47] I welcome this allusion as it opens a much needed perspective on a better appreciation of Merton's late poetry and its similarity to, as well as a difference from, the American avant-garde poetics of the 1950 and 1960s.

This insight is deepened by Deba Patnaik, who aligns Merton's photography with the sparing poetry of Robert Lax and Louis Zukofsky, as well as the art of 20th century minimalist photographers. The common denominator for all those artists is avoidance of self-projection and referentiality and concentration on "pure seeing" instead. Such seeing becomes possible when, in Merton's words, "the smoke of ideas clears."[48] Patnaik's organizing idea for the essay comes from Merton's comment on Zen: "If Zen has any preference it is for glass that is plain, has no color, and is 'just glass'."[49] Recovering the innocence of vision that allows things to exist in their own right, rather than as projections of human desires, the contemplative photographer becomes transparent to the world and sees it, as it were, from within: seeing "through a glass purely" parallels Rilke's "inseeing." Patnaik advances the theory that Merton's photography can be called "photographing degree zero," by an obvious analogy with Roland Barthes' "writing degree zero"[50] that renounces all "messages" and contraptions of art. "We are what we are" proclaim the images in the McGrath Art Gallery. "See. See without the smoke of theories and symbolisms."[51]

The Zen idea of becoming all eye, along with the possibility of piercing illusions and reaching the very "suchness" of things, is further explored in the collection's third essay. Bonnie B. Thurston calls Merton's photographs "a sort of *satori*," an intuitive illumination which the monk achieved—and captured with his camera—because he was wholly present to the immediate reality. She remarks: "Direct awareness of and response to the minute details of daily living are fundamental aspects of Zen discipline... Merton's photographs invite us to 'one aesthetic illumination' in which we see the 'mundane' and the 'spiritual' as one."[52] Obviously, the emphasis on the ordinary as a potential vehicle of spiritual enlightening that Thurston attributes to the influence of Zen on Merton's art was part of a broader and more complex phenomenon. On the one hand, William Carlos Williams in his belief that

so much depends
upon

a red wheel
barrow

glazed with rain
water

beside the white
chickens[53]

endorses the same understanding of the poetics of the real, a return to "the thing itself," however ungainly, in search for aesthetic illumination. On the other hand, there is the whole contemplative tradition of early Cistercians, influenced by the *Theoria Physike* of the Greek Fathers that taught Merton to perceive the simplest and most ordinary reality as imbued with Presence. Merton's Zen photography, his "anti-poetry," and his Cistercian spirituality are different facets of the same, integrated, artistic-contemplative vision of reality—a "stereoscopic vision" produced by the process of cultural translation. Such a vision cannot but result in a truly "universal embrace."

The World in My Bloodstream: Thomas Merton's Universal Embrace is the title of a collection of papers originally presented at the Fourth General Conference of the Thomas Merton Society of Great

Britain and Ireland. While corroborating most of the above-discussed insights, the volume extends the range of concerns beyond art and spirituality to explore the significance of Merton's message for the post-9/11 political, economic, and social issues. Some authors are quite outspoken in their critique of the hypocrisy and short-sightedness of the current American policy, others make a similar point in a more nuanced manner. All go to Merton for answers to the fundamental question about the place of the individual in troubled times. The answers, they all agree, are to be found in the ethical vision of life, in becoming responsible for oneself and others, in relating to others not within the abstract framework of globalization, but through altro-centeredness, personalism and compassionate love. In the context of the cross-cultural misunderstandings attendant on the "war on terror," Merton's tender embrace of Islam explored by Bonnie B. Thurston is of particular relevance. All the essays collected in the volume show Thomas Merton as a person who had the entire world in his bloodstream and whose universal embrace forged a new transcultural consciousness—one would almost wish to add that he was like a transparent glass, without the accumulated smoke of ideas and theories, which reflected the world "purely."

The Beatnik-Monastic Fringe of the All-American Trio: Thomas Merton, Robert Lax, and Edward Rice

Merton's association with the Beat Generation of the 1950s and 1960s has lately become another fertile ground of research. Quite predictably, Merton found himself in sympathy with those writers, self-excluded from the consumerist utopia of the "square" society and contesting its values by casting themselves in the roles of beaten—as well as beatific—artists of life. In Merton's language they qualified as "monks in reverse."[54] This theme is explored by David Belcastro and Angus Steward in two stimulating essays from *The World in My Bloodstream*. Belcastro asserts that through his life and writings Merton redefined monasticism to include the "subterranean" world of the body the Beats represented. To prove the point he quotes Merton's poem on the five (Beatnic) virgins who came to the Wedding Feast with disabled motorcycles and were allowed to stay. Angus Steward examines the Merton-Kerouac connection, calling both figures Dharma Bums.

Well in advance of the movement, however, Merton and his Columbia friends, chief among them being Robert Lax and Edward Rice, had already been living the Beat experience without knowing it. This fact is alluded to in Arthur Jones's article "A Poet, a Monk and a Journalist."[55] Reviewing the three books on the "all-American trio" published in the last few years—S.T. Georgiou's *The Way of the Dreamcatcher*, the letters of Robert Lax and Thomas Merton edited by Arthur W. Biddle, and *Circus Days and Nights* by Robert Lax—Jones savors the climate of jazz and experimental writing and living characteristic of the three friends' Columbia days. Commenting on their status as "the first hippies," he says: "They were hippies who could write—initially for each other, then for wider audiences . . . finally, cumulatively, to the future as epilogue and epitaph writers for the generation."

The relationship between the three "monks" and artists becomes the focus of attention of James Harford, a long-time friend of Lax and Rice, in his article "Merton and Friends in the 1940s"[56] excerpted from a book he is currently working on. Harford places his memories of the trio in the context of Wilfrid Sheed's comment: "Much of the Beat life style existed among a small group at Columbia University as early as 1939."[57] The other date bracketing the decade Harford is focusing his lens on, 1949, was the time Lax got reunited with his other fellow Columbia bohemians: Ad Reinhardt, the budding abstract painter, and Bob Gibney, then married to Lax's former girlfriend, Nancy Flagg, at the Gibney's Virgin Island abode. It is Flagg who years later compared the mood of the Olean days in the life of the Merton-Lax-Rice trio with the quartet's Carribean experience in her 1972 article "The Beats in the Jungle." In between the two dates Harford traces the lives of Merton, Lax, and Rice, highlighting the antiestablishment attitudes they owed to their Columbia experience and their resulting dedication to explore cultural and spiritual alternatives to mainstream values, combined with their self-imposed marginality: Merton's in the monastic enclosure, Rice's and Lax's in their nonconformity and relative obscurity. Prior to launching his groundbreaking, dogmatically challenging religious magazine *Jubilee*, Rice was striving unsuccessfully to be a writer. In the meantime Lax had been fired from the *Time* because his film reviews were apparently too subtle for the editors, felt that he was made "unholy" by his two-year-stint in Hollywood, finally joined the Cristiani Brothers circus as a reporter-at-large, but the article he was to write never materialized. Instead, the reworked experience was published in 1959 as a volume of poetry *Circus in the Sun*. Of the three Columbia friends only Merton was secure in his monastic withdrawal from the world and, paradoxically, becoming a celebrity with the publication of *The Seven Storey Mountain* in 1948.

On December 1, 1949, Rice remarked that the "best art of the present" is "spot art. . . Good because it is used as an aid to other things just like medieval and Byzantine wall drawings and decorations were used as an aid to worship."[58] This comment captures an important aspect of the three ex-Columbia bohemians' sense of art, as well as elucidating the relative lack of critical acclaim they suffered from when their most authentic artistic voice was concerned. Just like Rice, Merton and Lax treated art as a cognitive tool, an instrument to access the hidden wisdom of things, rather than a goal in itself.

As regards the spiritual quest the three of them were pursuing in the 1940s, Merton speculated in his autobiography that Lax had a deeper sense of God's closeness than he did.[59] It is difficult not to think about this remark reading the beautiful tribute Moschos Lagouvardos write for his late friend, "Memories of Robert Lax." The author had met Lax on Patmos in 1968 and since then visited him often. His lyrical essay seems to touch on the very mystery of holiness. Remembered as a person who loved even inanimate beings and never said a bad word about anyone, "Roberto" Lax enjoyed the company of simple people, knew waiters, fishermen, and hotel staff by their names, and was at peace with himself and with the world. One can hardly read these recollections without being reminded of the Sermon on the Mount and seeing the beatitudes at work in the life of that man. There are some humorous touches in the essay too, but they only reinforce the sense of "Roberto's" almost otherworldly innocence and kindness. Thus for example, Lax did not care for the clothes he was wearing, but, Lagouvardos says, "unkemptness was part of his charm."[60] And so was his awkwardness, at which he often laughed. Dividing his time on Kalymnos and then on Patmos between praying, writing, answering voluminous mail, and traveling or walking, Lax became what Thomas Merton was striving hard to be: an authentic monk, though a monk *in* the world. In the purity of his heart, his meek disposition, simplicity, peacefulness, and love of wisdom and beauty, Lax was fee from attachments and oblivious to his own needs—like transparent glass that allows light to pass through without deflecting it. Recollecting Lax's words that "art makes all things bright," Lagouvardos remarks: "He himself was that art which he had just talked about that afternoon. He touched the earth as if he were nothing more than a tender look."[61] Such poetic moments are frequent in this heartfelt verbal portrait sketched by somebody who knew and loved Robert Lax and felt happy writing the essay because he was writing "about Roberto."[62] It is good these memories can be shared because the fate of the world depends on its saints, their mercy, and their joy. Robert Lax was among those who make the world brighter. Holiness may be marginal *in* the world but it is absolutely central *to* it.

Public Intellectual in the Margin

The fact that Merton's extended definition of the monk proves to be consonant with many contemporary intellectuals' understanding of their role in the technological society is the focus of J.S. Porter's essay "Thomas Merton as Public Intellectual," published in the summer issue of *The Merton Seasonal*. Porter first situates Merton in a long line of Columbia public intellectuals, from Mark Van Doren to Edward Said, "noted for critique and dissent,"[63] which qualities he attributes to "a legacy of enlightened humanism."[64] Next he quotes Morris Berman's description of the "new monastic individual" as "a sacred / secular humanist, dedicated not to slogans or the fashionable patois of postmodernism, but the Enlightenment values that lie at the heart of our civilization: the disinterested pursuit of the truth, the cultivation of art, the commitment to critical thinking."[65] Having thus established a link between the intellectual and the monk as persons marginal to and critical of the power structures and illusions of the world, Porter evokes one of the most celebrated intellectuals of the last half-century, the Palestinian scholar Edward Said, to demonstrate how closely Merton's concept of marginality corresponds to Said's belief that the intellectual should always side with the poor, the silenced, the outlawed, the excluded, and raise uncomfortable questions to confront the apparently unshakeable certitudes of the established centers. All in all, the monk as public intellectual—as well as the public intellectual as monk—must be an exile, literal or metaphorical, from a one-dimensional technopoly (society dominated by technological values). The main body of the essay examines Merton's challenge to technopoly as represented by Merton's parodies of Adolf Eichmann, the technological man *par excellence*. Eichmann, who was in charge of the Auschwitz genocide project, is a prototypical techno-man, "a rational man without feeling, without compassion and without guilt or anxiety"[66] who speaks the language of officialdom. In our times, says the author, his voice can be heard, for instance, in the pronouncements of Cheney and Rumsfeld.

While the whole essay is lucidly organized and cogently argued, there are two occasions when it falls short of the high standard the author sets for himself. First, Porter advances a risky thesis that Merton was an "heir to a legacy of enlightened humanism," which needs to be qualified to be properly understood. Without this qualification the reader may mistake the "Enlightenment values" Porter's public intellectual is to cherish with Merton's wholesale acceptance of the Enlightenment, which is simply untrue. Merton, quite predictably, had a problematic relation with the Age of Reason, which, to put it bluntly, replaced metaphysics with physics and so launched the Western world towards technopoly and the postmodern void. It is sufficient to revisit Merton's essays on Camus and Faulkner to realize how much Eichmann's "sanity" was the product of the Enlightenment itself: of the rational, Apollonian, "enlightened" mind that, as Merton saw it, "recoils from Dionysian dread."[67] Porter, seemingly oblivious to the inconsistency within his argumentation, fails to show that Eichmann's sanity without love is seen by Merton as frequently vested in the most "enlightened" individuals (Faulkner's Jason would be a literary case in point Merton commented on[68]).

Moreover, Porter identifies four Merton pieces that revolve around the figure of Eichmann, while Merton wrote only three.[69] The fourth one, "Chant to Be Used in Processions around a Site with Furnaces" (1963), performs not Eichmann but Rudolf Hess, the first Auschwitz concentration camp commander, who started organizing mass murder in a technical way. Merton must have known how easily people confused the two criminals and so he made it clear that "Chant" was about Hess in his letter to Lawrence Ferlinghetti, the editor of *Journal for the Protection of All Beings*, who was publishing his poem.[70] The letter to Cid Corman that Porter quotes as, supposedly, identifying the poem as "a sort of Eichamnn's own double talk about himself" refers to "A Devout Meditation."[71] Having said that, I want to stress once again that these are minor flaws in an otherwise admirable essay, and even the confusion of Eichmann with Hess is quite a legitimate mistake, as both represent two almost identical realizations of the same "technological man" type. In the optics of the essay the intellectual-monk's task is to demystify the "new man" of technopoly as enslaved to slogans and dominated by machines, and to present creative, authentically *new* alternatives to such a solipsistic, fragmented existence.

The same issue of *The Merton Seasonal* features another thought-provoking, post-conference paper that identifies Merton as an intellectual exceptionally sensitive to the *Zeitgeist* and, consequently, living at the religious edge. In "Thomas Merton: A Parable for Our Time" William Reiser, SJ, identifies a number of fault lines in the Gethsemani monk's thinking, which anticipate the "disjunctions, dislocations, and relativism" of our postmodern times.[72] One of the tensions resulted from Merton's early recognition of the multiple ways in which God's mystery manifested itself in the world: "The business of becoming fully human and of creating a world order marked by justice and peace," remarks Reiser, "is far too important for God to entrust it to just one religion."[73] This recognition situated Merton at the "edge of Christian identity,"[74] and demanded solidarity with the victims of power politics of most diverse sorts. There is no doubt that Merton's heightened sensitivity to the spirit of his age that has ultimately made him "a parable for our time" can be largely attributed to his belonging to a number of, apparently at least, discontinuous worlds. Reiser enumerates the following: "the world of the Desert Christians, the world of the Cistercian spiritual tradition, the world of cultural Catholicism of post-war America, the cultural world of Europe, the world of the preconciliar Church, and the world of other major religious traditions."[75] The creative tensions between these worlds could not but lead to some dislodging of traditional assumptions and to producing what I baptized Merton's "stereoscopic vision"—a vision that continues to inspire us in the twenty-first century. In the face of our own struggles and dislocations we can still find strength in the reassurance that "Thomas Merton had been there before me."[76]

Centering Perspectives: *Peace in the Post-Christian Era*

"But my position loses its meaning unless I can continue to speak from the center of the Church. Yet that is exactly the point: where is the true center?"[77] asked Merton in exasperation, confused about the ban on his peace writing issued in 1962 by Abbot General of the order, and challenged by E.I. Watkins to disobey and follow his conscience. It is a revealing moment. Although Merton did obey the ban, realizing that an authentic change in the Church's official position on war and on the nuclear threat could come only form inside the institution, the thought about the "true center" of the Church continued to bother him. In a letter to Jim Forest, Merton insisted that his silencing "reflects an insensitivity to Christian and Ecclesiastical values, and to the real sense of the monastic vocation." Considering his banned book, he added with bitterness that "it might just possibly salvage a last shred of repute for an institution that many consider to be dead on its feet."[78] In the same letter Merton commented once again on the monastic vocation and rearticulated his deepest conviction that the monk's position should be in the advance guard of the Church and that his first allegiance was to his conscience.[79] Years later he would define the monk's life in terms of a "free floating existence under the state of risk."[80]

Believing that only obedience would make his witness to peace credible, however, Merton chose a sort of inner emigration.[81] Renouncing the idea of publication, he managed to circumvent the ban by sending self-published copies of his peace book to friends, peace activists, and theologians participating in *Vaticanum Secundum*. It is only recently that, after decades of its existence on the margin of the Merton *opus*, the long suppressed Merton essays gathered in *Peace in the Post-Christian Era* have finally been released by Orbis Books, establishing themselves where in fact they have always belonged: in the center of the Merton canon. The Gethsemani monk frequently expressed his conviction that universal peace must have its origin in the human heart and that unless the individual consciousness has been rebuilt and the heart purged of hate and self-absorption no lasting peace can prevail. *Peace in the Post-Christian Era* once again brings those considerations into sharp focus, but while commenting on the totalitarian state of mind that has lead Western Christians to consider waging a nuclear war on their Communist enemy, the author sets himself the task of examining the Church's official position on the bomb and her attitude to war and peace in general. In his recourse to the Fathers of the Church, papal encyclicals, and prominent theological voices of the twentieth century, he truly speaks "from the center of the Church," finding there the very message of peace and nonviolence that many Western priests and religious apparently chose not to hear in the troubled 1960s.

"The purpose of the present book," says Merton about the now forty-two-year-old volume that is still as topical as ever, "is to stand back from the imminent risks of the Cold War crisis, seeking to judge the problem of nuclear war . . . in the light of moral truth."[82] In other words, Merton the Church intellectual retreats to the contemplative margin of the activist, war-crazed society to take a broader view of the totalitarian mind and to ground his political and ethical considerations in an all-embracing spiritual perspective. Doing this he notices that even in the so-called Christian countries Christian ethics is universally ignored, that violence has become the norm while the once normative ethics of charity has acquired an exotic status, and that Christianity itself has been reduced to "a materialistic neopaganism with a Christian veneer." In what he considers to be a post-Christian age Merton prophesies that "life in Christ will become a matter of extraordinary heroism, a venture and an unconditional commitment of which very few will be capable." [83]

Although Christianity has been contaminated by naked power and Christian politicians tend to follow Machiavelli rather than Christ, Merton proclaims his and every conscientious believer's dissent from this line of reasoning by identifying love, including the love of enemies, not power, as the keystone of authentically Christian policy. In this eschatological perspective Christian peace becomes the fruit of the Spirit—it belongs to the new life of the Resurrection, while war and hatreds are remnants of the old life under the Law. Addressing "the dwindling and confused Christian minority in the West,"[84] Merton asks them to muster heroic courage and become peacemakers, that is, nonviolent witnesses to the eschatological norm. Voicing his belief in the power of the spiritual weapon of prayer and witness, Merton quotes Cardinal Newman's belief that "the greatest victories of the Church were all won before Constantine, in the days when there were no Christian armies and when the true Christian soldier was the martyr, whose witness was nonviolent."[85] Such a witness consists, as it did in the early days of Christianity, in proclaiming the hidden presence of the kingdom of peace right in the middle of the violence of history. The secret kingdom, this hidden center of the world from which God seems to be otherwise singularly absent, belongs to those who "will take no direct part in the struggles of earthly kingdoms. Their life is one of faith, gentleness, meekness, patience and purity,"[86] says Merton. (At this point it is difficult not to think

of Robert Lax.) Only by centering their lives in love, this fundamental truth of the Gospel, can such marginal witnesses facilitate
the larger world's access to the life-giving truth and initiate a much-
needed spiritual revolution that would enable others to choose
peace and become responsible before, and give a conscientious
response to, the Lord of History.[87]

In his foreword to the book Jim Forest opines: "it would dis-
tress [Merton] that, far from being a poignant memento of a by-
gone era, it [*Peace in the Post-Christian Era*] remains both timely
and relevant."[88] Even though Merton concentrated on a particular historical situation and could not even imagine the collapse of
Communism, no post-Cold War reader can fail to register a shock
of recognition when perusing his prophetic words. Attunement to
the spiritual dimension of history allowed Merton to capture the
hidden dynamics of totalitarian mentality which, like the mythical hybrid, keeps growing ever new heads. In this context our
struggle against the external enemy—be it Communism, terror-
ism, or other "isms"—can succeed only when we decide to wage a
war on "our own violence, fanaticism, and greed" first.[89] Merton's
"new" book, *Peace in the Post-Christian Era*, is a bitter reminder
that victory over evil is still as distant as it was when Merton started
to pen these essays.

Conclusions

This brings me back to the relationship between the false center of
the *polis* and the margin of authenticity. In my essay I have been
arguing that Merton redraws the lines between living in the world
and the monastic life and, in the broadest context, between the
center and the margin. Most of the publications I have been reviewing explore Merton's vision of the solitary who withdraws to
the margin of society to become a diaphanous center of awareness
and in whom the divine and the natural intersect.[90] Faced with
the postmodern lack of stable centers, the solitary becomes a center him-/ herself. It is a new center that is nowhere and everywhere, that is open and inclusive, and that can, therefore, transcend the opposition between centrality and marginality in a higher
synthesis that embraces all.

Questions about the true center of life led Merton away from
the "proud world" he had once been immersed in to a Trappist
monastery situated on the periphery of the world's concerns.
Puzzlement about the true center of the Church made him leave

the relative safety of rigorously and uncritically accepted dogmatic solutions concerning vital problems of his time and placed him on a narrow path close to the religious edge. In this "free-floating existence under the state of risk" Merton was thought to be drifting to the margin of Church orthodoxy, but it was in this very margin that he rediscovered the core of the authentically Christian message and reclaimed it for the Church. Here again Merton seemed to be ahead of his time, anticipating the postsemiotic discovery of marginality as a process, rather than a fixed position. In the materials reviewed in this essay marginality and centrality refuse to remain safely confined to oppositional concepts and become instead two states in an endless process of reinterpretation that parallels the early Christians' understanding of faith—and life—as pilgrimage, a dynamic reality open to the new and the unexpected. Everyday experience likewise confirms this pivotal truth of the Gospel that the marginal is central. I can only wish for a similar transformation in the realm of Merton Studies in Poland.[91]

Notes

---

1. Thomas Merton, *A Search for Solitude* (ed., Lawrence S. Cunningham; Journals III, 1952-60; San Francisco HarperSanFrancisco, 1997), p. 230.

2. M. J. "Popularny trapista," *Znak* 5 (1949), pp. 429-430; reprinted in *Studia Mertoniana* 1 (ed., Krzysztof Bielawski; Bydgoszcz: Homini, 2002), pp. 31–33.

3. Jozef Zycinski, "Merton and Ecology of Human Spirit," tr., Anna Muranty, *Studia Mertoniana 2*. Collected Papers of the first Merton Conference in Poland. Lublin, Oct. 24-27, 2002 (ed., Krzysztof Bielawski; Krakow: Homini, 2003), p. 8.

4. "Building History One Stone at a Time," *National Catholic Reporter*, July 27, 2001, online.

5. Maciej St. Zieba, preface to the Polish edition, Thomas Merton, *Mysli o Wschodzie* (tr., Adam Wojtasik; Lublin-Krakow: Homini, 2003), p. 11, translation mine.

6. Paul Hourihan, *The Death of Thomas Merton. A Novel*, (Redding, CA: Vedantic Shores Press, 2003).

7. See Paul Ricoeur's illuminating essay "Religion, Atheism, and Faith," tr. C. Freilich, in *The Conflict of Interpretations* (Evanston: Northwestern University Press, 1974), pp. 440-467.

8. Recently a similar conclusion has been reached by Ron Dart in his article "Thomas Merton and Alan Watts: Contemplative Catholic and Oriental Archivist," *The Merton Journal* 11.2 (Advent 2004), pp. 12–15.

9. *The Last of the Fathers: Saint Bernard of Clairvaux, Passion for Peace: The Social Essays, Survival or Prophecy: Letters of Thomas Merton and Jean Leclerq, Dialogues with Silence*, and a re-edition of *Raids on the Unspeakable* (first published in 1997).

10. Thomas Merton, *Aby odnaleźć Boga. Antologia* [To Find God. An Anthology] (sel. and tr. Aleksander Gomola; Poznan: W drodze, 2004).

11. *O milosierdziu* [*Parole di misericordia*], tr. Irena Burchacka (Warszawa: Wydawnictwo Ksiezy Marianow, 2004).

12. Paul M. Pearson, "Book Round-up," *The Merton Journal* 11.2 (Advent 2004), p. 35.

13. See, for example, *Anthology of Modern American Poetry* (ed., Cary Nelson; New York and Oxford: Oxford UP, 2000).

14. David Perkins, *A History of Modern Poetry. Modernism and After* (Cambridge, Mass.: Harvard UP, 1987), p. 387.

15. Recently this field has been explored with interesting results by such scholars as Claire Hoertz Badaracco, Lynn Szabo, and David Belcastro.

16. Thomas Merton, *Wybor wierszy* [Selected Poems] (ed., Jerzy Illg; Krakow: Spoleczny Instytut Wydawniczy Znak, 1986).

17. Maciej Bielawski, "Merton's Margin," transl., Anna Muranty, *Studia Mertoniana 2*, p. 83.

18. Bielawski, *Studia Mertoniana 2*, p. 85.

19. Bielawski, *Studia Mertoniana 2*, pp. 86-87.

20. Bielawski, *Studia Mertoniana 2*, p. 86.

21. The essay was reprinted as "Czeslaw Milosz on Merton" in *The Merton Journal* 11.2 (Advent 2004), pp. 2-4.

22. Czeslaw Milosz, "Merton," transl., Anna Muranty, *Studia Mertoniana 2*, p. 47.

23. As defined in *The Captive Mind*, Ketman, by analogy with the practice known under this name in the Islamic world, is a strategy that allowed Eastern intellectuals to hide and defend their true beliefs by confessing belief in contrary values. Milosz evokes Gobineau's book *Religions et Philosophies dans l'Asie Central*, which claims that in Islam one is obliged to protect one's faith from being contaminated by contact with the infidel. Ketman, therefore, makes it possible for the Muslim to be silent about the truth or even preach the opposite in order to mislead the enemies of faith.

24. Elzbieta Kislak, "Merton and Milosz in the Face of Totalitarianisms," transl. Anna Muranty, *Studia Mertoniana 2*, p. 171.

25. Kislak, *Studia Mertoniana 2*, p. 172.

26. Czeslaw Milosz, *Rok myśliwego* [The Year of the Hunter] (Paris: Instytut Literacki, 1990).

27. In the English translation of this article the mystic's name is wrongly spelled as "Julianna."

28. Theresa Sandok, "Thomas Merton's Contemplative Vision," *Studia Mertoniana 2*, p. 137.

29. Mary Jo Weaver, "Conjectures of a Disenchanted Reader," *Horizons* 30/2 (2003), p. 290.

30. I quote this lucid definition after Susan Muzruchi in "Fiction and the Science of Society," *The Columbia History of the American Novel* (ed., Emory Elliott; New York, Columbia UP, 1991) , p. 198.

31. Paul M. Pearson's article appeared in *US Catholic Historian* 21.2 (Spring 2003): 414-62, Stanislaw Obirek's essay, under the title "A Second Round of Merton's Beer, or Mysticism Incarnate," in *The Merton Journal* 10.1 (Easter 2003), pp. 43-49.

32. For example—and I blush to quote: "In this way he enters in his stormy youth, full of contrast events." *Studia Mertoniana 2*, p. 180.

33. Salman Rushdie, "Imaginary Homelands," *Imaginary Homelands: Essays and Criticism 1981-1991* (London: Granta Books, 1992), p. 17.

34. Milosz, *Studia Mertoniana 2*, p. 46.

35. Roger Collins, "Fronting up to the American Public: Owen Merton's Exhibitions In the United States," *The Merton Seasonal* 26.2 (Summer 2001), p. 36.

36. Rushdie, *Imaginary Homelands*, p.19.

37. Roger Collins, "A New Zealand Painter in Medieval France," *L'offrande du coeur: Medieval and Early Modern Studies in Honour of Glynnis Cropp* (Christchurch: Canterbury Press, 2004), p. 144.

38. Collins, "A New Zealand Painter in Medieval France," p. 154.

39. Quoted in Collins, "A New Zealand Painter in Medieval France," p. 153.

40. Merton, *The Seven Storey Mountain* (New York: Harcourt Brace, 1948), p. 43.

41. Jon Simpson, "An Astonishing Variety," Rev. of *Owen Merton: Expatriate Painter*, Catalogue of the Exhibition: 11 June—26 September 2004, by Roger Collins, *The Merton Seasonal* 29.3, p.36.

42. Michal Ziolo, introduction to Thomas Merton, *Ostatni z Ojcow: Sw. Bernard z Clairvaux. Encyklika Doctor Mellifluus* [*The Last of the Fathers: Saint Bernard of Clairvaux* and the encyclical letter, *Doctor Mellifluus*] (Skoczow, Wydawnictwo Sw. Bernarda, 2004), pp. 9-23.

43. Ziolo, introduction to Thomas Merton, *Ostatni z Ojcow*, p.16.

44. The latter view was held by Czeslaw Milosz. See *Studia Mertoniana 2*, p. 46.

45. Quoted in Paul M. Pearson, "Thomas Merton: Photographer," *A Hidden Wholeness: The Zen Photography of Thomas Merton* (ed., Paul M.

Pearson; Louisville, Kentucky: Thomas Merton Center at Bellarmine University, 2004), p. 4.

46. *A Hidden Wholeness*, p. 7.

47. *A Hidden Wholeness*, p. 9. The same point was made by Katarzyna Bruzda in her essay "Thomas Merton—An Artist," *Studia Mertoniana 2*.

48. Thomas Merton, *The Other Side of the Mountain: The End of the Journey* (ed., Partick Hart; San Francisco: Harper Collins, 1999), p. 286.

49. Thomas Merton, *Zen and the Birds of Appetite* (New York: New Directions, 1968), p. 4.

50. Thomas Merton, "Roland Barthes—Writing as Temperature," *The Literary Essays of Thomas Merton* (ed., Patrick Hart; New York: New Directions, 1985), pp. 140–146.

51. Deba Patnaik, "Through a Glass Purely," *A Hidden Wholeness*, p. 15.

52. Bonnie Thurston, "'One Aesthetic Illumination:' Thomas Merton and Buddhism," *A Hidden Wholeness*, p. 17.

53. William Carlos Williams, "The Red Wheelbarrow," *The Norton Anthology of American Literature* (sixth edition, ed., Nina Baym, vol. D; New York: W. W. Norton & Co, 2003), p.1271.

54. For a detailed discussion of this phrase see David Belcastro, "Merton and the Beat Generation: A Subterranean Monastic Community," *The World In My Bloodstream. Papers of the Fourth General Conference of the Thomas Merton Society of Great Britain and Ireland, Oakham School* (ed., Angus Stuart, Abergavenny, Monmouthshire: Three Peaks Press, 2004), pp. 79-91.

55. *National Catholic Reporter*, NCRonline (October 8, 2004). Surprisingly, the text contains a number of imprecise figures concerning Merton. Jones mistakenly claims that Merton died at the age of 63 (actually, he was 53), that he entered Gethsemani in 1944 (it was in 1941), and was naturalized a U.S. citizen in 1950 (1951).

56. *The Merton Seasonal* 29.3 (Fall 2004), pp. 9–23.

57. Quoted in Harford, "Thomas Merton and Friends," p. 20.

58. Harford, "Thomas Merton and Friends," p. 23.

59. Quoted in Moschos Lagouvardos, "Memories of Robert Lax" (transl., Fanee Karatzu, ed., Paul J. Speath), *The Merton Seasonal* 29.3 (Fall 2004), p. 31.

60. *The Merton Seasonal* 29.3, p. 25.

61. *The Merton Seasonal* 29.3, p. 28.

62. *The Merton Seasonal* 29.3, p. 32.

63. *The Merton Seasonal* 29.2 (Summer 2004), p. 16. It was originally presented as a talk at Canadian Memorial United Church, Vancouver, BC, on January 20, 2003.

64. *The Merton Seasonal* 29.2, p. 17.

65. *The Twilight of American Culture* (New York: Norton, 200), p. 10; quoted in *The Merton Seasonal* 29.2, p.17.

66. *The Merton Seasonal* 29.2, p. 20.

67. Merton, "Baptism in the Forest," *Literary Essays* 120-21

68. See especially Merton's "Baptism in the Forest: Wisdom and Initiation in William Faulkner" and "Time and Unburdening and the Recollection of the Lamb: The Easter Service in Faulkner's *The Sound and the Fury*, *Literary Essays*, pp. 92-116 and 497-14 respectively.

69. "Devout Meditation in Memory of Adolf Eichmann" (1964), a fragment from *Conjectures of a Guilty Bystander* (1966), and "Epitaph for a Public Servant" (1967).

70. "This piece is by the way not about Eichmann, but about the commandant of Auschwitz, [Rudolf] Hess." Thomas Merton, *The Courage for Truth. The Letters of Thomas Merton to Writers* (ed., Christine M. Bochen; New York: Farrar, Straus & Giroux, 1993), p. 268. Accidentally, Lynn R. Szabo, the editor of the just released collection of Merton's selected poems makes the same mistake. See *In the Dark Before Dawn. New Selected Poems of Thomas Merton* (ed. Lynn Szabo; New York: New Directions, 2005), p. 242.

71. Merton, *Courage for Truth*, p. 248. Incidentally, the letter was written on September 5, 1966, not 1965 as Porter claims.

72. *The Merton Seasonal* 29.2 (Summer 2004), pp. 3-13; the paper was first delivered at a conference at Holy Cross College in Worcester, Massachusetts, on December 10, 2003.

73. *The Merton Seasonal* 29.2, p. 7.

74. *The Merton Seasonal* 29.2, p.9.

75. *The Merton Seasonal* 29.2, p.7.

76. *The Merton Seasonal* 29.2, p. 11. Accidentally, Reiser's emphasis on Merton being "in many respects so noticeably preconciliar" (p. 3) strikes me as unjust. The author apparently chooses not to remember how seriously Merton was involved in preparing the ground for the opening of the Church to the world that the Second Vatican Council implemented. Likewise, Merton's Christ: "the Lord of the Songs" who broke bread with the pre-Columbian Maya (*The Geography of Lograire*, p. 763), the Christ who "went down to stay with them Niggers and took his place with them at table" (ibid., p. 516), and "Christ Our Mother" of Lady Julian of Norwich's revelation—seems to be very much the Jesus of the gospel and everyday life and not, as Reiser claims "the Christ of the dogmatic tradition" (p. 4).

77. Thomas Merton, *Turning toward the World* (ed., Victor A. Kramer; San Francisco: HarperSanFrancisco, 1997), pp. 244-45.

78. Quoted by Jim Forest in foreword to Thomas Merton, *Peace in the Post-Christian Era* (ed. Patricia A. Burton; New York: Orbis Books, 2004), p. x.

79. Incidentally, this point was elaborated in detail by one of Merton's early guides in the world of the spirit, Cardinal Newman, in his famous 1874 letter to the Duke of Norfolk. Explaining to its Anglican critics the controversial doctrine of papal infallibility accepted by the First Vatican Council in 1870, Newman made a distinction between the pope's *ex cathedra* pronouncements, which acquire the value of infallible decrees, and papal pronouncements dealing with practical matters, which can be erroneous. On the basis of his careful theological and historical inquiry, Newman could generalize the problem, claiming that the voice of conscience, through which God speaks to the believer, should take precedence over the voice of the superiors, who, being human, are always susceptible to misjudgments.

80. *Thomas Merton's View of Monasticism (Informal talk delivered at Calcutta, October 1968)* in: Thomas Merton, *The Asian Journal of Thomas Merton* (London: Sheldon Press, 1974), p. 308.

81. Patricia Burton, "The Book that Never Was," introduction to Merton, *Peace in the Post-Christian Era*, p. xxxv.

82. Merton, *Peace in the Post-Christian Era*, p. 4.

83. Merton, *Peace in the Post-Christian Era*, p. 72.

84. Merton, *Peace in the Post-Christian Era*, p. 9.

85. Merton, *Peace in the Post-Christian Era*, p. 129.

86. Merton, *Peace in the Post-Christian Era*, p. 30.

87. The nonviolent witness of Pope John Paul II's life and death, and the almost global spiritual renewal triggered by his funeral, seem to be most spectacular proofs of this proposition in recent history.

88. Merton, *Peace in the Post-Christian Era,*, p. vii.

89. Merton, *Peace in the Post-Christian Era*, p. 11.

90. Compare Donald P. St. John, "Technological Culture and Contemplative Ecology in Thomas Merton's *Conjectures of a Guilty Bystander*," *Worldviews: Environment, Culture, Religion* 6.2 (2002), pp. 159-182.

91. I owe a debt of gratitude to Edward Jan Michowski, SVD, for his invaluable help in accessing materials crucial to my research for this essay.

Reviews

In the Dark Before Dawn[;] *New Selected Poems of Thomas Merton*, Edited with an Introduction and Notes by Lynn R. Szabo. Preface by Kathleen Norris (New York: New Directions, 2005) 253 pages with Index. ISBN 0-8112-1613-6. $16.95. (Paperback).

This completely reconceived New Directions selection of Thomas Merton's poems will eventually replace the earlier *Selected Poems* (1959, Enlarged Edition 1967) edited with an introduction by Mark Van Doren. The editor of these newly "selected" poems, Lynn R. Szabo, has done a very successful job by choosing and arranging Merton's poems thematically, and while to some degree chronologically, above all aesthetically. To do such a job well is to write a variety of literary criticism. To do such a job with complete approbation from all the different Merton circles of readers would be impossible. It should therefore be understood that this review is designed not to imagine what other kinds of "selected" Merton poetry books might have been fashioned. This book is valuable.

In the Dark Before Dawn will inevitably be compared to the preceding *Selected Poems* yet that is not the purpose of this analysis. Szabo has sought a new way to present Merton for a 21st century audience. Thus, we do not have here just an historical document (an anthology) but a new reading too.

The "Preface" by Kathleen Norris is graceful. It is attentive to the listening of Benedict and to the work of the monk-artist who must learn to listen "with the ear of the heart (RB Prologue; 1)" (p. xv). Hospitality, Plenitude, Worship, yet an attitude of no nonsense are the elements of Merton which Norris isolates and comments upon.

Szabo's "Introduction" places Merton among his poetic contemporaries. One of her criteria for choosing these particular poems is revealed in her argument that in Merton's best poetry there is always a

> refusal to dichotomize the secular and the sacred.... His identity became grounded in his vocation, engendering the language by which to represent his experience beyond the realm of empiricism and metaphysics and birthing a sophisticated

and penetrating wisdom arising from the analogous world of the poet and mystic (p. xxvii).

To choose poems which best demonstrate this accomplishment is a tall order, and, of course, another editor would have chosen differently. Some examples clearly had to be omitted. Arranged thematically, these few selections, about 125, in relation to the bulk of the 1,046 pages in *The Collected Poems of Thomas Merton* are less than a quarter of what Merton has written. (And we might also remember sometimes his journal entries or parts of his essays also scan like poems.)

Szabo has arranged the book in this order: 1) Geography's landscapes; 2) Poems from the Monastery; 3) Poems of the Sacred; 4) Songs of Contemplation; 5) History's Voices; 6) Engaging the World; 7) On Being Human; 8) Other Languages. Each of these groupings gives us a different variety of Merton, as a seeker. Each of the themes which the editor has chosen for this collection could, I am sure, have been expanded by the addition of other poems, yet we realize that publishing constraints of space made it necessary to limit the number of pages in this book.

The title *In the Dark Before Dawn* establishes a tone present throughout the book. The book's title suggests how in maturity Merton came to honor the earliest hours of the day when clarity, in and with God, seemed to be nearest. Szabo's title is meant to reflect "Merton's love of the predawn hours, after the night vigils monastic office, in which he found the silent darkness to be the ground of his creative energies…" (p. xxxiii).

Each section gives a feeling, usually chronologically early and late, for Merton's loves. In part one, "Geography's Landscapes," we find Merton's speaker rejoicing and lamenting. Poems from "Figures for An Apocalypse" (p. 9) and "Darjeeling" (p. 19) are included. The "Monastery" section selects from the first volume (1944) and includes the late ironic, "A Practical Program for Monks," which did not become available until 1977.

To put together a new and selected volume of Thomas Merton poems had been necessary for decades and this new selection is welcome. It is a totally different kind of book than the earlier "Selected" which has been in existence for approximately 40 years. In this arrangement as devised by Lynn Szabo, we have a new concept which gives us a more comprehensive view of the multifaceted Merton. Instead of a chronological record, we have a mosaic produced by its overlapping and interrelated themes.

What other themes might have been included? All of the following: 1) Vocation; 2) Simplicity; 3) Saints; 4) Sinners; 5) Mercy; 6) Anger. My point is simply that Szabo had a tremendous editing job to do and lots of material was excluded. To me, a surprising yet understandable thing does occur in the selections included in the section called "On Being Human." Most of those poems (13 of 19) are from the heretofore more or less hidden *Eighteen Poems*. Such a large selection from these *Eighteen*, sometimes called "Love Poems," is justifiable because while they are late and interesting poems which allude to romance, they are more than poems about being human. Rather, it seems to me these poems are very much about the Mystical Body of Christ as well as human love. Many others in the *Complete* (or indeed within other sections of this *New*) could have been introduced in this section. Perhaps the first poem in the book "Geography's Landscapes," "The Night Train" could have been utilized in this section. Certainly other categories or selections might well have been made. Much was available after Merton's earlier *Selected Poems* appeared. In fact, if we count pages from *Cables to the Ace*, *Lograire* and the other materials in the *Collected Poems*, the editor had perhaps 500 pages from which to choose. We can, therefore, well imagine "selected" early and "selected" late volumes of Merton such as New Directions once did for William Carlos Williams. One more peculiarity is the limited batch of translations—ten poems only.

Also it appears in the desire to include "new" poems, a few of those chosen are not so polished. "Songs of Experience" (echoing William Blake) jars, yet it clearly demonstrates Szabo's point about sacred and secular. It seems a "found" observation, not yet made into a finished poem—closer to a journal entry. It is interesting but does not seem finished. On the other hand, the poem "[untitled]" at p. 73 "Fire, breath..." is excellent. Both of these selections stand as proof of Szabo's conviction that for Merton the holy and ordinary are here merged.

This thematic arrangement or the grouping of these selections is an excellent choice. The editor has accomplished several things by this imposition of limitations. Clearly we are allowed to see how earlier themes remained fundamental to Merton's development and as well we are able to trace these themes into maturity. *In the Dark Before Dawn* is a success. It makes us want to find our quiet times and places so we can make poetry of contemplation.

Szabo's editing does Merton a service. She treats his poetry as if it were part of the American canon. It should be. From these careful selections we see a "vastness in God's mercy" and an ambitiousness in Merton the poet which is as every bit as valuable as the contributions of T.S. Eliot, Ezra Pound, Denise Levertov or Charles Olson. Organizers of American literature courses and anthologies would do well to digest what Szabo has given us in her thoughtful editorial arrangement. Then, more readers would come to Merton.

Victor A. Kramer

MONTALDO, Jonathan, editor. *A Year with Thomas Merton: Daily Meditations from His Journals* (San Francisco: HarperCollins, 2004), pp. xv + 381. ISBN 0-06-075472-9 $19.95 (hardcover).

The HarperCollins publishing company is apparently getting its money's worth from its exclusive rights to Thomas Merton's complete journals. After the publication of the seven volumes of journal (1995-1998), it has issued the one-volume compilation *The Intimate Merton: His Life from His Journals* (1999), followed by *Dialogues with Silence: Prayers and Drawings* (2001), which matched journal excerpts with examples of Merton's line drawings, and now *A Year with Thomas Merton: Daily Meditations from His Journals*. The principal guiding spirit behind all the recent volumes is Jonathan Montaldo, former director of the Thomas Merton Center at Bellarmine University and past president of the International Thomas Merton Society, who probably knows the Merton journals better than any other person alive. After editing *Entering the Silence*, the second volume of the complete journals, he co-edited *The Intimate Merton* with Brother Patrick Hart and was sole editor of *Dialogues with Silence* and now of *A Year with Thomas Merton*. His long familiarity with the material has produced in this most recent volume a wonderful collection of excerpts for daily reading and reflection.

The title *A Year with Thomas Merton* is appropriate not only because it includes a selection for each day (except for February 29!), but because the nature of the journal material lends itself so naturally to the temporal pattern of a daybook. Unlike previous compilations of this type, Thomas P. McDonnell's *Blaze of Recognition: Through the Year with Thomas Merton* (1983) and Naomi Burton Stone's *Keeping a Spiritual Journal with Thomas Merton* (1987), which draw on a broad range of Merton's published writing (and of course appeared before the complete journals were available), all the selections here (with one exception—the December 30 excerpt from an unpublished letter to Merton's Louisville friend Tommie O'Callaghan on the death of her mother) are drawn from the journals, which gives the book a certain consistency of tone even as it samples the rich variety of Merton's reflections on his inner and outer life, on his relationships with himself and his God, with his monastic community and his wider community of friends dispersed throughout the country and the world.

The design of the book is attractive, with the smaller-than-standard 5 1/2" x 7 1/4" page size making reflection while walking, as well as sitting, an inviting possibility. Each of the entries is given its own page, preceded by the date and a descriptive title provided by the editor, and followed by the original entry date with its volume and page number from the compete journals. Significant events in Merton's life, such as his birthday (January 31), his permanent entrance into the hermitage (August 20), or his arrival at Gethsemani—and the day of his death (December 10) are also noted on the appropriate days. The months are divided from one another by a page (or two) featuring a photograph or drawing by Merton. The book proper is preceded by a brief introduction by the editor in which he proposes that the journals were a primary way in which Merton was able to discover and articulate the language of love, and suggests that reading these entries can assist the reader in learning that same language.

Montaldo wisely doesn't attempt to match the dates of the journal entries exactly to the dates of the daybook, which would have been artificially restrictive and probably impossible, as there were no doubt some dates for which Merton, who didn't make journal entries every day, had never written a journal entry in the more than two decades for which journals are extant, and other dates for which no appropriate material would have been available. But he does find passages from the same month, usually only a few days before or after a given date, so the flavor of a particular time of year is always preserved, and for some dates, particularly important ones in his own life, like the famous "Fourth and Walnut" experience (81 [March 19]), or the day of his ordination (152 [May 26]), journal and daybook dates coincide. Successive passages do not follow a chronological order. They move forward and backward through the years to create interesting juxtapositions of Merton at various stages of his life, but at the same point in the annual cycle, though there are occasions when a single entry or contiguous entries are spread out over successive days, as when a reflection on the Indian Buddhist sage Shantideva from June 29, 1968 is continued over two days (June 18 and 19).

Montaldo frequently abridges an entry to include only the core material he wants (without indicating omissions by ellipses, which would be a distraction given the nature and purpose of the book, but which makes it unsuited for quotation in any sort of academic context), and on occasion will include material from two separate journal entries, which can create fascinating and insightful juxta-positions, as in the entry for February 21 (53), given the title "Where Your Treasure is," which combines a passage from February 4, 1961 on Merton's "[t]remendous discovery" of the *Brihad-Aranyaka Upanishad*, which he calls a "new door," with an entry ten days later (from the next page of the journal) on "the splendor of my Mass" that includes the Gospel verse "Where your treasure is, there your heart is also," thus reflecting the compatibility for Merton of his unwavering commitment to his own Catholic Christian faith with his openness to the wisdom of other religious traditions, and allowing the reference to "your treasure" to reach back to include the *Upanishad* as well.

The entries are distributed over the entire chronological range of Merton's journals (with the exception of the pre-monastic pe-riod, represented only by three entries from 1941), with the final decade of Merton's life being most heavily drawn on (1965, with 61 entries, is the most thoroughly represented, more than double the number of selections of any other year except for 1961, with 32 entries; all years from 1947 on have at least ten excerpts, except 1948, 1951, 1957, 1959 and—perhaps surprisingly—1967). The range of topics is narrowed somewhat by the nature of the vol-ume—there are no grumblings about the abbot, and no fantasies about the nurse—but still reflects the amazing range and depth of Merton's interests and commitments and his conception of a jour-nal as "a book into which everything can go" (a famous passage from July 1956 that Montaldo appropriately places at the very cen-ter of the book, on July 1 [191]).

Those acquainted with the journals already will find many fa-miliar and famous passages—Fourth and Walnut, of course, tak-ing a writing pad to purgatory (255 [September 1]), the vision of the deer at the hermitage (265 [September 11])—but also hidden gems like the role of the Holy Spirit in contemplation (88 [March 26]), or St. Irenaeus on being the work of God (228 [August 6]), or the influence of Islam on the conversion of Louis Massignon and Charles de Foucauld—to Christianity (320 [November 22]). There are of course passages on nature and the cycle of the seasons, on Merton's enthusiastic responses to his reading, on liturgy, and solitude, and old and new selves, and interreligious dialogue, and the Kingdom of God, on social issues—perhaps not as numerous as they might be (Merton's interest in racial justice is largely absent), but those that are included are striking and powerful—see for example the passages on peace and realized eschatology (71 [March 9]), on Chuang Tzu and commitment to peace (112 [April 18]), on Vietnam and Christ's passion (130 [May 4]), on non-violence in spirit (244 [August 22])—on technology, on humorous and slightly surrealistic monastic events (see "Another Lost Customer": 338 [November 20]), on "St. Benedict's Sanity" (289 [October 3]) and four days later on "America, the World's Mad Abbot" (293 [October 7]). Above all there is the ongoing story of Merton's successes and failures—neither of them absolute and definitive—in his ongoing efforts to surrender himself entirely to God and to God's mercy in humility and gratitude and *hesychia*—the peace that passes understanding.

In assembling these selections, Jonathan Montaldo has provided a precious resource both for long-time readers of Merton and for those encountering him for the first time. *A Year with Thomas Merton* is certainly worth spending a year with, and worth returning to, in part or in whole, for many subsequent years thereafter.

Patrick F. O'Connell

KOWNACKI, Mary Lou, *Between Two Souls: Conversations with Ryokan*, Introduction by Joan D. Chittister. Calligraphy by Eri Takase. (Grand Rapids: Wm. B. Eerdmans Publishing Company, 2004). xxii + 191 pages. ISBN 0802828094. (Hardcover) $20.00

Between Two Souls is a striking and a singular book. It is, as the subtitle suggests, a "conversation"—one that spans more than two centuries, bridging East and West and plumbing the depths of the human spirit beyond geography.

Joan D. Chittister's "Introduction to a Dialogue on Life" introduces readers to two monks and poets: Ryokan, a Japanese Buddhist, who moves back and forth from the solitary quiet of the forest to the village where he goes to beg for food and play with the village children, and Mary Lou Kownacki, a Catholic Benedictine, who finds solitude and community in an American inner-city where she administers a program in the arts. Chittister situates the book within the larger monastic tradition. "Both these poets," she writes, "are monks, *monastics*, a man and a woman, devoted to finding the One Thing Necessary in Life" (p. xii). Each is a seeker and their seeking forges a link between them.

Interspersed throughout the book are calligraphies by Eri Takase. The calligraphies serve as chapter headings, previewing themes of poems that follow: "Two Souls," "Heart," "Poem," "Rain," "Saint," "Pine," "Wind," "Ball," "Dream," "Bowl," "Children," "Letter." Indeed, these brush drawings might be likened to the tolling of a bell—a call to stop and attend to what is at hand. Such attention to the present moment, which characterizes the way of the Buddhist monk and the way of the Christian contemplative alike, marks Ryokan's poems and Kownacki's as well.

Ryokan's poems, translated by John Stevens, are reprinted from *Dewdrops on a Lotus Leaf: Zen Poems of Ryokan* (Boston: Shambhala Publications, 1993). Kownacki's poems offer a contemporary counterpoint to those of the Zen master. In her "Prelude," Kownacki tells how she came to know Ryokan (1758-1831) and enter into a poetic dialogue with him. Confessing that she "fell in love" with him, Kownacki tells how Ryokan was summoned by a friend to speak to his "wayward" son. The monk said not a word but as "the boy was helping tie Ryokan's sandals, he felt a warm drop of water on his shoulder. Glancing up, the boy saw Ryokan, eyes full of tears, looking down on him. Ryokan departed silently and the boy mended his ways." In this story and the poem that captures its lesson, Mary Lou Kownacki writes that she found "all the scriptures" she "needed to live as a monk." The poem is short and to the point: "Oh, that my monk's robes were wide enough to embrace the whole world."

Over the course of two years, reading Ryokan's poems became for Kownacki an exercise in *lectio divina*. *Between Two Souls* is the product of this "slow reading" which led to meditation and, in turn, gave rise to poetry. Presented alongside Ryokan's poems, Kownacki's poems are at once responses to Ryokan, reflections on her own experiences, and forays into the deepest recesses of the human heart. The result is a rich and nuanced exchange that invites the reader to imitate Kownacki's exercise of "slow reading"— perhaps with pen in hand.

It is apparent that in Ryokan, Mary Lou Kownacki found a kindred spirit: a poet to be imitated, a muse to inspire her, and a spiritual master to guide her journey. Sometimes, she takes her cue from the nineteenth century Buddhist monk's first lines, re-writing them as she reflects on her own experiences. So, Ryokan's "Thinking back, I recall my days at Ents?-ji ..." evokes Kownacki's memory of her year as a novice. And a poem Ryokan wrote on returning to his native village after a long absence prompts Kownacki to write about returning to her monastery after a year's leave. But Kownacki's poems are much more than the work of one poet imitating another. Ryokan's poems spark a memory, a feeling, or an experience that takes shape in the lines of a poem and the poems draw the reader into her world, where, as in Ryokan's world, the boundaries between monastery and world disappear and being a monk becomes a way of being *in* the world.

Like Ryokan, Kownacki shares the story of her spiritual journey. Despite all that Kownacki discovers that she has in common with the nineteenth-century Buddhist, their poems highlight some significant differences in lifestyle. Ryokan wrote:

In my youth I put aside my studies

And I aspired to be a saint.
Living austerely as a mendicant monk,
I wandered here and there for many springs.
Finally I returned home to settle under a craggy peak.
I live peacefully in a grass hut,
Listening to birds for music.
Clouds are my best neighbors.
Below, a pure spring where I refresh body and mind;
Above, towering pines and oaks that provide shade and brushwood.
Free, so free, day after day –
I never want to leave!

In response, Mary Lou Kownacki writes:

In my youth I put aside my talents
And aspired to be a saint.
I fasted on bread and water,
Prayed long hours into night,
Gave loaves of bread to the poor,
Was dragged to jail trying to stop war.

Finally, I found a single room in the inner city.
Outside my window
Police sirens, screams . . . footsteps in the night.

Three in the morning, children roaming the street.
I fold my hands and bow.
I pick up a pen and write.
All is well. All is well.

Both discover that their spiritual practice, however solitary, awakens within them deep compassion and a sense of solidarity with others. The needs of others penetrated and expanded Ryokan's solitude as they do Kownacki's.

For both the world is at once a place of beauty and of suffering, of innocence and ignorance. Each tends a garden—mindful of the fragility of the plants they raise: Ryokan surrendering plants and flowers "To the will / Of the wind" and Kownacki surrendering her tulips and daffodils "To the mercy / Of neighborhood children."

Inspired by Ryokan, Mary Lou Kownacki eloquently expresses her pleasure and gratitude for gifts at once simple and profound:

First blooming in the month of May,
The lilac pours perfume over my inner city street
Like God's mercy.

Soon the children are writing poems
On mirrors, balloons, rocks, kites . . . .
Soon the room smells
Of fresh words and ideas.
A bold phrase or image
Pops out of a child's hand and struts across the page,
So free and alive
That I feel the movement of a tickle inside of me.
Do you want to know the secret of life?
Listen a child is reading a new poem.

But the world in which Kownacki lives is a world in which children also suffer and die:

After a two-day search
We found five-year-old Lila's
Battered body in the dumpster
Her cotton underpants
Draping from one ankle.
How dare the wild violets
Continue to bloom.

It is a world in which people suffer from poverty and injustice and a world which makes martyrs of women like Ita, Dorothy, Maura and Jean who work to lessen that suffering. It is a world in which we experience loss and come to know the nearness of death.

There is a realism to Kownacki's poems (as there is in Ryokan's) but there is hope too as we come to see things as they are and as they can be—if we wake up and act with compassion. There is grace and healing.

Reading these poems we move easily between two worlds, invited to see our own world with new clarity. Ryokan and Kownacki have pared life to the basics—each in their own way. Ryokan writes:

> I have an old staff
> That has well served many.
> Its bark is worn away;
> All that remains is the strong core.
> I used it to test the waters,
> And often it got me out of trouble.
> Now, though, it leans against the wall,
> Out of service for years (p. 168).

And Kownacki:

> I have an old wooden
> Bookcase that folds flat
> For easy carrying. Whenever
> I move it becomes my backpack.
> Right now it sits
> In the corner of my room
> Holding all my worldly possessions:
> A half-burnt white candle,
> An icon of Our Lady of Tenderness
> (replica of one that hung in Saint Seraphim's cell),
> A gong to summon prayer,
> A framed colored photo
> of an angel tossing incense with abandon.
> My four favorite poetry books, A pen and lined notebook,
> A card with this quote by Saint Romould,
> "Sit in your cell as in paradise" (p. 169).

Reading *Between Two Souls* and especially the lines quoted above, I am reminded of Merton's *Day of a Stranger*, written to offer Latin

American readers a glimpse of his day in the hermitage and the inner world of his heart. Like Merton, Kownacki invites us to observe the outer landscape of our world and nurture the inner landscape of our spirit as we enter into this amazing conversation "between two souls."

Christine M. Bochen

CHITTISTER, Joan, *Called to Question: A Spiritual Memoir*, (Sheed & Ward, 2004). pp. 260. ISBN # 1580511430. (Hardcover) $21.95.

In *Called to Question: A Spiritual Memoir*, Sister Joan D. Chittister, a well-known spokesperson for social justice, calls for a spirituality which continually questions hierarchy, orthodoxies, and traditional religious assumptions, while celebrating the sacramentality and holiness of daily life. This little book consists of 25 brief chapters, each 6-8 pages in length, suitable for daily devotional reading. The chapters cover topics such as prayer, solitude, gender, justice, friendship, and the dark night of the soul.

The chapters are built around Sister Chittister's journal entries responding to quotations she found in a diary she used for a period of time (*In Good Company: A Woman's Journal for Spiritual Reflection*, published by Pilgrim Press, 1998). Every chapter in Chittister's book begins with a quotation she found in the journal, usually quotations of scripture or from women such as Teresa of Avila, Ann E. Carr, Thérèse of Lisieux, and Madeleine L'Engle. Each chapter's epigraphic quotation is followed by an excerpt from Chittister's own journal entry, responding to the quote. The chapter then expands on the theme begun in the journal, forming Chittister's conversation with the women quoted in the journal.

Called to Question is heavily autobiographical in style, as it opens with a discussion of Chittister's upbringing by parents in a "mixed marriage" and her questioning of fellow Roman Catholics who believed her Presbyterian stepfather would go to hell. Many chapters relate Chittister's wrestling with what she believes to be many Christians' rigid and hierarchical interpretation of their tradition. She describes her struggle to remain within the Roman Catholic Church, even as she finds resources within the tradition, especially monasticism, to be beneficial.

In many instances, her prose is insightful and profound, as she contrasts "real prayer" with escapist "self-induced hypnotism": "Real prayer plunges us into life, red and raw. It gives us new eyes. It leaves us breathless in the presence of the living God. It makes demands on us—to feed the hungry and clothe the naked, give drink to the thirsty and take care of the sick. It requires that we become the hands of the God "we say we have found" (p. 47). Particularly insightful are Chittister's reflections on commitment (chapter 10) and finding the sacred within "dailiness" (pp. 200-205). Chapter 11, on "balance," is a very fine reflection on the nature of one's vocation and calling.

Unfortunately the opening chapters of the book present a simplistically sharp dichotomy between "religion" (frequently characterized by institutions, rules, hierarchy, and oppressive judgmentalism), on the one hand, and "spirituality" (life-giving connection with the Divine), on the other hand. For instance, she says on page 16, "When religion makes itself God, when religion gets between the soul and God, when religion demands what the spirit deplores—a division of peoples, diminishment of the self, and closed-mindedness—religion becomes the problem. Then, spirituality is the only valid answer to the cry of the soul for the kind of life that makes life possible." Or, on pp. 21-22, "Religion is, at best, external. Spirituality is the internal distillation of this externalized witness to the divine." This overly sharp differentiation between spirituality and religion might appeal to the numerous folks who are inclined to say, "I'm spiritual but not religious"; however, Sister Chittister could have offered her readers a more nuanced use of these terms.

Chittister is most engaging when she shares the wisdom and spiritual lessons she learned as a young woman religious from older sisters who were her mentors. While strongly deploring society's tendency to sentimentalize and romanticize nuns, she introduces her readers to elderly Sister Hildegund, a mystic who talked to God (sometimes singing to God, sometimes scolding God) while standing over metal washtubs of wet linen, making pleats in the nuns' headgear. The author likewise celebrates Sister Marie Claire's love of symphony and opera music, listening to records on Sunday afternoons. Marie Claire, she said, was "steadfastly opposed to the suppression of joy in the name of holiness" (p. 216). Chittister is moved "by the model of such bold and wanton delight in the face of such institutional negation of it" (p. 216).

I would commend *Called to Question* to readers looking for an account of a spirited engagement with the Christian tradition and guidance for those seeking contemplative experience in the midst of everyday activity.

Joy A. Schroeder

KIRVAN, John, *Grace through Simplicity: The Practical Spirituality of Evelyn Underhill* (Notre Dame, IN: Ave Maria Press, 2004), pp. 7-206. ISBN 1594710260 (paperback). $8.95.

This little book, one in the series "30-Days with a Great Spiritual Teacher," elaborates and explores in prayerful form the insights of an extraordinary lay spiritual teacher, scholar of mysticism, guide to the contemplative life, and pioneer in the retreat movement. Evelyn Underhill (1875-1941) was a prolific author and editor, who both reclaimed the treasures of the mystical tradition and translated their wisdom, making them accessible to what she called "normal" people. Her most influential book, *Mysticism: A Study of the Nature and Development of Man's Spiritual Consciousness*, was published in 1911 and has remained in print continuously. In 1921 at mid-point in her writing career she moved from the life of scholarship to one in which she interpreted the mystical tradition for clergy and laity through popular writing, lecturing, and the giving of retreats. At the end of her life she became a pacifist, applying literally the mandate of the love of God that she discovered first in the mystics. Her corpus was very large, focusing not only on the mystical tradition but also on holiness, prayer, worship and the spiritual life. It established her as one of the early twentieth century foremothers of the contemporary burgeoning interest in spirituality. Among others, she influenced T.S. Eliot and the young Columbia University student, Thomas Merton.

Kirvan, who conceived of the 30-Days series and has authored most of its titles, wrote *God Hunger, Silent Hope, Raw Faith,* and *There is a God, There is No God.* The purpose of *Grace Through Simplicity* is to make the spiritual experience and wisdom of Underhill accessible and to invite the reader to meditate and pray her words daily for a month. Each meditation is structured in the same tripartite way: "My Day Begins, " "All Through the Day" and "My Day is Ending."

"My Day Begins" includes some ten to fifteen lines from Underhill. "All Through the Day" recapitulates one line from that selection, and "My Day is Ending" is Kirvan's prayer emerging from meditation on her words. As envisioned by Kirvan, the book is a "gateway" into Underhill, steeping the reader in her insights and then leading into prayer. The quotes selected focus heavily on what Underhill calls Reality and the individual's lifelong journey to bring oneself into correspondence with that Reality. This focus is consonant with Underhill's principal contribution, namely to establish the human need to be in relationship with its source. As such the book serves to companion one on a spiritual journey through life. There are disappointments, however. Nothing is delineated by quotation marks, and no citations are given to enable the reader to track down the source for further examination. Nonetheless, this very brief and portable book will serve to introduce one of the foremost twentieth century writers about the life of the spirit.

Dana Greene

PATTERSON, Richard B., *Writing Your Spiritual Autobiography* (Allen, TX: Thomas More Publishing, 2002), pp. 175. ISBN 0-88347-488-3 (paperback). $12.00.

In this practical, hands-on book, Richard B. Patterson, a clinical and consulting psychologist, suggests that writing one's spiritual autobiography is an effective way to cultivate and deepen one's awareness and understanding of his or her spirituality in relation to life's many dimensions. *Writing Your Spiritual Autobiography* consists of twenty-two chapters plus an annotated bibliography. Each chapter focuses on particular topics including prayer, thinking and doubting, parenting, one's image of God, addiction, suffering, and ethics, to name a few. On each topic, Patterson shares his own experience and insight as a "struggling traveler" versus a religious expert or theologian, then asks reflection questions and provides space to write. The nature of the questions encourage sober reflection upon oneself in relation to religious beliefs, spirituality, family, careers, morality, ethics, prayer, sex, suffering, and more.

A particularly attractive characteristic of Patterson's approach is his partially psychodynamic orientation and desire for the reader to *learn* rather than simply to feel inspired or motivated about spiritual growth. Key to such learning requires facing fears, mistakes and loss through thoughtful exploration and patience. A true mark of spiritual maturity shows itself when Patterson suggests that writing one's spiritual autobiography should ideally lead to richer questions rather than pat answers. Patterson states, "By writing your spiritual autobiography, hopefully you will clarify for yourself first of all exactly what you believe .... Perhaps you will also discover that what you actually believe and what you thought you believed are a little different, that difference coming to light only when you take the time to examine your beliefs" (p. 13).

Chapter five, "On Mysticism," for example, underscores the dual nature of spiritual exploration, and how this characteristic makes such an endeavor challenging if not intimidating. Patterson rightly notes that mysticism and mystical experiences can be both positive and negative, meaning that mysticism is not limited to a safe, intimate encounter with God. A mystical experience may also occur within a tragedy such as September 11, 2001, where horrifying wonder strikes, leaving those affected momentarily speechless and psychologically paralyzed. The point, however, is that we grow and develop spiritually as a result of such life experiences, assuming God's equal presence and availability.

Patterson, who is Catholic, writes from an ecumenical perspective, exploring religion as metaphor rather than dogma. He says the latter tends to complicate psychological and spiritual growth while the former encourages wonder and intrigue. Beyond family, friends, colleagues and acquaintances, Patterson's influences range from Thomas Merton, C.S. Lewis and Teilhard de Chardin to Zen Buddhism, Harold Kushner and Jewish mysticism to Viktor Frankl, Carl Jung and psychoanalysis. As a "self-help" book, *Writing Your Spiritual Autobiography* stands out due to its author's broad interests, influences and ecumenical spirit.

Glenn Crider

NOUWEN, Henri J.M., *Out of Solitude: Three Meditations on the Christian Life* (Notre Dame, IN: Ave Maria Press, 2004), pp.64. ISBN 0-87793-495-9. $7.95.

FORD, Michael (ed.), *Eternal Seasons: A Liturgical Journey with Henri J.M. Nouwen* (Notre Dame, IN: Sorin Books, 2004), pp.190. ISBN 1-893732-77-0. $18.95.

I am grateful for the opportunity to review these two recent publications from Henri Nouwen as it is unlikely that I would otherwise have picked them up. Not that I am unfamiliar with Nouwen's writings; that's the point, in a way I am too familiar with him and perhaps feel that I have heard all he has to say. Also I am not predisposed towards books with soft-tone filtered pastoral scenes (*Out of Solitude*) or Van Gogh reproductions (*Eternal Seasons*) on the covers. It smacks of that artificial beauty and insincerity of certain self-help books that we all love to hate and whose market, I suspect, these two publications are aimed. Which is a pity because they're both better than that.

Out of Solitude is a re-release of a book published thirty years ago (it's a "30ᵗʰ Anniversary Edition") based on three sermons Nouwen gave at Yale University drawing on three moments in the life of Jesus: finding a lonely place to pray before dawn amidst a busy schedule (Mk 1:32-39); feeding the five thousand (Mk 6:32-44); and the part in the last supper where Jesus tells his disciples that in a short time they will see him no longer but then they will see him again (Jn 16:16-22). From these Nouwen focuses on solitude, care and expectation: the need to find a center of solitude and silence in one's life; how this can then lead to real care of those who suffer; and the need for such care to be fed by the expectation (hope) of an end to suffering. It is "classic Nouwen" and therefore nothing very startling—all very familiar, no surprises.

For all its familiarity (and despite the cover), I found *Out of Solitude* strangely edifying—perhaps *because* of its familiarity. I found myself being reminded of things I already knew and of how easily it is to lose sight of them, particularly in the first meditation on solitude—though the ending is a bit weak: "let us not forget to once in a while get up long before dawn to leave the house and go to a lonely place" (p. 30), to say nothing of the dreadful split-infinitive. In the second section on care I found his distinction between care and cure a bit forced and suspect it relates to specific negative experiences he himself had. Whilst valid it seems to have become a bit of a bee in the bonnet—as it does for Thomas Moore in his not particularly inspired foreword. The last section on expectation is perhaps the weakest. It comes across as commonplace and a bit labored, also very preachy—you can see that it started out as a sermon. It does however contain this gem concerning what he calls the paradox of expectation: "those who believe in tomorrow can better live today … those who expect joy to come out of sadness can discover the beginnings of a new life in the center of the old … those who look forward to the returning Lord can discover him already in their midst" (p.59). It also provides a much needed corrective to those who would simplistically overemphasize living in the present moment or "the power of now."

It is not a book I would have bought, nor have even picked up, but one that I am glad to have become acquainted with. It is the sort of book that is ideal to give to someone who is getting baptized or confirmed, someone unfamiliar with Nouwen or who is searching for some "spiritual space" in their lives.

If *Out of Solitude* suffers from being over familiar this is far from true in the case of *Eternal Seasons* which I find to be a rich resource full of surprises. Michael Ford, an Anglican from Taunton in Somerset, England, has drawn widely from Nouwen's writings and skillfully crafted a book that is a work all of its own. Ford picks up on the prominence of time and season in Nouwen's work and uses it to produce a selection of readings that consciously follow the liturgical year. There are nine sections in all plus a very helpful introduction in which even the use of van Gogh for the cover makes perfect sense. Van Gogh, like Nouwen another Dutchman, was also acutely conscious of the passing seasons and sought to express this in his painting and re-painting of familiar landscapes in southern France.

The various sections include both a selection of readings for each season, Advent, Christmas, Epiphany etc. plus readings for the various feast days within each season. The book therefore becomes a rich resource both for individual devotions and for those putting together meditation series and celebrations for churches and groups. I particularly enjoyed Michael Ford's own introductions to each season which provide a helpful context for the selections that follow and somehow enhance them in a way that enables the reader to engage with them more meaningfully.

It has been a delight for me to re-engage with Henri Nouwen through *Eternal Seasons*. That which is familiar has been good to rediscover but there is much also that I have found fresh and new, or that has struck me in a new light, not least because of the way the readings have been selected and put together. Like precious stones, the setting and the arrangement seem to be as important as the beauty of the gems themselves. This is an anthology that I am pleased to recommend both for newcomers to Henri Nouwen and (even more so) to those (like me) who are familiar with him and think they have heard all he has to say.

Angus F. Stuart

O'MALLEY, John W., *Four Cultures of the West*, (Cambridge, MA, Harvard University Press, 2004): pp. 261. ISBN 0674014987. (Hardcover) $24.95.

I am inclined to describe this book as a "eureka experience." I use the term because John W. O'Malley seems fond of it (he uses it four times in the first quarter of the book, though, alas, from that point it disappears). A eureka experience is the joyful sensation one has at suddenly hitting upon something new and exciting. This was my experience in reading this book, as I hope it will be for other readers. It struck me as a new and refreshing way of reading the history of the Christian Western world.

The book provides interpretative categories for responding to the question that looms over its entire content (a question first posed by the brilliant, eccentric Latinist of the second-third century, Tertullian): "What does Athens have to do with Jerusalem?" By relating four cultures to Tertullian's question, O'Malley provides a road map through areas of Western history, with religion as the central highway. The author contents himself with identifying "four cultures," not *the* four cultures. Cultures, the author describes as "configurations of symbols, values, temperaments, patterns of thinking, feeling, and behaving, and patterns of discourse" (p. 5). There is an introductory section offering a general discussion of all four under the rubric of "Athens and Jerusalem." This is followed by a separate section on each of the cultures. A final brief section invites the reader to think of culture in terms of her or his own experience.

Culture one is the **Prophetic Culture**. It is the culture of protest, of reform. It is a Jeremiah for whom the Word of God is a fire burning inside that he cannot hold in. It is the culture that must speak out. It is about protest, decrying the present times, yet promising better times to come. Its language is the imperative. It cannot compromise or go to the negotiating table. This culture embraces such disparate figures as Tertullian, the monks of the desert, Pope Gregory VII and the monumental Gregorian reform, Martin Luther ("Here I stand. I can do no other"), William Lloyd Garrison and the Abolitionist Movement; Martin Luther King Jr. and his dream of a better future. Prophets are not easy people to live with; yet we need them. They shake us out of our complacency, our gradualism, our tendency to put things off. They insist that we look at NOW and deal with it.

Culture two is the *Academic Professional Culture*. Its methodology is that of the question, with one question inevitably leading to another. The style of this culture is analytical and logical. Its quest to understand is relentless. Highest honor is given to sound argument. Plato and Aristotle are its bright luminaries and the medieval universities its "monumental turning point." Scholasticism found a home in culture two. In fact, this culture represents the triumph of the philosophers and the scientists: Descartes, Galileo, Kant, Freud, Einstein, etc. "To probe beyond the status quo is the essence of culture two and the source and expression of its dynamism. Why, otherwise, do lectures always end the same way: 'Are there any questions?'" (p. 125).

Culture three is the *Humanistic Culture*. This is the culture of literature and rhetoric (oratory). Where culture two has a special zeal for the Truth, culture three's yearning is for the Good; Culture two delights in *good argument*, culture three in *good literature*. The style of culture two is linear, moving from point to point. Culture three's style is circular and meandering and many-layered. Its classical antecedents are the glories of Greece (Homer, Sophocles, Euripides, Demosthenes, Hesiod, etc.) and Rome (Virgil, Cicero, Quintilian, etc). These were *adapted* by early Christian writers, such as Origen, Ambrose, Augustine and others and *recovered* in the Renaissance of the mid fourteenth century, the "eureka moment" of culture three. That moment witnessed an outburst of literary creativity; at the same time it marked a return to the sources (pre- Christian and Christian).

It shone with such geniuses as Petrarch, Dante, Boccaccio, and Chaucer. Inevitably Renaissance humanism locked horns with Scholasticism. In the early sixteenth century, Erasmus in the *Praise of Folly* directs his strongest invectives against academic theologians. He anticipated the biblical movement of the 20th century by producing a critical edition of the Greek New Testament with a Latin translation. Moreover, he offered as an alternative to Scholasticism a return to the more literary and rhetorical style of the early Church Fathers. In the seventeenth century there was an explosion of geniuses writing in the vernacular: Cervantes, Montaigne, Moliere, Shakespeare, Milton, etc. In the schools "Latin remained a staple in the program, but its piece of the curriculum pie became ever smaller as vernacular works cut out for themselves more and more of it" (p. 171). The most significant religious and theological expression of culture three in the twentieth century were the documents of the Second Vatican Council. They are written in a style never before used in any previous church council: a style that is rhetorical rather than dialectical, a style that invites dialogue and seeks understanding. It is easy to see how a style of this sort bewilders people who are used to looking to councils for definitions and condemnations. This is a good example of one of the theses of O'Malley's book: the difficulty one culture experiences in understanding another.

Culture four is the artistic culture. This is an intensely visual culture, expressing itself in dance, painting, sculpture, music and architecture. It was a culture highly evident in the Greco-Roman world—with its temples to the gods, its sculptures, gladiatorial contests, chariot races—into which Christianity was born. Because it was visual and had no need for words, it readily reached a population that was largely illiterate. For Christians, especially after the time of Constantine, culture four found expression especially in worship—church architecture and art (icons, frescoes, statues, altar, ambos) and the ritual of the Mass. The Iconoclast Controversy that lasted through the eighth century generated much image-smashing but also a rich volume of literature that in the light of the Incarnation justified and encouraged the use of images. Monastic communities—with their churches, illuminated manuscripts, and ornate vessels for liturgy—made their contribution to culture four. An even greater contribution came with the revival of cities and the building of huge cathedrals. Liturgy involved not only churches and cathedrals and the accoutrements of worship, it also included performance: the ritual action of the Mass and sacraments with the accompaniment of the art of music. Music is the only verbal manifestation in this culture that is otherwise mute. In our day, works of art have also found a place, apart from liturgy or special occasions, in museums and concert halls where people go to visit and enjoy. The art of Leonard Bernstein, Alvin Ailey, Georgia O'Keeffe, Frank Lloyd Wright—and, yes, pop stars—are at home in culture four (cf. 233).

This necessarily inadequate summary of O'Malley's "four cultures" will offer some inkling at least, of the rich treasures stored in this book. In a valuable insight, he offers a caveat about the approach he has taken to the history of the Western world. The "four cultures" have their limitations. No one of the cultures, not all of them taken together, tell the whole story. In a helpful comparison, O'Malley writes: "If you imagine Western civilization as a vast ocean, you might imagine the four cultures as four Gulf Streams flowing through it. The streams help us to understand many phenomena, but they are not the ocean" (p. 6). Hardly any of the cultures exist in pure form. They are by no means sealed off from one another. Sometimes partners, sometimes rivals, they may blend with one another or borrow, complement or contradict. Some people are imbedded in all four cultures. Liturgy is an excellent example of the way in which one culture may use another or even take it captive. Most properly liturgy belongs to culture four, yet is coveted by all the other three. "Culture one wants it as a bully pulpit, culture two as a classroom for instruction in orthodoxy, culture three as an expression of religions or religious political solidarity within a given milieu" (p. 25).

If there is anything I would like to see added to this book it would be a section discussing more explicitly, and in more detail, the interaction of these four cultures with one another. This is offered as a comment, not a criticism, as examples of this intermingling do appear in various parts of the book.

I found this book a delight: an enlightened and enlightening approach to the history of the Christian Western world. It is eminently readable: a trait one would expect in a book that clearly belongs to culture three.

William H. Shannon

Contributors

Dennis Beach is a monk of The Abbey of St. John's, Collegeville, Minnesota. He is also Associate Professor of Philosophy at St. Ben's College / St. John's University.

Christine M. Bochen, Professor of Religious Studies, holds the William H. Shannon Chair for Catholic Studies at Nazareth College. A founding member and past president of ITMS, she is the editor of *Courage for Truth, Learning to Love, Thomas Merton: Essential Writings* and a co-author of *The Thomas Merton Encyclopedia*.

Ernesto Cardenal was a novice under Thomas Merton's direction at The Abbey of Gethsemani. "Time of Transition: A Selection of Letters from the Earliest Correspondence of Thomas Merton and Ernesto Cardenal" was published in Volume 8 of *The Merton Annual*. This Nicaraguan priest, poet and revolutionary has published volumes of poetry including "Homage to the American Indians" and "Cósmic Cantico" which first appeared in 1989 and was translated into English and published as "Cósmic Cánticle" in 1994. He read from this massive work at the 2004 Poetry Reading which preceded the commentary transcribed here.

Jeff Cooper, CSC, is a priest in the Congregation of Holy Cross and is finishing a 6 year term on his community's Novitiate Formation staff in Cascade, Colorado. In 2006 he will begin PhD studies in Spirituality at the Catholic University of America. He has published several times in *The Merton Seasonal* and most recently gave a paper at the 9th General meeting of the ITMS on Gandhi, Merton and Satyagraha.

Glenn Crider, Production Manager and Editorial Contributor for *The Merton Annual*, served as chair of the Atlanta Chapter of The International Thomas Merton Society, 2001 to 2003. He holds an MA in psychology and a Master of Divinity from Candler School of Theology, Emory University.

Daniel Durken, OSB, is a Benedictine monk and priest of Saint John's Abbey, Collegeville, Minnesota. He is the senior editor of Liturgical Press where he edits the *New Collegeville Bible Commentary* and contributes Homily Hints for the *Loose-Leaf Lectionary*. He is also the editor / publisher of *The Abbey Banner*, the magazine of The Abbey.

Anthony Feuerstein graduated from St. Edward's University in Austin, Texas (1961) and has been interested in spirituality and prayer since he first read Merton's *Seeds of Contemplation* in 1958. He is familiar with Centering Prayer both through instruction at the Abbey of the Holy Spirit, Conyers, Georgia, and at Sacred Heart Monastery in Cullman, Alabama. Last year he published book reviews in *The Merton Annual*.

Dana Greene, former Dean and CEO of Oxford College of Emory University, is author of *Evelyn Underhill: Artist of the Infinite Life*. She has edited *Evelyn Underhill: A Modern Guide to the Ancient Quest for the Holy* and *Fragments from an Inner Life: The Notebooks of Evelyn Underhill*.

Michael Griffith is Associate Professor of Literature at the Australian Catholic University in Sydney. His teaching explores the relationship between contemplative and artistic practice and he sees Merton as a touchstone for this. He is currently completing a study of William Blake's impact on spirituality in the Arts in Australia and is supervising a PhD candidate on "Merton: Poet and Contemplative."

Patrick Hart, one of the original founding editors of *The Merton Annual*, has edited many collections of Merton's writing. He was recently recognized with an honorary doctorate from Bellarmine University, Louisville.

Eric Hollas is a monk of Saint John's Abbey, Collegeville, MN, and he currently serves as Senior Associate for Arts & Cultural Affairs at Saint John's University. He helped to plan and speaks widely on The Saint John's Bible, which is the first hand-written, illuminated, monumental Bible to be commissioned by a Benedictine Abbey in nearly five hundred years.

Ross Keating is a Senior Lecturer in the Faculty of Education at Australia Catholic University. He lectures in world religions, and in spirituality. His interests are in poetry and theatre. He has published *Francis Brabazon Poet of the Silent Word* and has won the International Bishop Burton Essay Prize for "Spirituality and the Passage from Adolescence to Adulthood."

Victor A. Kramer began study concerning Merton in 1972 and has remained active as a Merton scholar since then. He edited Merton's journal *Turning Toward the World: The Pivotal Years, 1960-1963* (1996). Presently he teaches for Spring Hill College (Mobile, Alabama) in its MA Extension Program in Atlanta. He is also a graduate student in a two year Certificate Program for Spiritual Direction.

Dewey W. Kramer was a founding editor of *The Merton Annual* and has made frequent contributions over the years. She is also author of *Open to the Spirit*, a history of The Abbey of the Holy Spirit (1986, revised 1996). In 2003-2004 she was a Research Scholar at the Institute for Ecumenical and Cultural Research at St. John's University, in Minnesota where she worked on the relationship between the Illuminations, Text and Music of Hildegard of Bingen.

Roger Lipsey is the author of *Angelic Mistakes: The Art of Thomas Merton* (Shambhala Publications, April 2006), a book on Merton's previously unexplored ink drawings and prints of the 1960s. Dr. Lipsey's prior publications include *The Spiritual in Twentieth-Century Art* (1988, reissued by Dover Books in 2004) and a trilogy of books by and about Ananda K. Coomaraswamy (1977 with later editions).

Patrick F. O'Connell teaches English and Theology at Gannon University, Erie, PA. A founding member and former president of the International Thomas Merton Society, he serves as editor of *The Merton Seasonal*. He is co-author of *The Thomas Merton Encyclopedia* (2002), and editor of *The Vision of Thomas Merton* (2003) and *Cassian and the Fathers* (2005), the first volume of Merton's novitiate conferences.

Chris Orvin has been exploring the relationship between lay life and monastic spirituality. To deepen this interest, he has visited Mepkin Abbey in Moncks Corner, SC. The paper revised for publication here, "The Conflict Not Fully Faced: Thomas Merton as Reader" recently won the Edmund Perry prize at Northwestern University. Mr. Orvin is currently serving with the Peace Corps in Panama.

Paul M. Pearson is Director and Archivist of the Thomas Merton Center at Bellarmine University, and President of the International Thomas Merton Society. His most recent book, *Seeking Paradise: Thomas Merton and the Shakers*, was published by Orbis. He is a regular contributor to Merton conferences in Europe and the USA. In 1999 he was awarded a "Louie" by the ITMS for his contribution on an international level to the promotion of Merton's life and writings.

Malgorzata Poks teaches courses in American Literature at the English Teacher Training College in Sosnowiec and the Academy of Business Administration and Foreign Languages in Katowice, Poland. She was an ITMS Shannon scholar in 2001/02; contributed an article to *The Merton Annual* (2001), and wrote her doctoral dissertation on Thomas Merton and the poets of Latin America.

Corey Shouse is an Associate Professor of Spanish at St. John's University, Collegeville, Minnesota.

Joy A. Schroeder holds the Bergener Chair in Theology and Religion at Capital University and Trinity Lutheran Seminary in Columbus, Ohio. Her areas of research include medieval mysticism, women in Church history, the history of the Church's response to sexual and domestic violence, and the history of biblical interpretation.

R. Kevin Seasoltz is a Benedictine monk of Saint John's Abbey in Collegeville, Minnesota. He teaches Liturgical Studies and Systematic Theology at Saint John's University and is the editor of the liturgical journal *Worship*. He is the author of the recently published *A Sense of the Sacred: Theological Foundations of Christian Architecture and Art* (Continuum 2005).

William H. Shannon is Professor Emeritus at Nazareth College in Rochester, New York. He is the Founding President of the International Thomas Merton Society. In addition to numerous articles on Merton and spirituality, he is the author of *Silent Lamp: The Thomas Merton Story* and *Silence on Fire*.

Angus F. Stuart is the Rector of St Francis-in-the-Wood Anglican Church, West Vancouver in British Columbia, Canada. Formerly he was Senior Chaplain at the University of Bristol in

England and is a former chair of the Thomas Merton Society of Great Britain & Ireland. He edited the papers from the 2002 UK Merton Conference, *The World in my Bloodstream: Thomas Merton's Universal Embrace* and has contributed to the UK *Merton Journal* and other publications.

Marilyn Sunderman, RSM, is Associate Professor / Chair of Theology at Saint Joseph's College of Maine. She has contributed articles to *The Merton Annual* (1999); *The Paradox of Place: Thomas Merton's Photography* published by the Thomas Merton Center, Bellarmine University, 2003; and *Groundings, St. Michael's Theological College Publication*, Jamaica, West Indies, January 2004.

Methodius Telnack is a Cistercian monk and priest at The Abbey of the Holy Spirit, Conyers, Georgia. He has been active for many decades both as a composer and stained-glass artist. He also manages the Stained-glass Shop at Conyers and serves as its principle designer. His work has been installed in hundreds of churches and other buildings throughout the Southeast.

Stefanie Weisgram, OSB, is the Collection Development Librarian for the College of Saint Benedict and St. John's University in Minnesota. For the last fifteen years, one month each year, she has been the cataloger in the library the monks of Abadia de Jesucristo Crucificado in Esquipulas, Guatemala, opened to the public.

Charlotte Anne Zalot, OSB, is a liturgist, teacher and liturgical musician. She holds a PhD in Liturgical Studies from Drew University. She is presently working on a book manuscript to record Frank Kacmarcik's contributions to the development of American Roman Catholic liturgical space and furnishings. She is active in the music ministry at Mount Saint Benedict Monastery, Erie, PA, where she resides.

Index

A

L'Abbaye Notre-Dame de New
   Melleray 32
The Abbey Banner 59
Abbey of Our Lady of the Holy
   Spirit 96
Abbey of Gethsemani 29, 96, 169,
   239
Abbey of Melleray 103
Abbey of New Melleray , Peosta,
   Iowa 24
Abbey of Our Lady of New
   Melleray 27
Abdesalam, Sidi 227
Aby odnalezc Boga 322
Acadèmie de la Grand Chaumière
   23
*Ace of Freedoms: Thomas Merton's
   Christ* 203
Adams, Ansel 167, 182, 185, 253
   *Ansel Adam's Guide: Basic
      Techniques of Photography* 188
   Letter to Alfred Stieglitz 188
Adams, William Seth 49, 52
   Theology and Liturgical Space 57
Aeschylus
   Prometheus Bound 226
*The Aesthetic of Beuron and Other
   Writings* 31
After God: The Future of Religion
   204
Agnes Scott College 80
St. Augustine
   City of God 222
Ailey, Alvin 369
Albers, Josef 288
Alberti, Rafael 141
Alcuin Library 11

Almy, Ruth Case
   Stained Glass For Amateurs 83
Alteizer, Thomas
   *The Radical Vision of William
      Blake* 113
Altizer, Thomas
   *The New Apocalypse: The Radical
      Vision of William Blake* 125
St. Ambrose 141
America 64
America a Prophecy 110
American Liturgical Movement
   42
American Roman Catholic 43
Americas 143
*An Astonishing Variety, Rev. of
   Owen Merton* 345
Mount Analogue 135
Andersen, Hans Christian 325
de Andrade, Carlos Drummond
   141
*Angelic Mistakes: The Art of Thomas
   Merton* 309, 312, 314
Angelico, Fra 240
The Annunciation 176
Another Space 326
Ansel Adams 188
*Ansel Adam's Guide: Basic Tech-
   niques of Photography* 188
*Ansel Adams: The Grand Canyon
   and the Southwest* 188
*Ansel Adams: The Role of the Artist
   …* 188
*Ansel Adams: The Spirit in Wild
   Places* 188
St. Anselm 217
   De Casu Diaboli 217
*Anthology of Modern American
   Poetry* 344

Antonucci, Emil
    Original Child Bomb 310
Apologia 25
Apologia to William of St. Thierry
    107
Aquinas 119, 120
    Thomistic 123
Architecture for Worship 50, 57
*Architecture of Silence: Cistercian
    Abbeys of France* 32
The Archives of American Art 312,
    313
Arendt, Hannah
    The Human Condition 222
Aristotle 368
Armstrong, Karen
    A History of God 112, 125
*The Art Comics and Satires of Ad
    Reinhardt* 313
The Art of Thomas Merton 186
Art and Scholasticism 55, 241
Art and Spirituality 185
Art and Worship 19, 302, 306
*Art-as-Art: The Selected Writings of
    Ad Reinhardt* 313
The Ascent to Truth 246
Ashtavakra Gita 230
Asia 143
The Asian Journal of Thomas Merton
    186
Astavakra Gita 133
Mount Athos 278
Atkins, Father Anselm 85, 87
Atlanta University
    Lyke Catholic Center 95
Atlas and the Fatman 164
Aubade - Harlem 175
Aubade - The City 175
Auguries of Innocence 119
Auschwitz 154, 337
Autobiography 55
Aztec 60, 67

B

Backhouse, Janet
    The Illuminated Manuscript 32
Badaracco, Claire Hoertz 344
Bahama Islands 63
Baker, Russell
    Growing Up 62
Balliol College 128
von Balthasar, Han Urs
    Herrlichkeit 214
Baltimore Cathedral 88
Baptism in the Forest 347
Bardstown 98
Barnett, James Monroe
    *The Diaconate: A Full and Equal
        Order* 56
Barron, Robert
    *Bridging the Great Divide:
        Musings of a Post-liberal* 31
Barth 220
Basho 197
Baudrillard, Jean 200
    Simulations 204
Beach, Dennis 65
The Bear 221, 234
Beat Generation 334
Belcastro, David 10, 334, 344
Bellarmine University
    McGrath Art Gallery 331, 333
    Thomas Merton Center 331
St. Benedict 59, 60, 68, 160
    Order of 68
Benedictine 68
Benjamin Franklin 61
The Berakah Award for 1981 56
Berdyaev, Nikolai 215
    Slavery and Freedom 226
Bereza, Konrad 327
Berkeley, Bishop 265
Berman, Morris 337
St. Bernard 15, 25, 26, 27, 87, 88,
    89, 92, 97, 111, 215, 216, 218,

277, 303, 327, 330
Apologia to William of St. Thierry 107
On the Love of God 216
Bernstein, Leonard 369
Berone, Ludo 94
Between Two Souls: Conversations with Ryokan 355
Bhagavad-Gita 133
2004 Bibliographic Survey 318
Biddle, Arthur W. 335
Biddle, Arthur W. ed.
When Prophecy Still Had a Voice 313
Bielawski, Krzysztof 321, 323, 327
Aby odnalezc Boga 322
Bielawski, Maciej 325
Merton's Margin 344
Blake and the New Theology 165
Blake, William 8, 21, 109, 110, 113, 114, 115, 116, 120, 123, 168, 169, 198, 223, 241, 351
America a Prophecy 110
Auguries of Innocence 119
Four Zoas 119
Jerusalem 123
The Laocoön 123
The Marriage of Heaven and Hell 110
Vision of the Daughters of Albion 110
Blaze of Recognition: Through the Year with Thomas Merton 352
St. Bleb 274
Blenko, Bill 83
Blenko Glass Company 83
Boccaccio 368
Bochen, Christine M. 257, 360
Learning to Love: Exploring Solitude and Freedom 125
The Thomas Merton Encyclopedia 257
Bodhidharma 266

Bois, Yve-Alain 246
St. Bonaventure 219, 221, 224
St. Bonaventure University 168, 172, 239
A Book of Luminous Things 204
The Book that Never Was 348
Book of Psalms 209
Book Round-up 344
St. Boris 274
Botz, Paschal 23, 47
The Saint Paul Statuary 57
Boulgakov, S. 21
Bound to Books 55
Bourdon, David
Master of the Minimal 313
Bouyer
Le Mystère Pascal 222
Breuer, Marcel 94
Bridging the Great Divide: Musings of a Post-liberal 31
Brihad-Aranyaka Upanishad 354
Brother Ephrem 251
Brother Frank Kacmarcik Obl.S.B. 1920-2004 31
Brown, Christy
My Left Foot 62
Brown, Steven Ford 143
Jorge Carrera Andrade in America 163
Bruzda, Katarzyna 328
Thomas Merton—An Artist 256, 326
Buber, Martin 265
Ten Rungs 230
Building History One Stone at a Time 343
Bulgakov, Sergei 215
Bultmann, Rudolf 212
Bunt i gwalt [Rebellion and Violence] 163
Bunting, Madeline
When the Meaning Boils Down to a Brand Name 204

Burden, Shirley
    God Is My Life 250
    Monastic Peace 250
Burgundy 26
Burton, Patricia
    The Book that Never Was 348
Butler, Theodore 28, 30, 31

C

Cables to the Ace 170, 323, 351
Calder 239
Callaghan, Henry 253
Called to Question: A Spiritual
    Memoir 360
Cambridge University 250
campesinos 70
del Campo, Anna 160
Camus, Albert 144, 161, 162, 215,
    325, 338
    The Myth of Sisyphus 212, 226
    The Stranger 162
Cannon, Basil
    Ansel Adams 188
Cantares Mexicanos 67
Cap and Bells, The Poetry of Francis
    Webb 126
Capra, Fritjof 321
The Captive Mind 318, 326, 344
Cardenal, Ernesto 8, 65, 66, 69,
    141, 162
    Cantares Mexicanos 67
    Cosmic Canticle 66, 67
    Frater Lawrence 65
Cardenal, Fernando
    Minister of Education 66
Carey, Graham
    Eric Gill: 1882-1940 55
Carol 177
Carpentier, Alejo 142
Carr, Ann E. 360
Carrera Andrade, Jorge 140, 141,
    143, 144, 145, 146, 147, 148,
    149, 150, 151, 155, 156, 157,
    158, 159, 160, 162

Biografía para uso de los pájaros
    143
Boletines de mar y tierra 143
Crónica de las indias 143
Ecuadorian Consul General
    143
El fabuloso reino de Quito 164
El libro del destierro 143
El tiempo manual 143
Hombre planetario 143
País secreto 143
Secret Country 143
The New American and His Point
    of View toward Poetry 143
The Weathercock on the Cathedral
    of Quito 166
Carter, President Jimmy 183
Cartesian 142, 218
Cassian, John 224
Catching the Soul of Frank
    Kacmarcik 55
Catechism of the Catholic Church,
    Libreria Editric 56
Cathedral of Chartres 240
Catherine Spalding College 243
The Catholic and Creativity 56
Catholic Monarchs 142
Catholic University of Lublin
    Ecumenical Institute 326
Centre d'Art Sacré 23
Cervantes 368
Cezanne, Paul 20, 237, 240
Chadwick, Nora 225
A Chant Historian Reads Liturgiam
    Authenticam 31
Char, René 141, 212
de Chardin, Teilhard 364
Chaucer, Geoffrey 368
Cheney, Richard 338
Chicago 70
Chicago Music College
    Roosevelt College 72
China 70

Chittister, Joan D. 355
  Called to Question: A Spiritual Memoir 360
Chouinard 85
Christchurch Art Gallery 329
Chuang Tzu 141, 355
The Church Against Itself 220
Church Fathers 207
Cicero 368
Cincinnati Art Museum 297
Circus Days and Nights 335
Circus in the Sun 335
Circus of the Sun 299
Cistercian Architectural Tradition 22
Cistercian communities
  Moncks Corner, South Carolina 27
  Peosta, Iowa 27
Cistercian Europe: Architecture of Contemplation 32
Cistercian Glass 89
Cistercian life 7
Cistercian Order of the Strict Observance 111
Citeaux, Burgundy, France 24, 25, 27, 103
City of God 222
Civil Rights 250
Civil War 27, 99
Claire, Marie 361
Clairvaux 25
Clarksville, Tennessee 72
Claudel, Paul 213
Clement of Alexandria 141
Clément, Olivier
  Transfigurer les Temps 214
Cloud of Unknowing 222
Cluniac Benedictinism 96
Cluny 59
Coke, Van Deren 253
Cold War 248, 341
The Collected Poems of Gerard Manley Hopkins 125

The Collected Poems of Thomas Merton 125, 126, 141, 145, 163, 165, 186, 187, 259, 313, 350, 351
The College of St. Benedict 15
Collins, Roger 329, 330, 331, 345
  A New Zealand Painter in Medieval France 345
The Columbia History of the American Novel 345
Columbia University 65, 168, 241, 260
  Rare Book and Manuscript Library 312
Commonweal 240
Communism 262
The Complete Poems (Dickinson) 165
The Complete Poetry and Prose of William Blake 124
The Conflict Not Yet Fully Faced 205
The Conflict of Interpretations 343
Congdon, William 285, 306
Congregation of the Sisters of the Divine Savior 311
Conjectures of a Disenchanted Reader 206, 345
Conjectures of a Guilty Bystander 139, 142, 161, 173, 186
Constantine 341
Constitution on the Sacred Liturgy 42
Contemplation in a World of Action 203
Contemporary Architectural Witness to the Lived 96
Conze, Edward 321
Coomaraswamy, A.K. 55, 112, 119, 242, 265, 282, 312
  Selected Papers Traditional Art 204
  Transformation of Nature in Art 124

Cooper, David D.
  Thomas Merton's Art of Denial:
    The Evolution of a Radical
    Humanist 203, 314
Cooper, David D. ed.
  Thomas Merton and James
    Laughlin: Selected Letters 313
Cooper, Jeffrey A. 127
Corman, Cid 338
Cornell, Judith
  Mandala: Luminous Symbols for
    Healing 108
Cortés, Alfonso 141
Cosmic Canticle 66, 67
The Courage for Truth 163, 313, 347
Cousineau, Phil
  The Way Things Are: Conversa-
    tions with Huston Smith 203
Crichton, James 22
Crider, Glenn 15, 77, 364
The Crisis of Scientific-Technical
  Civilisation ... 324
Cristiani Brothers 335
Crivelli, Carlo 278
  Venetian painter 304
Cuadra, Pablo Antonio 65, 141
Cunningham, Dick
  He Teaches Clergy Their Artistic
    ABCs 57
Cupitt, Don 193
  After God: The Future of Religion
  204
Curzon, Lord 287
Cyprian, Father 80, 81
St. Cyril of Jerusalem 218

D

Daggy, Robert E. 315
Daggy, Robert E. ed.
  Dancing in the Water of Life 231,
    232, 258
  Monks Pond: Thomas Merton's
    Little Magazine 313

Dante 127, 368
Darío, Rubén 65, 162
  Lo Fatal 69
Dark Night of the Soul 249
Darwin, Charles 66
Daumal, René
  Mount Analogue 130, 138
Davenport, Guy 252
Davis, Stuart 288
Day of a Stranger 188, 359
Dayton Art Institute 279
De Casu Diaboli 217
The Death of Thomas Merton: A
  Novel 343
Del Prete, Thomas 201
  Thomas Merton and the Education
    of the Whole Person 204
Demosthenes 368
Descartes, Rene 368
Devout Meditation in Memory of
  Adolf Eichmann 347
Dewdrops on a Lotus Leaf: Zen
  Poems of Ryokan 356
The Diaconate: A Full and Equal
  Order 56
Dialogues with Silence: Prayers and
  Drawings 8, 352
Dickinson, Emily 224
  The Complete Poems 165
Dictionnaire de Spiritualité 211
Diekmann, Godfrey 22
Dimier, Anselme
  Stones Laid before the Lord 32
Dionysius 246
Directions 17 145
Dirge for the City of Miami 174
A Discovery 72
Discovery of the Mind 214
Disputed Questions 249, 257, 304
Do I want a small painting? 260
Doctor Mellifluus 345
Dogmatic Constitution of the Church
  57

Don Juan 160
Donald, David H.
  Lincoln 60
Dostoyevsky 325
Duckett, Eleanor 225
Duffy, Eamon
  Saints & Sinners: A History of the Popes 60
Duke of Norfolk 348
Dunne, Frederic 100, 101, 102
Duns Scotus 224, 228
Durham 59
Durken, Daniel 59
Durkheim, Emile 327

E

Early Blizzard 170
Ecclesiastes 226
Ecclesiasticus 208, 210
Eckhart, Meister 118, 222
Ecumenical Institute 326
Editions Zodiaque 298
Eichmann, Adolf 337
Eighteen Poems 351
Einstein, Albert 368
Elegy for the Monastery Barn 117
Eliade, Mircea 135
Elias 159
Elias—Variations on a Theme 150, 171
Eliot, T.S. 69, 352, 362
Ellis, Joseph
  Founding Brothers: The Revolutoinary Generation 60
Ellman, Richard
  The Norton Anthology of Modern Poetry 138
Emblems of a Season of Fury 141, 142, 143, 144, 150, 161
Emerson, Ralph Waldo 331
Eminent Victorians 214
Emmanuel, Pierre
  Qui est cet homme? 224, 226

Encounter in a Secret Country 140
The End of Education: Defining the Value of School 190, 203
The End of Knowing 203
Ends and Means 223
L'Engle, Madeleine 360
Enitharmon 119
Entering the Silence: Becoming a Monk and Writer 58, 231, 352
Environment and Art in Catholic Worship 43
Erasmus 368
Erdman, David V. et al.
  The Complete Poetry and Prose of William Blake 124
Eric Gill: 1882-1940 55
Esse Quam Videri: Notes on the Building of Churches 57
Eternal Seasons: A Liturgical Journey 364
Euripides 368
Europe 70, 143
Evagrius 218
Evdokimov, Paul 232
Eyck, Van 240
Ezekiel 212

F

El fabuloso reino de Quito 164
Faithful Dissenters: Stories of Men and Women 61
The Family Album of Lucybelle Crater 254
The Family of Man 223
Farrar Straus 240
Father Louie: Photographs of Thomas Merton 259
Faulkner, William 222, 338
  The Bear 221, 234
  The Sound and the Fury 347
Fehrenbacher, Henry
  Catching the Soul of Frank Kacmarcik 55

Felix culpa 326
Fénelon 218
Ferlinghetti, Lawrence 338
Ferry, W.H. "Ping" 317
Feuerstein, Anthony 72
Figures for an Apocalypse 175
Finnegans Wake 293
First Epistle of John 200
Fischer, Balthasar 22
Five Days Old 121
*Five Unpublished Letters From Ad
   Reinhardt* 257
Flagg, Nancy 335
Folie 300
Ford car company 200
Ford, Michael
   *Eternal Seasons: A Liturgical
      Journey* 364
   *Wounded Prophet: A Portrait of
      Henri J. M. Nouwen* 61
Forest, Jim 340, 342
   Living with Wisdom 319
de Foucauld, Charles 354
*Founding Brothers: The
   Revolutoinary Generation* 60
Four Cultures of the West 367
Four Zoas 119
Fourth and Walnut 353
Fox, James 94, 102
St. Francis 228
Franciscan Publishing House 319
Frank Kacmarcik: A Mepkin
   Tribute 58
Frater Lawrence
   Ernesto Cardenal 65
French Cistercian Grisaille Glass
   108
Freud, Sigmund 368
Frischauf, Clement 36
Frishauf, Clement 22
Frost, Robert 69
Furlong, Monica 220
   Thomas Merton: A Biography
      124, 233

G

Galileo 368
Garaudy, Roger 220
Gardner, W.H. 132
   *Gerard Manley Hopkins: Poems
      and Prose* 138
   *The Collected Poems of Gerard
      Manley Hopkins* 125
Garrison, William Lloyd 367
Gaul 62
Gelassenheit 327
Genesis 152
The Gentle House 62
The Geography of Lograire 176, 187,
   323
*Geography of Holiness: The Photog-
   raphy of Thomas Merton* 187
Georgiou, S.T.
   The Way of the Dreamcatcher 335
*Gerard Manley Hopkins: Poems and
   Prose* 138
Gergen, Kenneth 192
Gershwin Memorial Award
   Pastorale and Allegro 72
Gethsemani 65, 134, 142
Gibney, Bob 335
   Virgin Island abode 335
Gill, Eric 34, 36, 55
   Autobiography 55
Gilligan, Martin T. 108
Gilson, Étienne
   Spirit of Medieval Philosophy 223
Ginsberg, Allan 69
Giotto
   Florentine painter 304
Giroux, Robert 305, 306
Gobineau
   *Religions et Philosophies dans
      l'Asie Central* 344
God Hunger, Silent Hope, Raw Faith
   362
God in Search of Man 214
God Is My Life 250

Good Friday 209
Good Work 241
Gorres, Ida
    The Hidden Face 62
Grace through Simplicity: The
    Practical Spirituality 362
Granada, Nicaragua 65
Grand Canyon 185
The Great Voyage 238
Greece 70
Greene, Dana 363
St. Gregory of Nyssa 218
Griffin, John Howard 134, 178,
    183, 243, 250, 251
    A Hidden Wholeness 187, 254,
    258, 316
Griffith, Michael 109
Griffith, Michael and James
    McGlade
    Cap and Bells, The Poetry of
    Francis Webb 126
Griffiths, Bede 321
Grillmeier, Aloys
    Dogmatic Constitution of the
    Church 57
Grisaille 90, 104, 105
Growing Up 62
Guardini, Romano
    Sacred Images and the Invisible
    God 58
Guareschi, Giovanni
    The Little World of Don Camillo
    61
Guggenheim Fellowships in
    Music Composition 72
Gy, Pierre-Marie 22

H

Hagia Sophia 144, 148, 159, 177
Hagia Sophia, The Collected Poems
    203
Hall, James Baker 253
Hammer, Victor 246, 247

Harding, Stephen 78, 87
Harford, James 335
    Thomas Merton and Friends 346
Hart, Patrick 65, 173, 315, 324,
    352
    The Literary Essays of Thomas
    Merton 204
    Thomas Merton: First and Last
    Memories 186
Hart, Patrick and Jonathon
    Montaldo
    The Intimate Merton 203
The Haunted Castle 238
Hays, Bryan Beaumont 7, 73, 74,
    76
Hays, Bryan Beaumont, OSB 72
Hays, H.R.
    Jorge Carrera Andrade: Magician
    of Metaphors 164
He Teaches Clergy Their Artistic
    ABCs 57
Heraclitus 69
Heretic Blood: The Spiritual Geogra-
    phy of Thomas Merton 109,
    124
Hernandez, Miguel 141
Herrlichkeit 215
Heschel, Abraham 220
    God in Search of Man 214
Hesiod 368
Hess, Rudolf 338
Hess, Thomas B.
    The Art Comics and Satires of Ad
    Reinhardt 313
Hesse, Hermann
    Steppenwolf 218
Heyerdahl, Thor
    Kon-Tiki 61, 62
The Hidden Face 62, 213
The Hidden Ground of Love: The
    Letters of Thomas Merton 314
A Hidden Wholeness: The Visual
    World of Thomas Merton 187,
    254, 258, 346

A Hidden Wholeness: The Zen Photography of Thomas Merton 316, 331, 345

Higgins, Michael 115
  Heretic Blood: The Spiritual Geography of Thomas Merton 109, 124

Hildegund, Sister 361

Himalayas 131, 134

Hindu and Muslim Mysticism 214

Hinduism 112

Hiroshima 154

Hirsch, Edward
  How to Read a Poem and Fall in Love with Poetry 204

An Historical Sketch of the Abbey Church 32

A History of God 112, 125

A History of Modern Poetry 323

A History of Modern Poetry: Modernism and After 344

The History of The Abbey of Our Lady of The Holy Spirit 77

Hollas, Eric 59

Holy Week 207

Homan, Daniel and Pratt, Lonni Collins
  Radical Hospitality: Benedict's Way of Love 64

Homer 368

homo postmodernus 324

Homo Viator 222

Hopkins, Gerard Manley 8, 115, 127, 128, 129, 130, 132, 136, 137, 138, 169, 223, 241

Hori, Victor Sogen
  Zen Sand: The Book of Capping Phrases 313

Hourihan, Paul
  The Death of Thomas Merton: A Novel 343

How to Read a Poem and Fall in Love with Poetry 204

Hoyle, Sir Fred 66

Hryniewicz, Waclaw, OMI 326

Hui-Neng 266, 295

Hulme, Kathryn
  The Nun's Story 61

The Human Condition 222

Hurley, Archbishop Denis 22

hurricane Hugo 30

Husted, Wayne 85

Huxley, Aldous
  Ends and Means 223

Hymn to the Pearl 326

hyperreality 200

I

St. Ignatius
  Spiritual Exercises 221

The Illuminated Manuscript 32

Imaginary Homelands: Essays and Criticism 1981-199 345

In Good Company: A Woman's Journal for Spiritual 360

In My Disc of Gold: Itinerary to Christ of William Congdon 306

In the Dark Before Dawn 347, 349, 350

Inglebret, Julie
  Bound to Books 55

The Inner Experience 201, 204, 246

insitum verbum 209

Instruction on the Ecclesial Vocation 45, 57

The Intelligible World 218

International Thomas Merton Society
  Eighth Conference 109

The Intimate Merton 203, 206, 352

invisible fecundity 194

St. Irenaeus 218, 354

Isaias 16, 17

J

Jaguar 200
James, Dom 79, 251
Japan 63, 70
Jeffers, Robinson 69
Jefferson and/or Mussolini 71
Jeffery, Peter
  A Chant Historian Reads
    Liturgiam Authenticam 3 31
Jerusalem 123
Jewels Upon His Forehead 167
The Jewish Museum 263
Joachim, Father 86
Joan of Arc 329
Job 212
St. John of the Cross 216, 217, 226,
    227, 239, 246, 263, 301
  Dark Night of the Soul 249
St. John the Baptist 316
Jones, Arthur 335
Jorge Carrera Andrade 164
Jorge Carrera Andrade in
    America 163
Jorge Carrera Andrade: Magician of
    Metaphors 164
Joshu 266
Jounel, Pierre 22
Journal for the Protection of All
    Beings 338
Journals Vol. 1 231
Journals Vol. 1, p. 135 234
Journals Vol. 1, p. 98 235
Journals Vol. 1, pp. 297-8 233
Journals Vol. 2, p. 195 234
Journals Vol. 2, p. 344 233
Journals Vol. 2, p. 345 236
Journals Vol. 2, p. 353 232
Journals Vol. 2, p. 384 234
Journals Vol. 2, p. 435 235
Journals Vol. 3, p. 135 236
Journals Vol. 3, p. 204 232
Journals Vol. 3, p. 256 231

Journals Vol. 3, p. 364 235
Journals Vol. 3, p. 89 233
Journals Vol. 3, pp. 94-5 234
Journals Vol. 4, p. 122 236
Journals Vol. 4, p. 189 235
Journals Vol. 4, p. 202 232
Journals Vol. 4, p. 278 234
Journals Vol. 4, p. 322 233
Journals Vol. 5, p. 149 232
Journals Vol. 5, p. 235 235
Journals Vol. 5, p. 306 236
Journals Vol. 5, p. 52 233
Journals Vol. 5, p. 55 232
Journals Vol. 6, p. 153 235
Journals Vol. 6, p. 312 233
Journals Vol. 6, p. 86 232
Journals Vol. 7, p. 18 236
Journals Vol. 7, p. 182 235
Journals Vol. 7, p. 259 233
Joyce, James 296
  Finnegans Wake 293
Jubilee 240, 241, 265, 267, 287,
    294, 297, 335
Julian of Norwich 10, 155, 224,
    326, 327
Jung, C.G. 296
  Man and His Symbols 108
  Mandala Symbolism 108

K

Kacmarcik, Frank 7, 11, 22, 24, 27,
    30, 31, 33, 37, 38, 39, 40, 41,
    42, 43, 45, 47, 48, 49, 50, 51,
    52, 53, 54, 55, 56, 93
  The Berakah Award for 1981 56
Mt. Kanchenjunga 127, 135, 253
Kant, Immanuel 368
Kao Tzu 218
Kapleau, Philip 321
Karen 62
Kavanagh, Francis X.
  Oral History 108
Keating, Ross 189

Keeping a Spiritual Journal with Thomas Merton 352
Kelly, Marcia 312
Kelty, Matthew 108
Kennedy Airport. 86
Kentucky 131
Kierkegaard 253, 325
Kilcourse, George 194
  Ace of Freedoms: Thomas Merton's Christ 203
Killilea, Marie Karen 62
Kinder, Terryl N.
  Architecture of Silence: Cistercian Abbeys of France 32
  Cistercian Europe: Architecture of Contemplation 32
King, Martin Luther, Jr. 309
King of Israel 71
Kirvan, John
  God Hunger, Silent Hope, Raw Faith 362
  Grace through Simplicity: The Practical Spirituality 362
  There is a God, There is No God 362
Kislak, Elzbieta 325, 344
Klee, Paul 20, 307
Klein, Francis
  Frank Kacmarcik: A Mepkin Tribute 58
Kocka, David 317
Kon-Tiki 61, 62
König, Franz Cardinal 22
de Kooning, Willem 261, 312
Kownacki, Mary Lou
  Between Two Souls: Conversations with Ryokan 355
Kramer, Dewey Weiss 8, 96
Kramer, Victor A. 7, 15, 77, 352
  Open to the Spirit 107
  The History of The Abbey of Our Lady of The Holy Spirit 77

Thomas Merton: Monk and Artist 55, 56
Turning toward the World 347

L

La Trappe in France 98
Labrie, Ross 118, 121
  The Art of Thomas Merton 186
  Thomas Merton and the Inclusive Imagination 109, 124
Lagouvardos, Moschos
  Memories of Robert Lax 346
Lahey, G. F. 223
di Lampedusa, Giuseppe
  Prison Meditations of Father Delp 214
  The Last of the Just 214
  The Leopard 214
The Land of Urlo 326
Lao Tzu 325
The Laocoön 123
The Last of the Fathers 330, 345
The Last of the Just 214
Latin America 70
Latin Vulgate 200
latreutic 301
Laughlin, Jay 294
Lawrence, C.H.
  Medieval Monasticism: Forms of Religious Life ... 31
Lax, Robert 245, 260, 294, 332, 334, 335, 337, 342
  Circus Days and Nights 335
  Circus of the Sun 299
  Estate of 313
Learning to Love: Exploring Solitude and Freedom 125, 258
Leaves of Grass 67
Leclercq, Jean
  Otia Monastica 226
  The Love of Learning and the Desire for God 207, 209
lectio divina 25, 206, 209

Lee, Muna
  Secret Country 143
Lentfoehr, Sister Thérèse 240, 314
  Schwester Therese 311
Lenz, Desiderius
  The Aesthetic of Beuron and Other
    Writings 31
The Leopard 214
Lercaro, Giacomo Cardinal 22
Let Your Life Speak 56
Letter to Alfred Stieglitz 188
Levertov, Denise 352
Lewis, C.S. 364
Lexington Camera Club 253
Life 263, 311
Lincoln 60
Lipsey, Roger 9, 260
  Angelic Mistakes 312, 314
  Coomaraswamy: Selected Papers
    Traditional Art … 204
  Thomas Merton and Ulfert
    Wilke: The Friendship of
    Artists 314
The Literary Essays of Thomas
  Merton 204
The Little World of Don Camillo 61
Liturgical Arts 108
Liturgy of the United States
  Catholic Conference o 43
Living with Wisdom 319
Lo Fatal 69
locus theologicus 147
logos 306
Lograire 351
Los 119
The Lost World of the Kalahari 62
The Love of Learning and the Desire
  for God 207, 209
Love and Living 186
Love Winter When the Plant Says
  Nothing 76, 171
Luce, Henry and Clare Booth 30
Luckman, Syd 281

Lumen Gentium 44
Luther, Martin 44, 367
Lyke Catholic Center
  Atlanta University 95

M

M 161, 206
Machiavelli 341
Mad 253
Mai Mai Sze 225
  Tao of Painting 212
Maitland, David J.
  Vocation 56
Malys, Konrad 327
A Man in the Divided Sea 187
Man and His Symbols 108
The Man Who Got Even with God
  61
mandala 104, 108
Mandala Symbolism 108
Mandala: Luminous Symbols for
  Healing 108
Marcel, Gabriel 156, 157, 158, 219
  Homo Viator 222
  Reality, Man, Existence: Essential
    Works 165
Marcus Aurelius 325
Maritain, Jacques 34, 119, 218, 265
  Art and Scholasticism 55, 241
  Notebooks 225
Maritain, Raïssa 141, 221
The Marriage of Heaven and Hell
  110
Marshall, Willoughby 28
Martin's Predicament or Atlas
  Watches Every Evening 164
Marx, Michael 23, 35
Mary Magdalene 239
Masheck, Joseph 314
  Five Unpublished Letters From Ad
    Reinhardt 257
Massignon, Louis 136, 354
Master of the Minimal 313

Mauck, Marchita 51
Mauck, Marchita B.
  Places for Worship: A Guide to Building and Renovation 58
May, Robert C. 253
Maynard, Theodore
  St. Benedict and His Monks 61
McClory, Robert
  Faithful Dissenters: Stories of Men and Women ... 61
McDonnell, Thomas P.
  Blaze of Recognition: Through the Year with Thomas Merton 352
McGann, Robert 78, 79, 80, 81, 82, 84
McGrath Art Gallery 331, 333
McManus, Frederick 22
McMillan Hall, Columbia University, New York Cit 72
Meatyard, Ralph Eugene 252
  Father Louie: Photographs of Thomas Merton 259
  The Family Album of Lucybelle Crater 254
Mediator Dei 42
Medieval Monasticism: Forms of Religious Life 31
meditatio 208
Van de Meer, Pierre 225
Memories of Robert Lax 346
Mencius 218
Mendes, Guy 253
Meng Tzu 141
Mepkin Abbey, South Carolina 24, 29
Merleau-Ponty 253, 332
The Merry-Go-Round 198
A Merton Connection 33
The Merton Annual 93, 186, 315, 371
The Merton Journal 258, 343, 344
The Merton Seasonal 186, 314, 319, 322, 337, 339, 345, 346, 347

Merton and Ecology of Human Spirit 343
Merton Legacy Trust 187, 273, 289
Merton, Owen 168, 237, 329, 330
The Merton Poem Cycles 76
Merton, Rev. M Louis 288
Merton, Ruth 168, 237
Merton, Thomas 11, 15, 19, 33, 77, 88, 94, 140, 205, 237, 238, 242, 252, 255, 260, 263, 273, 289, 307, 311, 317, 321, 326, 329, 335, 343, 350, 362, 364
  A Discovery 72
  A Search for Solitude 138, 231, 257, 314, 343
  Art and Spirituality 185
  Art and Worship 302, 306
  Atlas and the Fatman 164
  Aubade - Harlem 175
  Aubade - The City 175
  Baptism in the Forest 347
  Blake and the New Theology 165
  Cables to the Ace 170, 323, 351
  Carol 177
  Conjectures of a Guilty Bystander 139, 142, 161, 173, 186
  Contemplation in a World of Action 203
  Dancing in the Water of Life 231, 232, 258
  Day of a Stranger 188, 359
  Devout Meditation in Memory of Adolf Eichmann 347
  Dirge for the City of Miami 174
  Disputed Questions 249, 257, 304
  Early Blizzard 170
  Eighteen Poems 351
  Elegy for the Monastery Barn 117
  Elias—Variations on a Theme 150, 171
  Emblems of a Season of Fury 141, 142, 143, 144, 150, 161

Entering the Silence 58, 231, 352
Figures for an Apocalypse 175
Hagia Sophia 144, 159, 177
*Hagia Sophia, The Collected
  Poems* 203
In the Ruins of New York 175
Jorge Carrera Andrade 164
*Learning to Love: Exploring
  Solitude and Freedom* 258
letter to Clayton Eshleman 163
letter to Ernesto Cardenal 163
letter to Esther de Cáceres 163
letter to Stefan Baciu 163
Lograire 351
Love and Living 186
*Love Winter When the Plant Says
  Nothing* 171
*Martin's Predicament or Atlas
  Watches Every Evening* 164
Message to Poets 164, 185
Midsummer Diary 327
Monks Pond 312, 314
My Argument with the Gestapo
  329
Mystics and Zen Masters 113,
  125
New Seeds of Contemplation 110,
  124, 130, 138, 139, 154, 185,
  204
Night-Flowering Cactus 172
No Man Is An Island 240, 318,
  320
Notes of a Parachute Jumper 165
Notes on Sacred and Profane Art
  185
Peace in the Post-Christian Era
  340, 342, 348
*Poetry and Contemplation: A
  Reappraisal* 114, 115, 125, 148
Poetry and Imagination 204
Praying the Psalms 204
Prólogo 165
Raids on the Unspeakable 243,
  249, 257

Ravenswell 238
Reality, Art, Prayer 185
Redeeming the Time 204
*Roland Barthes—Writing as
  Temperature* 346
Run to the Mountain 231, 244,
  257, 313
Seeds of Contemplation 188, 318,
  320
Selected Poems 250, 349, 351
Sign of Jonas 61
Song: If You Seek 172
*Spiritual Direction and Medita-
  tion* 140, 163
Stranger 174
The Annunciation 176
The Ascent to Truth 246
*The Asian Journal of Thomas
  Merton* 186
The Catholic and Creativity 56
*The Collected Poems of Thomas
  Merton* 125, 126, 141, 145,
  163, 165, 186, 187, 259, 313,
  350, 351
The Courage for Truth 313, 347
The Geography of Lograire 176,
  187, 323
The Great Voyage 238
The Haunted Castle 238
*The Hidden Ground of Love: The
  Letters* 314
The Inner Experience 201, 204,
  246
The Last of the Fathers 330
The Other Side of the Mountain
  128, 138
*The Other Side of the Mountain:
  The End of the Journey* 232,
  259, 346
*The Plague of Albert Camus: A
  Commentary* 163
*The Quickening of St. John the
  Baptist* 177

The Road To Joy 126, 187, 257, 258, 313
The School of Charity 58
The Secular Journal of Thomas Merton 186
The Seven Storey Mountain 54, 128, 135, 138, 186, 223, 237, 238, 241, 244, 318, 320, 330, 336, 345
The Sign of Jonas 173, 186, 320
The Strange Islands 295
The Tower of Babel 175
Thirty-Seven Meditations 298
Thomas Merton's View of Monasticism 348
Thoughts in Solitude 298, 319
Thoughts on the East 320
Three Saviors in Camus: Lucidity and the Absurd 166
Turning toward the World 257, 314, 347
Waters of Siloe 271
Witness to Freedom 258
Woods, Shore, Desert 127, 130, 131, 135, 139
Zen and the Birds of Appetite 320
Merton: A Biography 124
Mertonana, Studia 321
Mertoniana 319
Merton's Margin 344
Message to Poets 164, 185
Mexico 60, 67
Meyer, Richard 93
Middlebury College 270
Midsummer Diary 327
Milosz, Czeslaw 196, 325, 328, 344
A Book of Luminous Things 204
Another Space 326
Hymn to the Pearl 326
Ketman 326
Rok my´s liwego 344
The Captive Mind 318, 326

The Land of Urlo 326
The Year of the Hunter 326
Milton, John 368
Minneapolis 28
Minneapolis College of Art and Design (MCAD) 34
Miro, Joan 239
modernitas 324
Moliere 368
Moltmann, Jürgen 45
What Is A Theologian? 57
Monastic 7
Monastic Peace 250
A Monk with the Spiritual Equipment of an Artist 237
The Monk and Sacred Art 15
Monks Pond 264, 312, 313, 314
Montaigne 368
Montaldo, Jonathan 8, 352
Dialogues with Silence 9, 352
The Intimate Merton 352
A Year with Thomas Merton 352
Moore, Marianne 69
Moore, Thomas 365
Morgan, Edmund S.
Benjamin Franklin 61
Motherwell, Robert 309
Mott, Michael
The Seven Mountains of Thomas Merton 258
Mounier, Emmanuel 225
Mount Analogue 130, 131, 138
Muir, Edwin 241
Mullany, John 27, 28
Murti, T. R. V. 218
de Musset, Alfred 73
Mussolini 71
Muzruchi, Susan 345
My Argument with the Gestapo 329
My Left Foot 62
Myshkin, Prince 325
Le Mystère Pascal 222
Mysticism: A Study of the Nature and Development 362

Mystics and Zen Masters 113, 125
The Myth of Sisyphus 212, 226

N

Nagarjuna 218
Nash, Erich Peter
  Ansel Adams: The Spirit in Wild Places 188
National Catholic Reporter 319
  Building History One Stone at a Time 343
National Catholic Reporter, October 8, 2004 346
Nature and Art in William Blake 124, 125
Neo-Platonism 112
Neruda, Pablo 211
Netzahualcoyótl 67
A New Zealand Painter in Medieval France 345
The New Yorker 238
The New Apocalypse: The Radical Vision of William Blake 125
New Directions Books 294
New Melleray Abbey: Cistercians of the Strict Observance 32
New Mexico 130
A New Order According to Michelangelo 57
New Seeds of Contemplation 110, 124, 130, 138, 139, 154, 185, 204
New York School 261
Newman, Cardinal 341
Newman, Fred and Lois Holzman
  The End of Knowing 203
Nicaragua 66, 70
Nicholas of Cusa 246
Nicoli, Armand M., Jr.
  The Question of God: C.S. Lewis and Sigmund Freud 61
Nieset, Frank E. 47
  A New Order According to Michelangelo 57

Nietzsche, Friedrich 324
Night-Flowering Cactus 172
Nineveh 84
Nishida
  The Intelligible World 218
No Man Is An Island 240, 318, 320
Nobel laureate 325
Norris, Kathleen 349
The Norton Anthology of Modern Poetry 138
Norwid, Cyprian Kamil 325
Notebooks 225
Notes of a Parachute Jumper 165
Notes on Sacred and Profane Art 185
Nouwen, Henri 366
  Out of Solitude: Three Meditations 364
The Nun's Story 61

O

Oakham 168
Obirek, Stanislaw 328
O'Callaghan, Tommie 353
O'Connell, Patrick F. 257, 355
O'Conner, Flannery 73
O'Gorman, Ned 285, 309
O'Keeffe, Georgia 369
Old Testament 150, 219
Olean, New York 172
Olson, Charles 352
O'Malley, John W.
  Four Cultures of the West 367
On the Love of God 216
One Aesthetic Illumination: Thomas Merton and Buddhism 346
Open to the Spirit 107
Opus Dei 99
Oral History 108
Orate Fratres 36
Orbis Books
  Peace in the Post-Christian Era 340

Origen 223, 225
  The Treatise on Prayer 223, 226
Original Child Bomb 310
Orvin, Chris 9, 205
The Other Side of the Mountain 128, 138, 232, 259, 346
Otia Monastica 226
Our Lady of Vladimir 29
Out of Solitude: Three Meditations 364
Oxford 128

P

Palmer, Parker J. 41
  Let Your Life Speak 56
Pan American Union 65
Panelists Say Artists, Clergy Need Each Other 57
Panofsky, Erwin 270, 298
Saint Panteleimon 274
The Paradox of Place: Thomas Merton's Photography 331
Parousia 153
Parra, Nicanor 141
Pasternak, Boris 224, 241
Pastorale and Allegro Gershwin Memorial Award 72
Patnaik, Deba P. 331, 332
  Geography of Holiness: The Photography of Thomas Merton 187
Patterson, Margot 319
Patterson, Richard B.
  Writing Your Spiritual Autobiography 363
Paulus Diaconicus 141
Pax 265, 267, 294, 299
Le Pays de France 330
Peace in the Post-Christian Era 340, 342, 348
Pearson, Paul M. 9, 237, 312, 314, 322, 328, 331, 345

A Hidden Wholeness 346
  Thomas Merton: Photographer 345
Pearson, Paul M. et al.
  Thomas Merton: Poet, Monk, Prophet 124
Pecklers, Keith
  The Unread Vision, the Liturgical Movement 56
Pennington, Basil M.
  Thomas Merton: Brother Monk 327
  Towards Discerning the Spirit 124
Pepler, Conrad
  The Life and Teaching of Eric Gill 55
Perkins, David
  A History of Modern Poetry 323
  A History of Modern Poetry. Modernism and After 344
Pessoa, Fernando 141
Petisco, Sonia
  Recovering our Innocence 109
Petrarch 368
Phillipe, Paul
  La Très Sainte Vierge et le Sacerdoce 212
Picasso, Pablo 239
du Pin, Patrice de la Tour 213
  The Hidden Face 213
Places for Worship: A Guide to Building and Renovation 58
The Plague of Albert Camus: A Commentary 163
Plato 218, 368
Plotinus 119, 123
Poe, Edgar Allan 157
Poetry and Contemplation: A Reappraisal 114, 115, 125, 148
Poetry and Imagination 204
Poetry of the Sneeze: Thomas Merton and Nicanor Para 258

le point vierge 136
Poks, Malgorzata 10, 140, 318
polis 325, 342
Polish Association for American
    Studies 322
Pollock, Jackson 261, 312
Polonnaruwa 170, 182
Pope Gregory VII 367
Pope John Paul II 348
Pope Paul VI 44
Pope Pius XII 42
Porter, J.S. 337
Postman, Neil 189
    *The End of Education: Defining
        the Value of School* 190, 203
Pound, Ezra 67, 69, 70, 71, 352
Praying the Psalms 204
Presley, Elvis 270, 298
Prison Meditations of Father Delp
    214
Prólogo 165
Prometheus Bound 226
Psalm 85 209, 210
Psalm 86 210
Psalms 209, 212
Puerto Rico 63

Q

St. Quentin 62
*The Question of God: C.S. Lewis and
    Sigmund Freud* 61
Qui est cet homme? 224, 226
*The Quickening of St. John the
    Baptist* 177
Quietism 304
Quietist 278
Quintilian 368

R

The Radical Vision of William Blake
    113
*Radical Hospitality: Benedict's Way
    of Love* 64

Raids on the Unspeakable 243, 249,
    257
Rambusch, Robert 50, 51, 54, 87,
    90, 226
    *What Mean These Stones? A
        Theology of Church Buildings*
        58
de Rancé, Armand 98
Rare Book and Manuscript
    Library 312
Ravenswell 238
Raymond, M.
    The Man Who Got Even with God
        61
*Reading Merton from the (Polish)
    Margin* 318
Reality, Art, Prayer 185
*Reality, Man, Existence: Essential
    Works* 165
Recovering our Innocence 109
The Red Wheelbarrow 346
Redeeming the Time 204
Redwoods 133
Regan, Patrick 35
Reinhardt, Ad 246, 247, 260, 262,
    268, 273, 289, 291, 307, 308,
    311, 312, 335
    Estate of 273, 289, 312
    Reinhardt Black Painting 301
Reinhardt, Anna 273, 289, 312
Reinhardt Black Painting 301
Reiser, William 339
Religion, Atheism, and Faith 343
*Religions et Philosophies dans l'Asie
    Central* 344
Revelation 1: 6 44
Rice, Edward 238, 250, 260, 294,
    297, 334
Richards, David 85
Ricoeur, Paul
    Religion, Atheism, and Faith 343
Rilke, Rainer Maria 169, 196, 197,
    241, 242

Selected Poems 204
The Merry-Go-Round 198
The Road To Joy 126, 187, 257, 258, 313
St. Robert of Molesmes 24
Robinson, Leonard 280
Roettger, Gregory 23
Rok mysliwego 344
Roland Barthes—Writing as Temperature 346
Romans 222
Romantic Movement 98
Rome 70
Roosevelt College
Chicago Music College 72
Rose, Anna Perrott
The Gentle House 62
Rose, Barbara ed.
Art-as-Art: The Selected Writings of Ad Reinhardt 313
Rothko, Mark 261
Rouault 240
Rousseau, Le Douanier 20
Rudolph, Conrad
The "Things of Greater Importance": Bernard 32
Ruether, Rosemary Radford
The Church Against Itself 220
In the Ruins of New York 175
Rule of Benedict 24, 26, 27, 59, 97
Rumsfeld, Donald 338
Run to the Mountain 231, 244, 257, 313
Rushdie, Salman
Imaginary Homelands: Essays and Criticism 1981-199 345

S

Sacred Images and the Invisible God 58
Said, Edward 337
St. Anthony Messenger 64
St. Antonin 238

St. Benedict's Monastery 62, 63, 64
St. John, Donald P. 348
St. John's 59, 60, 94
St. John's Abbey 22, 33, 41, 54, 72, 76
St. John's Monastery 36, 37, 38
St. John's University 15, 23, 41, 65, 66, 76
Alcuin Library 11
St. Mark's Cathedral in Minneapolis 72
Saint Benedict and His Monks 61
Saint Bernard: The Aesthetics of Authenticity 107
The Saint Paul Statuary 57
Saints & Sinners: A History of the Popes 60
Samsel, Roman
Bunt i gwalt [Rebellion and Violence] 163
Samuel, Book of 71
Sandburg, Carl 70
Sandinista government 70
Sandinista Minister of Culture 66
Sandinista revolution 70
Sandok, Theresa 327
Thomas Merton's Contemplative Vision 345
Sartre, J.P. 217
Saulieu 16
Schapiro, Meyer 261
Schickel, William 108
The School of Charity 58
School of Fine Arts, San Francisco 183
Schroeder, Joy A. 362
A Search for Solitude 138, 231, 257, 314, 343
Seasoltz, R. Kevin 22, 93
A Tribute to Frank Kacmarcik 32
Brother Frank Kacmarcik Obl.S.B. 1920-2004 31

L'Abbaye Notre-Dame de New Melleray 32
Second Vatican Council 24, 62. *See also* Vatican II
The Secular Journal of Thomas Merton 186
Sedulius 141
Seeds of Contemplation 188, 318, 320
Selected Poems 204, 250, 349, 351
Seneca 325
Sengai 307
Senior Society of Sachems 305
Sergius 265
Sergius of Moscow 269
The Seven Mountains of Thomas Merton 258
The Seven Storey Mountain 54, 128, 135, 138, 186, 223, 237, 238, 241, 244, 318, 320, 330, 336, 345
Shakers 250
Shakespeare, William 368
Shannon, William H. 257, 370
Shantideva 354
Sheeler, Charles 250
Shoes of the Fisherman 229
Shouse, Corey 65
The Sign of Jonas 61, 173, 186, 320
Simpson, John 330
An Astonishing Variety, Rev. of Owen Merton 345
simulacrum 200
Simulations 204
Siskind, Aaron 253
Slate, John Hampton 270, 298
Slavery and Freedom 226
Smith, Henry Holmes 253
Smithsonian 245
Snell, Bruno
Discovery of the Mind 214
Socrates 218
Song: If You Seek 172

Sophocles 368
Sortais, Gabriel 84
The Sound and the Fury 347
Sovik, Edward 47, 49
Architecture for Worship 50, 57
Esse Quam Videri: Notes on the Building of Churches 57
Sowers, Robert 86
Spaeth, Eloise 240, 305, 306
Spanish Conquest 66
Spirit of Medieval Philosophy 223
Spiritual Direction and Meditation 140, 163
Spiritual Exercises 221
Sponsa Regis 7, 15, 240, 249
Stained Glass For Amateurs 83
Steppenwolf 218
Stevens, John tr.
Dewdrops on a Lotus Leaf: Zen Poems of Ryokan 356
Steward, Angus 334
Stieglitz, Alfred 185
Stiegman, Emero
Saint Bernard: The Aesthetics of Authenticity 107
Stillman, Andrea S.
Ansel Adams: The Grand Canyon and the Southwest 188
Stone, Naomi Burton 251
Keeping a Spiritual Journal with Thomas Merton 352
Stones Laid before the Lord 32
Strachey, Lytton
Eminent Victorians 214
The Strange Islands 295
The Stranger 162, 174
Stuart, Angus F. 366
Studia Mertoniana 325, 327
Studia Mertoniana 2 256, 323, 343, 344, 345
Summa theologiae 219
Sunderman, Marilyn 167
sunyata 302

Suzuki, D.T. 265, 282, 294
  The Zen Doctrine of No Mind
    295
  Zen and Japanese Culture 204
Suzuki, Daisetz 39
Szabo, Lynn R. 344, 350
  In the Dark Before Dawn 349

T

The Tablet 70
Taiwan 63
Takase, Eri 356
Tanglewood 72
Tao of Painting 212
Telnack, Methodius 8, 77
Ten Rungs 230
Teresa of Avila 360
Tertullian 367
theology
  Augustinian 218
  Thomistic 218
Theology and Liturgical Space 57
Theoria Physike 333
The Theory and Practice of the
  Mandala 108
There is a God, There is No God 362
St. Theresa 225
St. Therese 239
St. Therese of Lisieux 62
Thérèse of Lisieux 360
The *"Things of Greater Importance"*:
  Bernard 32
Thirty-Seven Meditations 298
St. Thomas 18, 224
  Summa theologiae 219
The Thomas Merton Encyclopedia
  257
Thomas Merton and Alan Watts:
  Contemplative Catholic 343
Thomas Merton and Friends 346
Thomas Merton and James Laughlin:
  Selected Letters 313

Thomas Merton and the Education of
  the Whole Person 204
Thomas Merton and the Inclusive
  Imagination 109, 124
Thomas Merton and Ulfert Wilke:
  The Friendship of 314
Thomas Merton Center 164, 245,
  252, 310, 315, 316, 317, 331
Thomas Merton Papers 299
Thomas Merton Society of Great
  Britain
  Oakham Conference 109
Thomas Merton to Ad Reinhardt,
  July 3, 1956 257
Thomas Merton to Ad Reinhardt,
  October 31, 1963 258
Thomas Merton—An Artist 256,
  326
Thomas Merton: A Biography 233
Thomas Merton: Brother Monk 328
Thomas Merton: First and Last
  Memories 186
Thomas Merton: Monk and Artist
  55, 56
Thomas Merton: Photographer 345
Thomas Merton: Poet, Monk,
  Prophet 124
Thomas Merton's Art of Denial: The
  Evolution of a Radical Human-
  ist 203, 314
Thomas Merton's Contemplative
  Vision 345
Thomas Merton's View of Monasti-
  cism 348
Thoughts in Solitude 298, 319
Thoughts on the East 320
Three Prayers 11
Three Saviors in Camus: Lucidity
  and the Absurd 166
Thurber, James 161
Thurston, Bonnie B. 331, 333, 334
  One Aesthetic Illumination:
    Thomas Merton and Buddhism
    346

Tillich, Paul 265, 282
Time 335
Time of Transition: A Selection of Letters 371
Times (London) 237
Titus 210
Tobey, Mark 309
Togliatti 265, 269
Tomb Cover of Imam Riza 141
Towards Discerning the Spirit 124
The Tower of Babel 175
Transfigurer les Temps 214
Transformation of Nature in Art 124
The Trapp Family Singers 61
Trapp, Maria
  The Trapp Family Singers 61
Trappist Order 68
The Treatise on Prayer 223, 226
La Très Sainte Vierge et le Sacerdoce 212
A Tribute to Frank Kacmarcik 32
tricherie 217
Tucci, Giuseppe
  The Theory and Practice of the Mandala 108
Tun Huang 270
Turnage, Robert
  Ansel Adams: The Role of the Artist in the Environment 188
Turning toward the World 257, 314, 347
The Twilight of American Culture 347
Tygodnik Powszechny 318
Tylovich, Alexander 30
tympan of Vezelay 18

U

U.S. Catholic 64
U.S. Marine Corps 77
U.S. Navy 262
Unadorned Ideal 77

Uncommon Daisies 73
Underhill, Evelyn
  Mysticism: A Study of the Nature and Development 362
Ungaretti, Giuseppe 211
United States 70
University of Louisville 276, 303
University of Mexico 65
The Unread Vision, the Liturgical Movement in the United States 56
Urizen 119
Urtecho, José Coronel 65, 66

V

Vallejo, César 141
Van der Post, Laurens
  The Lost World of the Kalahari 62
Van Doren, Mark 116, 168, 261, 337, 349
Van Gogh, Vincent 365, 366
Vancouver 123
Varick Street 268
Vatican II 22, 42, 43, 53, 100, 102, 113, 222, 301. *See also* Second Vatican Council
Vaticanum Secundum 340
videntes 18
Vietnam 248
Virgil 368
Vision of the Daughters of Albion 110
Vocation 56

W

Warde, Beatrice 35
Waters of Siloe 271
Watkins, E.I. 339
Watts, Alan 321
The Way Things Are: Conversations with Huston Smith 203
The Way of the Dreamcatcher 335

The Weathercock on the Cathedral of Quito 166

Weaver, Mary Jo
  Conjectures of a Disenchanted Reader 206, 345

Webb, Francis 122
  Five Days Old 121
  Lancaster Bomber air-gunner 123

Wechsler, James 280

Weil, Simone 225, 325

Weisgram, Stefanie 15, 59

West, Morris
  Shoes of the Fisherman 229

What Is A Theologian? 57

What Mean These Stones? A Theology of Church Buildings 58

When Prophecy Still Had a Voice: The Letters of Thomas Merton and Robert Lax 313

When the Meaning Boils Down to a Brand Name 204

White, Minor 253

Whitman, Walt 70, 331
  Leaves of Grass 67

Wilke, Ulfert 276, 286, 303, 309, 310

Willett, Henry Lee 83

Willett, Muriel 83

William, Benedictine abbot of Saint-Thierry 25

Williams, Jonathan 252

Williams, William Carlos 69, 333, 351
  The Red Wheelbarrow 346

Wisdom, Sapiential Poetry, and Personalism 189

Witness to Freedom 258

Woods, Shore, Desert 127, 130, 131, 135, 139

The World In My Bloodstream 333, 334, 346

World War II 37, 72, 102, 149

Worship 40

Wouk, Herman 280

Wounded Prophet: A Portrait of Henri J. M. Nouwen 61

Wright, Frank Lloyd 369

Writing Your Spiritual Autobiography 363

wu-nien 295

Y

Yang-Yin 134

A Year with Thomas Merton 9, 352

The Year of My Life: A Translation of Issa's Oraga 204

The Year of the Hunter 326

Yellowstone National Park, 184

Yhung Mandala 267, 296

Yoga 113

Yuasa, Nobuyuki
  The Year of My Life: A Translation of Issa's Oraga 204

Z

Zaehner
  Hindu and Muslim Mysticism 214

Zakin, Helen Jackson
  French Cistercian Grisaille Glass 108

Zalot, Charlotte Anne 33, 93

Zarebianka, Zofia 327

zazen 302

The Zen Doctrine of No Mind 295

Zen 167

Zen Sand: The Book of Capping Phrases 313

Zen and Japanese Culture 204

Zen and the Birds of Appetite 320

St. Zieba, Maciej 320, 343

Zieba 321

Ziolo, Michal 330
  Doctor Mellifluus 345

*The Last of the Fathers: Saint
    Bernard of Clairvau* 345
Zitzen 302
Znak 318, 320
Znak 5
    Popularny trapista 343
Zukofsky, Louis 194, 195, 241, 332
Zycinski, Jozef 318
    *Merton and Ecology of Human
        Spirit* 343
    *The Crisis of Scientific-Technical
        Civilisation* 324